the Council and House

the State of Massachusetts

ed

us the Subscribers Inhabi

art of the town of Sudbury

any & great Difficulties and

unavoidable by us in

esent connected Situation

r Town Affairs with the

dbury) lay with peculiar

n us; which we shall

set forth in this Petition

ht as the Nature of the

mit of.

ik meetings to transact

The Puritan Village Evolves

The 1848 Town Bridge, one of the two four-arch stone spans which replaced wooden bridges over the Sudbury River.

The Puritan Village Evolves

a history of Wayland, Massachusetts

by

Helen Fitch Emery

Helen F. Emery

Published for the

WAYLAND HISTORICAL COMMISSION

by

PHOENIX PUBLISHING

Canaan, New Hampshire

Emery, Helen Fitch.
The Puritan village evolves.

Bibliography: p. 336
Includes index.
1. Wayland (Mass.)—History. I. Wayland (Mass.).
Town Historical Commission. II. Title.
F74.W35E43 974.4'4 81-5185
ISBN 0-914016-78-4 AACR2

Printed in the United States of America
by Courier Printing Company
Binding by New Hampshire Bindery
Design by A. L. Morris

Dedicated to

the memory of three of my friends

each of whom had a singular interest in Wayland

ROBERT MARSH MORGAN 1901 / 1976

who was responsible for my coming to Wayland in 1946

MABEL SMALL DRAPER 1887 / 1970

first curator of the Wayland Historical Society

who encouraged me to study less well-known aspects

of our local history

and

MARGARET BENT MORRELL 1901 / 1980

source of lore and memorabilia and my

enthusiastic companion in

historical research

Contents

Acknowledgments

First I want to express my gratitude for the faith of my colleagues on the Wayland Historical Commission–George K. Lewis, Nancy Hart, Rosalind G. Kingsbury, Dorothy S. Walsh, Jane H. Sciacca, and Elizabeth G. Goeselt–who voted in the fall of 1979 to have this history of Wayland published. Special thanks are due to Chairman Jane Sciacca for taking responsibility for and guiding the publication effort. To Elizabeth Goeselt I am particularly indebted for compiling two original maps and working closely with me in the search for illustrations. For general endorsement of the project I wish to thank the officers and board of the Wayland Historical Society and especially former president Elizabeth C. Sweitzer. I am indebted to curator Isabel Wight for giving me easy access to the society's documentary collections and permission to copy photographs. Grace I. Bowen, Town Clerk, and Edward N. Perry, Executive Secretary, welcomed me to the town building and gave me access to all of the town's historical books and papers. The staff of the Massachusetts Archives Search Room has been very helpful over the years. I am also indebted to the staff of The Morse Institute (Natick Public Library) for letting me wear out numerous microfilm reader light bulbs during months of reading Natick newspapers in search of material on Cochituate and Wayland.

My colleagues and several Wayland citizens read the manuscript, gave me encouragement, and made valuable suggestions and criticisms. Among these were Howard S. Russell and Margaret B. Morrell who are now deceased. Those whose reactions and criticisms were particularly helpful included Forrest D. Bradshaw, dean of Sudbury historians; Barbara Robinson who has delved into and written Wayland history; Bruce B. Kingsbury who contributed his editorial experience; Marcia Storkerson who lent her publishing expertise; and George K. Lewis who brought a professor's critical approach to scholarly writing. Paul F. Foskett of the finance committee carefully read the manuscript to see if it would be enlightening and of interest to Wayland's citizenry. Selectman L. Thomas Linden gave the project a boost when he assured the finance committee that the history was worth reading. I thank them all.

Lastly I express my thanks to my husband who has been a discerning critic and helper at various crisis points in the arrangements for publication. He made no complaint when for a number of years our house was strewn with boxes of notes and his wife very preoccupied.

H.F.E.

Preface

SEVERAL YEARS AGO this writer, after doing extensive research in the original records of the first two centuries of Sudbury and Wayland's history, concluded that a complete account of the eighteenth-century events leading to the April 1780 separation of East Sudbury from Sudbury had never been written. Alfred S. Hudson, who wrote *The History of Sudbury, Massachusetts*, published by the Town of Sudbury in 1889, devoted only seven pages to the actual division. A section of a chapter on 1775-1800 begins with the matter-of-fact sentences: "A prominent event of this period was the division of the town. The proposition came before the town by petition . . ." This writer found that one of the strong threads of history of Sudbury in the eighteenth century had been the events leading up to the division which gave birth to Wayland as a separate town.

Having analyzed the new Town of East Sudbury in 1780 from most of the available angles, it was decided that an in-depth look at Wayland in 1880, when it had been a town on its own for one hundred years, would show the course of development to an interesting point in the town's history. Owing to the availability of statistics and particularly good newspaper material, it happens that 1880 is a good time to look at Wayland's then burgeoning village of Cochituate with its shoe industry and also at various events and features of the whole town which elucidate its nineteenth-century history and set the stage for some of what is present a century later. It also is a fact that no one has written an account of Wayland as a town in the late nineteenth century.

Thus, this history has evolved with Part I devoted to the eighteenth century and birth of the separate town and Part II to the quite considerably changed town of one hundred years later. Founding of the Town of Sudbury and subsequent seventeenth-century history is presented in detail with documentation in Hudson's *History* and in Sumner C. Powell's *Puritan Village, The Formation of a New England Town*, published in 1963. That era of our town's history has here been summarized in the Prologue.

The Epilogue skims over the major events and changes that have occurred in Wayland in the first eight decades of the twentieth century. It is brief and contains no documentary references. However, it is the author's hope that, without going into detail on every change and trend, she has written a perceptive and balanced account of what happened from 1900, when the town's population was 2,303 and there were 413 houses, until 1980 when the population stood at 12,633 and there were about 4,000 households.

Personal observation over thirty-four years and interviews with older and long-term residents, as well as with citizens who are particularly well informed about recent changes in the town, helped with interpretation. Perusal of certain key town records such as the town reports and valuation lists gave the author an overview which seemed to make a good ending to this book. The author hopes that a future historian will do for the twentieth century the kind of exhaustive research she did on the eighteenth and nineteenth centuries. A detailed account of the twentieth century would make this book too long; the research to document such an account would require several years, and perhaps time must elapse for historical perspective.

Most of what is described is purely local and does not pertain to famous people and events. In all aspects of the history an attempt was made to see Wayland's events in the larger setting of Massachusetts. The author would have liked to have been knowledgeable enough about the affairs of many other specific towns to be able to point out more similarities and contrasts. Some have been brought out, and she hopes that they will lead to a better understanding of our town. An effort has been made to see Wayland as related to its neighbor towns and as compared with other communities and thus avoid the old-fashioned tendency to describe and discuss the town as a world apart with all of its affairs seemingly unique.

Despite the focus on birthdays in 1780 and 1880 in the outline, the main events of the eighteenth and nineteenth centuries are related. However, when there exists another and excellent study of a subject such as the founding of the Wayland Public Library, that subject has been treated more briefly in favor of telling at considerable length the story of the shoe industry, which has been recorded in detail.

The reader will find that the author scarcely mentions the town's involvement in wars and military expeditions. Sudbury had a narrow escape in King Philip's War, and Sudbury men were numerous in the military events of 1775. A book was published in 1871 by the Town of

Wayland as a memorial to seventy-two men of the town who served in the Civil War. This author is less interested in American history told primarily in terms of wars as was common in her youth. Her training as an economic historian gives her a different focus of interest.

Except for a few scholars who see in local history the fabric of American social and economic life, the readers of a history of a town like Wayland are mostly residents or former residents of the town, genealogists searching for information on families, and persons interested in some especially prominent feature such as a dominant industry. This history is primarily directed to Wayland townspeople, present, past, and future. It tries to answer their questions about more than three centuries of life in the town which are frequently asked and on some of which material is not easily available.

Helen Fitch Emery

Wayland, Massachusetts
February 1, 1981

The Puritan Village Evolves

Prologue

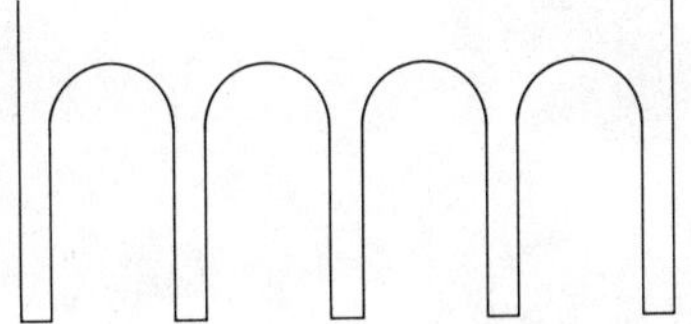

Sudbury's Founding and Early Growth

OUR TOWN, to which the name Wayland was given in 1835 nearly two hundred years after its founding, was officially incorporated in September 1639 and was the site of the original settlement of Sudbury Plantation. By the late 1630s, with the continuous swarm of Puritan English arrivals at coastal towns around Massachusetts Bay, places like Watertown were becoming crowded, and there was pressure to found new towns such as Dedham in the hinterland or to move farther afield to Connecticut. In 1637 one group of inhabitants of Watertown petitioned the colonial legislature for the right to settle a new town directly to the west, giving as their reason "straightness of accommodation and want of more meadow." The fertile meadowlands along the Sudbury River, then called the Musketahquid, looked to the explorers, fur trappers, and travelers along the Indian paths which traversed it, like good grazing land which would not require too much clearing. It was over this land that Thomas Hooker had led his band to Connecticut in 1637, and because of that route taken to the southwest, we have today a road, Old Connecticut Path, which follows that trail.

In 1638 four citizens of Watertown were directed by the General Court to lay out a plantation suitable for fifty or sixty families along the river directly upstream from Concord. The first settlers arrived in 1638 and 1639. Some, including Thomas Cakebread, Henry Curtis, John Grout, and John Stone, had lived in Watertown. The larger number had come directly from England in the summer of 1638 on

The Sudbury River meadows.

such ships as the *Confidence*, which brought the Haynes, Noyes, Bent, and Goodenow families. Their first crude dwellings were mostly clustered along the south-facing bank on what is now Bow Road and Old Sudbury Road. This came to be known as the Mill Road with its east side lined with early house lots. Other early house lots were laid out on Northwest Row and East Street, near present Glezen Lane, Moore Road, and Training Field Road. Still other first settlers lived on the road to Bridle Point. This road ran from the point where Bow Road now meets Concord Road across the meadow and over the rise on which the Raytheon Laboratory now stands. By the fall of 1640, there were about one hundred settlers and three hundred cattle in the part of Sudbury which is now Wayland.

The original grant from the colonial legislature was roughly five miles square astride the river—an area constituting the present towns of Wayland and Sudbury and parts of Maynard and Stow. It was named Sudbury for the shire town in Suffolk, England, near which the first pastor, Edmund Browne, and others of the company had lived. Sudbury was the nineteenth town to be incorporated as part of the Massachusetts Bay Colony, the third inland town, Concord and Dedham having preceded it. An additional mile of land was added to the southern end of the town in 1640, and a third grant, two miles wide along the western boundary, came from the colonial court in 1649. For each of these grants payment was made to Carto (Goodman) and other Indian owners with deeds drawn up and signed. The larger part of the territory was granted to the settlers collectively, who thus formed the plantation and established the town. However, it was stipulated that the town grants were not to encroach on some six private farm grants previously made by the legislature. Herbert Pelham's farm was surrounded by Sudbury town land, but other farms—those of Henry Dunster, William Jennison, and Mrs. Glover—were south of the Sudbury 1640 grant. All of these persons granted individual farms had performed important services for the Massachusetts Bay Company.

At the outset each townsman had a house lot, usually of four acres. Further allotments of meadow and other land depended on status, family size, cattle ownership, and other estate, thus varying for individual families. As in England, the settlers first tilled their fields in common, and extensive cow commons were established on public domain on both sides of the river. For more than one hundred years, subsequent allotments of land from the town to the individual inhabitants bore a complicated but definite relationship to the original grants of meadowland.

Sudbury's (and thereby Wayland's) seventeenth-century history is well documented by official records of the town's activity dating from the very beginning. These records, owned by the Town of Sudbury, are still in existence and are carefully kept in a special vault.

As in all Puritan Massachusetts Bay Colony towns of the seventeenth century, the church was of prime importance, a regular duty of the town government being to maintain the pastor and the church building. In 1640 Sudbury townsmen drew up a covenant to organize a church and appointed a minister, the Reverend Edmund Browne, a Puritan divine educated at Cambridge University, England. The first meetinghouse was built in 1643 in what now is the North Cemetery in Wayland on Old Sudbury Road. In addition to church services, the crude building, only 30 by 20 feet, was used as a gathering place for the men of the town when meeting as a municipal body. Growth and prosperity led to the decision in 1653 to build a larger meetinghouse in the same general location. This was a frontier town, and town records

The Noyes-Parris House, built in 1669.

indicate that the second meetinghouse had a watchtower and later a palisade.

An early economic need was supplied in the spring of 1639 when Thomas Cakebread established a gristmill on the Mill Brook. The town still dams the stream there, and now there is a skating pond. By a grant of meadowland in 1646, Richard Sanger was persuaded to set up a blacksmith shop not far from the gristmill, but this first smithy did not continue for very long. To help with the building of frame houses and barns, a sawmill was established with town encouragement on the west side of the Sudbury River in 1677. Other gristmills and sawmills followed as homesteads began to dot all sections of the town, but for nearly one hundred years all families, no matter how remote their farms, came faithfully to church on the Sabbath on Old Sudbury Road in Wayland.

Growth of population all too soon led to a feeling of crowding. By 1649 many of the younger generation, sons of the first settlers, felt that they were not fairly treated in the matter of land allotments. This led to political trouble in the town and involved the Reverend Edmund Browne. From the first settled area around the mill and meetinghouse, settlers had spread first to the southern part of the town. Then, starting about 1650, with a bridge across the river already built in

1643, the territory on the western side of the river was gradually settled. In addition to settling Sudbury lands to the west of the river, a group from Sudbury petitioned the General Court for more land even farther west and in 1656 founded the plantation of Marlborough, which included present Northborough, Southborough, Westborough, and Hudson. Marlborough became a separate town in 1660. In the eighteenth century settlers from Sudbury would help to found the Massachusetts towns of Framingham, Worcester, Grafton, and Rutland.

After Marlborough and other settlements farther west were established, Sudbury was not so isolated or exposed to Indian attacks as such towns as Lancaster and Deerfield. But Sudbury was still a frontier town, and six garrisonhouses were built for protection from hostile Indians. Five were on the west side of the river. The sixth, in what is now Wayland, was the home of the Reverend Edmund Browne and stood on Timber Neck on the northern edge of the Sandy Burr golf course. Sudbury was definitely endangered, and many of the houses and barns on the west side were burned during King Philip's War. One of the decisive battles of the war was fought in April 1676 on Green Hill in what is now South Sudbury. The major fighting occurred west of the river, but a skirmish took place at the Town Bridge on Old Sudbury Road in Wayland. There were smaller losses from burning on the east side of the river. The guns and the smoke of burning houses were heard and seen to the east in Weston, then outer Watertown, as eastern Sudbury residents sought shelter at the Browne garrisonhouse.

The only house built well before 1700 which is now standing in Wayland is not visible from a town road. Its early features, both exterior and interior, have been well preserved, and it is beautifully located overlooking a river meadow on a large estate. This house was built in 1669 by Peter Noyes, a son of the Peter Noyes who was the leader of town government from its inception until he died in 1657. The house is known locally as the Samuel Parris house because a minister of that name married Dorothy, daughter of Peter Noyes, as his second wife and came to live there. Parris had been pastor of the church in Salem Village but left that town because of his family's involvement with witchcraft. He was acting as one of Sudbury's early schoolteachers in 1717.

Part I

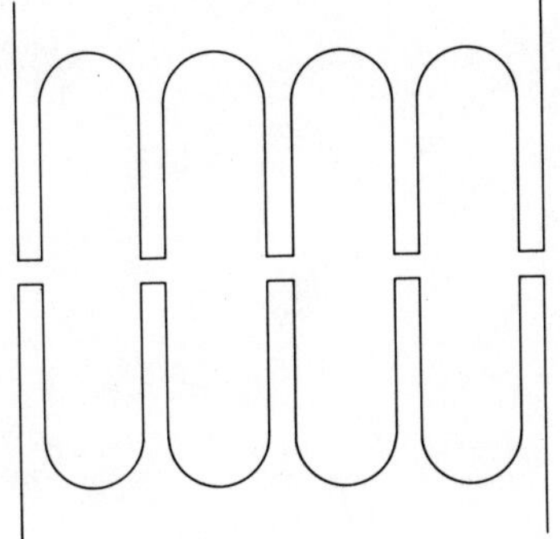

Wayland Becomes a Separate Town

The separation petition of February 22, 1779.

To the honorable the Council and House
of Representitives of the State of Massachusetts
Bay, in New-England

The Petition of us the Subscribers Inhabitants of the easterly Part of the town of Sudbury
humbly sheweth.

That whereas many & great Difficulties and
Inconveniencies intirely unavoidable by us in
Consequence of our present connected Situation
(being united in all our Town Affairs with the
westerly Part of Sd. Sudbury) lay with peculiar
and heavy Weight upon us; which we shall
hereafter endeavour to set forth in this Petition
in as clear and just Light as the Nature of the

1

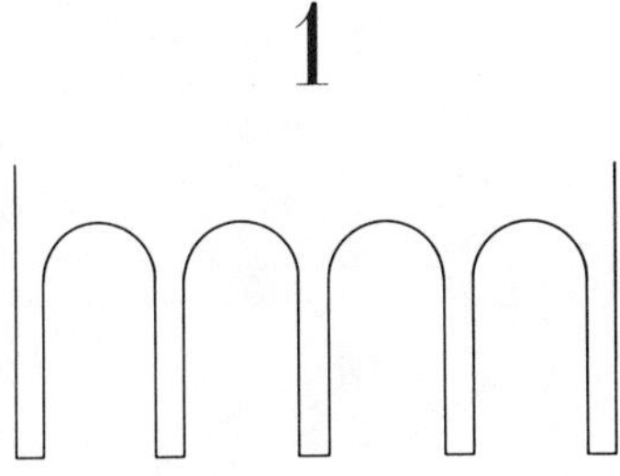

Two Meetinghouses East and West

THE TWO SUDBURYS did not separate until 1780, but the first decade of the eighteenth century saw the initial step in the breaking apart of the closely knit entity which had been organized as Sudbury Plantation in 1638 and the Town of Sudbury in 1639. From the beginning Sudbury had had definite grants of land from the Massachusetts Bay Colony, and its founders formed a united and exclusive group of inhabitants centering their community life on a Puritan church.

If attention is focused solely on geography, it would seem as if the Sudbury River, which cut the town roughly in half as it flowed from south to north, was entirely the cause of the eventual split into two towns. To a considerable extent the river did become the dividing line, and the difficulty of crossing it was an argument for division into two precincts. Divisions of towns following the line of rivers were logical and common enough so that in her book about the early Puritan churches, *Meeting House Hill 1630-1783*, published in 1952, Ola E. Winslow entitled a chapter "East Side—West Side." But it is important to realize that in those same years many early settled towns without significant rivers or natural features to make division lines were breaking into smaller towns all over the province of Massachusetts and in the rest of New England.

Weston, our neighboring town to the east, had broken off from Watertown, first as a precinct in 1698 and then as a town in 1713. Sudbury's early grants of land—1638, 1640, and 1649—gave the town a

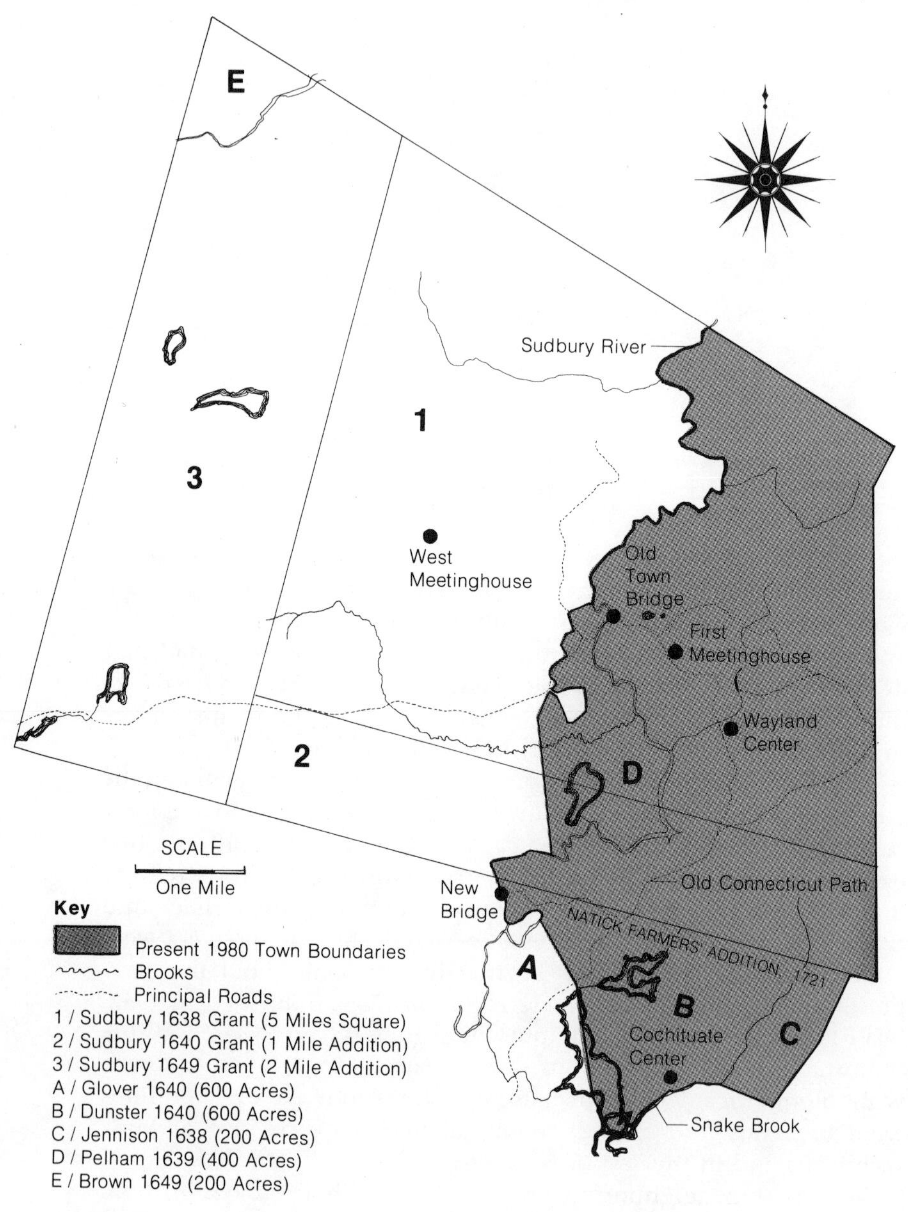

Sudbury town grants, southern farms and meetinghouses.

rectangular area roughly 5 miles by 7, or 35 square miles. This area, while somewhat larger than the 23 square miles which is the present-day area average of the 351 Massachusetts towns, is nowhere near as large as present Petersham (68 sq. mi.) or Belchertown (55 sq. mi.) or several large-area Plymouth colony towns like Plymouth (103 sq. mi.), Middleboro (73 sq. mi.), and Dartmouth (62 sq. mi.). However, it must be realized that because of the spreading out of inhabitants, their increased numbers by the eighteenth century, and a desire not to have to travel great distances to attend church and town meetings if they could afford a separate building and a minister, there was in the eighteenth century a general movement to break the larger, original towns into smaller ones. Weston's separation from Watertown followed the most common procedure by having the area first set off as a church precinct and then made a separate town.

In Sudbury a group west of the river first tried to initiate a division into two precincts in 1707. It was not until fifteen years later, 1722, that what were at first called two precincts were attained, this when a meetinghouse and minister were arranged for on the west side of the river. The division into two towns—Sudbury and East Sudbury—was not to come until 1780. Since the separation of parish or precinct to eventual separate towns was a very common pattern, occurring throughout the province, one might wonder why the story cannot be told in a paragraph. It certainly was not the unique event that Hudson's *History of Sudbury*, published in 1889, made it seem. It was traumatic in Sudbury, as it was in many another town, since it caused controversy and represented the first falling apart of the early town entity which had started out three generations before as a well-organized unit of families who had banded together to form a town. In this connection it is interesting to note that in his *History of Andover, Massachusetts*, published in 1959, Claude Fuess entitled the chapter about the division of Andover into two precincts "The Great Andover Schism."

The story of how Sudbury was divided has importance to those interested in Wayland history because the particular way the division happened in Sudbury explains why our town, the first settled part of Sudbury, now bears a different name. Also, the present location of Wayland's village center and the inclusion of the section of Wayland known as Cochituate in the town's territory is part of this story.

In 1707, after the loss to Framingham of the "outdwellers" beyond the southwest border in 1701, Sudbury's population was well under

The North Cemetery, Wayland, site of the first three Sudbury meetinghouses.

1,000—perhaps between 650 and 750 persons. Only twenty years earlier a new and especially nice third meetinghouse had been built close to the site of the first two meetinghouses in what is now the North Cemetery in Wayland. The town had reason to be proud of this building upon which it had lavished £200 and much effort. The second minister, the Reverend James Sherman, who was hired after the Reverend Edmund Browne died in 1678, had turned out to be difficult and undesirable. The town fathers had finally dismissed him and, after careful consideration, had in November 1706 ordained a promising and satisfactory Harvard College graduate, Israel Loring, as the new minister.

The townsmen might have been expected to be content with their 1688 meetinghouse because they needed to solve the pressing problem of developing more adequate schools for the town. Unlike another offshoot of Watertown—Dedham—or such towns as Ipswich and Newbury, Sudbury had not in the seventeenth century got off to a very early start with schools and at the beginning of the eighteenth century was scarcely meeting the Massachusetts requirements. One would have hoped that the legacy to the town of £50 of the first minister, Edmund Browne, could be used to build a schoolhouse and upgrade the quality of Sudbury's reading and writing (elementary) as well as the grammar (college preparatory) school for which Browne's bequest was specifically left. Instead, in 1707 the town plunged into a drawn-out controversy about whether it could or would establish a meetinghouse on the west side of the river.

One of the great problems was that the meetinghouse on the east side (at the North Cemetery on Old Sudbury Road, Wayland) was very far from being in the center of the town either geographically or in terms of population. In 1701 the so-called Sudbury outdwellers just beyond the southwest corner of the town had succeeded in being set off to the new Town of Framingham. Their satisfaction in not having to trek all the way to Sudbury meetinghouse on the Sabbath and for midweek lectures and town meetings must have been great. Floods had been bad on the river in the spring of 1691, and the winter of 1697 had been a particularly severe one. By 1706 or 1707 a group of inhabitants of the west side of the town was ready to try to get a meetinghouse and minister nearer their farms on the west side of the river.

In the early 1700s, indeed throughout the eighteenth century, the rural towns were still expected officially to have and to be centered on an Orthodox (Puritan) church. (It should be noted, however, that the larger, seaport town of Boston had much earlier begun to have a multiplicity of churches of different denominations, supported by their own congregations.) If, for convenience or any other reason, additional parishes were contemplated for the rural towns, permission had to be sought from the General Court of Massachusetts. The records of the General Court throughout the eighteenth century are full of petitions for, controversies about, and acts and resolves allowing the setting up of new church precincts. The controversies were often about precinct lines and the location of meetinghouses. These matters were of great importance to the inhabitants of the various towns because church attendance, both morning and afternoon on Sundays, was required by law whether or not people were full-fledged church members. The meetinghouses served additionally both for midweek church lectures and as places where town meetings were held and, in many cases, as storage places for town ammunition for the militia. It must always be borne in mind that the building and maintenance of a meetinghouse and payment for the original settling and continuing salary of a minister were major expenses for the rural towns, comparable to the late-twentieth-century burden of providing public schools which overshadows all other present-day town expenditures. There was, of course, a greater tendency for a town to break

The Sudbury River and Nobsot Hill.

into precincts or even districts[1] if the original town area was very large (as in Dedham or Rutland), if remote villages had sprung up in outlying sections (as in the "Farmers' Precinct" of Watertown, which eventually became the Town of Weston), or if the early meetinghouse was not in the center of the town.

There is no mention in the Sudbury town clerk's record of discussions in 1706 at any town meeting of establishing a church on the west side of the river, but there undoubtedly had been discussion among church and town leaders in this year as to the desirability and feasibility of having a west parish when the town arranged for a replacement of the Reverend Sherman in 1706. The first official step toward a west side church was a petition dated January 15, 1707, originated by John Goodenow, John Haynes, and John Brigham and was signed by twenty-eight other inhabitants of the west side of the town. There were Goodenows on both sides of the river; the Haynes family had tended to gravitate to the west side of the river. John Brigham, brought up in Marlborough, had rather recently settled on the far western side of Sudbury. He had been Sudbury's deputy to the

General Court in 1705 and, while attending sessions, had probably become increasingly aware of new precincts and procedures and strategems for attaining them. Four of the seven-man board of selectmen elected on March 19, 1706, were signers of the petition. This document is to be found in the Massachusetts Archives, Volume XI, pages 221-222, and is printed on pages 284 and 285 of Hudson's *History of Sudbury*.[2] This is a fairly short and simple petition, stressing that because of winter ice in the river, the flooding at various times in the year, and the great distances (up to six miles) families were obliged to travel to church, young children and old and weak people could rarely travel to church at those times. The petition asked that the General Court appoint a committee to come to consider their problem. This January petition was read in the House of Representatives on March 20, 1707, and read again to the Legislative Council at the new session on June 4, 1707. At this time the Council ordered that the "Town of Sudbury be served with a copy of the petition and notified to attend the court [legislative session] on the first Friday of the next session if they have any objection."

Meanwhile a town meeting had taken place in Sudbury to discuss the proposal to create a west precinct. Apparently some of the west side inhabitants who favored the new precinct felt that they had not been properly notified about this town meeting. Feeling ran high. In the Massachusetts Archives there is an affidavit dated June 2, 1707, by John Haynes (who had signed the petition for the West Precinct) that John Rice, the town clerk, had refused to give or even show him a copy from the town clerk's record warning of the meeting. The forces against establishing a West Precinct were organizing. It is interesting to note that among the selectmen chosen for town office on March 18, 1707, none was a signer of the January petition.

The matter stood unresolved during that summer. Apparently, the west side petitioners failed to realize that they were expected to appear before the General Court to present their case. Edward Rice of the east side, the town's deputy to the General Court, may have deliberately failed to remind them. In the Massachusetts Archives[3] there is a second petition (October 1707) signed by John Brigham and John Balcom, "on behalf of the rest" of the petitioners for a west precinct asking that the matter be taken up, explaining that they had misunderstood that they were to go to an earlier hearing, and asking that they be heard at the same time as the committee which was planning to come before the legislature. The October 16 warrant for an

October 21, 1707, town meeting reads "to see if the town will do anything by way of answer or objection as to the petition that is lodged in the General Court by some of our neighbors on the west side of the river for a precinct, we being served with a copy of the petition."[4] At this town meeting a committee of six was appointed to go to the General Court to discuss the petition for a precinct. The committee comprised three leading men from the east side—Deacon Joseph Noyes, who had been prominent in the town, especially in the 1690s and was now the east side's elder statesman; James Barnard, the Reverend Edmund Browne's heir and a large landowner; and Ens. Samuel King—and three from the west side, Lt. Hopestill Browne, Noah Clapp, and Thomas Plympton. It should be noted that none of the three men from the west side had signed the petition for the West Precinct.

The next week, five of this committee drew up a petition to the General Court, dated Sudbury, October 29, 1707, against dividing the town into two precincts. The original petition is in the Massachusetts Archives. With its signatures of twenty-four men from the west side and thirty-six from the east side, it is printed in Hudson's *History of Sudbury* on pages 286-287. This document says that the number petitioning for the west precinct was small and that such a move would be "unseasonable and unreasonable," especially in view of the great expense the town had just undergone to depose a minister and settle a new one. They mentioned also the expense of the present war (Queen Anne's) and argued strongly that they deemed the town incapable of supporting two ministers. They added that they were ready to take steps to raise the causeway so that passage to the church across the river would be easier. They ended by pointing out that if a west meetinghouse were to be placed at the center of Sudbury's territory west of the river, it would be just as remote from some west side dwellings as the east meetinghouse then was.

On October 30, 1707, both the petitioners for the West Precinct and the town committee attended a hearing before the General Court. It can be supposed that John Brigham, one of the leaders of the movement to establish a west precinct, brought to this hearing his rather crude map of the town of Sudbury, the original of which is in the Massachusetts Archives, bearing the date 1707 and Massachusetts Archives No. 228. At the bottom is the title, "The plat of Sudbury Township Jno Brigham." A later copy of this map with printed rather than handwritten titles and bearing the date 1708 appears opposite page 124 in Hudson's *History of Sudbury*, but there is no reference to this having been a document supporting the petition for a west precinct, nor is there evidence that Hudson realized this.[5] If one refers to the Massachusetts Archives, one finds that two similar but not identical maps actually were submitted, the second one now designated with Massachusetts Archives No. 230 and the date 1708. Both maps show by the letter *h* the location of the early houses in the town and were obviously submitted in connection with the petition for the West Precinct. Map No. 230 has the river less exactly drawn and a larger number of houses on each side of the river. Both are extremely interesting because they represent the earliest extant contemporary maps of the whole town. The roads are not shown, but it is apparent that an effort was made to locate the *h* symbols where the houses were actually situated. One can see where houses clustered and where some of the roads must have gone. The handwriting on both maps is the same; both must have been the work of John Brigham, who called himself a surveyor. There is considerable discrepancy between these two maps as to the placement of the houses, especially on the New Grant lots on the western edge of the town. These are crude maps. They were drawn to show the General Court how far from the center of the town the meetinghouse stood and that by this time there were more houses on the west side of the river than on the east.

Map No. 228 (1707) shows 57 houses on the west side of the river and 32 on the east side. Very interestingly, the 1708 map included beyond Sudbury's south border on the east side of the river, twelve *h*'s designated as "the farmers." This very important group of houses will be discussed below when we come to the "Natick farmers." A note on the margin of No. 230 says, "It is understood that in several houses one [*sic*] each sid the river two families dwells in the same." The mapmaker was trying to assure the legislators that there were enough families on each side of the river to support separate ministers. At this period the province was specifying that new townships could be incorporated only if they had a minimum of sixty families for the support of a minister.

On November 1, 1707, the day after the hearing, *The House Journal* shows that, owing to the fact that the House did not consider that it had received enough information, it appointed a committee of three—Col. Samuel Checkley of Boston, Capt. Thomas Oliver of Cambridge, and Capt. Jonas Bond of Watertown—to go to Sudbury to study the question. The Governor's Council concurred and added two men to the committee: John Phillips and Joseph Lynde, Esq., both of Charlestown.

The record shows that on March 15, 1708, a town meeting was ordered to choose men to meet with the committee of the General Court who wanted to come to Sudbury March 17 to consider the petition for a west precinct. The town chose a committee of twelve distinguished citizens[6]—six from the east side of the river and six from the west side. Three of these were incumbent selectmen: Hopestill Browne, Samuel King, and Thomas Plympton. Of the six west siders, all had signed the petition against the west precinct.

A report was made to the General Court on May 13, 1708, stating, in part:

Considering the badness of the causeway, the difficulty of the way and the Distance they are from the meeting house, we are of [the] *opinion that it is needful, there should be a meeting house upon the west side of the River. But yet considering the Present Greatness of Publicke Charges, the division their is between the Inhabitants of the west side, and the obligation that the whole Town are under to their Present minister . . . we are . . . of the opinion that the whole Town continue to assemble at the Present meeting house until those obstructions be removed. (Mass. Archives, Vol. XI, p. 250c)*

The proponents of a west precinct were not to be defeated. A second petition, dated May 26, 1708 (probably accompanied by the second map, No. 230), was sent to the legislature, signed by John Brigham and John Balcom, "in behalf of the rest." This petition is printed on page 288 of Hudson's *History of Sudbury*. After reiterating the difficulties of crossing the river and saying that there are 356 persons on the west side, it asks that they be allowed to have a meetinghouse and minister at such time as the General Court shall deem appropriate. The figure of 356 people on the west side is interesting. If the houses were correctly plotted on the west side—60 in number— this means that there was an average of 5.9 persons per house; and if this average can be relied upon, the 49 houses on the east side of the river contained about 290 persons.

This petition got better results. The General Court decided in June 1708 that if the west side inhabitants should be in a position to erect a meetinghouse and present to the General Court a subscription of £ 50 per annum for the minister's salary for the first seven years, they could go ahead and build a meetinghouse and invite a minister. This legislative order, dated June 23, 1708, and cited on page 289 of Hudson's *History of Sudbury*, specified that such action for a new meetinghouse and a second minister should in no way infringe on the contract the town had with Mr. Loring unless the town or General Court should make other arrangements.

It appears possible that when the first petition was circulated in very early 1707, Mr. Loring had already indicated some interest in going to a new precinct on the west side or at least that a group on the west side wanted him to move there. Just as the petitions for and against a West Precinct came up, the house on the east side of the river which the town had provided for its second minister, James Sherman, became available to the town for Mr. Loring. In December 1707 the selectmen called a town meeting "to take care that our Reverend Pastor Mr. Israel Loring have a ministerial place . . . and so see that our meeting house be mended." At a December 17, 1707, meeting, the town confirmed Mr. Sherman's house and lands for Mr. Loring. Immediately, twenty-three men, mostly west siders who had signed the January 1707 petition for a West Precinct, recorded in the town book their dissent against the settling of Mr. Loring in Mr. Sherman's former house, because "we are now in the General Court's hands." However, many inhabitants who were prominent in the town did not suspect that Mr. Loring would go to the west side when a church was established there. This is shown by the fact that on March 12, 1711, the Sudbury Proprietors granted six acres of land near Smithfield (on the east side of the river, near the present Wayland Public Library) to Israel Loring and six acres (location not designated) "to the first orderly settled minister that shall be settled on the west side of the river."[7] These grants were not the same as the ministerial lands which the proprietors were also laying out, but were outright gifts forever to Israel Loring and his prospective colleague.

When towns created second precincts, it was not uncommon for the incumbent minister to be allowed to choose which precinct he would serve. This was the stipulation made in Chapter 83 of Province Laws IX 34, passed November 3, 1708, that divided Andover into North and South precincts. The early Andover church was in the North Precinct, and the Reverend Thomas Barnard was ordered by the General Court to choose which precinct he would serve. Unlike Mr. Loring, he found it difficult to make up his mind, although it was fairly clear that the new, South Precinct did not want him. Barnard procrastinated so long that the General Court ordered him to reach a decision before December 11, 1710. He finally decided to stay where he was, in the old, North Precinct.[8]

It cannot be positively determined whether for the next few years it proved impossible to raise the funds stipulated by the General Court. There was considerable excitement, controversy, and activity from 1706 to 1708, when the Sudbury proprietors decided to divide up a large part of the town's extensive common lands on both sides of the river. This decision may have diverted the town's attention from the meetinghouse problem and could even have been a deliberate tactic to delay the campaign for a west precinct. It is interesting to note, however, that as soon as they sat down to divide the town's common and undivided lands, the Sudbury proprietors started planning for a minister on the west side of the river. On November 2, 1708, the proprietors voted at their meeting to grant forty acres from the common land on each side of the river for the use of the respective east and west ministries.[9] Deacon Noyes (east side) and Deacon Haynes (west side) were to work with the surveyor in picking out "convenient land." The surveying and laying out of this land took place around 1720.

The next time the matter of a west side church appears in the town clerk's record is five years later, during 1713. In January of that year there was an article in the warrant "to see if the town will do something that the inhabitants on the west side of the river may be in a way to hear the word of God preached, they being under extreme difficulties . . . and hear what proposals may be made." Nothing was done at this meeting, but at a town meeting called for February 20, 1713, there was a proposal "to see if the town will do anything to bring the house into the center of the town or within a quarter of a mile of the center . . . the Town of Sudbury being seven miles long [wide from east to west] and the meeting house . . . but about a mile and a half from the east end." For this meeting, which was held in midwinter but was probably well attended, John Rice (1651-1717), one of the town's older, distinguished leaders who had served seventeen years as selectman and was then town clerk, was chosen moderator. In the usual laconic style in which town clerks (and especially John Rice) reported even the most controversial town meetings, he recorded that "the major part of the town did not act as to moving of the meeting house." Again, in May 1713 the matter of moving the meetinghouse to a central place was put in the warrant. However, there is no record of a discussion or a decision on the article. In the fall of 1713 it was proposed that the town provide one or more boats to transport people across the river. Apparently, nothing was done about this expedient, and they were still discussing the building of a boat in 1718.[10]

Two Meetinghouses

In the spring of 1714 proponents of a west precinct were again pressing for a west meetinghouse. On March 15 at the regular spring election meeting a petition to build a meetinghouse on the west side of the river was brought up by a group of west side inhabitants. The meeting did not consider this petition on that day, but a special meeting was called for March 29 to consider the petition. The question of a west meetinghouse must have been discussed at this meeting, but Town Clerk John Rice's record mentions no discussion or action.

The failure of the town to act on the west siders' petition to the town in the early spring of 1714 must have infuriated west side inhabitants who wanted a west meetinghouse. By May 1714 a substantial group of west side inhabitants were submitting a petition to the Massachusetts General Court asking to be set off as a separate township. Their petition is not to be found in the Massachusetts Archives, but from the wording of Chapter 6 of Province Laws IX 350, passed June 2, 1714, the petitioners prayed to be made a township "that they may be in the way to establish ye word of God among themselves." Chapter 6 ordered these petitioners to serve the Town of Sudbury with a copy of their petition and ordered a hearing for objections to be held at the fall session of the General Court.

The petition was probably presented to the Sudbury selectmen in the early summer. However, the town clerk's record shows that it was not until October that a meeting was called to consider objecting to this drastic petition. There is no doubt that there was tension and unpleasant discussion over a fraction of the west side's attempt to become a separate township. The east siders and those advocating that they remain a united town seem to have tried to call a meeting of east side inhabitants only. That this was not legal or allowable and that in the end it was supposed to be a full town meeting is evidenced because Joseph Noyes, constable of the west side, asked to have recorded in the town clerk's book that he had had a very (too) short time to be able to warn the inhabitants of the west side of this particular meeting. A peculiarly worded warrant, dated October 1714, ordered "the people on the East Side to meet at the Meeting House October 26, 1714 . . . to answer the petition of Inhabitants of the West Side of the river to be heard at Boston October 27th." This was the very next day.

At the town meeting of October 26 a committee of four—Ephraim Curtis, Noah Clapp, William Jennison, and Hopestill Bent—was appointed to attend the General Court the next day to present the town's objections. All were east siders except Clapp, who lived west of the river but had in 1708 petitioned against building a meetinghouse on the west side.

The petition for a separate township was not allowed. However, it is interesting to speculate, in view of what happened in 1778-80, as to whether, if the petition had been granted, the western offshoot would have borne the name Sudbury and retained the early town and church records as happened in 1780.

On October 28, 1714, the day after the hearing at which the chief petitioners for a separate, west township and the town committee were both heard, the General Court in Chapter 83 of Province Laws IX 374 rejected the separate township idea but made the basic decision that "there be a distinct Precinct and a Meeting House erected for the publicke worship of God on the West Side of Sudbury River." In this connection, a legislative committee was appointed to go to Sudbury to look at possible places for this meetinghouse and to "hear the Inhabitants on both sides of the River what they propose referring to the support of the Ministry and Acomodating both Parts of the Town with Schools." This committee was to report its recommendations at the next session of the General Court, in the spring of 1715, "unless the Town shall agree . . . and return their Agreement in writing to the Chairman of the Committee within two months" (by late December 1714). Here we see the provincial legislature trying to get the town to settle its own controversy.

Apparently, in November attempts were made to decide this issue within the town. A town meeting was called for November 18 to debate the question. The town clerk, John Rice, recorded that Capt. Hopestill Browne, who had very recently served as a selectman and was this year the town's deputy to the General Court, was chosen moderator of the meeting. However, the town clerk recorded nothing else about this meeting, unless the record was later destroyed. Eleven days later, on November 29, 1714, the town met again, this time "to elect or depute one or more persons to represent them at the General Court . . . referring to ye precinct in Sudbury." At this meeting it was voted that the two deacons of the church, James Haynes (who had favored the west precinct) and Edward Rice (who had not favored a west precinct), should go to the General Court to tell it that the town was not agreed about the present division but had agreed to let the legislative committee come and would entertain it.

One might have expected that the legislative committee would have brought in its report at least by mid-1715, but as the report shows this was a difficult matter and the report was not presented to the

General Court until December 8, 1715. In the meantime, the record of the town clerk, still John Rice and now quite elderly, shows no discussion of the precinct division or the placement of a meetinghouse on the west side at the various town meetings of 1715. In late March 1715 the town's first schoolhouse, a small building at the Gravel Pit at the western end of the causeway, was finished and accepted by the town. During that spring the town was much concerned with stoppages and flooding of the river and on March 7 voted £ 150 for raising the causeway. Later in the spring and throughout the summer, Sudbury was rocked by a scandal about the theft of the town's supply of ammunition, which had presumably been stored in the meetinghouse on the east side. One senses the tension over this and the division of the town when one reads in the town clerk's record of a town meeting on September 6, 1715, that "if the town is ever divided into two the supply of ammunition would be divided [between the two towns]."

The report that was finally made on December 8, 1715, to the General Court by its committee[11] is most interesting. It shows that there had been considerable discussion, as well there should have been, about the land division, how the two ministers could be maintained, and whose responsibility and expense it would be to build the west meetinghouse. This report reads, in part:

The Inhabitants on the East Side are willing to give one half of the land in Sudbury to make the West Precinct and so each to maintain their own minister which the Inhabitants in the West Side of the River do refuse and instead the west proposed to build a Meeting House at their own Charge and settle a minister. And the Ministers on both sides of the River should be supported equally by the whole Town.

This represented a departure from the usual arrangement whereby, if there were separate precincts, each precinct supplied its own minister. Although it contained a smaller land area, the per acre tax valuation of the section of Sudbury on the east side of the river was higher. This fact must have influenced the west siders to vote for a less than precinct arrangement that the two ministers be supported by the whole town.

The report was read and accepted in the Council and concurred to in the House, and it was ordered that a place on the west side called Poplar Swamp Gutter on the north side of the Lancaster Road be the place for the west meetinghouse. No mention was made in the legislative order of an exact land division of the two precincts or of the proposal that the west siders erect their own meetinghouse. It was, however, ordered that "the Inhabitants of the whole Town do in common maintain and pay both of their ministers."

Nearly another four years passed without agreement about who would pay for the west meetinghouse. If the inhabitants of the west precinct were to pay for their own meetinghouse, the precinct line would be a matter of permanent importance. One of the articles before a town meeting of July 21, 1719, was to see if the town would choose a committee to agree to a dividing line for the two precincts so that a petition could go to the General Court. The town clerk's record shows no such committee appointed or any action taken, and no petition for a precinct dividing line can be found in the Massachusetts Archives.

In the year 1720, thirteen years after the drive to divide the town into two church precincts began, a group petitioned the town at a town meeting on May 12

that although the act of the General Court ordered that a meeting house be erected . . . on the west side of Sudbury and employing two separate congregations . . . we are humbly of the opinion that if the town can agree upon other methods more conducing to their own peace and welfare it will be very satisfactory to the Court, therefor we the subscribers [not named in the record] *do request that you call the town . . . together . . . to see if . . . when met by a vote . . . will remain one town entire and have but one meeting house and build a meeting house large enough for the whole town . . . and place said meeting house . . . and build a meeting house on the west side of . . . Sudbury River at or near the Gravel pit at the westerly end of the long causeway . . . and to see if the town will raise the long causeway a foot or foot and a half for convenient passage and mend the way.*

On May 12, 1720, the major part of the town approved the above proposals and agreed to submit them to the General Court. However, forty-nine men, including two selectmen, Ephraim Curtis and John Woodward, both east siders, signed a written dissent to this vote and entered it on the town clerk's record. They had two chief arguments. One was that it was unreasonable under present conditions to so arrange a church that the inhabitants of the east side should have to encounter the difficulties the inhabitants of the west side had been experiencing; the second was the uncertainty of success of such a project as raising the long causeway.

This rather massive dissent apparently discouraged the idea of petitioning the General Court for a change of plan to build one meetinghouse for the use of the whole town. No petition and no action on this matter is found in the legislative record.

By the spring of 1721 there were renewed efforts to have a meetinghouse built for west side inhabitants. David Haynes and sixty-three others preferred one petition to the General Court that spring, and Edmund Browne and sixteen others preferred another petition about the placing of the west meetinghouse and the combined maintenance of the ministers. These petitions, not extant, were read in the House on May 31, 1721, and led to an order of June 9, 1721,[12] that there be a new meetinghouse built on the place called Poplar Swamp Gutter, as arranged by a former committee in December 1715. This time the General Court was very definite about payment for the new meetinghouse when it ordered that a new meetinghouse be erected at Poplar Swamp Gutter and that the old (east) meetinghouse be put in good repair, both to be done "at the charge of the whole Town and that the Ministers on both sides the River be Maintained and Supported by a Town Tax." The question of a precinct dividing line was ducked, and wisely so, because the river, which was the natural barrier, divided the town far from evenly, giving much more land to the west parish.

Ephraim Curtis was a peppery opponent of changing the status and later the location of the east church. He strongly opposed involving the east siders in any obligation to help build a west meetinghouse. *The Journal of the House of Representatives* shows that in March 1721 a committee of the House recommended to that body that a petition by Ephraim Curtis, signed by fifty-four inhabitants of the east side, should be dismissed as groundless; the petition opposed the order for building a west meetinghouse at Poplar Swamp Gutter and proposed instead that the Town of Sudbury be divided into two distinct townships.[13] Ephraim Curtis died in 1759 and thus did not live to see the town division which took place in 1780 and to know of his son Joseph's importance as leader of the newly formed East Sudbury. In 1721 the time was not ripe for a town division.

By the summer of 1721 the east meetinghouse, although only thirty-four years old, seems to have fallen into rather bad repair, and we find a town meeting of October 21, 1721, voting that the town "will mend the steps of the meeting house where it has fallen down."

Meanwhile, the west siders were anxious to get their meetinghouse built. However, by late 1721 it had become apparent that the Poplar Swamp Gutter location was not popular with the majority of west siders and that they had determined that they preferred to locate their meetinghouse on Rocky Plain, the present Sudbury Center, near where the proprietors had laid out a west side burying ground in 1717. The location of the burying ground here in early 1717 may mean that the Poplar Swamp Gutter location proposed by the legislative committee was never seriously considered by the west side residents of Sudbury.

Records show that on December 26, 1721, a town meeting was called at George Pitts's tavern near the present Sudbury Center on the west side, to see (1) if the town would grant money to support preaching on the west side and (2) whether, in view of the fact that not even a third of the inhabitants of the west side liked the Poplar Swamp Gutter location, the town would appoint a committee to prefer a petition to the General Court that the west side inhabitants be allowed to place their meetinghouse at a location on Rocky Plain they had recently agreed upon. At this meeting the town granted £25 to carry on preaching on the west side for the present and then chose a committee to prefer the petition to the General Court for the Rocky Plain location. This committee of five included three men from the west side—Lt. David Haynes, Ens. John Balcom, and Daniel Estabrook—and two men from the east side—William Jennison and Samuel Graves.

Apparently there were those in town who thought the meeting on the west side was out of order. The town clerk's record shows that on the complaint of Benjamin Parmenter, Sr., and eighteen others, Francis Fulham, justice of the peace for Middlesex County, was requested to order the constables to issue a warrant for a town meeting "at the Meeting House" on December 28 to discuss repairing the east meetinghouse and building the west meetinghouse as ordered in June 1721 and to vote on the size of the new meetinghouse. The townsmen assembled for the December 28 meeting, but a majority seems to have resented the way the meeting had been called, for, by a vote of 87 of the inhabitants (a clear majority), they refused to act on any proposals in this warrant.

Finally, at a town meeting held one month later, on January 19, 1722, the town voted a sum of £5 to prefer a petition to the General Court asking that Rocky Plain be the location of the west side meetinghouse. Without waiting for General Court permission, some of the west siders built a temporary meetinghouse where church services were held that winter and spring. In other towns, one of them being Framingham, groups had taken matters into their own hands and built meetinghouses before official permission was granted or before a location was officially approved. Although the petition for the formal change is not to be found in the Massachusetts Archives, there obviously was one which the House of Representatives was not inclined to grant. However, on March 20, 1722, Chapter 87 of Massachusetts Province Laws (Resolves) 1721, Volume X, states that the Council did not concur with the House and, "having considered the great dissatisfaction of the Inhabitants on the West Side of the . . . Town with the order of the General Court . . . of December, 1715 voted a committee of three men from the Council with such men as the House will appoint once more to view the several places proposed for the west meeting house . . . [and] that always the Salary of the Reverend Mr. Loring be no way diminished." This time the Council appointed one man from Newton, one from Concord, one from Lancaster, and one from Lexington.

This committee brought in its report in June stating that, having viewed the place proposed and also having seen the several parts and quarters on the west side of the river, it agreed that Rocky Plain was the most convenient place for a meetinghouse and that "it accordingly be placed some 30 rods to the westward of a House Newly Erected on Rocky Plain and where there has been preaching for some Sabbaths." This place was described as "near the place where a Road from Concord to Wood's Mill crosses the Public Road to Lancaster and to stand to the Northeast of Said Road." This is the location of the present Sudbury Unitarian Church, a successor building to the first west meetinghouse.

Reasons given in the report were that although Poplar Swamp Gutter was fairly near the center of the land area on the west side, the quality of the land to the east was capable of accommodating more inhabitants than the westerly land. The report ended with a recommendation that because the inhabitants living on the north side of the Stow (Assabet) River were remote from this location and much nearer to the Stow meetinghouse which they generally attended, these families be set off to Stow as to ministerial charges.

That summer (1722) the town refused to raise funds by tax collection for the west meetinghouse. This led to a petition to the General Court by three west side leaders—David Haynes, David Estabrook, and John Haynes—that the General Court help them. This in turn led to an order of November 27, 1722 (Chapter 191 of Massachusetts Province Laws [Resolves], Volume X, pages 225-226) "That a New Meeting House be Erected . . . at a place called Rocky Plain . . . and that a Sum of £500 be raised by and assessed on the Town of Sudbury." The land on which the new Rocky Plain meetinghouse was placed was common land which was not officially laid out by the Sudbury proprietors for this purpose until the meetinghouse was well under way. The proprietors record contains a map ("plat") of 2 acres and 127 rods laid out on June 2, 1723, on Rocky Plain, "where the New Meeting House stands." The files of the Massachusetts Historical Society contain a diagram of this land taken from page 25 of the second book of proprietors records.[14]

The west side inhabitants obtained permission to erect their meetinghouse where they wanted it on Rocky Plain after they built a temporary house there; held services on Sunday; and, as previously mentioned, persuaded the General Court to send another committee to the west side of Sudbury. By April 1722 the town was providing money for the ministry on both sides of the river, although the west meetinghouse was not built in 1722. The *Sudbury Westerly Precinct Record* tells us that the west meetinghouse was framed on April 24, 1723. The first meeting of the West Precinct organization was held in the new meetinghouse on July 15, 1723. The West Precinct record states that the last part of the payment of £400 to the builders, Abraham Wood and Joseph Dakin, was not made until May 31, 1725.[15] At a town meeting held on August 5, 1723, in the west meetinghouse, it was voted that warnings of future town meetings be posted for the west side inhabitants on the meetinghouse doors —good evidence that the building was then essentially finished.

The legislative order of November 27, 1722, went on to the matter of repairing the east meetinghouse, "at the Charge of the Whole Town." This leads us to the subject of the so-called Natick farmers and the considerable controversy over the east meetinghouse: whether to repair it in its original location, move it, or replace it.

NOTES

1. A district carried on its own municipal business with separate meetings, clerk, records, and financing as well as a separate church. It differed from a town only in being unable to send a representative to the General Court.

2. There seem to be several errors in the transcription of the signatures. Richard Sanger is given as Richard Taylor. Prefer Haynes should be Peter Haynes.

3. *Massachusetts Archives* Vol. XI, p. 228.

4. *Sudbury Records* (Mary Heard edition) Vol. II, p. 101. Note the tone of this in saying "Our neighbors to the west."

5. In the list of illustrations at the beginning of Hudson's *History of Sudbury* the map opposite page 24 is mistakenly called "By Haynes."

6. From the east side: Maj. Thomas Browne, Dea. Joseph Noyes, Mr. James Barnard, Ens. Samuel King, Lt. William Jennison, and Lt. Samuel Graves (Town Clerk). From the west side: Lt. Hopestill Browne, Samuel Wright, Noah Clapp, Joseph Stanhope, Thomas Plympton, and Joshua Haynes.

7. Sudbury Proprietors, *Book of Grants*, p. 67.

8. Claude Fuess, *Andover, Symbol of New England: the Evolution of a Town*, Andover, 1959, p. 121.

9. Sudbury Proprietors, *Book of Grants*, pp. 40-41.

10. *Sudbury Records*, Vol. II (M.H. ed.) pp. 158-173.

11. *Massachusetts Province Laws* [Resolves], Vol. IX 1708-1719, Appendix IV, p. 451.

12. *Massachusetts Province Resolves*, Chapter 4, 1721.

13. *Journal of the House of Representatives of Massachusetts*, Massachusetts Historical Society edition, Boston, 1922, pp. 176-177.

14. Massachusetts Historical Society, *Sudbury*, No. 1, 69.

15. Town of Sudbury, *Westerly Precinct Record*, pp. 21 and 34.

2

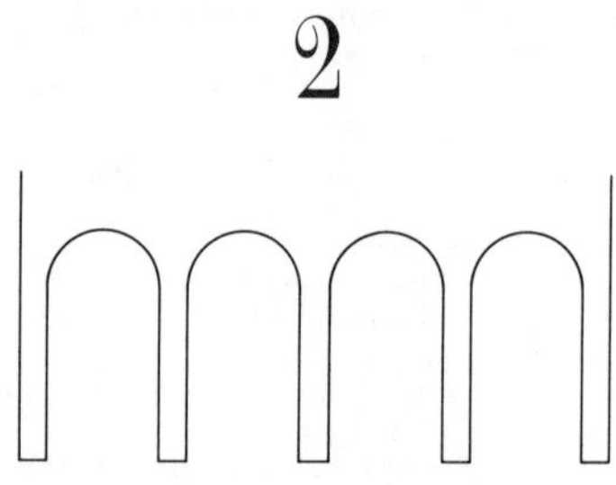

Natick Farmers and the East Meetinghouse

AT A TOWN MEETING held on March 5, 1705, a committee of three—Cornet William Browne, Jonathan Rice, and Thomas Plympton—was appointed to meet with agent John Leverett to run Sudbury's southern bound with Natick. On April 21 of that year a town meeting voted that "the farmers adjacent to Sudbury that lie between Sudbury and Natick should still continue with us." This continuation must have meant church affiliation and possibly parish taxation for schools. It was also voted at this meeting to petition the General Court that "the farmers adjacent to Sudbury may be confirmed to the town of Sudbury." It is not known whether as early as 1705 the idea that there might be a west precinct served as a spur to Sudbury inhabitants to try to have included officially on their southeast flank the group of families who had spread into the area south of Sudbury's legal south border. At this time Sudbury's south border was contiguous with Natick's north border only for five hundred yards near the southeast corner of Sudbury and the northeast corner of Natick. Most of the households in the intervening land between towns were connected by marriage and descent with the Rice family.

These families living over the border toward Natick but who were closer to Sudbury would be considered valuable additions to the eastern side of the town. John Brigham was Sudbury's deputy to the General Court in 1705 when the matter was first discussed in town meeting. It is clear that by the time Brigham showed them on his 1708 map, their twelve households were considered as actual or potential contributors to the support of an east precinct. It is conceivable that with the loss in 1701 of the southwest outdwellers to the newly established Town of Framingham, the town merely was anxious to keep as much of the population on its southern fringe as possible. These households had a strong bond of kinship with Sudbury families. Natick, to the south, was still an Indian town under guardianship of the General Court, and the twelve families would not have wanted to cast their lots with that political entity.[1]

The complete list of the twelve families is not known, but, as has been pointed out, John Brigham's 1708 map accompanying the petition for a west precinct had indicated at least in a rough way the location of the twelve houses of these farmers. The twelve farms were on land originally part of the Glover, Dunster, and Jennison private farm grants, (see map on page 10) rather than in the Sudbury or Dedham township land grants. Caleb Johnson, one of the twelve, had bought some of the Glover land and lived near Dudley Pond, then called Johnson's Pond. The Rice family had acquired much land south of Sudbury's border. The so-called Natick farmers of 1721 included Phineas Brintnal who had married Sibella Rice, a granddaughter of Matthew Rice. Natick farmer John Graves's wife, Sarah Loker, was also a granddaughter of Matthew Rice. John and Sarah (Rice) Loker lived in that area, and their son Isaac Loker later married Ann Brintnal. Micah Bent (a somewhat later occupant of some of the land) also married a Rice, and both the Duntons and Collars, edge-of-Natick families, had intermarried with Rices.

There is no extant evidence that a petition was sent to the General Court for the inclusion of these families in Sudbury in 1705. Moreover, it has not been determined why the town waited until a meeting on March 20, 1721, to vote again to petition the General Court "for the farmers and farm lands lying between the town of Sudbury and Natick who have laid to the town of Sudbury to duty for years past may now be laid to the Town of Sudbury forever."

It is interesting to note that on the same day (June 9, 1721) the General Court passed its order that a meetinghouse be built on the west side of the river and that the east meetinghouse be put in good repair, *both* meetinghouses to be at the charge of the whole town, Chapter 2 of the same General Court session was an order that:

Upon reading a petition of William Jennison and Ebenezer Rice praying that several farms lying adjacent to the Town betwixt Sudbury and Natick may be added to the Township of Sudbury for Ever, the Inhabitants dwelling in those farms having desired to be joined to the said town, the Committee are of the Opinion that the Farms petitioned for be annexed from henceforth and made part of the Township of Sudbury and the Inhabitants thereof to pay their proportion to all rates and Taxes and Enjoy Equal Priviledges with the rest of the Inhabitants of the Town of Sudbury.[2]

At the town meeting of March 20, 1721, it had been voted to petition the General Court that the farmers and farmlands lying between the towns of Sudbury and Natick be joined to Sudbury. The committee elected to manage the petition included William Jennison, who lived on the southeast side of Sudbury near the present junction of Woodridge Road with Cochituate Road in Wayland and whose forty-six acres of land may have extended to the official south boundary of the town, and Ebenezer Rice, who may have had a house south of the legal border and been one of the Natick farmers. Ebenezer Rice's only office held in Sudbury was that of selectman in 1722. He died in 1724. This order,[3] entitled "Order for Adding Farms Near Natick to the Town of Sudbury," brought the 2,141 acres of land constituting the present south precinct of Wayland into the town.[4] Surprisingly, no map and boundary description seems to have accompanied this legislative action; at least, none was referred to in the official record. This boundary, part of which is Snake Brook, dipped down from the old, straight south boundary of Sudbury starting at the still recognizable old southeast corner of the early grant.

It was not shown on any map of Sudbury that can be found in the Massachusetts Archives until that made by Matthias Mossman as part of the general town-by-town survey of the Commonwealth of Massachusetts submitted in May 1795.[5] As far as this author can determine, except for an almost negligible adjustment made in April 1850 after the Cochituate Aqueduct was built, this line has stood as the southern boundary of East Sudbury (Wayland) and Natick ever since 1721 when an act so vague, in its wording at least, as to describe the land as "several Farms lying adjacent to the Town of Sudbury" brought this territory into the town. This is the section of the town later known as Cochituate. It can be assumed that the 1721 addition included all land between what had been officially granted to Sudbury as a southern addition in 1640 and the northern bound established for the Indian plantation at Natick in May 1660.[6] The map on page 10 shows this land as including William Jennison's 1638 grant of two hundred acres, the six-hundred acre farm granted Harvard College President Henry Dunster in 1638, and part of Mrs. Glover's six-hundred-acre farm acquired from the Massachusetts Bay Colony in 1640.

If one can believe the house count of the 1708 Brigham map, this addition of twelve houses did much to even the number of houses on the two sides of the river and made a significant though not equalizing addition to the much smaller land area east of the river. But, although the families thus added to the town seemed to want to be included officially, the "old south bound" was remembered and referred to in deeds and documents for many years. Moreover, very soon a controversy arose as to whether these farmers would remain with the town of Sudbury after all.

The above-cited General Court order (Chapter 2), passed on June 9, 1721, mentions nothing about the location of the east meetinghouse. However, on January 22, 1722, after some steps had been taken the previous October to repair the east meetinghouse in its original location, a petition was brought before a January 29, 1722, town meeting, "to see if the town will . . . pull down the old meeting house and carry it more south and set it up and finish it at the town's cost to accommodate the new east side inhabitants . . ." and "to see if the town will choose a committee to prefer a petition to the General Court to obtain liberty to do the same." At the January 29 meeting it was voted to move the east meetinghouse south within five years if the General Court would approve. A committee was chosen for this, including William Jennison and Ebenezer Rice, who had handled the 1721 petition to the General Court to get the Natick farmers included in the town, and Samuel Graves from the east side, some of whose land bordered on Natick. There were also three men from the west side: Capt. David Haynes, John Balcom, and Daniel Estabrook. Seventy men apparently voted to petition the General Court to move the east meetinghouse south (also to change the west meetinghouse location to Rocky Plain), but twenty-eight men, many of them prominent east siders and town officers (including Selectman Ephraim Curtis and Town Treasurer Samuel Abbott), entered their dissent. The location of both meetinghouses was by now a matter of extreme controversy in the town.

Nothing in the June 1721 act of the General Court or in the town action of March 1721 authorizing William Jennison and Ebenezer Rice to petition the General Court for inclusion of the Natick farmers' territory in Sudbury indicates that the admission of these families was officially contingent upon moving the meetinghouse to a more convenient location. However, from later records and documents it is fairly apparent that a promise was made to this group by the selectmen or by the committee chosen to petition the General Court.

This writer has found no evidence that a town committee made any move to petition the General Court to be allowed to move the east meetinghouse south in the year following the annexation of the farms of the twelve Natick farmers. A year after it had been voted to mend the steps and underpinnings of the east meetinghouse, the warrant for an October 22, 1722, town meeting contained an article "to see if the town will put the old meeting house into good repair pursuant to the order of the General Court." No funds were voted for this purpose at that meeting. But when on November 27, 1722, the General Court ordered that the new west meetinghouse be built at Rocky Plain at an expenditure by the town of £ 350 to £ 500, the General Court again stated that the east meetinghouse must be repaired by the town.

In January 1723 the east meetinghouse was still in bad repair. The Reverend William Cook, who had been on trial as minister for the east side that winter, was to be ordained and also married in this meetinghouse in March. We find a town meeting called for January 22, 1723, with a warrant article "to see if the town will well and sufficiently repair the old meeting house according to the order of the General Court." At this meeting £ 150 was voted to repair the east meetinghouse. However, apparently little if anything had been done by March 23, the date of the Reverend Cook's ordination and marriage. The East Precinct record contains a warrant article for its April 5, 1723, meeting "to see whether the Precinct will have the Old Meetinghouse repaired agreeable to the order of the General Court . . . and to let it to workmen and draw money from the Town Treasurer."[7] At this meeting the precinct organization voted to repair the meetinghouse and chose a precinct committee of five men—Ephraim Curtis, Capt. Joshua Haynes, Mr. Thomas Taylor, Mr. Ephraim Rice, and Lt. John Noyes—to supervise the work.

After the ordination celebration we find that there was an article in a town meeting warrant for April 8, 1723,

to see if the Town will desist from repairing the old meeting house because of its location . . . and to see if the town will remove said meeting house more south easterly where it may better accommodate the inhabitants of the easterly precinct if the General Court will allow.

In March 1722 William Jennison and Ebenezer Rice, the original petitioners to the General Court for the taking in of the farmers near

Natick, were both on the board of selectmen, and in 1723 William Jennison was still a selectman. The board of selectmen that year also included John Dunton, one of the Natick farmers.

By the spring of 1723 a complicated townwide controversy had arisen over whether to repair the third meetinghouse in its original location or move it south, as had apparently been promised when the twelve farms near Natick were taken into the town. The East Precinct leaders appear not to have wanted to accommodate the Natick farmers by moving their meetinghouse south. The East Precinct record shows that they remained intent on repairing the meetinghouse where it was.

No town committee went about petitioning the General Court for permission to move the meetinghouse south. Thus, by this time, after all the indecision, the Natick farmers decided to act. At least two petitions were sent to the General Court during the summer of 1723. Neither of these petitions is to be found in the Massachusetts Archives; however, the legislative record of the Council and *The House Journal* quoted from these documents.

In June 1723 a petition was presented by John Dunton, John Graves, and

Others who Dwell in Farms within the Town of Natick and adjoining to Sudbury shewing that wheras the General Court was pleased to sett them to the East Precinct in Sudbury in answer to the petition of William Jennison and others in which it was suggested that it was the desire of the present petitioners to be placed there, they think it proper to Inform this Court that the Inhabitants of the . . . East End of Sudbury did Engage to the petitioners to remove the Meeting House nearer to the petitioners and passed a vote. But that they are now repairing the Meeting House where it now stands so that the petitioners are defeated as to the Grounds and reasons of their willingness to be joined to Sudbury and therefore praying that the . . . East Meeting House . . . may be removed nearer to them or that they may lie to Natick as formerly. (Chap. 55, Mass. Acts and Resolves, Vol. X)

The General Court ordered that the East Precinct of the Town of Sudbury be served a copy of this petition and give an answer. The petition and its answer are not consistent with the June 9, 1721, act of the legislature which had attached the Natick farmers, not to the East Precinct merely with respect to church duties, but had "annexed [them] from henceforth and made [them] part of the Township of Sudbury."[8]

From the General Court record one learns of a second petition by the Natick farmers in August 1723 by "Caleb Johnson and the rest lately placed by an order of this Court to the Eastern precinct in Sudbury." This petition said that

the only reason that induced them to apply to the General Court to be sett to the said precinct was a vote of the Inhabitants of . . . the town and an agreement under the Hands of the Principal persons of ye said Precinct that the Meeting House should be removed more southerly which would very much accommodate the petitioners. That the Inhabitants of the said precinct are repairing the said Meeting House where it stands and refuse to move it notwithstanding the vote and agreement and therefore praying that this Court would either order the removal of the said Meeting House more South or that they may be sett off again to the Town of Natick from whence they were taken or that a Committee may be appointed to view and consider the situation and circumstances.

In August 1723 the General Court ordered "a committee to repair to the Easterly Precinct in Sudbury and consider whether it will be most reasonable to remove the Meeting House there and to what place it is to be removed and whether the Petitioners ought to be taken off from Sudbury and putt to Natick."

The East Precinct leaders did not go along with this petition to move the meetinghouse south. On August 5 we find the precinct choosing a committee of three men—Ephraim Curtis, Capt. Joshua Haynes, and Lt. Samuel Graves—to go to the General Court to give reasons against the petition.

While the petition was before the General Court, an August 5, 1723, town meeting was called. One of the articles in the warrant read:

to see if the Town [not just the East Precinct] *will act or do anything either by a petition to the General Court or other ways that so the petitioners that was laid to ye Town of Sudbury by ye General Court June, 1721 may still be continued to ye Town that so ye Town may not be weakened and disabled as to their publick charges it being very heavy on them.*

The town record goes on to say that there is now a petition in the General Court either that the old meetinghouse in the East Precinct be removed, "so to accommodate them in some manner according as was promised before they moved to be layed to ye Town or else they may be layed from Sudbury to Natick." As usual, the town clerk's record did not describe the bitter argument that must have occurred at that meeting. Nor does the record enlighten us as to whether any real promise had been made to the Natick farmers that the east meetinghouse would be moved. Noah Clapp, the town clerk, simply recorded that the town voted to do nothing.

It should be noted that although the petition to add the southern land drawn up in the spring of 1721 was described in the Sudbury town record as "for the farmers and farm lands lying between the town of Sudbury and Natick," and the legislative act of June 1721 taking in these farms referred to them as "farms near Natick," the two 1723 petitions sent by the Natick farmers to the General Court apparently referred to these farms as having belonged to Natick, and threatened that they would return to Natick. The annotator of the legislative record referred to the Dunton and Graves petition of June 1723 as John Dunton, John Graves, and "others who dwell in Farms within the Town of Natick." The General Court record quotes Caleb Johnson's petition as asking that the meetinghouse be moved south or that "they may be sett off again to the Town of Natick from whence they were taken." It has not been possible for this author to determine whether these statements about having belonged to Natick and returning to Natick meant that in 1721 the transfer of 2,141 acres could be said to have been a transfer of land which could ever have been legally a part of Natick. The offical Commonwealth of Massachusetts document, *Historical Data Relating to Counties, Cities and Towns in Massachusetts,* prepared by Kevin H. White, secretary of the Commonwealth in 1966, does not mention this transfer under Natick. Under Sudbury, the June 9, 1721, action is referred to simply as "Certain farms annexed."

If the Rice family acquired the Dunster farm, which had been a private, colonial grant to Harvard College President Henry Dunster in 1638, it is difficult to see how these lands could have come to be included in Natick unless official action was taken to do so at some time before 1721. The most plausible explanation seems to be that in 1723, when the meetinghouse was not moved south as agreed, the twelve families tried to use a threat to leave Sudbury to gain their end and phrased their petitions so that it seemed as if they would be returning to Natick to strengthen their case.

Whereas the leadership of the East Precinct seemed to want to hold out and not move its meetinghouse south, the record of the West Precinct organization shows that the west siders considered it so important to try to retain the Natick farmers in the town that they were willing to pay their share of the expense of moving the east meetinghouse. The record of a meeting of that precinct on August 12, 1723, shows that they chose John Haynes and David How to go to the General Court,

yt [that] *ye farmers on ye East Side of Sudbury River now Petitioners in ye General Court may be continued and remain to ye Town of Sudbury yt so ye heavy charge now on said Town may be more easily and comfortably supported, the Town now having two ministers to maintain besides all other charges; said farmers having now a Petition in ye General Court that ye old meeting house of ye East side . . . may be removed for their accommodation according as was agreed on and promised before they moved to be layed to Sudbury otherwise they move to be layed to Natick.*

These men must have gone to Boston to the General Court, as the record of the West Precinct shows a March 30, 1724, payment of £1 3s. 9d. to John Haynes for attending the General Court by order of the precinct.[9]

The town finally had to cooperate with the committee ordered in August by the General Court to come to the East Precinct. At the town meeting of October 21, 1723, it was voted to entertain at the town's expense the committee the General Court was to send "to settle the East Precinct meeting house." On this same day the East Precinct organization met, probably at an earlier hour, "to see if the Precinct will choose a committee to attend on the General Court's Committee when they come to Sudbury and to gain such records as will be necessary to enlighten them in the affair." When it met, the precinct voted not to choose such a committee. However, at an East Precinct meeting held on November 4, probably on the eve of the arrival of the General Court's committee, the precinct did choose a committee of three: Lt. Samuel Graves, Capt. Joshua Haynes, and Ephraim Curtis. The General Court's committee must have come to Sudbury around November 10. Its report, made to the legislature on November 16, 1723, stated in part that:

having viewed the Precinct and Maturely considered the circumstances of the whole Town with regard to the support of both ministers out of a joint stock and the accommodation both of the farmers and the major part of the East Precinct are . . . of opinion that the . . . Meeting House be removed about a mile South east from the place it now stands to the land of Mr. James Ross and to be placed nigh to the Meeting of the four roads as the ground will admit and, in consideration of the Great Expense the Town have been at in Building a Meeting House in the Westerly Side of the river, are further of opinion that the Town be allowed the space of 18 months to complete the work.[10]

Thus it was decreed in mid-November 1723 that the east meetinghouse be moved south, a project ordered to be accomplished by the middle of 1725. The order officially stated that the Town of Sudbury shall pay the whole charge that "shall arise in Removing the meeting house together with the sum of £7, 17 sh., 9 d to the committee for their time and expense." In this way and owing to promises made to lure twelve large landholders and taxpayers into the town, the east meetinghouse, and eventually the town's east center, which is now Wayland Center, were moved south from the original North Cemetery location selected in 1639.

There was to be more objection and controversy before the east meetinghouse was actually relocated. If the 1688 meetinghouse was going to be taken to pieces and moved south, the easiest way to do this was by means of sleds, drawn over the winter snow. Preliminary work of taking down the meetinghouse seems to have begun very soon after the November 1723 General Court order. A town meeting was called for January 13, 1724, to choose a committee "and fully empower them to agree with workmen and go on with the work to remove the old meeting house . . . and to agree with James Ross for the land to set the meeting house on." James Ross's land extended south of the Mill Brook along Cochituate Road from the entrance to the present Town Office Building at least as far as the present Trinitarian Congregational Church. Ross's house is said to have been a little to the southwest of the Unitarian Parish House. The Mill Brook at this time was often called Ross's Brook. Not much could have been done yet to repair the old east meetinghouse because this January 1724 town meeting voted to use the £150 formerly voted to repair the meetinghouse for the expense of moving it. The warrant for this meeting had an article "to see if the town will order another fashion roof to said meeting house when removed." No action was recorded on this question, but a committee of five (all from the east side and one a Natick farmer, Phineas Brintnal) was appointed to manage the removal. The word "removal" was used several times in this meeting's record.

Apparently the committee of five—William Jennison, Zachariah Heard, Isaac Glezen, Elisha Smith, and Phineas Brintnal—tried to see that the building removal was accomplished while snow was on the ground. This attempt is responsible for traditions such as the one that appears in the booklet, *A Brief History of the Town of Sudbury in Massachusetts 1639-1939*, originally compiled by the Federal Writers' Project of the Works Progress Administration (WPA) and republished by the Sudbury Woman's Club under the auspices of the Sudbury Historical Society, that the old meetinghouse was pulled south over the snow in the winter of 1724. It did not happen that easily and quickly however. First, James Ross refused to sell the land that had been designated by the General Court for the new meetinghouse location. James Ross (1664-1739) was the son of a James Ross, a Scotsman, who came to Sudbury and married Elizabeth Goodenow in 1658. It is not known whether pressure was put on him by influential east siders to refuse to sell to stop the meetinghouse removal. Second, various prominent citizens of the East Precinct became very excited about the demolition of their meetinghouse when there was no place on which to reerect it. Third, as the old meetinghouse was taken down, it became more and more apparent that a large proportion of the timbers and boards were too rotten to be used in building another meetinghouse.

Two most interesting petitions to try to stop the precipitate tearing down of the meetinghouse in the winter of 1724 are to be found in the Massachusetts Archives.[11] One, dated February 12, 1724, was written by Joshua Haynes (1669-1757), who had been a selectman seven different years before this (most recently in 1721) and was then captain of the militia. He lived on the western side of the river but continued to have a strong allegiance to the east church. This petition indicates that a Monday in the middle of February had been set as the day for pulling down the building. The petition reads as follows and shows how dissatisfied certain leaders of the town were, not only with the idea of tearing down this meetinghouse, but with the methods and attitudes of the town committee:

That whereas . . . the General Court was pleased to order the meetinghouse . . . should be pulled down and removed to the Land of James Ross about a mile south-eastward principally to accomodate about a dozen farmers. . . . Now it is . . . that last night we have the news . . . that the committee of the Town appointed to see the . . . order complied with being persons designed to accomplish it with marks of severity and therefore not so much designing the removal of the Meeting house to the place intended by the General Court as the destruction *of the place of Divine Service and have appointed next Monday to pull down the present meeting house though they have not purchased the ground of . . . Ross to set it on . . . nor have they provided any other place, nor prepared any boards, nails, stones, shingles nor any other material . . . nor can they conveniently in this winter season do it.*

May it please your Honor therefore only to defend us from such unreasonable proceeding and take such necessary orders . . . as the place of Divine Worship may not be destroyed but they may first provide all things needful to erect a meeting house at or near the place intended within the time limit before they demolish the house we now enjoy.

This petition is signed: "Joshua Haynes in behalf of himself and many others of the East Precinct of Sudbury."

There is another petition, undated, but clearly submitted to the General Court at about this same time. This document refers twice to the General Court's allowance of eighteen months for the work of moving the meetinghouse and in part says:

and whereas a committee appointed by the Town . . . to pull down and remove the said Meeting house are now entered upon the work which now in this winter season is a great damage and impediment to sundry persons who cannot attend the public worship if it should now be removed and since there is 18 months time allowed to perform . . . work which may be done at a better season, . . . It is most humbly prayed that a stop may be put to it by the order of the Honorable Board as the removal of it now will very much prejudice each of us the Subscribers and other inhabitants of the East Precinct of Sudbury.

This petition is signed first by Lt. John Noyes, who had been a selectman in 1711, 1714, 1717, and 1720, and may have been its author. Joshua Haynes's name came sixth. There were forty-three signers, all but Joshua Haynes from the east side and including James Ross.

It is interesting to note that in February, William Jennison, chairman of the committee to remove the meetinghouse, received a letter from a distinguished and influential Bostonian, Judge Samuel Sewall, objecting to the winter removal of Sudbury's east meetinghouse. This letter, transcribed from Sewall's letter book, appeared in print in an 1888 publication of the Massachusetts Historical Society.[12] It was addressed to "Mr. William Jennison and others, a Committee chosen by the Town of Sudbury, To Remove the Old Meeting-House, pursuant to an Order of the General Court."

Judge Sewall's niece, Jane Sewall, was the young wife of the east side's new minister, William Cook. The couple were married at Cook's Sudbury ordination ceremony. Although Samuel Sewall's diary does not indicate that its author attended the joint marriage and ordination ceremony on March 20, 1723, Sewall had probably attended services in this meetinghouse and was to take a special interest in this parish's welfare during his niece's husband's pastorate. Sewall ordered four large folio volumes of the works of the Reverend Richard Baxter to be bound in London and planned to give them to the east church in Sudbury. He died before they were delivered from England, but his executor sent them to the east parish after writing on the flyleaf: "For the use of the Church and Congregation in the East Precinct of the town of Sudbury now under the care of the Rev. Mr. Cook—Boston July 19, 1731." Three of these volumes are in the rare book section of the Wayland Library. The fourth is lost. Sewall's gift of books to the East Precinct may have been inspired early in 1725 by a gift of books to the West Precinct by Thomas Plympton.

The legislative record implies that there was a third, later petition by east siders against the meetinghouse removal before a place was acquired and also that the town removal committee was compelled to petition the legislature. On April 24, 1724, the Council, "after reading the petition of John Woodward and forty-six other inhabitants together with a Petition of William Jennison and others, a committee appointed to remove the Meeting House . . . and upon consideration of the dissatisfaction of the . . . Inhabitants at the placing the Meeting House on the land of James Ross and the difficulty of obtaining the land of said Ross," ordered a new legislative committee to view other places and report at the legislative session in May.

The General Court record shows that this legislative committee repaired to Sudbury on May 12, 1724, and found James Ross unwilling to sell land for the meetinghouse.[13] The committee reported on May 29 that its members were unanimously of the

opinion that the most commodious Place for that use is a piece of rising ground about 17 rods [280 ft.] *northward of the bridge over the Brook called Mill Brook on the West side of the way and at about 30 rods* [ca. 500 ft.] *distance from the place agreed upon by the former committee.*

This committee wanted no further difficulty about the exact site and reported having placed two stakes fifty-five feet apart to mark the location. The land was claimed by Hopestill Bent but was partially in

Third Sudbury Meetinghouse, 1688.
Copyright 1963 by Wesleyan University. Reprinted from *Puritan Village: The Formation of a New England Town,* by Sumner C. Powell, by permission of Wesleyan University Press.

the highway, and Bent was willing to waive his claim to it. The wording of this May 30, 1724, order is significant in that it no longer speaks of moving the old meetinghouse but of "placing" a building which was to cost the same as the new west meetinghouse.

In spite of the General Court's very definite May 30 order about proceeding to build a new east meetinghouse, the summer of 1724 saw further delay and controversy. Noah Clapp's town clerk's record is not entirely clear as to the sequence of events. Whatever happened, the building of the fourth east meetinghouse in its new location, which was on the corner of the present Cochituate Road and Pelham Island Road, south of the present Collins Market, was not left to the inhabitants of East Precinct with a sum of money provided by the town. Instead, the whole town in town meeting concerned itself with the extent to which this meetinghouse would be newly built or a reconstruction of the old. The town clerk's record shows that the town voted on July 13 against the proposal for setting up the meetinghouse "in ye form of ye same demensions as it was before," except for gables. Further, the town on this occasion voted against a proposal to have a committee "improve the timber" and instead voted to go ahead with building a meetinghouse where the General Court had ordered.

More petitioning of the legislature was contemplated; one wonders whether other towns sent such a rain of petitions to the General Court about the placement of one church building. The warrant for a July 18, 1724, town meeting contained an article

to see if the town will choose a committee to prefer a petition to the General Court that so the town may go on in their proceeding in building and finishing the meeting house on the east side . . . to prevent the extraordinary charges that may come to the town under their now difficult circumstances. Likewise to prevent the great contention that is now likely to arise in the town.

The town seems to have been in a turmoil, but it is not clear exactly what the trouble was.

The third meetinghouse must have been completely torn down by the late summer of 1724 or perhaps earlier. In the East Precinct record there is reported a March 5, 1724, precinct meeting for the election of officers held at "Lt. Noyes is Old Hous where the East Precinct meetes on Sabbath Days." An entry in the East Precinct record book for April 30, 1725, shows that John Noyes's house was used for services in the interim between the demolition of the third meetinghouse and the building of the fourth. The record shows that Noyes was paid £3 "for the yous [use] of his house."

Articles in the warrant of a town meeting of September 24, 1724, were:

(1) *to receive a report of the committee to pull down the East Meeting House;*
(2) *to see what to do with the old timbers and other materials of the East Meeting House; and*
(3) *to see if the town will grant £200 toward the building of a new East Meeting House.*

At this September 24 meeting a new committee was empowered to dispose of the old timbers but not of the town's bell. Instead of appropriating new funds (the £200 asked for in the warrant) it was ordered that the £150 appropriated to "repair the old meeting house be put towards building the new one." Thus, it would seem that as recorded in the town, the precinct, and the Massachusetts records, the story cited in some historical accounts, and of general currency that what was essentially the third meetinghouse was taken apart, a few rotten timbers replaced and rebuilt at the Wayland Center location is untrue. This had been the plan at one time, but it had not proved feasible.

The burden of paying two ministers and building two meetinghouses in three or four years was so great that the September 24, 1724, meeting did not grant the £200 asked for the east meetinghouse. The committee appointed to pull down the old meetinghouse rendered an accounting of £41 expense for their work. In December it was voted to use the money obtained after much difficulty in payment of the Reverend Edmund Browne's 1687 legacy for a grammar school, to pay the committee which had torn down the third meetinghouse. The final charge made by William Jennison, Zachariah Heard, and Phineas Brintnal for tearing down the meetinghouse was £29 1s.

The above-mentioned £150 (minus £29 1s. for tearing down the meetinghouse) was not enough to build the new east meetinghouse. The town meeting of April 5, 1725, granted a further £250 for carrying on the building and finishing of "the new meeting house in the east precinct." It is not known exactly when the fourth or new east meetinghouse was actually finished. At the April 5, 1725, town meeting it was proposed and voted that town meetings would henceforth be held alternately at the west and east meetinghouses. This practice was followed regularly until 1780.

The first East Precinct meeting held in the new meetinghouse was called for December 7, 1725. However, during 1726 work must have been proceeding to finish the building. The formal vote to accept the house from the building committee took place on January 30, 1727. On this date the precinct organization also addressed itself to the questions of seating and of allowing pews to be privately built. Town treasurer's records show a receipt dated June 3, 1728, for £400, "in full granted by said town to carry on the building of a meeting house in the east precinct." The building committee had consisted of Joshua Haynes, the west sider who preferred to belong to the East Precinct and was very active in it; Ephraim Curtis; John Noyes; Samuel Graves; Jonathan Rice; Dennis Hedley; and Hopestill Bent. Final settlement of £400 for the west meetinghouse had been made on May 31, 1725.

Drawing by Rita Anderson of Sudbury's East Meetinghouse, completed in 1726 and used until 1815.

David Baldwin was the builder of the east meetinghouse. The plan, adopted at an East Precinct meeting on August 3, 1724, called for building and finishing a meetinghouse

as near as they can of the same dementions of the new Meeting Hous in the West Precinct . . . as to length and bredth and height and all so the finishing with in side and with outside of the same dementions of the afore said meeting Hous as near as they think convenient and to youse [use] *as much of the old meeting Hous in said building and finishing said meeting Hous as they shall think fit for to put into the building . . . as the Town or their comtte will Deliver up to them for that yous.*

The West Precinct record shows that on December 28, 1722, the precinct voted to have built a meetinghouse 46 feet long and 38 feet wide, with 21 feet between joists.

When the building was accepted by the East Precinct meeting, it was voted that David Baldwin should at extra cost "make better steps than is at the west side Meeting House and bring in his Bill." The warrant article for this January 30, 1727, meeting of the precinct had been "to see if the precinct will ad anything toward making of the steps at the meeting Hous Doors hansomer than the steps at the West Side Meeting Hous is." On May 11, 1727, David Baldwin was paid £ 5 6s. 10d. for making steps.

At a later date and in retrospect, the fourth meetinghouse was described as a rather undistinguished, square-built structure. Nineteenth-century town historian James Sumner Draper in a historical appendix to a booklet on the 1878 dedication of the Wayland town hall described the fourth east meetinghouse as follows:

The frame of the building known as the "old green store" [now the house called Kirkside at 211 Boston Post Road] *is that of the "old meeting house of 1814" with partially diminished proportions and excepting the timbers of the roof. . . . In place of its present hip-roof erect a common gable with slight pediments and coving. Construct a projecting porch in the front side and also on each end and with eight windows in front, four on each end and four on the back with one large circular-top window back of the pulpit and a semi-circular one in each gable end. This structure, with neither steeple, turret nor chimney to relieve its plainness . . . was the old meeting house of 1814.*

Draper was born in 1811, so he could not have remembered this meetinghouse building very clearly. However, his father and older associates probably described it to him, and he surely made inquiries about its appearance when he undertook to write a description of the town center as of 1814.

In 1865 the Reverend John Burt Wight, who had been the pastor of the East Sudbury church for twenty years (1815-35), wrote reminiscences of his earlier life and work in Wayland. He began his preaching in East Sudbury in October 1814 before the fifth (present Unitarian) church building was finished. He was thus familiar with the old fourth meetinghouse when it was still in use. He had the following to say about this building:

The old house had been standing more than ninety years. It was a wooden building, about forty feet square, with a plain barn-roof, old fashioned, much time-worn, and, for the last few years intentionally left without much repairing. . . . At the west end of the interior was a plain pine pulpit, over which was suspended a large, hollow, rectangular canopy called a sounding board, which, by its vibrations, tended to deepen the tones and increase the volume of the speaker's voice. The pulpit was furnished with a large, rectangular, heavy cushion, covered with green plush, without fastening, so that the preacher had need to be careful lest it should fall on the heads of the people seated below. On the floor in front of the pulpit were several benches with sufficient backs, for the accommodation of the deaf and aged, who were thereby better enabled to see and hear the minister.

The first Damon House, built in 1737, was moved to Dover after 1900.

Being in the body of the house, they were called body-seats; and the instances of longevity at that time so numerous that they were usually well filled. The remainder of the floor was filled with small, square pews ornamented at the top with open rundle-work. There were loosely hinged seats, raised at the commencement of the prayer and lowered again at its close. When there was a full assembly, partly composed of lively boys, this process occasioned a great clatter. The principal entrance to the aisle was a folding door in two parts, facing the East; and in the South East corner was a rude stair-case, leading to a gallery. . . . Outside the building was a large mounting-block for the accommodation of those who came to meeting on horse-back. In the front gallery was a large bass-viol to accompany the singers. During the hot summer afternoons the pulpit was pleasantly shaded by a fine old Button-wood Tree that stood very near the west side of the house.

It cannot be determined whether the fourth east meetinghouse or its counterpart at Rocky Plain (Sudbury Center) were really inferior to the 1688 third meetinghouse building in the North Cemetery in which the town had taken such great pride and had gone to great effort to copy from Dedham's then much-admired meetinghouse. One senses in reading the precinct and town records that the two buildings, finished in 1723 and 1726, respectively, were built along economy lines, the one on the west side to provide a house of worship for the west siders who had struggled for well over a decade to attain their own meetinghouse, the one on the east side to be almost exactly like it. The effort to build the third meetinghouse (voted 1686 completed 1688) had been a uniting experience for the town, with some of the outdweller families who were later attached to Framingham taking an active part. The need to build two new meetinghouses for the town in the 1720s and the controversies over their location and how they would be paid for were, by contrast, a bitter and burdensome experience.

This writer has not found an exact accounting of the monies realized from the sale of the timbers and other materials from the third meetinghouse. The money was slow to come in and probably did not amount to much. Cash was always scarce in Sudbury, and some of the timbers of this meetinghouse had been authorized to be sold in April 1725 so the receipts could be used to help support an indigent widow. Some of the timbers and (according to tradition) the doors of the third meetinghouse doubtless were incorporated into the fourth meetinghouse, even though it was essentially a new building. Its congregation included thrifty Yankee farmers, and there was no wealth to support unnecessary expenditure. The Wayland Historical Society owns what is thought to be part of the pulpit of the third meetinghouse. The present owners of Kirkside at 221 Boston Post Road in Wayland believe that they, with the help of an architectural historian, have identified certain very large beams in that house as having been first hewn for the 1688 third Sudbury meetinghouse.

The fourth meetinghouse was complete enough to be used for a town meeting in April 1726. It must have been hard indeed for the Reverend William Cook to commence his pastorate in a part of the town which had been disappointed that Israel Loring chose to go to the West Precinct; in a building that was rotting and falling down, and over which much controversy raged as to whether to repair, move, or replace it, and to conduct services in makeshift quarters, possibly some of the time outdoors. This author looked but could not find in the Sewall manuscript letter collections any comments by William Cook about the meetinghouse controversy. One must bear in mind that difficult precinct divisions and meetinghouse location controversies were taking place all over Massachusetts during those years.

Referring again to Andover's history, there was much uncertainty around 1710 as to whether to repair the older, north meetinghouse for the North Precinct. Although the land division of Andover's two precincts had been about equal, the population of the later settled part of the town—the South Precinct—was greater at this time. The General Court advised the North Precinct to repair its existing meetinghouse, but the inhabitants of the North Precinct, not to be outdone by the South Precinct, went ahead and built a new north meetinghouse. To twentieth-century readers it may seem strange that the provincial legislature concerned itself with, and had to give approval of, the location, repair, and replacement of meetinghouses in the various towns. The separate towns were autonomous to some extent, but, especially in matters which concerned Puritan churches, the rocks on which the towns were founded, the General Court had supervision and took part in decisions if they were at all controversial, as can be seen in the Sudbury experience.

The controversy about moving the east meetinghouse south and its connection with the inclusion in our town of the Cochituate section is a little written-about chapter of Sudbury and Wayland history. Of the two men whom the town appointed in 1721 to petition the General Court to include this area in the town, William Jennison ceased to hold town office after 1724 and by 1726 had moved to Worcester. Jennison was a man of great energy and action. He could well have been the person who made the promise to move the east meetinghouse south for the accommodation of the Natick farmers. After leaving Sudbury he became a leader in Worcester and was the chief petitioner for setting off Worcester County from Middlesex and Norfolk counties in 1731. The two men were not around to see the eastern village center of Sudbury (now Wayland Center) grow up in the area where it is now located. Ebenezer Rice died in 1724.

It turned out that the location of the fourth meetinghouse was a low and swampy one. Attempts to drain the land and roads near the structure with ditches led in 1731 to emergency measures to refill ditches and lay stones around the meetinghouse foundation. The village center which grew up around this fourth and the nearby fifth (1815) meetinghouses has continued to be plagued with problems of wetness resulting from its low elevation.

Natick Farmers

NOTES

1. See Michael J. Crawford, *History of Natick, Massachusetts 1650-1976*, 1979, pp. 24-36.
2. *Acts and Resolves of Massachusetts Bay*, Vol. X, Resolves, Appendix 5, Chapter 4.
3. *Ibid*, Chapter 2, p. 797.
4. Acreage estimate (1969) by Town Engineer Lewis L. Bowker Jr.
5. Massachusetts Archives Map No. 1181.
6. See Commonwealth of Massachusetts, *Historical Data Relating to Counties, Cities and Towns in Massachusetts*, Boston, 1966.
7. Town of Sudbury, *East Precinct Record*, W.P.A. transcription owned by Wayland Historical Society, pp. 14-15.
8. *Acts and Resolves of Massachusetts Bay*, Vol. X, Resolves Appendix 5, Chapter 55.
9. Town of Sudbury, *Westerly Precinct Record*, pp. 23, 24 and 27.
10. *Massachusetts Province Laws* [Resolves], Vol. X, Chapter 270.
11. *Massachusetts Archives*, Vol. XI, pp. 404 and 404a.
12. Massachusetts Historical Society, *Collections*, 6th Series, Vol. II, Boston, 1888, pp. 159-160.
13. *Massachusetts Province Laws* [Resolves, Orders, Votes, etc.], Chapter 3. General Court session begun May 24, 1724.

3

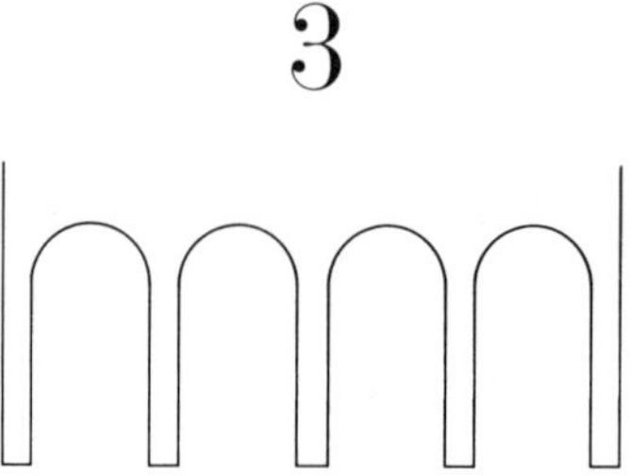

Precincts, Parishes, and Religious Societies

REFERENCE HAS BEEN MADE in the previous chapter to an East and a West Precinct and to the records kept by them. When in 1715 the General Court ordered that there could be a west precinct in Sudbury, it was undoubtedly thought that the west and east precincts would follow the usual precinct structure. Each would be based on a church and would provide its own elements which made up the church, that is, a meetinghouse building and a minister with his salary and settlement, and also certain of what we now consider to be municipal functions such as the provision of schools. This did not happen in Sudbury. The ministers' official salaries were voted and paid by the town government at all times. Settlement of a minister was a lump sum, usually greater than a year's salary, paid to him when he was ordained. The settlement fee for each of the Sudbury ministers, Israel Loring in 1722 in the West Precinct, and William Cook in 1723 in the East Precinct, was paid by the respective precincts. As was explained in the previous chapter, in the end the whole town paid for the first west meetinghouse, finished in 1723, and for the fourth east meetinghouse, finished in 1726.

The two Sudbury precincts organized, kept records, and had meetings as prescribed under Chapter 10 of Province Laws of 1702 for roughly ten years but then ceased to keep formal records, presumably because it was realized that they were not operating as true precincts. The East Precinct record ends with the annual meeting of March 23,

1730. The last annual meeting recorded for the West Precinct was on March 27, 1732. The records of the two precincts, which were apparently not available to Hudson, are interesting documents. The Town of Sudbury owns the original West Precinct record. This record comprises fifty-six handwritten pages covering 1722-32 with five additional pages on the hiring of the Reverend Jacob Bigelow in 1772. The original of the East Precinct record is missing, but fortunately, before it disappeared, the Works Progress Administration's Middlesex County Historical Survey made a typewritten transcription of this record in 1937. This runs to sixty pages and is labeled "First Parish Church Wayland Records 1722-1782." In 1937 it was given to the Wayland Public Library but was later turned over to the Wayland Historical Society and a copy made for the First Parish Church.

These formal records, kept by a clerk much as the town clerk kept the town records, show that the West Precinct held its first meeting on December 18, 1721, at the house of Deacon John Clapp. Page one of the record shows that on November 27, 1721, Justice of the Peace Francis Fulham of Weston ordered Josiah Hayden to call the first meeting of the West Precinct. Hayden, a town constable from the west side, warned the west siders of the December 18 meeting on December 11. John Balcom was elected moderator and clerk, and a precinct committee of seven was elected. This meeting concerned itself with hiring a Mr. Minott to preach for six weeks, two Sundays at the house of Mr. Pitts and four at the house of Deacon John Clapp. Like the town, the precinct had an annual meeting, the first being held on March 29, 1722, at "ye new hous on rocky plain." At this meeting three assessors and a treasurer were elected, and it was clear that the precinct expected to pay its own expenses.

The first meeting of the East Precinct took place on June 25, 1722, six months after that of the West Precinct. Ephraim Curtis was chosen moderator and clerk, and a committee of five was elected to operate the precinct until the following March. At this meeting the first business was to arrange to deliver thirty-five cords of wood to the Reverend Loring, who was still the East Precinct's minister. A month later, on July 26, a second meeting was called to hear Israel Loring's decision to accept the call to the West Precinct and to choose a committee to provide a minister. At subsequent meetings held during 1722 the East Precinct decided to try, then to give a call to William Cook to be their minister. The first annual meeting of this precinct took place on May 21, 1723, to choose officers. Ephraim Curtis was chosen clerk, Samuel Abbott treasurer, and Joseph Parmenter collector, the immediate business being "to make a rate of £100 for Cook's settlement." Cook did not get his settlement payment on time and apparently had to sue for it. The precinct committee consisted of Capt. Joshua Haynes of the west side, Hopestill Bent, and Ephraim Curtis.[1]

Aside from concerning themselves with the building and relocation of the east meetinghouse, the two precincts made arrangements to provide wood for their ministers and in both precincts to supplement the official, town ministerial salary. They also concerned themselves with arrangements for allowing a certain number of top taxpaying members to stake out and build themselves pews at their own expense and according to their own designs. The custom of granting a certain floor area for a pew but of not controlling its design otherwise led to quite a hodgepodge appearance inside the meetinghouses. In one case in the Sudbury east meetinghouse access to one man's pew was through another's. Pews tended to be located under the galleries along the outside walls of the building, and permission was sometimes given to allow a window to be cut in the wall over a pew.

In the 1720s both precincts provided room in inhabitants' houses for school purposes, and during the recordkeeping period built schoolhouses for their precincts. It must be noted, however, that although at the town meeting held on May 17, 1725, it was voted that "each precinct would provide places to keep school," at a November town meeting it was voted that the school buildings in the separate precincts would be provided "at the Town's charge." On March 17, 1729, the East Precinct voted to build a schoolhouse between "Mill Brook and the Little Swamp on or near adjoyning to the Center Roade." The West Precinct had voted to build a schoolhouse on Rocky Plain in 1728, 22 feet long by 18 feet wide. The East Precinct school was ordered to have the same dimensions. In this decade, the 1720s, considering the facts that the fourth east meetinghouse was built to be like the west meetinghouse and that the school buildings had the same measurements, there seems to have been a great effort to provide equal, virtually identical church and school facilities on the two sides of the river.

Before becoming minister of the church in the West Precinct in 1722, Israel Loring had served the whole town for sixteen years, preaching in the meetinghouse on the east side and living on that side of the river. The fact that the West Precinct was organized six months before the East Precinct allowed Loring to refer to the west church as the First Parish Church and the east church as the Second Parish

Church. Those designations must have disturbed members of the east church considerably because they were convinced that their church, which began occupying its fourth building in 1726, had come down in direct succession from the original Sudbury church established in 1640. Loring's terminology infuriated James Sumner Draper, the nineteenth-century historian of Wayland, who was particularly interested in church history. We find him holding forth bitterly on this subject in the "Appendix to The Annals of Wayland" in Alfred S. Hudson's *Annals of Sudbury, Wayland and Maynard,* published in 1891. In a section entitled "Succession of Meeting Houses," Draper said, in part:

During the controversy in the first quarter of the eighteenth century concerning the division of the town into precincts, nothing occurred, that we have yet discovered, which caused the church on the east side to lose its identity as the First Church of the town. There was a separation from it, but not a removal of it. . . . The one element . . . was already worshipping in the west precinct, and the remaining element, we infer, without evidence to the contrary, continued on in the east precinct as the original church, with all the traditions, associations, and prestige. It is true that the records were subsequently in the possession of the west precinct church, and are now in the hands of the Unitarian parish in Sudbury; but this may be accounted for on the supposition that Mr. Loring, having kept the scanty records that were then made of church matters, may have taken them with him on his removal to the west side as a matter of no consequence to either church.

When Andover was permitted to have a North and a South Precinct, with the old meetinghouse continuing to serve the North Precinct, the incumbent minister, the Reverend Thomas Barnard, was, by order of the General Court, given the right to choose which precinct he would serve. It was therefore not completely at variance with practice for Loring to choose to accept the call to the new West Precinct. It appears, however, somewhat high-handed that Israel Loring chose to designate the west parish of Sudbury as the First Parish, Sudbury. In the early years of Massachusetts, the church books were considered to be the property of the ordained minister rather than of the church or the town which owned the meetinghouse building and paid the minister. Mr. Loring took Sudbury's church books, dating back to his ordination in 1706, with him when he moved to the west side of the river in 1722. Technically, if ordained in

Sudbury when the only meetinghouse was on the east side of the river, he was carrying on Sudbury's ministry when he moved to the more populous west side; but the meetinghouse and the precinct there had to be newly planned and petitioned for, and in no sense was it Sudbury's first parish. Loring had an arrogant, chauvinistic side and wanted his part of the town to stand first with respect to its historical heritage. He did succeed in perpetuating the myth that Sudbury's west parish was the first parish in the town. In 1970 a detailed study of the records of the early Congregational (Puritan) churches in Massachusetts was published by a scholar at the Harvard Divinity School. His compendium, entitled *An Inventory of the Records of the Particular Churches of Massachusetts Gathered 1620-1805,* compiled from an examination of the extant records of churches in the various towns including those of Sudbury and Wayland, designates the Sudbury church as the older and first church in the town.[2]

It is not known whether in towns where the precincts were more distinctly divided as to responsibility for their ministers there was much if any crossing of precinct lines. No exact line was ever designated between the two Sudbury precincts. The river was considered the boundary in that there was much reference to the west and east sides. In Sudbury it is said that there was a fair amount of crossing the river to go to church, with families on the east side attending Mr. Loring's church and certain west siders regularly worshiping at the meetinghouse on the east side. Supposedly the Reverends Cook and Loring were friendly, espoused similar Puritan doctrine, and exchanged pulpits with each other rather regularly.

Dissatisfaction about the location of the meetinghouse continued, however. All was not well now that there were two churches, one on each side of the river and both placed where they would supposedly accommodate the population. No sooner had the west meetinghouse been finished than it became apparent that it was much easier for the families living north of the Assabet River in the northwest corner of the town to go to church in Stow than it was to attend church in Sudbury. Agitation for a horse bridge across the Assabet had started at the March town meeting in 1714, but it was not until December 1715 that arrangements were made for determining its location with a committee chosen to handle the matter. The bridge was apparently finished in 1716 but was not a very substantial one, as in 1727 there was again mention of the lack of a bridge.

By the summer and fall of 1725, when tax collections for the two new meetinghouses were very heavy, John Jewell and other inhabitants on the west side of the Assabet River petitioned the General Court to be annexed to Stow. The requirement that they pay taxes for the new east meetinghouse as well as for the west meetinghouse, which they could not reach very easily, led them to petition that the money they had been required to pay in taxes toward the building of the new east meetinghouse be refunded to them. At the town meeting of November 24, 1725, a committee of three, including Ephraim Curtis, who was a selectman, was appointed to answer this petition by a counterpetition by the town that these northwest inhabitants be continued to Sudbury and their money not refunded. There is no evidence that the General Court acted on the 1725 petition, but those living beyond the Assabet continued their agitation; and, at a town meeting held on October 27, 1729, it was voted that "the inhabitants of the west [northwest] be eased on the assessment for the minister's pay." They apparently then attended the Stow church. This measure failed to satisfy the residents of that corner of the town, and in 1730 a petition of Peter Luce and Timothy Gibson and others asked the General Court that they and certain other families be annexed to Stow. On December 15, 1730, Ephraim Curtis and David Estabrook were chosen as a committee to go to the General Court. Their attempt to keep these families and their land in Sudbury failed. On December 29, 1730, by Chapter 170 of Province Laws [Resolves], 2d Session, 1730, this northwest corner of Sudbury, with six families, now a part of Maynard, was annexed to Stow.

By this time, the practice of carving up townships to make additional ones, thus placing a given population nearer to a proposed new meetinghouse, was rife in Massachusetts. With the increase and spreading out of the population on the west side of Sudbury, the meetinghouse on Rocky Plain seemed to some churchgoers too far away. Moreover, the burden of sharing in the payment for two ministers appeared to be great. At this point a group of Sudbury west siders, along with some inhabitants of Marlborough, Framingham, and Stow, petitioned the General Court in March 1740 to be set off as a separate township four miles square, which they claimed would include nearly seventy families. This petition, signed by forty-three men, is to be found in the Massachusetts Archives and is referred to in Hudson's *History of Sudbury*.[3] On March 20, 1740, the legislature ordered that the petitioners serve their respective towns with this petition. At a town meeting on May 19, 1740, Capt. John Haynes and John Woodward were chosen to go to the General Court to protest in behalf of the Town of Sudbury. Haynes was the town treasurer and Woodward a selectman; both men were assessors that year. Their lengthy petition opposing this new township before the General Court is found in the Massachusetts Archives and is liberally quoted in Hudson's *History of Sudbury*.[4] After stating that the March 14, 1740, petition did not make it clear how many inhabitants and how much land would be taken away from Sudbury, they based their objections on the following arguments:

(1) That a loss of inhabitants would discourage their present ministers who were applying for more salary.
(2) After the great expenses of the recent building of two meetinghouses and two schoolhouses and with recent bridges and difficult causeways, they could not afford to lose any tax base.
(3) That the west meetinghouse had been officially placed where the west side petitioners wanted it.
(4) That the town often had quite a heavy relief burden (in lieu of tax revenue) because of river overflow ruining hay and other crops.

The petition ended with the claim that the royal charter under which the original Sudbury town grants had been made was intended to be "forever hereafter held and enjoyed according to the import and patent of such respective grant." It would be interesting to know how many other towns fell back on the thesis of the inviolability of an original grant as an argument against fragmentation. That the leaders of Sudbury did so shows a certain desperation after one hundred years of existence as a municipal entity. The Massachusetts Archives contain Framingham's objections, which did not, as Sudbury's did, use general economic and philosophical arguments. Framingham contended that the placement of their new meetinghouse, over which a tremendous controversy had raged, had been to accommodate the inhabitants of the northern part of the town—the very ones who now proposed to merge with some neighbors as a separate township.[5] The petition of David How of Sudbury and his group and the towns of Sudbury and Framingham objecting to this proposed township were referred to the fall session of the Court.[6] The matter never came up again. We note that David How, leader of the proposal for this new township, was elected a selectman of Sudbury in March 1741. This could have been a consolation or reward for his dropping the agitation for the new township.

The inconvenience of having to go some miles to attend church services and the idea of setting up new municipal entities based on nearer meetinghouses continued to threaten Sudbury in the eighteenth century. Sudbury's town clerk's record shows a proposal made in 1768 as a petition to the General Court. The winter of 1768 may have been one of prolonged snows when it was difficult to travel from the southern end of town to the east meetinghouse. In any case, we find in the warrant for the town meeting of May 9, 1768, an article "to see if the Town will excuse a number of persons belonging to said Town and living near to Natick from paying rates to the ministers in the years 1767 and 1768 agreeable to the petition of Lt. Brintnal and others." This article was passed in the negative.

A month later a petition, the original to be found in the Massachusetts Archives, was sent to the General Court saying that a number of inhabitants of the west part of Needham, the north part of Natick, the south part of Sudbury, and the southwest part of Weston "are very remote from their respective places of publick worship to which they belong." The petition goes on to say that John Jones, Esq., had made a survey on January 30, 1768, suggesting an area, which as far as Sudbury was concerned would start at Eliakim Rice's house and go "as far northerly as 'Natick old Line' " (the old south boundary of Sudbury)—formerly between Sudbury and Natick and so running westerly to the Framingham line—to be incorporated into a "District Society" as other district societies in this province.[7]

Agitation for this new parish district must have started well before the May 9 town meeting in Sudbury when the town refused to excuse those who dwelt in the south part of Sudbury. The document was signed for Sudbury by Phineas Brintnal (1696-1772), an original Natick farmer, and by Thomas Damon and would have taken the whole of the area acquired in 1721 out of the east parish, thus losing to this church the very families and lands the support of which it was deemed so necessary to keep in 1723 that the General Court had ordered the third meetinghouse moved south.

Thomas Damon was the first of the Damons to come to Sudbury. He was born in Reading in 1703, married Abigail Rice, daughter of Isaac and Sebella Rice, and in 1731 bought Brintnal land where he built two houses (neither of which is still standing) near the southeast corner of the town. In the nineteenth century the junction of the present Rice Road with Commonwealth Road was known as Damon's Corner, location of the first Damon houses.

According to the petitioners, they had already, when writing this petition of June 4, 1768, received the consent of the towns of Needham and Natick. On June 7 the House of Representatives ordered the petitioners to supply the towns of Sudbury and Weston with the petition and to ask these towns to answer at the next session of the Court. No further record of this matter could be found in Sudbury's town records or in those of the General Court. It can be concluded that the petitioners were persuaded to abandon their petition when it was realized that the erection of such a "district," as it is termed in *The House Journal*, would remove a large area from the support of the east church and perhaps out of the Town of Sudbury.

We find in the record of the town meeting of March 2, 1761, that the town voted that the "land of Robert Jennison [of Natick] and of Col. Elisha Jones [of Weston] adjoining Sudbury might be laid to the town of Sudbury agreeable to their petition." This boundary change did not go to the General Court and did not go through. Robert Jennison, who had married Sibylla Brintnal, daughter of Phineas Brintnal, the Natick farmer, probably attended church at the east meetinghouse of Sudbury. In 1792, a few years before he died, he tried again to have his property included in East Sudbury, as is evidenced in the Massachusetts Archives. A map is entitled "Land of Robert Jennison to be set off from Natick to East Sudbury, 1792." Again the attempt to add a piece of land adjoining East Sudbury on its southeast corner failed. One of Robert Jennison's daughters, Eunice, had married Isaac Baldwin of the eastern part of Sudbury in 1761, and another married William Grout. This Jennison family had very strong ties to Sudbury, but their property near Nonesuch Pond continued as part of Natick.

The term "precinct" was not used in connection with the Weston-Needham-Natick-Sudbury appeal for a separate church. "District society" was the term devised for this proposed arrangement. It is not known to this writer whether other such district societies actually were set up. By the late 1760s East Precinct and West Precinct had long since ceased to be used as terms in Sudbury, and provision for church buildings and the ministers had become a municipal function of the town as a whole, although the town had east-of-the-river and west squadrons to assist the constables in handling tax collections, as well as districts on one side of the river or the other for which local highway surveyors were responsible. Equal salaries continued to be paid to the ministers by the whole town regardless of the unequal numbers of parishioners or area served. Likewise, the two meetinghouse buildings continued to be the property and concern of the whole town, with the town meeting considering necessary repairs to both from time to time.

Resentment, for a different reason, that the whole town was supporting two ministers, came to the surface in the early 1760s. At a town meeting on May 14, 1760, it was ordered that the precinct books be delivered to the town clerk. The church groups on both sides of the river were then concerned about what would happen when their now quite elderly ministers would die and have to be replaced. They were maneuvering to avoid having to share the settlement costs of two ministers on a town-wide basis. The Reverend Cook, pastor of the east church, died in November 1760. A proposal was quickly made in the town meeting, by a warrant article instigated by west siders, that settlement of Cook's successor be an expense of the east parish alone, not of the whole town. This led to much controversy over whether to continue the practice of having the whole town support its two ministers. By this time the west side was more populous and could better afford to support its own minister and collect funds when a settlement would be needed for Loring's successor. The east side was apparently afraid that the west side would not contribute toward settling Cook's successor. Deacon Andrews Stone of the east church had petitioned the General Court asking that that body make a requirement that the settlement of Cook's successor be at the cost of the whole town. At the June 30, 1761, town meeting a compromise was reached when it was voted not to oppose Deacon Stone's petition but to uphold it, provided the General Court would "grant and confirm the same privilege to the west church when there should be occasion." Israel Loring was then well along in years, and the west parish knew it would soon be faced with settling his successor.

This rather bitter controversy led, in July 1761, to the passage of Chapter 13 of Province Laws entitled "An Act Making Special Provisions for the Settlement and Support of the Gospel Ministry in the Town of Sudbury." The preamble of Chapter 13 says that "whereas there are two distinct *societies* for religious worship . . . in the town of Sudbury . . . and each . . . desirous of being authorized and impowered to contract with and proceed to the settlement of a gospel minister . . . as fully as by law they might do if they were distinct *parishes.* . . ." The last phrase indicates that at this time it was not considered that the east and west churches served either distinct parishes or precincts. They were merely religious societies.

Section 1 of the act goes on to say that such inhabitants as usually attend public worship on either side of the river and are qualified to vote in parish affairs

be . . . incorporated into distinct and separate societies as to be enabled . . . to call, contract with, and settle a gospel minister . . . in manner and form as the ministers of the churches of this province are called, contracted with and settled and such . . . shall be valid and effectual . . . as if such societies had been . . . distinct and separate parishes.

Section 2 says that whenever the east church and congregation or the west church and congregation shall be destitute of a minister, the deacons of that church shall notify the inhabitants, qualified to vote in parish affairs where such destitute church is, to meet, choose a moderator and clerk, and act as parishes do toward settling a minister. But it also states that assessors, collectors, and other *town* officers of Sudbury are empowered to "assess, lay and collect all rates and taxes for the support and maintenance of such minister from all the inhabitants of . . . Sudbury in manner as if such ministers had been chosen and contracted with by the said town."

On October 20, 1761, the town meeting was asked and granted Josiah Bridge, Cook's successor on the east side, "his settlement and salary as he has contracted with the East Society." This action was taken by the whole town, as was a comparable action in the summer of 1772 when the Reverend Jacob Bigelow was chosen by the west society to succeed the deceased Israel Loring. Town money was voted toward the funeral expenses of both ministers, Cook and Loring, although the town meeting had at first refused to make a contribution toward Cook's funeral.

NOTES

1. The election of precinct officers at annual meetings was taken very seriously and led sometimes to controversy as is evidenced by Chapter 103 of *Province Laws (Resolves,* Vol. XI, p. 42) when the General Court was called upon to settle a dispute about choosing officers at a West Precinct meeting.

2. Harold Field Worthly, *An Inventory of the Records of the Particular (Congregational) Churches of Massachusetts Gathered 1620-1805,* Cambridge, 1970, p. 604.

3. *Massachusetts Archives,* Vol. XII, P. 137 and Alfred S. Hudson, *History of Sudbury,* 1889, pp. 308-309.

4. *Massachusetts Archives,* Vol. XII, pp. 134-135.

5. *Ibid,* p. 158.

6. *Massachusetts Acts and Resolves,* Vol. XII, Chapter 2, p. 671.

7. *Massachusetts Archives,* Vol. IV, pp. 521-523.

4

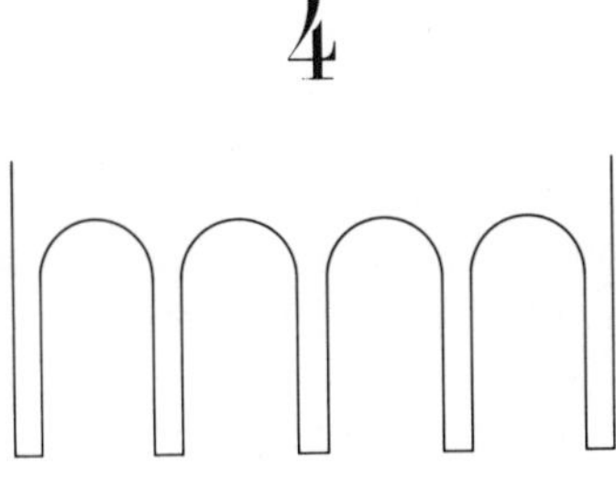

Separate Towns

BY THE 1770s the town as a whole was going along paying its two ministers identical salaries, with added gratuities to make up for wartime inflation after 1775. It was also taking full financial responsibility for the repair, alteration, or enlargement of the two meetinghouses which were still being used in alternation as places for town meeting. The population of the west side of town had come to exceed that of the east side by an appreciable number. This had led to a proposal at the March 2, 1771, town meeting "to see if the Town will enlarge or rebuild the West Meeting House." A committee was appointed to consider this question, but nothing was done to enlarge the now crowded building until the 1790s.

Along with two churches, by mid-century the town was supporting grammar schools at five places, albeit for short intervals at each, two on the east side and three on the west. There were what were called "town schools," one near each meetinghouse, and various outlying schoolhouses. By the late 1770s reading and writing schools were kept in eight schoolhouses. It cannot be determined whether more than half of these eight schools were on the west side, but this was almost surely the case. At this same period there was agitation and much controversy over a new schoolhouse in the southwest corner of the town. That there was friction over the arrangements for teaching more children on the west side is shown in the warrant for the town meeting of March 7, 1763. A petition of Josiah Richardson of the west side and others requested that money for the support of a grammar school shall in future "be equally divided between the west side and the east in proportion to their pay." The meaning of "in proportion to their pay" is not clear. The measure did not pass. In reading the town clerk's record one cannot ascertain whether differences and distinctions over schools became a source of serious difficulty between the two sides of the town.

Although the east side was smaller in land and population, properties there were more highly developed and there was a certain accumulation of wealth. The fragmentary tax lists which have come down to us show that in the latter half of the eighteenth century, as had been true at the end of the seventeenth century, the east side had a higher total assessed valuation than the west side. If the richer east side was carrying more of the tax burden but getting only equal benefits from ministers and meetinghouses and perhaps schools, and was threatened with having to pay more per capita for enlarging the west meetinghouse, there was cause for strain between the two sides of the town. Whatever can be deduced about church- and school-related economic strains, it is clear that additional stress and difficulty over handling Sudbury's part in the Revolutionary War brought to a head the decision in 1778 by the east siders that they would like to form a separate township.

When the War of Independence was in the offing in the early 1770s, there was definite east-west controversy over the erection of a powderhouse for the town's ammunition. At a town meeting held on October 14, 1771, it was voted to build the powderhouse on the east side on land between the property of William Baldwin and that of Maj. William Curtis. This would have been in the Glezen Lane-Baldwin's Pond area. However, a later meeting, on March 2, 1772, overturned that vote, and it was voted to build the powderhouse on the west side of the river on the west training field.

When war finally came, the economic dislocations and strains were enormous. After the first rush of patriotic involvement in 1775, the town leaders had an increasingly difficult time filling provincial manpower requirements levied on the town. Heavy levies of beef, a chief product of the area, were also made. There were difficult problems of paying those who served as soldiers and of supporting their sometimes indigent dependents while they were away on expeditions to Rhode Island, New York, and elsewhere.

In 1776 and 1777 the large roster of town officers chosen at the

March town meeting was filled about equally by east and west side inhabitants, but by March 2, 1778, the strain of local public service combined with military service was beginning to cause tension. The number of town meetings required to handle problems directly related to the war or owing to the growing population became burdensome, and of course the selectmen had to meet much more often. Three of the seven selectmen chosen in March declined to serve or were dismissed at their request, and substitutes had to be found for them. Caleb Moulton of the east side had been chosen as an assessor in March, but William Baldwin was chosen to take his place on June 25 because Moulton was "engaged in public service."

Apart from the economic question whether it was necessary or desirable for the smaller, more heavily assessed side of the town to be paying for more than its share of church buildings, bridges, highways, schools, and other town facilities, this writer has not found reasons additional to those cited in the petition to detach the eastern part of Sudbury as a separate town. Whereas in the seventeenth and early eighteenth centuries ownership by an individual of lands on both sides of the river was very common, personal holdings had been consolidated, and families had gravitated to one side of the river or the other. Among direct male descendants of the original settlers, branches of certain families, such as the Parmenters, Bents, and Goodenows, were to be found on both sides of the river. But certain other families were almost exclusively on one side of the river: the Curtises and Lokers on the east, the Hayneses and the Hows on the west. Families who had come later than the proprietors, usually marrying daughters of original settlers, tended to be on one side of the river or the other—the Damons and Reeveses on the east side, the Willises and Puffers on the west. Despite the fact that their churches were separate only as church societies and not in the important matter of financial support which very often led on to town separation, among the leaders of the east side there arose a strong desire to break the municipal ties which had been carefully nurtured long after the church separation. The east side had had enough of being combined with the west side, and in 1778 it initiated a drive to break away from the west side.

It is not known why John Tilton (1707-79) was the man who presented the petition which came up at the June 25, 1778, town meeting or who "the others" were that the town clerk recorded as sponsoring the article. John Tilton was a newcomer to Sudbury from Essex County in the mid-eighteenth century, having bought a house and farm just east of the Five Paths Corner on what is now known as Old Connecticut Path from his brother Samuel, who had lived there briefly, then moved to Hopkinton. John Tilton must have been a man of dignity and substance, because in 1764 he was elected tithingman and for several years thereafter was an overseer of the poor. He had served as a selectman in 1773 and 1774. It may have been easier and more appropriate to have a man whose roots did not go far back in Sudbury's history make the radical proposal. Being in a position to be more objective, he may have seen more clearly the advantages of making the eastern part of Sudbury a separate town. Or perhaps his highly respected personality made him the wise choice to introduce a controversial measure. He died in 1779 and did not see his proposal realized.

Article 2 at the June 25 town meeting read: "To see if the Town will vote to Divide the Town of Sudbury and make it two towns and take the necessary steps therefor." There is no way of knowing how well the late June town meeting at the east meetinghouse was attended, but the article passed in the affirmative, and a committee of six men was appointed to agree on a dividing line. Three were from the east side, Capt. Richard Heard, Phinehas Gleason, and John Merriam; and three from the west side, Col. Ezekiel How, Nathan Loring, and John Maynard.

On July 6, less than two weeks later, an adjournment of this same town meeting was held to hear the report of the division line committee. The committee reported that it had not been able to agree as to the land division, after which the town voted "to reconsider the vote for the division of the town." The town clerk's record does not indicate whether a larger number of voters attended the July 6 meeting, but it can be presumed that such was the case. At this time the population on the west side of the river was at least 50 percent greater than that on the east side, and if a majority of west siders wanted to oppose a town division, they had the balance of power in the town meeting.

The east siders who were in favor of splitting off their part of the town as a separate municipality tried again at a special town meeting called for February 1, 1779. Article 1 of the warrant was to see if the town would vote for a division and agree on a line of division. At this meeting a committee of five—this time two from the east side, Maj. Joseph Curtis and Capt. Richard Heard, and three from the west side, John Balcom, Thomas Plympton, and Capt. Jonathan Rice—were appointed to agree on a line of division. The committee members retired, deliberated, then returned and informed the town that they could not agree on a line. The town voted to discuss the matter at a later meeting. Then they voted that the town be divided by the Sudbury River and that Pelham's Island, west of the river and then owned and occupied by the Heard family, be annexed to the east side and the land on the east side be set off from Sudbury.

This February 1, 1779, vote represented an acquiescence on the part of the west side that the east side could be permitted to be a separate town, and the meeting was adjourned to February 15 to consider the matter further. At that meeting the question was raised whether more land could be added to the newly conceived eastern town. However, although the land area west of the river was very much greater than the land to the east of the river with Pelham Island, the vote was negative. Although town clerks' records for this era seldom reveal controversy or even debate, the town clerk recorded this decision as having been taken "after a long debate."

Even though they clearly were going to have to settle for less than half of the territory, by this time the east siders had been persuaded almost to a man that they wanted a separate township. The next move was a petition to the General Court, dated February 22, 1779, that the General Court appoint a committee to help settle a fair line of division between the two towns. The petition asks help with the division line but devotes most of its space to the reasons why the town should be divided. The original of this petition, in Joseph Curtis's handwriting, is in Massachusetts Archives, Volume 225, pages 89-91. It appears in printed form, without its long list of signatures, in *Massachusetts Province Laws 1769-1780* in a section called "Revolutionary Period—State Notes."[1] (It is of special importance in the history of Wayland—indeed, it is East Sudbury's declaration of independence.) It is interesting to note that with the first signatures, those of town leaders who were its authors—John Noyes, William Barker, Joseph Curtis, William Bent, Richard Heard, John Merriam, and Jacob Reeves—there are in all 122 signatures. These signers constituted almost all of the men of voting age in the eastern part of the town.

The petition's first argument is that the distance needed to travel to transact town affairs is just too great and that this fatiguing and demanding situation is of special prominence "in the present exigencies of publick affairs," by which is meant in time of war. In the year 1779 there had been nineteen town meetings or meetings with adjournments to another date. The petition goes on to use the argument, popular in Massachusetts in the Revolutionary War era, that to have meetings which voters cannot attend is "taxation without representation." The second argument is that, owing to the extensiveness of the town and thus the distance to meetings, capable men are discouraged from accepting public office. This paragraph goes on to point out that difficulty in securing good town officers and the extensiveness of the town make it more difficult and expensive to recruit good men for military service in the present war, a rather strained argument.

The petition next points out that town meetings have been held on the subject and that "it is the general opinion of the Inhabitants of the Town that it is sufficient in Dimentions and numbers to make two Towns." But then the petition goes on to point out that the voters on the west side of the river are many more in number than those on the east side and that they (of the west) have repeatedly granted the request for an eastern township but that they are insisting that the river be the boundary, with the exception of two farms on the west side which would go to the east side. This, the petitioners point out, would be a very unequal division, giving the westerly town over two thirds of the land. The petitioners pray that the legislature take this problem of inequality into consideration and appoint a committee to settle a fair line between the two towns. The petition ends with the following disarmingly poignant N.B.: "We suppose a just and equal Division may be made without the removal of either Meeting House or the laying out of a new Road."

It had apparently been the hope of the petitioners for an east side township and the thought of the town officers that the February 22 petition would be acted upon quickly. The annual town meeting for the election of officers, required by law to be held in March, was put off from the first week of March until March 29, 1779. On this date a slate of officers, carefully balanced between men from the east and west, was elected.

The East Sudbury petition was apparently not read in the House until April 23 and was then committed to a three-man committee, which submitted a report to the House on May 3, 1779. This report was lost, and nothing more was done about it during this session of the legislature. This may have been deliberate stalling on the part of the General Court, as is known to have occurred in the matter of the separation of other towns. The east side petitioners were alert to see that the next session of the legislature, beginning in June, received their petition. This time, on June 11, 1779, steps were taken in the

Legislative Council to appoint a committee to view the Town of Sudbury and report on a division line.

It is not known exactly when during the summer of 1779 the General Court's committee of both houses, headed by Samuel Austin of Boston and William Brown of Framingham, went to Sudbury, met with the selectmen, and heard a large number of the citizens of the western part of the town who had begun to oppose any separation. The town clerk's record shows that on September 20, 1779, a special town meeting was held at the west meetinghouse. The chief article was "To see if the Town will choose a committee to attend the General Court to hear the report of the Committee Appointed by the General Court on the Petition of a Number of Inhabitants of the Town living on the East Side of Sudbury River and Give their Committee so chosen such instructions relating to a Division of said Town as the Town may think proper when met."

The committee chosen to attend the General Court consisted of three west side residents—Thomas Plympton, Col. Ezekiel How, and William Rice, Jr. Their instructions, voted at this September 20 meeting, read as follows:

Notwithstanding a former vote of this Town dividing the same by the River, yet upon more maturely considering the situation and viewing the circumstances without prejudice to the one part or the other, you are therefore directed to use your utmost endeavors to preventing any division of said Town.

In the meantime the General Court's committee made its report to the Council on November 25, 1779, and to the House on November 26, saying:

After the most Deliberate Consideration your Committee are clearly and unanimously of Opinion that it will greatly contribute to the convenience and peace of both parties and serve the public intent that the Town be Divided into two separate Towns.

They then spelled out a boundary line which was similar to what was enacted in the final bill.

With a favorable report, the bill that led to Chapter 33, 4th Series Province Laws 1779-1780 was read for the first time on December 1 and referred to the next sitting of the General Court. As soon as it became known in Sudbury that the November report favoring a division into two towns had led to a bill for such in the legislature, a special town meeting was held at the west meetinghouse on December 6, 1779, to choose a committee "to act on behalf of the Town . . . to oppose a Division of the said Town and Give the committee . . . instructions . . . and to grant a sum of money to enable said committee to carry on said Business." The same three men—Ezekiel How, William Rice, Jr., and Thomas Plympton—were appointed to the committee and were granted £ 300 expenses.

At an adjourned meeting the next afternoon the town meeting instructed this committee "to prefer a Petition or Memorial . . . praying that the Bill for Dividing . . . may be set aside . . . setting forth the great disadvantages the westerly part of the Town will Labour under." The town went on to give instructions as to specific objections they were to make to the actual division proposed in the bill. The resulting petition started with the statement, "that it is with the greatest Regret and Concern that a Major Part of the Inhabitants . . . understand that a Bill has been brought forward . . . for dividing of said Town."[2]

They then gave two reasons why on behalf of the town they wanted to oppose the bill. First, "that a major part of the Inhabitants are greatly averse to the proposed Separation." They failed to say that the inhabitants of the west side who had a preponderant number of votes in the town meeting opposed the division. From what was stated in the petition, one could infer that inhabitants all over the town were opposed, which was not the case. The second reason was: "that at a time that a State Constitution was pending was a poor one to allow the multiplication of towns within the state." The towns had been asked to attend conventions and study drafts of the Massachusetts State constitution eventually adopted in 1780, but this did not stop various other towns from petitioning for division and would appear to have been a lame argument. The petition then goes on to raise objections to the pending bill for actual division as follows:

(a) that the provision that the westerly town support one half of the great causeway and Bridges even though they will be within the limits of the easterly town is unfair as it will saddle the Westerly Town with nearly double the highway expense the Easterly Town will have.

(b) that the Westerly Town will be cut off from the supply of gravel from the gravel pit which is needed for highway repairs.

(c) that with one exception all the town paupers will be the responsibility of the Westerly Town.

(d) that the proposed line of division will cut off from the Westerly Town a large training field that was especially appropriated for the use of the west parish.

On May 25, 1713, the Proprietors of the Common and Undivided Land of Sudbury had voted to lay out two convenient training fields, one on each side of the river. The Sand Hill Training Field on the west side of the river, then containing only three acres, was actually laid out by the proprietors on February 29, 1720.[3]

(e) that a number of Inhabitants will be greatly injured as individuals should the proposed line of division apply.

The petition ends with the plea that division proceedings be stalled, stating as follows:

Your petitioners, in behalf of . . . Sudbury pray that no Division . . . of said Town until a new Constitution shall be adopted may be made, and if this cannot be conceded to at least the said Bill may be recommitted and said Town . . . be further heard.

At the same December 1779 session of the legislature, four Sudbury citizens presented a remonstrance to the General Court.[4] Caleb Wheeler, whose farm on the west side of the river was to be incorporated in the eastern town, objected to being set off to the easterly town because he would lose the privilege of the town school on the west side. Wheeler had married Jerusha Dorr in November 1778, and at the time of this petition had just one child. He subsequently had at least seven more children, and the question of having to send them across the river to school when his property was a good bit nearer by road to the Rocky Plain School than to the town school near the east meetinghouse was perhaps a valid one. The other four men—Robert Emes, Isaac Hunt, Jr., Samuel Hunt, and Moses Stone—objected to the proposed division line because their houses would lie in the western town, whereas the greater part of their farms would be in the eastern town. This, according to them, would cause inconvenience and loss of value.

The House Journal between December 1779 and April 1780 is missing, and it is not known exactly when the two December petitions, the Town of Sudbury petition to oppose the division, and the petition of the five citizens who felt they would be adversely affected by the dividing line were heard. However, a memorandum attached to the report in the bill says that the committee for the bill fully heard the petitioners and considered their arguments and concluded that:

said Town of Sudbury in its present situation is Subjected to very great disadvantages which render it necessary that it should be divided which in the Opinion of your committee will conduce to the Interest of both Eastern and Western parts and that no other Line can be drawn which will do equal justice to each party better than the Line agreed upon by the Committee who reported the division and that the bill pass.

The editor of the notes appended to the printed *Province Laws 1769-1780* was unable to ascertain on what date the House committee endorsed the bill which became Chapter 34 of Province Laws 1769-1780, 4th Session, but supposed it to be in late March, probably on or just before March 23, 1780, when the bill was taken up in the House.

The Sudbury town clerk's record reveals very little about the pending question of whether a bill would be passed that would divide the town. If the west siders were hoping that the east siders would give up or be defeated in their effort to become a separate town and were trying to persuade the leaders of the east side to withdraw their petition, there is no extant evidence to show such activity. Whereas in March 1779 the annual town meeting was delayed to see if the division would come about in time to be taken into account in the March election, the town met on March 6 and elected the usual slate of officers, with a fairly equal balance between east siders and west siders. The board of seven selectmen included three east siders: Squire William Baldwin, Capt. Caleb Moulton, and Capt. Thaddeus Russell. It is significant that none of these men was chosen as selectman in the first election held by East Sudbury as a separate town. One concludes that these were men who, although they had signed the original February 1779 petition for a separate town, were less active in pushing the division.

It should be noted that at the March 6, 1780, town meeting a petition, a copy of which cannot now be found in the Massachusetts Archives, dated March 6, 1780, and signed by 116 inhabitants of the east side, was sent to the General Court objecting to the £300 expenses voted in December 1779 for the committee to oppose the town division. The only reference to this petition is in the Notes to *Province Laws 1769-1780*, page 1327, where the petition is described as making objection to the £300 appropriation and a subsequent second £300 because the Sudbury town meeting on December 6 was warned by posting a notice at the door of the meetinghouse on Sunday, December 5, and that most of the petitioners never saw the notice.

Maps must have been drawn in connection with the East Sudbury-Sudbury division, but none is extant. The existing maps which come closest to the 1780 date are surveys made for the Commonwealth of Massachusetts by Matthias Mossman of East Sudbury in 1795.[5] In these surveys Mossman stated that Sudbury, including roads and bodies of water, contained 18,030 acres, and that East Sudbury contained 8,123 acres. Although its boundaries have not been changed appreciably since Mossman's 1795 survey, modern surveying methods attribute 15.28 square miles or approximately 9,800 acres to Wayland.

The bill, which became Chapter 34, passed April 10, 1780, is Wayland's charter as a separate town. Section 1 spells out the boundary lines which have remained, with one very small exception on the Natick border, the same to this day and incorporates this area into a town by the name of East Sudbury.

Section 2 provides for joint maintenance of the bridges and causeway on what is now Old Sudbury Road, or Route 27. The bridges and causeway were within the bounds of East Sudbury, and this was one of the points objected to by the west siders. It also provides that the town's arms and ammunition be divided according to the proportion of men able to bear arms in the two towns. Further, it provides that, with the exception of the donation given by Mary Dean specifically for the inhabitants of the east side, all other donations for the poor, funds for schools, and all lands and monies in the treasury be equally divided. As to the support of the poor, which had been a point of objection to the division by the west side, it was provided that the poor should be divided according to the last tax act.

Section 3 satisfied some of the objections in the December 1779 petition in that Caleb Wheeler's farm and the training field adjoining it went to Sudbury. This explains the very uneven west border of Wayland. The training field did not make much change in the line which attempted to give East Sudbury a fairer share of the land than would have been the case if the river had been used as the boundary. However, the Wheeler farm, containing nearly fifty acres, caused a definite and peculiar jog in the boundary line, a subject of much curiosity since.

Section 4 provided that any property still in the hands of the Proprietors of the Common and Undivided Land of Sudbury should be the joint property of this group, as if the town had not been divided. This was the usual way of handling lands owned by the heirs of the original proprietors of towns when town divisions took place. In the case of Sudbury, there was very little undivided land in the joint ownership of the proprietors by 1780, and there was no problem. The proprietors from both sides of the river met a few times in the 1780s and 1790s. Finally in 1803, having disposed of all of their property, they voted to discontinue their organization.

Section 5 provided that the Town of East Sudbury should be held responsible for its proportion of town, county, and state taxes. Later in that year, in September 1780, Jonathan Rice, deputy to the General Court from Sudbury, requested that the state treasurer stay his execution against the collector of East Sudbury for a short time, that is, until the tax mechanism in East Sudbury could be organized.[6]

Section 6 directed that Josiah Stone, a justice of the peace from Framingham, be empowered to direct some principal inhabitant of East Sudbury to warn the inhabitants of the new town to assemble, choose the officers usually elected in a town in the month of March, and transact any other necessary business.

Much had to be done in the ensuing few years to divide the two towns' assets and liabilities and to make accountings for these purposes. As far as this writer could determine, the business of carrying out Chapter 34 and dividing donation funds, war levies, and the like, was conducted very amicably even though Revolutionary War calls for soldiers, levies of supplies, and the attendant statewide inflation had given rise to a very complicated array of accounts.

No town meeting was held in Sudbury between the above-described March 6, 1780, annual meeting when officers were chosen from both sides of the river until May 9 when, as was the annual custom at that time, a town meeting was called to elect Sudbury's representative to the General Court. This meeting was also to act on the Massachusetts State constitution. Article 3 in the warrant contains the first direct reference in the town clerk's record to the already accomplished town division. "To choose any or all such Town officers that the Town may Judge necessary by reason the Town having been

Divided." If the Massachusetts Archives had been burned and we had to rely on the town clerk's record, we would know very little about the process by which this division into two towns took place.

At a Sudbury town meeting held on May 22, 1780, Asher Cutler was added to the board of selectmen, making a board of five, and Capt. Samuel Knight was chosen as an assessor in place of William Baldwin, who lived in East Sudbury. The following year five selectmen were elected; the board of assessors continued with three men; but, as would be expected, there were only two constables and fewer surveyors of highways than when the town was larger.

At the May 22, 1780, town meeting Sudbury voted that the selectmen and James Thompson, town clerk and treasurer, would constitute its committee to settle the details of the division of property and obligations with East Sudbury. It was apparently decided not to charge the east siders with their share of the £600 expense account voted in December 1779 to oppose the town division and the east siders' petition against this opposition.

East Sudbury's first town meeting was held on April 24, 1780. Five selectmen were elected, but a few of the traditional minor offices Sudbury had been accustomed to have, such as deer reeve, were omitted. More will be said about the first officers of East Sudbury in the next chapter.

Some have not understood why, when it was the earlier settled part of the town—and where the central feature of a Puritan Massachusetts town, the only meetinghouse, was situated for the first eighty years of Sudbury's history—the earlier town took the name East Sudbury and did such things as leave the original town records in the hands of the slightly less old part of the original town. It was simply a matter of who initiated the splitting off. By the late 1770s the people east of the river had lost their feeling of oneness with the west side. The fact that almost every head of a household on the east side signed the 1779 petition to separate must have impressed the General Court and must have carried more weight with that body than the late 1779 town votes against division. It is clear that the east siders were extremely eager to disassociate themselves from the west side. This is shown by the fact that they were willing to accept a secondary name, a smaller land area, and even a ridiculously uneven western land boundary to accomplish this breakoff as soon as they could get it through the legislature. They knew they were going to be the smaller town, but now they wanted to go it alone.

It has required quite a few pages to give a complete account of the process of separation of the two Sudburys from 1707 to 1780. The details may not be of interest to all readers, but to the historian of Sudbury and of Wayland, the story, not all previously understood, has fascination as well as explanations of such important factors as the present location of Wayland Center and the inclusion of Cochituate in our town. One must, however, bear in mind that during the years from 1707 through 1780, when the separation of the two Sudburys was evolving, ninety-one other new Massachusetts towns were separated from earlier towns—in most cases from one town, in fewer cases from two or more adjacent towns. The legislature must have been busy indeed if many of the separations involved the number of petitions which came from Sudbury.

Starting with Plympton, which was established as a separate town from part of Plymouth on June 4, 1707, and ending with Milford, which broke off from Mendon in 1780, in these seventy-four years there were thirty-five separations of towns from one earlier constituted town, eleven more towns which were made from a part of an earlier town with the addition of unclaimed adjacent lands, and thirteen towns established from parts of two or more towns. These fifty-nine towns were established by individual acts of the Massachusetts legislature. In addition to these, there were thirty-three towns which were made such from districts by a general legislative act of August 23, 1775, under which districts became towns.

Throughout those years Sudbury's representatives to the General Court whom the town almost invariably elected and sent certainly were aware that the older, larger towns were being broken into more manageable or congenial entities. They also knew that in most if not all cases during this eighteenth-century period separations were led up to by the creation of a separate church precinct. The representatives were aware that controversies raged over many if not most of these divisions. They knew that the General Court was constantly having to act on petitions and send committees to the towns to judge the feasibility and fairness of the divisions.

Without doing enormous research into the history of many other towns it is not possible to determine to what extent the Sudbury experience differed from the ninety-one other divisions that occurred in this period. This writer is quite sure, however, that the failure to establish two real precincts was confined to Sudbury and, if to any other towns certainly to very few. It is hard to judge whether by

Judge Edward Mellen (1802-1875)

relating the two Sudbury church bodies to the town in this different way, the town thought it was remaining a more united entity than those towns which established and operated full-fledged precincts. This would seem to have been the case. In the end, economic strains occasioned by the fact that the smaller, eastern part of Sudbury carried a heavier per capita and per acre tax burden apparently pushed the east siders into petitioning for separation. Running a town with a larger population became more complicated, especially when there were war demands and disruptions. An attempt was made to consider a fairer division of the land, but the river was there; it did not cut the town equally, but cohesive groups had arisen and grown more distinct on each side of it.

This writer does not know whether there is a significant number of Massachusetts towns in which fragmentation led to the earliest settled section having an adjunct name, as did East Sudbury, or a different name, as Wayland, which the Town of East Sudbury chose to adopt in 1835. The Town of East Sudbury petitioned the General Court that its name be changed to Wayland in February 1835. By Chapter 50 of the Acts of 1835 the name was officially changed. A full discussion of the name change does not seem worthwhile here. Suffice it to say that no extant town record explains or even gives a clue to the reasons for the choice of the name. When in 1957 this writer undertook extensive research into the adoption of the name Wayland, no contemporary (1835) comment or explanation could be found. However, strong evidence was found that the town was named for the Reverend Francis Wayland, president of Brown University in Rhode Island. Statements made within the town at that time of or soon after Francis Wayland's death in 1865 seem to corroborate but do not absolutely prove the tradition that this was the case.[7] Judge Edward Mellen (1802-75), who came to East Sudbury in 1830 and bought the village home of Samuel Mann and also Mann's law office building across the street in Wayland Center,[8] can be supposed to have suggested the name Wayland. By 1835 he was active in Wayland affairs. Both Mellen and John Burt Wight, the Unitarian minister, were graduates of Brown University. Mellen was a personal friend and admirer of Francis Wayland.

The Town of Quincy, incorporated at its separation from Braintree in 1792, encompassed the earliest settled and thus oldest part of Braintree. However, most of the new towns of the eighteenth century were centered on younger church precincts which developed when the population became great enough to create a demand for a meetinghouse in what were at first outlying and sparsely settled areas of the older, larger towns. As the nineteenth century developed, new towns were incorporated for other reasons than the desire to center on a church. If this practice had not already ceased, the legal separation of church and civil government in 1834 would have precluded the repetition of Sudbury's experience. In April 1871 Maynard was incorporated as a town from parts of Stow and Sudbury. This new town was based on the concentration of population in that section occasioned by the sudden growth of industry at the waterpower site there.

It may be of interest to close this chapter with a few comments on the separation of Milford from Mendon in Worcester County, which was enacted into law the day after that of East Sudbury's, on April 11, 1780, by Chapter 35 of Province Laws of 1780. In Part I of the volume published by the town of Milford in 1882, entitled *History of the Town of Milford, Massachusetts from its First Settlement to 1881,* Adin Ballou related a story similar to that of Sudbury in telling how Milford became separated from Mendon. The topical summaries which head Chapter IV, "A Generation of Progress Down to the Establishment of the Precinct," and Chapter VI, "Induction, Incorporation and Organization of Milford," show considerable parallel to the Sudbury experience except that after a struggle which continued from 1727 to

1741 amid very bitter controversy, a true precinct which later became Milford was established. Ballou's account of this precinct seems to show evidence of greater controversy and bitterness than was the case in Sudbury. Section headings in Chapter IV are: "The Long Series of Town Meetings, Agitation, and Contention About the Meeting-House," followed by "The Mill River Aggrieved Party, their Protests and Efforts to get set off as a Town or Precinct," "Secession of the Aggrieved Members from the First Church and Pastor Dorr" and finally "Growth and Success of the Separation Movement—Copy of their Petition to the General Court." We also find the following in the outline of this chapter: "Proceedings for the Erection of a Meeting House—Disagreements Respecting its Location," "Referral to an Outside Committee to state the Spot," "Delays and Judgment of the Committee," and "Troubles in Getting the Edifice Begun." This indicates that Sudbury went through the same throes of trying to adjust to the need or desire for more than one church center as many another rural Massachusetts town did during the eighteenth century.

NOTES

1. *Massachusetts Province Laws 1769-1780,* pp. 1324-1325.
2. The petition of Sudbury's committee of Ezekiel How, Thomas Plympton and William Rice, Jr. is to be found in *Massachusetts Archives,* Vol. 186, p. 16. A partial transcription appears on page 1326 of *Province Laws 1769-1780.*
3. *Sudbury Proprietors Record, 1720-1780,* p. 1.
4. *Massachusetts The House*, No. 430 and *Province Laws 1769-1780,* p. 1326.
5. East Sudbury's map is Massachusetts Archives Map #1181; Sudbury's map is Massachusetts Archives Map #1198.
6. *Massachusetts Archives*, Vol. 229, pp. 171-172.
7. See paper "The Town That Bears His Name" by Helen F. Emery in files of the Wayland Historical Society.
8. The Mellen office, one of the few surviving examples of the typical two-room law office of the early nineteenth century is still standing on the village green, and is now owned by the town.

5

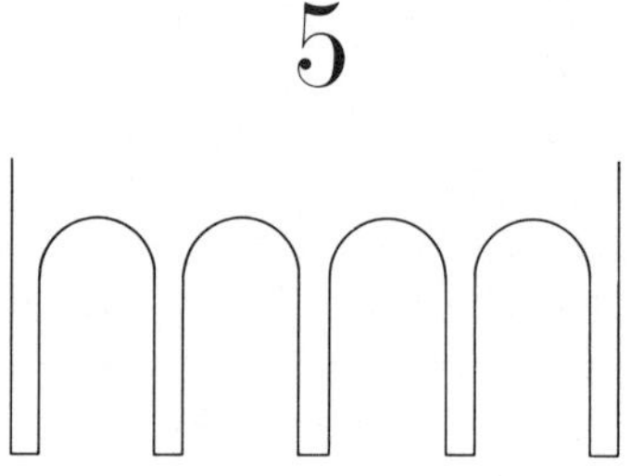

East Sudbury in 1780

If one reads with care and imagination pages 34 through 51 of the book *Wayland Historical Tours* published in 1976 by the Wayland Bicentennial Committee with text written by Barbara Robinson, one can get a good idea of the evidence that now exists of what the new Town of East Sudbury was like in 1780. There are no pictures or detailed descriptions of the town at that date. During the bicentennial celebrations in 1975 and 1976 there was exhibited in the Wayland Library a model representing Wayland Center at the time of the Revolutionary War. This was based on James Sumner Draper's reconstruction of the town as of 1775. There are, however, a nearly contemporary map, a list of families that made up the town, a census enumeration, and the town clerk's records of dates at, or not too far distant from, 1780, so that we can see quite plainly, if less vividly and in less detail than would be ideal, what East Sudbury was like during that year.

In June 1794 the Commonwealth of Massachusetts ordered all of its then constituted towns to make surveyor's maps showing boundaries; acreage; bodies of water; and location of meetinghouses, mills, and major highways. The originals of these survey maps are in the Massachusetts Archives. The surveyor employed to make the maps of both East Sudbury and Sudbury was Matthias Mossman, who at that time lived in East Sudbury. His survey map, dated May 20, 1795, is the only map of the town anywhere near contemporary with the time of separation.[1]

The main ("county") highways are shown providing an idea of the road network. No structures were shown except the bridges, the one meetinghouse, and two mills, Wyman's Grist Mill on the Mill Pond and a sawmill owned by Phinehas Gleason and Benjamin Adams on the upper part of Hazel Brook. Individual houses were not designated on the Mossman maps. Although a survey map of 1830 showed the houses and indicated the owners for Sudbury, as did those for a number of other towns, East Sudbury (Wayland) was to have no map indicating houses until a large wall map of Middlesex County, with insets for town centers, was published in 1856. An original copy of this map, published by Henry F. Walling, is on loan to the Wayland Historical Society.

Copies of a map, entitled "Plan of the Town of Wayland in 1776," made by James Sumner Draper (1811-96), are widely circulated in Wayland. The original of Draper's map, which measures 28 by 16 inches, is owned by the Wayland Historical Society. It is not dated, but there is evidence that it was constructed in the 1870s and was perhaps called forth by the celebration in 1875 of the centennial of the beginning of the American Revolution. This is not a contemporary map but is a reconstruction based on one man's conclusions about the layout of the town at the time of the Revolution. The original bears the label "Wayland in 1775." This map has been reproduced in reduced size at various times, once in 1880, and several times in the twentieth century, so that it is familiar to quite a few present Wayland residents. It may be noted that the reproductions of the Draper map do not include all of the place names (names of swamps, etc.) and house locations which are on the Draper original. The placement of dwellings was done after long study of the town records and of old roads and cellar holes, and after much inquiry around the town as to where the earlier houses were located. Except for indicating the homestead of Edmund Browne, the first minister of Sudbury, which no longer existed in 1775, the map shows homesteads in existence in 1775 according to Draper's calculations. There are a few errors, but the careful research that went into this project resulted in this map being considered by those who have studied the land titles through deeds to be correct in almost every particular.

The Mossman and Draper maps depict the physical layout of East Sudbury about 1780. One of the most important features of these maps is the roads. On Mossman's map every lane and byway was not shown, but one can study the through highway system and see how it differs from that of today. In 1780 there was no east-west highway equivalent to Route 30 going west from the present V where East Plain Street comes into Commonwealth Road. Farther north in the town it is important to note that the Boston Post Road as we know it did not extend west beyond Wayland Center. In 1780 and until the late 1820s, the Boston Post Road took a right-angled turn near the East Sudbury meetinghouse and went northwest on what is essentially the present Old Sudbury Road and over the Town and Canal bridges into Sudbury.

In 1780 East Sudbury had a population of about 750 to 775 persons. This estimate is based on the assumption that the population grew evenly from 1765 when there was a census count for the towns in the province of Massachusetts to 1790 when the first United States census was taken. Another assumption is that the same proportion obtained in 1780 as existed in 1790 between persons in East Sudbury and the total of the two Sudbury towns. Draper's map shows stores, a tavern, and a schoolhouse clustered fairly near the meetinghouse at the present village center, but the greatest concentration of dwellings was northwest of there, where a good many of the original house lots had been—along Bow Road and the part of Old Sudbury Road from Bow Road to Baldwin's Pond. The far northern end of the town was the most sparsely settled.

In 1781, a year after East Sudbury became a separate town, the annual March town meeting chose a committee of six to study the question of the number and placement of schoolhouses and to make a recommendation to the town. At a town meeting held on July 30 of that year, the committee, consisting of three of the selectmen—Jacob Reeves, Micah Goodenow, and Richard Heard—with three additional men—Isaac Stone, Jonathan Parmenter, and Isaac Loker—brought in the recommendation that there be "six squadrons of schools." Draper placed five schoolhouses on his map for 1775. If Draper was correct, the 1781 school study committee was recommending one new schoolhouse to be located at the northern end of the concentration of houses on the way to Sudbury and near Deacon William Baldwin's dwelling and tavern. The committee listed under each described squadron the households which would send children to or support the six schools. This list was copied into the town clerk's book after the record of the town meeting of July 30, 1781. We thus have a statement of households by neighborhoods or areas in East Sudbury a year after the town became separate. This list is available at the Historical Society and the library.

Twenty-one households were listed for the schoolhouse, "at the Meeting House where it now standeth or their abouts." Included in this squadron were the Heard houses on Pelham Island and the families in what during the recent century has been known as the Tower Hill area as well as those nearer the meetinghouse. Fourteen families were listed for the more sparsely settled southwest squadron with a school about where the present Wayland High School entrance is located. Eighteen families were listed in the south part of the town (present Cochituate). There were twenty families in the eastern part of the town, many of them on the Boston Post Road on the way to Weston with a school at the corner of the present Old Connecticut Path and Rice Road. Twenty-two families were to make up the squadron with a school near Deacon Baldwin's, and twenty-one families were to constitute the north school squadron with a building "where there had already been one" at the junction of present Lincoln Road with Concord Road. James S. Draper's map contains most of the names that appear on the school squadron list, but there are a few discrepancies, some of which arise because the list pertains to a period six years after the time of the Draper map. This writer feels quite sure that Draper used this list in compiling his map. A few names, such as that of the Roby family who lived just beyond the present Wayland Library on Concord Road, were omitted from the school list, but by and large this is a list of the families who made up East Sudbury at its beginning as a separate town. We are fortunate to have the list as written in the town clerk's handwriting roughly two hundred years ago.

It is interesting to analyze the school list as to the family names included. In 1781 there were thirty-five households which carried down the names of Sudbury's earliest settlers or original proprietors. There were many more families descended from the original proprietors because wives of relative newcomers were very often from proprietor families. In the list, Rice households, of which there were six, were the most numerous, followed by Lokers, Stones, Goodenows, and Rutters, of which there were three each. There were three Noyes households, but these Noyeses were descended from Joseph Noyes, who came to Sudbury from Newbury in 1662, not from the Peter Noyes founding family. Other numerous families in the town, by now intermarried with the proprietor families, were Shermans and Dudleys with four households each, and Cuttings, Moultons, Damons, and Carters with three each.

The 1781 school list with its 116 households compares with 144 families listed in East Sudbury in the United States census of 1790. This census enumeration, entitled *Heads of Families at the First Census of the United States Taken in the Year 1790*, was printed in 1908 by the Bureau of the Census and is readily available in research libraries. At that date 801 persons were counted as living in East Sudbury, and there were 112 houses. There was thus an average of 7.2 persons per house and 5.6 persons per family. The 1790 total of 801 for East Sudbury compares with 1,290 west of the river in the Town of Sudbury. It is no wonder that the Town of Sudbury then needed a new and larger meetinghouse. Wayland was not to come up to Sudbury's 1790 population figure until 1876, eighty-six years later.

By this time there were nine Rice households and six Damon households. The names of many of these late-eighteenth-century (and earlier) families have been perpetuated in the town with streets (Loker, Rice, Brackett, etc.), ponds (Dudley, Heard, Baldwin), and bridges (Stone's and Sherman's) bearing their names. Our current street names are of rather recent origin. In the late nineteenth century and earlier there were no standard street names such as we have now. Most roads named in deeds up to the twentieth century were "the road from the Meeting House to Deacon Draper's" (Plain Road, in part) or "the road to Concord" (Draper Road).

A few of the houses of the families living in the town in 1780 are still standing. Appendix B lists the twenty houses which are now recognizable dwellings occupied by East Sudbury families at the time the new town was created, even if since added to or remodeled. There are several other buildings in the town which contain remnants of pre-1780 dwellings but are not recognizable as houses of that era. The list does not include one present Wayland house, built about 1713, which was taken down and moved from Kingston, Massachusetts, to Wayland in 1941, or a house older than 1780 moved to the edge of Wayland from Weston. At least two houses which were standing in East Sudbury in 1780 are now located in other towns, one in Sudbury and one in Dover.

Almost all of the householders in the town owned land and considered themselves first and foremost farmers. With the exception of the Reverend Josiah Bridge, who would have been designated as a clerk, most deeds for the purchase or sale of land by these men designate them as yeomen. A few who, in addition to having their family farms had been trained in occupations such as blacksmith, wheelwright, or housewright, used these occupational titles on their deeds. William

Baldwin, Jacob Reeves, and other tavernkeepers of the time were designated as innholders. It was a rural town of owner-occupied, self-sufficient farms. The Yankee farmers and their wives with almost no exception were of English origin, and most of them were descendants of those English who came to Massachusetts in the great Puritan migration of 1620-40. The majority of the town's 750 men, women, and children were born in Sudbury. By checking the 1781 list against the *Sudbury Vital Records*, this writer found that 70 of the heads of the 116 households were born in Sudbury.[2] It can be assumed that an equal number of wives were born here. A much larger proportion of the children and the young, single adults were born in the town, and a significant proportion of old people living with relatives as well as of the children born to nonnative parents were also born in the town. One can estimate conservatively that at least 75 percent of the 1780 population had been born in the town.

The Reverend Josiah Bridge, who had come from Lexington to be pastor in 1761, and Deacon William Baldwin were Harvard College graduates; all other men had had only a common school education. It is not known how literate or well educated the wives were. Some signed their names on deeds in releasing dower rights to property; many marked with an X. The historical records of the late eighteenth century and earlier tell us very little about the women of the town.

The 1781 list contains quite a bit of information about status in the town. Josiah Bridge, the pastor of the town church, and the two deacons, William Baldwin and Samuel Parris, are listed with their church titles. From the beginning of Sudbury as a town militia positions represented status in the community. Especially at the end of the Revolutionary War period military titles were much used. Holders of these military ranks were proud of their titles; almost all of them had been paid by the town for serving in the Revolution. The school squadron list names the one colonel who was John Noyes (1715-85). In the latter half of the eighteenth century he was East Sudbury's most distinguished and influential citizen. When not called Colonel, he was John Noyes, Esquire, having been made a justice of the peace by the Middlesex County Court. Noyes's home was just northwest of the North Cemetery; the present house at 67 Old Sudbury Road is a later building on the same site.

The list shows two majors, Joseph Curtis (1721-91) and Jonathan Parmenter (1730-1807). Curtis and Parmenter were also entitled to use the title esquire. There were thirteen captains[3] and four lieutenants.

Three additional men not named on the school list as lieutenants were called lieutenants on the town officer roster for the year 1781 in the town records.

Let us now turn to the makeup of the East Sudbury government. It is likely that election of their first officers was an exciting event for the East Sudbury inhabitants. The first town meeting was held in the meetinghouse on April 24. This meeting was called in the usual way for a new town. The General Court saw to it that a justice of the peace from a neighboring town notified a distinguished citizen of the new town that a town meeting should be called. The first book of East Sudbury records tell us that on April 15, 1780, five days after the act of incorporation became law, Josiah Stone, justice of the peace of Framingham, notified Capt. Richard Heard to warn "all freeholders and other inhabitants qualified as the Law Directs to vote in Town Affairs . . . to meet at the Meeting House . . . on Monday, April 24 at 1:00 P.M."

With a population of 750 to 775, East Sudbury would have had about 150 males qualified to vote in town meeting.[4] Probably very few were absent that day. Joseph Curtis was elected moderator, and the following officers were elected:

Selectmen:	*Capt. Richard Heard* *Joseph Curtis* *Mr. Phinehas Glezen* *Mr. Jacob Reeves* *Capt. Isaac Loker*
Town Clerk:	*Joseph Curtis*
Treasurer:	*Joseph Curtis*
Assessors:	*Joseph Curtis* *William Baldwin, Esq.* *Lt. William Brintnall*
Constables & Collectors:	*Capt. John Noyes (Lt. Micah Goodenow to serve)* *Mr. Isaac Damon (Lt. Micah Goodenow to serve)*

Highway Surveyors:	*William Baldwin* *Lt. John Whitney* *Capt. Isaac Loker* *Lt. Jonathan Hoar*
Tithing Men:	*Mr. Phinehas Glezen* *Lt. Joseph Dudley*
Fence Viewers:	*William Barker* *William Dudley*
Fish Reeve:	*Mr. Ezekiel Rice*
Field Drivers:	*Mr. Samuel Griffin* *Mr. Nathaniel Reeves*
Hog Reeve:	*Mr. William Revis*
Sealer of Leather:	*Lt. Samuel Russell*
Surveyor of Boards and Shingles:	*Mr. John Merriam*

It will be noted that five selectmen were elected, a change from the larger board of seven selectmen, which had governed greater Sudbury, and that the minor offices were somewhat simplified. As constables and collectors of taxes, Capt. John Noyes, the colonel's son, who lived on the Boston Post Road where Lee's farm market now stands, was officially elected to collect taxes in the northern half of the town; Isaac Damon, who lived on the south side of what is now Commonwealth Road East, in the southern half. The job of tax collector was particularly difficult at this stage of the war. Micah Goodenow, probably on the promise that he would be elected as a selectman the next year, was accepted by the town meeting to serve "in the room of" those two men and thus do the real work of collecting the taxes.

The important offices involving leadership are interesting to analyze, along with the notable fact that one outstanding leader held several chief offices. The officer list shows Joseph Curtis to have been

The Fiske-Heard House, built in 1722 on Pelham Island Road, was torn down in the 1920s.

made the real head of the new town government that day—as selectman, as town clerk, as treasurer, and as assessor. Who was this man who was one of East Sudbury's two majors and was also, as was the other major, Jonathan Parmenter, known as Joseph Curtis, Esquire, or as Squire Curtis? At this time the title esquire did not have its more recent meaning of lawyer or gentleman but indicated that the man had been appointed as a justice of the peace or judge of small causes by the county authorities.

Joseph Curtis was born in the eastern part of Sudbury in 1721 and was a great-grandson of Henry Curtis, one of the original proprietors of the town. Joseph's father, Ephraim Curtis (1680-1759), was very prominent and, over a long span of years, a holder of many town offices of leadership in Sudbury. We have already encountered Ephraim as a leader of the East Precinct, one of those who unfailingly opposed relocation southward of the east meetinghouse. Before the meetinghouse controversy, in 1707 Ephraim Curtis had tried to challenge the proprietors' divisions of Sudbury's undivided common land according to town rights held, that is, according to the acreage of meadowland owned by an original proprietor ancestor in 1650 or to rights bought. Henry Curtis, Ephraim's grandfather, did not own much property when he joined the new Sudbury town and thus had had relatively small meadow allotments. His son, Joseph, Major Joseph's grandfather, had prospered and attained a higher status in the town than his father's. Ephraim went to court to try (unsuccessfully) to make it possible for Sudbury's inhabitants to share in the early-eighteenth-century divisions of the common lands on a basis other than that of the family's original holdings.

Maj. Joseph Curtis had followed the usual system in colonial towns of working up from lower town office; he had been elected a field driver in 1746. However, his father was prominent enough so that the son would be expected to follow in his father's footsteps to positions of real power. We find Joseph being elected selectman of Sudbury for five consecutive years, starting in 1757 when he was thirty-six years old. Before 1780 he had served as selectman fourteen times, as town clerk for two years (1766 and 1777), as assessor for three years in the 1760s and three years in the 1770s, and as town treasurer in 1767. He had been a selectman in 1779 and could thus bring continuity to the running of the town.

Joseph Curtis lived, as the fourth generation of his family, on the east side of Training Field Road at the location of his great-grandfather's house. By 1780 he had had three children by his first wife, Jane Plympton, and twelve children by his second wife, Abigail Baldwin. In 1780 two of his married children had households in the town and were shown on the 1781 school list. David Curtis, who had married Abigail Bent in 1777, lived on the Curtis property. Joseph's daughter Abigail Curtis was the wife of Ephraim Abbott, who had a blacksmith's shop and house on Concord Road near Sherman Bridge Road. Three children had died in an epidemic during August 1770. In 1780 there were several children at home, the youngest being Catherine, who had been born in 1775. The inventory of Joseph Curtis's estate shows that in 1791 his real estate holdings consisted of about 140 acres of land with two houses, two barns and other outbuildings, and a pew in the East Sudbury meetinghouse.[5]

In 1780 Joseph Curtis had a large stake in the new town. He had had also much to do with accomplishing the separation from Sudbury. In electing him to the chief offices of leadership, the town was both honoring him for past performance and relying on his ability and experience. He was to serve as selectman, town clerk, treasurer, and assessor through 1786. In 1786 the town elected him deputy to the General Court, a position which, with the exception of the year 1787, he held until his death. In 1787 Nathaniel Reeves took over as town clerk. In 1787 Curtis held no office and was perhaps ill. The following year he served as moderator and also as assessor and treasurer, and his son David began serving as selectman. He continued as treasurer and assessor in 1789, in 1790 as an assessor, and died in 1791. Thus we see that for a decade the new town had the benefit of Joseph Curtis's leadership but that his activity had to dwindle as he approached the end of his life. One has the impression from the records that the new town ran smoothly; for this Joseph Curtis must have been in large part responsible.

Richard Heard's name appeared first on the list of selectmen elected in April 1780, and although he was only a few months older than Curtis, it can be said that he was the distinguished elder statesman of the town. It was he who received the notification to call the townsmen to the first East Sudbury town meeting. Starting in 1765, he had served as selectman ten times up to 1777, six of those years together with Joseph Curtis on the seven-man Sudbury board of selectmen. He had labored hard to make the division work and had seen to it that the Heard lands on "The Island" west of the bow in the river were made part of the eastern town. At its second town meeting, in May 1780, Capt. Richard Heard was elected as East Sudbury's first deputy to the General Court. He served as moderator for several of the 1780 town meetings. Volume I of the *Wayland Town Records* has on its flyleaf, "East Sudbury's Book of Records The Gift of Captain Richard Heard 1780." The book had cost £55. We find that in May the town meeting voted £45 to purchase a book to record its proceedings. Perhaps Heard was reimbursed to that extent.

Richard Heard was born in the eastern part of Sudbury in 1720. His father, Zachariah Heard, arrived as a newcomer in Sudbury shortly after 1707 when he married Silence Brown, granddaughter of a prominent earliest settler. As had Joseph Curtis, Richard Heard had followed in his father's and father-in-law's (Jonathan Fiske) footsteps toward town leadership. In 1780 he was living in a house on the north side of Pelham Island Road just west of Jeffrey Road. This house had been built by Jonathan Fiske in 1722 and was in existence until sometime in the 1920s.

Heard had seven children, three of whom were listed as married and in separate households on the 1781 school squadron list. In 1773 Thomas Heard had married Elizabeth Reeves, daughter of Jacob Reeves; Abigail Heard had married Thomas Rutter; and Sarah Heard had married Jonathan Hoar. In the 1780s other children would marry a Damon, a Maynard, a Baldwin, and a Sherman.

Heard served for eight consecutive years through 1787 as a selectman. He was moderator of the annual meeting in 1781, 1782, 1786, and 1787. He served in the state legislature in 1780, 1781, and 1783. After 1787 he held no town office; he died in 1792. Richard Heard and his sons were large landowners. In 1798 the son Zachariah Heard had 115 acres of land on the tax list, sons Richard and David 213 acres.[6]

Phinehas Glezen, the third selectman, was younger than Curtis and Heard. Born in the eastern part of Sudbury in 1732, he was forty-eight in 1780. No Glezen (Gleason) was a proprietor of earliest Sudbury, but Phinehas's great-grandfather, Joseph Gleason (1642-1715), had moved to Sudbury from Watertown about 1675. Thus, Phinehas was of the fourth generation of the Gleason name in the town. His father had died as a young man and had not held a leadership office in the town, but his grandfather, Joseph Gleason, had served four times as selectman. Phinehas had no military titles. In later life he was called "Mister" because of his important economic status in the town. The *Direct Tax List of 1798* shows that Phinehas Glezen's property was assessed at $2,802, making him at that time the eleventh largest property owner in East Sudbury. His first town office had been as hog reeve in 1762. Then in 1764, 1766, and in 1771 he served as constable, the main duty being to collect taxes. By the 1770s he was showing himself capable of more responsible office and was elected an overseer of the poor in 1771 and tithingman in 1775. In 1776 and 1777 he was a selectman and in 1779 served on Sudbury's Committee of Correspondence, which served to communicate the town's view on Revolutionary matters to other towns. He served as selectman in 1776 and 1777 with Richard Heard and may have been a protégé of Heard. Jacob Reeves had also served as selectman in 1776 and 1777, and it is obvious that the three men constituted a team working for the interests of the east side and that they were elected in 1780 to carry on the work they had begun earlier.

Phinehas Glezen lived on Glezen Lane, a short distance east of Concord Road. His house, built by his father about 1730, was torn

Reeves Tavern, on Old Connecticut Path.

down in the mid-nineteenth century. From 1755 to 1774 he had ten children. His daughter Lucy married Capt. Jonathan Hoar, whose first wife (who had died young) had been Richard Heard's daughter. His son, Luther Gleason, who was born in 1771, was to become an extensive speculator in East Sudbury property in the early nineteenth century.

Glezen was to continue as selectman with Curtis, Heard, and Reeves through 1785. He was out of office in 1786. In 1787 he was both a selectman and town treasurer, but held no office after that year and died in 1799.

Unlike the other selectmen, Jacob Reeves had no roots in Sudbury, nor did his wife. Born in Salem and a resident of Roxbury for a number of years where deeds in 1746 and 1750 described him as a heelmaker,[7] he had come to the eastern part of Sudbury in 1762 and quickly established himself as a capable and substantial citizen. Nine years after his arrival in 1771 he was serving as an overseer of the poor. Earlier, in 1768 and 1769, he had been a highway surveyor in charge of road maintenance in his area. In 1774 he was elected a warden, and in 1776 he achieved leadership status when elected a selectman. The town recognized his business ability by electing him clerk of the market in 1778, 1779, and 1780, a position concerned with attempts to control prices during the Revolutionary War inflationary period.

Reeves, born in 1720 and thus sixty years old in 1780, was a contemporary of Heard and Curtis. His house is still standing in Wayland, at 126 Old Connecticut Path, and is known as the Reeves Tavern. The oldest part had been built about 1715. Jacob Reeves enlarged the house and began operating a tavern here in 1764. He had four children born in Roxbury and two born after his arrival in Sudbury. Within a year of his arrival in 1763, his daughter Naomi (called Amy) married Ephraim Carter of an established family in the eastern part of Sudbury. In 1780 the Carters were living with a family of several children in the school squadron based near Baldwin's Pond. In 1770 Jacob's son Nathaniel married Dorothy Hoar of Sudbury. She died two years later, and in 1776 Nathaniel married Eunice Noyes, daughter of Col. John and Tabitha (Stone) Noyes, perhaps the leading family of the town. In 1761 Col. John Noyes had petitioned the Sudbury town meeting to accept Jacob Reeves as an inhabitant. Reeves had been warned out, but this was probably a formality rather than a real intention or attempt to keep him out of town. Meanwhile Reeves's daughter Elizabeth had married Thomas Heard, a son of Capt. Richard Heard. In 1786 the son Samuel Reeves married Abigail Parris, daughter of Deacon Samuel Parris. We see that the Reeves children quickly married into the leading families of the eastern side of Sudbury. Reeves's grandchildren would go on marrying into East Sudbury families, and the family would be prominent in the town in the nineteenth century. Jacob Reeves served as selectman for six years, 1780 through 1785. By 1787 his son Nathaniel had become town clerk and assessor. Jacob died in 1794.

Capt. Isaac Loker, the fifth selectman, served only for the year 1780. He was a younger man of forty-one, having been born in 1739, and had never had an important civil office in Sudbury but had served as a field driver in 1768 and hog reeve in 1773. He was, however, one of Sudbury's more important military leaders in the Revolution, having commanded Sudbury's troop of horse. His election as selectman in 1780 was probably in recognition of his distinguished Revolutionary service and perhaps in part because he lived in the southern part of the town. His house is still standing at 36 Loker Street. He was a great-grandson of John Loker, one of the original proprietors of the town. Since both his mother and his paternal grandmother were Rices, his roots went back strongly to the founding families. In 1781 Loker was replaced as selectman by Micah Goodenow, a man of forty-eight whose mother also was a Rice and whose paternal line went back to an original proprietor of the town. Micah Goodenow lived across the river on River Road and had just barely been included in the Town of East Sudbury.

We have seen that, with the exception of Isaac Loker, the original board of selectmen of East Sudbury was a group of men, three of them around sixty years of age and the others somewhat younger, who had served the town extensively and were recognized leaders of the east side. They were all very active in bringing up, and getting support for, separation at the 1778 town meeting and in petitioning the General Court in 1779. We have already noted that Heard, Reeves, and Glezen had served together on the Sudbury board of selectmen in the 1770s. By electing them to the top office of the town, the inhabitants were both honoring them and putting the fate of their new government in their hands. Their repeated reelection together shows that they constituted a ruling group.

There is always politics. That the Curtis-Heard group was not or did not continue to be acceptable to the whole town is evidenced by the March elections in 1784. The annual town meeting for the election of officers and the conduct of other business was called for March 1, 1784. Richard Heard was elected moderator. Voting then proceeded for officers, and none of the 1780-83 men was elected selectman. The five selectmen elected that day were John Noyes, Esq., Isaac Stone, Robert Cutting, Samuel Griffin, and Thomas Heard. David Curtis, Joseph's son, was elected treasurer and assessor. The circumstances and reasons for this revolution in leadership are not known. With the exception of John Noyes, who was born in 1715 and thus in his seventieth year, the new officers were younger men born in the late 1730s and the 1740s. One can surmise that a faction of the town thought that the leadership was too old and that perhaps Colonel Noyes backed this move. The town clerk's record shows that on March 15, two weeks later, the town offices were reconsidered; this time the old slate of Richard Heard, Joseph Curtis, Jacob Reeves, Micah Goodenow, and Phinehas Glezen were elected as selectmen, and once again Joseph Curtis was elected to the positions of town clerk, treasurer, and assessor.

A detailed analysis has been made of East Sudbury's first group of selectmen because at this time leadership of a Massachusetts town of East Sudbury's size rested considerably with the selectmen, the moderator of the town meeting, the treasurer, and the town clerk. The office of representative to the General Court, usually voted at a separate meeting, was also a major one. With the exception of Isaac Loker, all of those elected in the first years of East Sudbury had been part of the pool of leadership when East Sudbury and Sudbury had been a single town. We have seen that, excluding Jacob Reeves, apparently an exceptional man, all had deep roots in the town's past. All were substantial property owners, and there was a certain amount of intermarriage among their children. They were a local elite with experience in town government, family status, and property. They were not, however, enormously well-to-do compared with the general run of East Sudbury householders. They worked their farms themselves and did rough physical work for the town like repairing bridges, just as other citizens did.

The town meeting was the seat of ultimate power in an eighteenth-century Massachusetts town. The separate Town of East Sudbury was not organized until late April 1780, so the record for the first municipal year was not a full twelve months. In that municipal year there were ten town meetings, several of them running to one or more adjourned sessions.

The town clerk and the two men who served as moderators at these meetings, Joseph Curtis and Richard Heard, had had experience in the affairs of the larger town. The "freeholders and other inhabitants of and belonging to the town of East Sudbury qualified as the law directs to vote in town affairs" were accustomed to attending town meetings at the east meetinghouse, which was then fifty-five years old. One has the impression from the rather brief record of 1780-81 meetings that the town's affairs were carried on very much in the way such meetings had been carried on in Sudbury for many years. The war was still on, and its business required long meetings with adjournments in both June and July. These two adjourned meetings were concerned with hiring soldiers. The record is sparse, but one reads between the lines that the procurement of soldiers was very difficult. In September we find the town having a meeting to elect state officers under the new Massachusetts constitution, which had been in the process of ratification during the drive for separation. Again in October a war levy was the chief subject of a meeting. It was not until November 20 that routine matters of local business such as appropriations for the Reverend Bridge's salary and for the schools and poor were voted upon.

With its concern over school districting and location in 1781, East Sudbury began to concentrate more on promoting its own progress, in this case education. There were twelve town meetings that year, and it was not until the mid-1780s that war levies, payments to soldiers or their substitutes, and business arising from the division of Sudbury ceased to require much town meeting time and attention. Later in the 1780s the small, rural, and very homogeneous town settled down to conduct its more normal affairs and eventually to meet the problems that further growth of population and changing economic and social conditions would inevitably bring.

NOTES

1. This map is Number 1181 in the Massachusetts Archives. Both the Wayland Library and the Historical Society have copies.

2. *Vital Records of Sudbury, Massachusetts to the Year 1850,* New England Historic Genealogical Society, Boston, 1903.

3. Elisha Brewer, Isaac Cutting, Robert Cutting, Jesse Emes, ________ Freeman, Richard Heard, Isaac Loker, Daniel Maynard, Caleb Moulton Jr., John Noyes, Joseph Payson, Thaddeus Russell, and Joseph Smith.

4. For this figure see Edward M. Cook Jr., *The Fathers of the Towns,* John Hopkins University Press, 1976. On page 24 he explains that because women did not vote and males voted only at 21, "to all intents and purposes . . ., the actions of the inhabitants of a town could mean no more than the actions of roughly one-fifth of the population who were adult males."

5. Middlesex County Probate #5474, First Series.

6. *1798 Massachusetts Direct Tax List,* Vol. IX, Sudbury, East Sudbury and Framingham, pp. 497-589.

7. *Suffolk County Deeds* Book 97, page 112 and *Middlesex County Deeds,* Book 58, page 556 when he bought his first property in Sudbury in 1762.

Part II

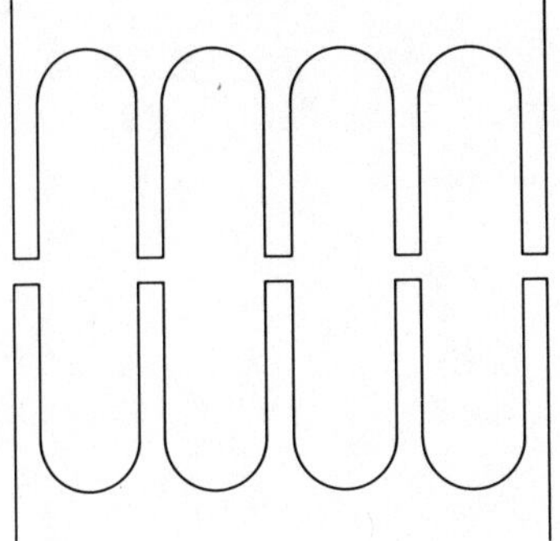

Wayland in 1880

Portion of lithograph of Cochituate and North Natick published in 1887 by Geo. F. Norris of Brockton, Mass.

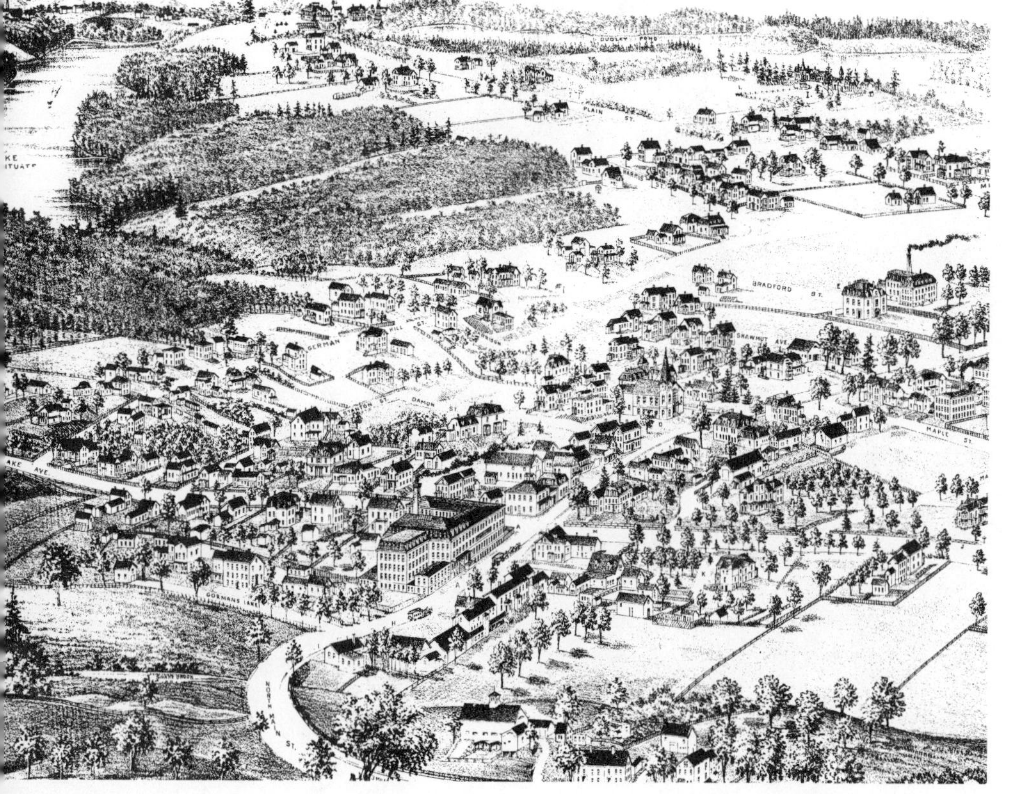

6

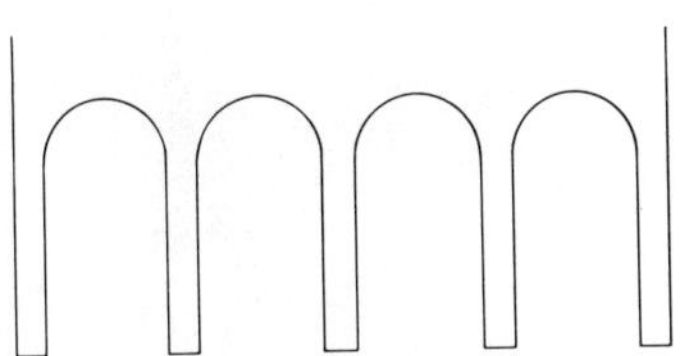

Changes during the Preceding Century

WHEN THE TOWN reached its one hundredth birthday in 1880, East Sudbury had been called Wayland for forty-five years. On March 11, 1835, the name of the town was officially changed.[1] This change of name, to avoid confusion between East Sudbury and Sudbury and to achieve separate identity, was alluded to as was this writer's attempt in 1957 to determine the reason for the choice of the name of Wayland on page 77 of Part I. No celebration of the milestone took place in 1880, for reasons which will be commented upon later. Centenary town celebrations were quite common at this time; Milford, our near-twin town, had such a celebration in 1880. In 1881 the neighboring town of Natick had an elaborate and well-planned celebration of its one hundredth birthday as a full-fledged town.

Entirely apart from its being a time traditionally noticed and celebrated, this date of 1880 was an interesting point in the history of our town. We shall therefore look in detail at the Wayland of 1880. Appendix A gives population figures for the town by decades from 1780 to 1850 and for five-year periods up to 1980. By 1880 Wayland had 1,962 inhabitants, compared with an estimated 750 to 775 in 1780 and a count of 801 in the census of 1790. The town had considerably more than doubled in population during this hundred-year period with essentially the same boundaries. This was greater growth than had been experienced by the adjacent towns of Weston and Lincoln, but the growth had not been anywhere near as large relatively as in the

The 1815 East Sudbury Town Church which later became the Unitarian Church, and the Town Hall built the same year which later became the "Kirkside" residence.

adjoining towns of Natick and Framingham or in the once-removed towns of Waltham and Marlborough.[2]

Wayland was still considered to be a rural town as opposed to towns like Natick and Waltham, which had become industrialized. In 1874 the Reverend Elias Nason, an educator and minister, who had been interested while editor of the *New England Historic Genealogical Register* in compiling material on New England towns, published his *Gazetteer of the State of Massachusetts.* Nason called Wayland "an agricultural town of pleasing natural scenery" but went on to mention a large shoe factory and a railroad being constructed through the town. The population given in Nason's article is the 1870 census figure; by the publication date of 1874 this figure was significantly increased.

Population Increase

The gazetteer article was written and published at a time of great population and other changes in Wayland. From 1870 to 1875 there was an increase of 526 persons, a very much greater increase than had been experienced in any five- or ten-year period since 1780. The population continued to grow between 1875 and 1880, but at a less dramatic rate. Analysis of population in the two parts of the town, Wayland Center and Cochituate, shows that from 1850 to 1875 in the north part of the town (which we shall call Wayland Center) the population stayed at around 775 persons, albeit with a somewhat changing makeup. The bulge in population which occurred between 1870 and 1875 came from an increase in the south part of the town (which we shall call Cochituate). This section went from 480 persons in 1870 to 1,000 in 1875 and to 1,161 in 1880. The burgeoning of Cochituate Village was the cause of Wayland's rapid growth in the 1870s. Thus, an important part of the analysis of the town as of 1880 will consist of the story of Cochituate Village. But before concentrating on the southern section of the town, some general observations are in order about overall changes in the town since 1780 other than population size.

Multiplicity of Churches

In 1780 there was one Orthodox (Puritan) church with its minister paid by the town and its town-owned meetinghouse in Wayland Center at the present northwest corner of Cochituate and Pelham Island roads. By 1880 there were four Protestant churches, none owned or supported by the town. Separation of church and state had been mandated by law in Massachusetts in 1834. East Sudbury was one of the last towns to have a single, town-supported church and did not discontinue voting the minister's salary in town meeting until 1833. In 1880 the Unitarian First Parish Church owned the presently standing building on the Boston Post Road which the town had had erected in 1814 by Andrews Palmer of Newburyport, using an Asher Benjamin design. The tower of this church held a bell ordered in 1814 from the Paul Revere foundry, which in 1980 still tolls the hour and is rung for celebrations. By 1880 a clock had been placed on the steeple (1850), heat had been installed, and considerable interior remodeling had occurred in the building.

In the 1820s a group had become dissatisfied with the Unitarian doctrines of the Reverend John Burt Wight's First Parish Church. In 1828 they had organized an Orthodox or Congregational Parish and built a chapel or vestry. In 1835 a church building and carriage sheds were erected next to the chapel on the west side of Cochituate Road.

Early view of the Lokerville School and Wesleyan Methodist Church.

This second church in town burned down in 1922; the present Trinitarian Congregational Church is on the same site.

By the 1840s residents of the south part of the town felt a need for a church in their part of town, and seventeen individuals organized a Wesleyan Methodist Society on February 15, 1846. For the first few years services were held in the South schoolhouse, located at the present intersection of East Plain Street with Commonwealth Road in the section then called Lokerville. There was some thought of building a church on Main Street in Cochituate Village, but the majority of members (dominated almost surely by Lokers) favored a site near the schoolhouse in Lokerville. A newspaper article of 1878, entitled "The Old Church at Cochituate," tells us of the controversy which arose in 1850 about which way this church would face. The first building, framed in July 1850, blew down in a strong wind. When rebuilt, the structure's front was turned toward Cochituate Village to secure the attendance of a member who had objected to the orientation of the first building.[3] After the establishment of the Methodist Episcopal Church in Cochituate, this small church building was used only intermittently by Baptists and for certain revival and nondenominational services. It fell into disuse in the 1890s and by 1900 was in ruins. However, it was left in place until 1902 when Jefferson Loker, who had been particularly devoted to this church, died in March at the age of ninety-three. Loker, who lived within sight of the church, had donated a mahogany table and two collection boxes to the church in 1850. Just before his death these were transferred to the Methodist Episcopal Church. In 1902 an auction was held at which Edgar B. Loker bought the building and Chester B. Williams bought the pews and underpinnings. In 1906 Loker moved the building to his property, where it is said to have become a henhouse. The land on which the church had stood was converted into an informal park.

Eventually a group broke off from the Wesleyan Methodist Church and organized a Sunday school in 1865, which met in William Loker's hall on Main Street with John C. Butterfield as superintendent. An organization meeting for a church was held on April 9, 1866, with Henry Coggin (later of North Natick but then living on Commonwealth Road in Cochituate) presiding. Twenty-two of the most prominent men in Cochituate Village signed a petition for the chartering of the Episcopal Methodist Society.[4] A half-acre lot on the west side of Main Street was bought from Charles R. Damon, who was one of this church's leading organizers and the society's first clerk.[5]

The original building, said to have been patterned after a Brighton church, was completed in 1868 and was dedicated on February 20, 1869.[6] The building, as it started out in 1868, was smaller, lower, and less impressive than the current structure, which took nearly its present form in a major rebuilding in 1896-98. It was not until June 1873 that donations were collected to put a modest, pointed spire with a bell on the building.[7]

It may be noted here that, although there was a Roman Catholic population in both Wayland Center and Cochituate in 1880, Catholic churches were not built until later. St. Zepherin's Church in Cochituate held its first service on March 2, 1890, and was dedicated on April 27 of that year.[8] The cornerstone of the first St. Ann's Church, which stood on the south side of the Boston Post Road near the present Wayland post office, was laid on August 20, 1905.[9] In 1880 Catholics attended services in Natick, Waltham, Saxonville, and Marlborough and were buried in Catholic cemeteries in those towns or in towns farther afield where they had formerly resided. Catholic parishes were constituted in both cases a few years before the building of the churches. Services were held for Cochituate parishioners in the Lokerville schoolhouse; for Wayland parishioners, in the vacated library headquarters in the town hall.

The Methodist Episcopal Church as it appeared in 1880 before addition of the present bell tower.

Diversity of Population

In 1880 the population of Wayland was much more diverse as to its origins compared with the very homogeneous town of 1780. The town was no longer dominated by founding early settler families, nor was a majority of Wayland residents Wayland-born, as was the case one hundred years before. Certain early families present and important in 1780 like the Curtises and the Noyeses had disappeared from the town. The census of 1880 shows that there were only three Rice households, although there were still a fair number of persons of Rice ancestry. By this time the most frequent "old names" were Loker, largely in the south part of the town, and Sherman, in the north part of the town. The Lokers were to turn out to be the most durable and long-lasting founding family in the town. As late as 1953 William A. ("Toke") Loker, the seventh generation from the first John Loker and great-great-grandson of Isaac Loker, a first East Sudbury selectman, was serving as the chairman of Wayland's board of selectmen. There are now no Lokers living in Wayland, but in 1880 there had been fifteen Loker households including forty persons bearing the name.

By 1880 quite a few families like the Deans, Fairbanks, and Bryants had moved into Wayland from nearby Massachusetts towns, especially from central Massachusetts. Also there had arrived in town various settlers—Marstons, Frenches, Folsoms—who thought that the Wayland area offered more opportunities than their native Maine or New Hampshire. These newer citizens were mostly of English Yankee stock. But by 1880 there had also been a considerable though not overwhelming admixture of persons of foreign birth or family origin, some from different ethnic and religious backgrounds, in some cases with different language and culture.

Irish

The Irish constituted Wayland's first wave of foreign-born, most of them filtering out to our town after they had landed in Boston in the great Irish migration which peaked in the year 1847. The United States census of 1850, which was the first to be concerned with birthplaces of residents of a town, showed eighty-five Irish-born individuals living in Wayland in June of that year. Of these thirty were single young men working and living as hired men (sometimes called handymen) on the farms of substantial landowners. Deacon James Draper, whose house is still standing at 116 Plain Road, had Patrick Rooney, age twenty-six, born in Ireland, as his hired man or "farmer." Jahleel Sherman in North Wayland had John Murfey,[10] and Jude Damon had Michael Glen, age twenty-five. In 1850 there were a few households headed by Irish-born laborers, but there was little or no ownership of real estate. Eleven households, including that of lawyer Edward Mellen, hired Irish girls to do housework. Since they were not paid much and were given miserably minimal living quarters, there was probably a large turnover as these Irish hired men and servant girls looked for better opportunities. A few of the Irish hired men stayed on in the town. John Coppithorn, who in 1850 at age nineteen was a handyman on Paul Loker's farm, had by 1860 become a shoe worker in Cochituate and was then living in the household of William Moore and Nancy Loker.

In 1865, fifteen years later, the Massachusetts State census showed seventy-three Irish-born persons in Wayland. Compared with most of the surrounding towns, there was less of an influx of Irish to Wayland. In 1865 Sudbury had 205 Irish-born, Weston 101, Natick 913, Framingham 768, and Concord 326. The Irish in Wayland did not reach substantial percentages of the total population as they did in Natick and Framingham, but they were a noticeable element.

By 1880 various Irish families had become established as property owners. Quite a few of them had by this time prospered enough to be able to buy the farms of some of the disappearing early Yankee families. A Wayland correspondent writing for the *Waltham Free Press* in 1868 had alluded to the Irish farmers as follows: "Real estate has diminished in value and some good, eligible places have fallen into the hands of foreigners whose style of life can hardly be called elegant."[11] The 1883 valuation list contains twenty Irish-born farmers whose combined land ownership totaled 762½ acres. All but Thomas Evans, whose farm was near the intersection of Commonwealth Road with Rice Road, were residents of the Wayland end of the town.

One of these families, the Rowans, have long since ceased to be farmers and were substantial landowners in Wayland in 1980. We first find Michael Rowan, age thirty-five, in the census of 1860 living as a hired man with the James Austin Draper family in the house now standing at 110 Plain Road. James A. Draper was soon to leave to serve in the Civil War, and his property was sold. By 1865 Michael Roan, as the name was then spelled, had married Bridget McGrath who was born in Ireland, and they had two small daughters. John Roan, Michael's father, came from Ireland to live with them on the small acreage they had acquired on the edge of the Draper property. By 1880 there were seven Rowan children. In 1883 Michael paid taxes on forty acres of land. A grandson of Michael and two great-grandsons are now Wayland property owners.

Another Irish family long on the Wayland scene was the Linnehans. In 1869 John Linnehan, who had been born in County Cork, Ireland, bought the farm of Samuel Baldwin on the Boston Post Road. John, who was then thirty-four years old, was newly married to Margaret Connolly, who had been born in County Galway, Ireland. When the deed to the farm was drawn up, John was illiterate and could sign only with an X, but he was ambitious to own land and to run his own farm.[12] By 1880 there was a growing family of five children. This farm, with its presently standing house at 156 Boston Post Road, remained in the Linnehan family until 1946. John's grandson, Thomas F. Linnehan, was prominent in Wayland town affairs. He served as a selectman from 1955 until his death in 1966; his widow is still a resident of the town.

In 1875, writing for the *Waltham Free Press*, Joseph A. Roby, who had just retired after a brief stint as Wayland's town clerk, commented on the buying up of Wayland farms by the Irish. For the February 26, 1875, issue he wrote: "Our farms are going two-forty into the hands of the Irish and why? Because the Irishman will thrive, pay for his farm, rear a large family and be thankful and satisfied while the Yankee boy is off to the crowded machine shop or store, anywhere but the farm. The Irishman has never seen the inside of a school, but he has been to the school of adversity and learned then and there the value of a homestead.'' In January 1875 Roby had written a story for the *Waltham Free Press* about ''Big John'' Linnehan going to Waltham to sell a load of hay, getting drunk there, and being put in the lockup for the night. Roby thought of Linnehan's propensity to drink as a great pity, and his comment was: ''Now this same Big John . . . had his house burned down a few years since, he rebuilt and then the lightning struck his barn and that went with all his hay and rye etc. Then the neighbors gave him a lift and a much better barn was the result. And John might do first rate if—''

Various early Wayland houses, which today have great appeal as homesteads of colonial families, were in the hands of Irish farmers in 1880. Some include the 1720 Samuel Griffin house at 184 Glezen Lane, then owned by Timothy Malloy; the house at 194 Glezen Lane, then owned by Timothy Coughlin; and the Benjamin Adams house at 34 Lincoln Road, which in 1880 was owned by Patrick McDonald (sometimes spelled McDonnell).

A third Irish farmer family which remained in Wayland a long time was that of Thomas Hynes. Living at what is now 74 Moore Road in a house built in 1822 by Luther Gleason, Thomas Hynes was in 1880 one of the largest Irish landowners, with ninety acres. From 1912 to 1962 Thomas Hynes's son Michael, then his son Tom, were Wayland postmasters. A grandson, William F. Hynes, was a selectman from 1941 to 1945.

The blacksmith trade, a most necessary service in Wayland or any town in the horse-dominated 1880s, was almost entirely in the hands of Irish smiths in 1880. Jeremiah Mullen, who had come to the United States in 1851 at the age of thirty and who lived in the center of Wayland in the double house at 29-31 Cochituate Road, had one of the two Wayland Center blacksmith shops. He had the failing of some Irishmen of drinking too much, and at one time the selectmen took him to court for drunkenness. When not drinking heavily, he was well liked in the town and was prosperous. He bought land on the Boston Post Road near the present Rich Valley Road where he did some farming. One of his daughters married Patrick Leary, the Cochituate blacksmith who was proprietor from 1869 to 1902 of the shop on the

The John Linnehan House on the Boston Post Road.

east side of Main Street near the brook which is the boundary between Wayland and Natick.[13] Leary Street is named for him, and the houses at 38 East Plain Street and at 17 Leary Street are thought to have been built by him.

Succeeding Jeremiah Mullen as blacksmith in Wayland Center was Lawrence McManus, whose Irish-born parents, Edward and Ellen McManus, were living in a seventeenth-century Rice house on a farm off Old Connecticut Path in the Charena Road area in 1880. The McManus presence was to last in Wayland for more than one hundred years. Edward McManus was recorded as a laborer of Wayland when in 1857 he married Elenor (Ellen) Fleming of Milford.[14] Lawrence, their oldest son, was born in Wayland in 1859. In the census of 1865 Edward was a farmer, and they then had four small boys; by 1880 there were eight children. Lawrence, then twenty-one, was working in a blacksmith's shop. In 1884 Lawrence McManus bought Jeremiah Mullen's blacksmith shop at the corner of the Boston Post Road and Pelham Island Road on land leased from Theodore S. Sherman.[15] Thus began the long association of the McManus family with that location. In 1915 Thomas McManus, a son of Lawrence, established here one of the two earliest Wayland automobile dealerships, for Overland cars. In 1924 Henry Ford signed him up to establish the Ford dealership, which stayed in McManus hands until 1979.[16]

In the Cochituate of 1880, in addition to the Thomas Evans farmer family with seven children (the four youngest born in Massachusetts), an Irish farmhand on Ebenezer Loker's farm, two Irish servant girls, and a carpenter, there were nineteen Irish shoe workers boarding in the village, all but one of them males. At this time a large number of shoe workers came daily from Natick to work in Cochituate. Since Natick had a large Irish population, a significant proportion of these factory workers would have been Irish-born or of Irish extraction.

In her history of Concord published in 1967, Ruth R. Wheeler wrote that Concord's Female Charitable Society helped poor Irish families acquire proper school clothing for their numerous children.[17] It is not known to what extent the Irish newcomers in Wayland had problems of real poverty. We have already noted the assistance given by neighbors to John Linnehan when fire destroyed his buildings. Neighbors were helpful to each other in those days, and it was not considered charity to help one's neighbor. However, of the five inmates of the town poor farm in 1880, two, a man and a woman who were there as paupers, had been born in Ireland.

Germans

Not long after the Irish farm laborers and farmers became a feature of the north part of Wayland, a small group of Germans came to Cochituate, attracted by opportunities in the shoeshops and by the village environment. Like the Irish, they spilled over from a substantial migration of Germans to Boston around 1850. Frederick Wendt, a brickmason, then age twenty-seven, was the first German to acquire property in Cochituate. This was in May 1851.[18] He was followed immediately by John G. Schleicher. They built houses on Pemberton Hill, and when other German families settled there the road laid out through Loker land, at first called High Street, came to be known as German Hill Street. There were two young German couples in Cochituate in 1850. By 1855 this first foreign-language group to be employed in the shoeshops had reached its peak of importance. As of 1855 three young, single, male Germans listed as shoemakers were living in the household of William Hammond. Wendt was still there and in part of his house lived both Jacob and Casper Corman, progenitors of a long-lasting German family in Cochituate for which Corman's Lane was named. Also living on German Hill Street (the name was changed to Pemberton Road in 1917 in the anti-German atmosphere of World War I) we find in 1855 George Schleicher, born in Germany, who had a small house and had his father, Antone

Schleicher, living with him. Members of this family were still on Pemberton Road and on Shawmut Avenue Extension one hundred years later, in 1955. Carl Gustav Groneveldt and his wife and two children were also in Cochituate in 1855. They had bought the early Bryant House at 24 Main Street from Henry Coggin in 1854.[19] Carl (Charles) was a jeweler by trade; it is not known how he made a living in Cochituate. Both he and his wife died of typhoid fever in the early 1860s.

By 1880 Casper Corman's family included eight children. John B. Yeager with wife, born in Saxony, and two young children, both born in Massachusetts, was a shoe worker in Cochituate in 1880. As early as 1860 there had been Yeagers in that village. A descendant now lives in the Wayland Center part of the town. A few other Germans were on the scene in 1880—Conrad Homer, Henry B. Fischer, and Joseph Imminck—all listed as farmers. Fischer had a small shoe-manufacturing shop at one time, and Imminck set up an upholstery business. On West Plain Street in Cochituate lived the Anton Schmeltz family from Bohemia. Anton was a furrier; a descendant was living there in 1955.

Despite the naming of German Hill Street, the number of Germans was never great. They have been discussed here because it has been supposed that they had importance numerically, and also because a few put down roots to become long-lasting Cochituate families. If they were shoemakers when they came to this country, the Germans were trained as workers on fine, expensive shoes. They would be expected to gravitate to such places as Philadelphia and not adjust easily to making the rough brogans which were the chief footwear product of Cochituate.

Nova Scotians

As was the case in many other eastern Massachusetts towns and in Boston, Nova Scotians were another foreign-born element in the Wayland of 1880. The 1880 census showed that sixty-seven persons living in Wayland were born in Nova Scotia. Several of Wayland's substantial farmers had young, single Nova Scotians rather than Irish farm laborers, there being eight such in Wayland and eight in Cochituate. Cochituate had more Nova Scotians because in addition to the farm laborers there were nine persons of that origin working in the shoeshops. Although that area came to be more the home of French shoe workers, the section around Leary Street was known in

Cochituate through several decades—the 1870s, 1880s, and 1890s—as Scotiaville, because at one time it was the home of several Nova Scotian families. Mention will be made later of the Griffins, who had become Cochituate's most prominent Nova Scotian family by the end of the nineteenth century.

The bulk of the Nova Scotian immigration to Massachusetts occurred during the 1870s and 1880s. At the time of the census of 1870 there had been nineteen Nova Scotia-born residents in Wayland, consisting of the Griffin and Coaldwell families and a few hired men on the farms. Samuel Maynard Thomas, one of the prominent farmers of Wayland, employed at this time both an Irish and a Nova Scotian farm laborer. The *Natick Citizen* of April 11, 1881, noted that eleven persons from Nova Scotia had arrived in Cochituate that week.

The Nova Scotians were very easy to assimilate. They had a similar background and culture to the old Massachusetts families and in many cases—the Dunhams, for example—were descendants of families which had left a too-crowded part of Massachusetts (Cape Cod) to settle in Nova Scotia one hundred years before.

French-Canadians

The latest, largest, and most conspicuous group of persons that were foreign-born or of foreign extraction which had come to Wayland by 1880 were the French-Canadians from Quebec Province. These people arrived in large numbers in the mid-to-late 1870s, mainly as shoe workers in the Bent shoe factory. All who came did not stay and put down roots, but many did. Cochituate was home for quite a few of these families for many years. Analysis of the 1880 census population enumeration reveals 45 families (and 12 single persons), a total of 245 persons, one or both adults of which were born in Canada or had parents born there. This represented about 22 percent of Cochituate's 1880 population and gave rise to the need for a Catholic church which, when it came in 1889-90, was a distinctly French church. Sermons at St. Zepherin's were often given in French rather than English despite the fact that some of the shoe workers and their wives had been born in Massachusetts or Vermont to earlier French-Canadian immigrants. Newspaper reports and vital records show that most of these people did not come directly from Canada to Cochituate but came here from North Brookfield, Spencer, Worcester, and other places where they or their parents had worked in shoe factories which made brogans, the chief product of the Bent and other

Cochituate shoe factories of that time. Many of the French-Canadian shoe workers in Cochituate had previously been employed at the huge Batchelder factory in North Brookfield, and some were to return there when hard times came to Cochituate.

It is impossible to determine which were the earliest French-Canadians to settle in Wayland. Several French-Canadians had temporary employment at the Bent factory in the 1860s. Israel Boudreau, who was born in Canada, had a Canadian-born wife and by 1880 had eight children, all born in Massachusetts. He was listed on the Wayland militia roll of 1865.[20] His may have been the earliest French family to stay in town. Up through 1875 there were births in Wayland to the Joseph Hooper, Nelson Matthews, Joseph Matthews, Hermine Huard, Anthony Roberts, Felix Derosia, Avila Lamarine, Eugene Matheu, Frank Basard, Henry Scott, Wallace Lupien, and Charles Tambo families. Nelson Matthews was born in Canada and his wife in North Brookfield, indicating that he was probably a shoe worker in that Worcester County town before coming to Cochituate. Charles Tambo was a harnessmaker and also one of the spectacular village drunks. The others mentioned here were shoe workers, and they were to be followed by other young, male French-Canadian shoe workers who were ready to settle down to rear families. It will be noted that some of these, like Henry Scott, had anglicized their names.

Among other French-Canadians who had also become parents of Wayland-born children by 1880 were three other Matthews couples—Moses, Jeremiah, and Wallace—and there were Frederick Lucier, Ralph Huard, George and Nelson Belmore, Frank Lupien, Moses Caswell, Theodore Potvin (wife born in Marlborough), Franklin Celorier, Albert Lepine (wife born in Grafton), Francis X. Daviau (wife born in Fiskedale, Maine), Philip White (wife born in North Brookfield), Alfred T. Dowdell, Louis Champigni, Louis Faneuf, and Narcise Normandin. Still other French-Canadian couples in Cochituate in 1880 were the Alphonse Allaires, the Charles Cheltras, the Amos Dusseaults, the Charles Dufresnes, two Tatros (Tatreault), Aleck who at age forty-nine worked in a shoeshop and had seven children, three of them sons—Wilfred, Edgar, and Napoleon—who also worked in the shoeshops, and Lucian Tatro, age forty, with five children.

In 1880 the French-Canadian population of Cochituate was not nearly as large relative to the total population as in nearby Marlborough or in the Worcester County towns of Southbridge, Spencer, and Webster, where the Canadian-born population was more than 40 percent of the total.[21] These people did come from a different language and religious background, and despite the fact that many of them had been in Massachusetts or other New England states for some time, they had strong cultural ties to the French communities which had been their homes in Quebec. When they could afford it, they visited old homes and relatives in Canada.

It is not known whether the French-Canadian shoe workers were a cheaper source of labor for the shoe factories of Cochituate or whether they were hired because they sought jobs in a town where the wage level was reasonably generous by the standards of that era. It is certain that they were hired because many of them had had experience in brogan manufacture and because in the 1870s the shoe industry was in a rapidly expanding phase in Cochituate.

Weekly newspapers which chronicled events in Cochituate made little mention of the French-Canadians at first. Many of them were very poor when they arrived, and some had a difficult time staying out of debt. Wayland town clerk's record books of personal mortgages contain numerous wage assignments to company officials, mostly to James Madison Bent's sons who ran the large company with their father. For a period of more than ten years, Jerry Matthews, Louis Cormier, Frank Davieau, Anthony Roberts, and others signed documents (sometimes with an X if illiterate) assigning their entire wages for most of the coming year to Myron Bent or, in a few cases, to the proprietor of a grocery store.

Records are not available to show how early and how widespread the practice of paying labor in store credit was in Cochituate. There is the tradition in the Bent family that this was a common practice in the 1850s and 1860s. By the late 1870s and 1880s wages were paid in cash; the practice of wage assignment was resorted to for only a small group of the French-Canadian workers, those who were improvident or who had misfortunes which pushed them into debt.

The 1880 census and the earliest voter registration book, that covering the years 1877-84, show some of the French-Canadian families occupying private dwellings but most of them living in multiple dwellings. The Wm. and J. M. Bent Company did not provide full company housing but, owing to the rapid growth of its work force and the scarcity of housing, erected a few tenement houses for their worker families. Most famous, but by no means the only one, was the building known as the Bee Hive, which stood on the corner of the present Winter Street (then called Madison Street) and Willard Street.

The name "Bee Hive" conveys the image of large numbers of workers swarming in and out of this building. This was not the case when the census of 1880 was taken or later. The June 15, 1885, "Cochituate Enterprise" news in the *Natick Bulletin* described a swarm of children when it reported: "The tenement house known as the 'Bee Hive' has five families with thirty children. There are eighteen children in the two families that occupy the lower floor." By this time, the Cochituate School, built in 1873, had become seriously crowded, and there was an awareness of the large size of the French families. The same issue of the *Natick Bulletin* commented that a French family had recently moved into town from Fiskdale with eleven children. One cannot be sure which building was the Bee Hive in the census of 1880 population enumeration. However, census dwelling number 61 contained five French families. Living there in June of that year were Moses and Emily Caswell with five children; Charles and Mary Dufresne with three children; and Lewis and Flora Cormier with five children and two brothers of Lewis, one of whom worked in a shoeshop, the other a blacksmith. Also there were Lewis and Emma Champney with one child and Charles and Adelaide Cheltra, an older couple with no children.

The Lewis (Louis) Cormier family became one of Wayland's largest French-Canadian families. Record of this family in the census of 1900 and a newspaper account of Louis Cormier's death appearing in the *Natick Bulletin* of November 2, 1900, gives us a picture of this family. Cormier was not born in Quebec Province but in New Jersey to Canadian-born parents. His wife, Flora, was born in Massachusetts, and one cannot be sure that she was of French-Canadian extraction. According to the newspaper account, they came to Cochituate from North Brookfield in 1874. By June 1900 when the census was taken, Lewis Cormier was fifty-five years old and his wife had borne him sixteen children of whom twelve were then living, eleven of them still in the household. In 1900 four sons ranging from age twenty-seven to seventeen were listed as shoemakers, and a daughter age fifteen was a shoeheel worker. At this time Cormier owned his house on Neale Street, now French Avenue. In addition to the large immediate family, two brothers and a sister were living with him.

In the 1870s and around 1880 there was a concentration of French-Canadians on the east side of Main Street, on Madison (Winter) Street and on the streets running off Madison, but records of the late 1870s show that the French families of Alphonse Allaire, Louis Gibeault, John Lamarine, and Napoleon Perodeau lived on or near German Hill

Street. By about 1890 French families who had prospered enough to move out of the tenements and boardinghouses had come to dominate the Scotiaville area north of East Plain Street. Patrick Leary, the Irishman, was there, but near him the houses were then owned by Lupien, Moreau, Sayers, and Tatro families, all French.

As has already been mentioned, the presence of French-Canadians in Cochituate led to the building in 1889-90 of St. Zepherin's Church. The process of organizing a parish had begun ten years before. The April 11, 1879, *Natick Bulletin* stated under Cochituate news that "The French Catholic Society have commenced holding meetings and prospects of a prosperous future as a society are before them." In December 1880 it was reported that a French priest from Canada was expected in a few days[22] and in April 1881 it was reported that a Catholic Sunday service was held in the upstairs hall of the Cochituate schoolhouse.[23] Meetings of the Catholic Society were suspended during February 1882, apparently as a temporary measure.[24] However, the May 23, 1885, issue of the *Natick Citizen* reported that the selectmen had given permission for the Catholics to hold services in the hall over the schoolroom in the Lokerville (South) schoolhouse and that a priest from Natick would officiate. The article went on to say: "This will be a great convenience to the people here who are now obliged to go to Natick or Saxonville to church, a distance of two miles to either place."

The *Natick Bulletin* of January 13, 1888, reported that the Reverend John Walsh had purchased a plot of land for a church. It has not been ascertained whether this was land on Main Street bought when it was contemplated that a Catholic church would be built just north of Lyons Corner. More than a year later, in March 1889, Father Rainville, the first priest assigned to the Cochituate parish, arrived from Marlborough, and the Albert Dean home on Main Street on the north corner of Willard Street was purchased to house him.[25] A few months later, in August 1889, ground was broken for St. Zepherin's on Willard Street behind the priest's residence. Completion of the church was a great event for the French and other Catholics in Wayland. A front-page article about it appeared in the *Natick Bulletin.*[26]

In the late 1880s, owing in part to their success in organizing a parish and with their own church becoming a reality, the French-Canadians in Cochituate became more self-consciously French. At this point the Natick newspapers began to report events of importance and interest to this element in Cochituate. In June 1888 an article stated that there had been a meeting of "the French citizens of the

The Albert Dean House and St. Zepherin's Church.

village" at which Napoleon Perodeau, Jean Charbonneau, and Leon Dion were chosen as delegates to an annual French convention in Nashua, New Hampshire.[27] In line with the movement in French communities all over New England, a St. Jean Baptiste Society, a mutual aid organization, was formed in the summer of 1888. Alphonse Allaire was the first president, Philip Le Blanc (who had been enumerated as Philip White in the census of 1880) and Anthony Roberts were vice-presidents, and Napoleon Perodeau was secretary.[28]

By 1888 the Canadians in Cochituate were organizing to promote their French culture. In April a French Theatre Company performed a French play called *Valduc* which was so well received that in May the company gave the play in neighboring towns. In December 1889 the local French Theatre Club produced a four-act play about the Canadian rebellion of Louis Rell in 1885 at the Knights of Labor Hall for the benefit of the Catholic parish. This play was repeated at the same hall in April 1890 and presented in Marlborough. The cast included A. H. Cormier, N. Normandin, H. Allaire, Dr. Moll, R. Nardeau, N. Perodeau, J. Charbonneau, A. Benoit, A. Allaire, A. Cormier, A. Moreau, Jacob Cormier, Stephen Cormier, Mrs. Dupuis, Mrs. Desaulnier, Mrs. Gladu, and Miss Eva Scott.[29]

In May 1893 the French Catholic Dramatic Club gave the play *Un Revenant* in the vestry of St. Zepherin's Church. In November 1893 the *Natick Bulletin* commented that many French citizens of Cochituate made a practice of reading *Le National*, a French newspaper published in Lowell.

Apart from a few remarks about the large size of the French families, there was no unfavorable comment on the French-Canadians in the local newspapers of the last three decades of the nineteenth century. Although a few fights took place in Scotiaville between the French and the Nova Scotians, there were no reports of serious ethnic friction between the French element and the Yankees, Irish, or Nova Scotians. They had their own church, but they integrated well into the community. The families of some of the French shoemakers put down deep roots in Cochituate, returning there to work after trying or being forced by economic necessity to take jobs in other shoe-manufacturing towns.

As far as political participation went, John Lamarine was the first French-Canadian to be placed on the jury list, this in 1886. By 1890 Alphonse Allaire had been elected assessor, but it was 1901 before a citizen of French-Canadian origin held high office in the town. That year Frank X. Lupien was elected selectman as the candidate of the French Naturalization Association. This was the first instance where ethnic considerations were introduced into Wayland politics. Cyrus Roake had become a political boss in Cochituate. He took the lead in mustering the French vote for Lupien in the preelection caucus. In March 1901 he was quoted as saying:

The French Canadian element in our village is very strong and it is only fair that it should have its representatives in the municipal government. May we hope that its success will lead to no stringent lines of nationality in our community. It is a gratifying fact that hitherto the French inhabitants have mingled freely and without friction with the other citizens of our village and we trust that this will continue. . . . And we think that it will so long as the French element is becomingly moderate in its demands in the way of town affairs.[30]

We shall summarize the subject of the immigrant groups present in Wayland in the 1880s with reference to a table showing the places of birth of Wayland's population as reported in the United States census of 1880.

1880 POPULATION OF WAYLAND BY PLACE OF BIRTH
from United States Census of 1880

Native Born		Foreign Born		Total
Massachusetts	1384	Canada[1]	105	
Maine	77	New Brunswick	3	
New Hampshire	72	Nova Scotia	74	
Vermont	19	Prince Edward Is.	1	
Connecticut	15	England	17	
Rhode Island	6	Ireland	118	
New York	25	Scotland	4	
New Jersey	2	Austria	5	
Pennsylvania	5	Germany	12	
Virginia	1	Denmark	2	
Ohio	1	Netherlands	1	
Illinois	2	Sweden	5	
U.S. not specified	5	China	1	
Total	1614		348	1962

1. Largely from Quebec Province.

The Massachusetts census of 1895 shows the 2,026-person population of Wayland in that year analyzed in terms of the native or foreign birthplaces of their parents. At that point Wayland's largest ethnic groups were the 271 (13.4 percent of total) of Irish-born parentage and the 298 (14.7 percent) of French-Canadian-born parentage. Nova Scotians were newer in Massachusetts, so their greater number in Wayland were foreign-born rather than native-born of foreign-born parents. The very large proportion of Irish parent residents in Waltham (29.2 percent) and in Watertown (34.4 percent) should be noted. Compared with the more industrialized nearby towns and cities, Wayland had remained more of a Yankee town.

The Preceding Century

NOTES

1. Commonwealth of Massachusetts, *Acts of 1835.* Chapter 34.
2. Changes in population for adjacent and neighboring towns from 1790 to 1880 (census figures) are as follows:

	1790	1880
Wayland	801	1,962
Sudbury	1,290	1,178*
Lincoln	740	907
Weston	1,010	1,448
Natick	615	8,479*
Framingham	1,598	6,235*
Waltham	882	11,712*
Marlborough	1,554	10,127*

* Indicates change of boundaries.

3. *Natick Bulletin* June 7, 1878.
4. Wayland, *Town Clerk's Record,* April 7, 1866.
5. James Madison Bent was the first moderator; the first trustees were Lafayette Dudley, John F. Felch and James N. Hammond.
6. *Natick Bulletin,* November 9, 1906.
7. *Ibid,* June 14, 1873. See poem by "Quill."
8. *Ibid,* March 7 and May 2, 1890.
9. *Ibid,* August 25, 1905.
10. The census taker was unfamiliar enough with Irish names as to spell Murphy this way.
11. *Waltham Free Press,* February 7, 1868.
12. South Middlesex Deeds, *Baldwin to Linnehan,* Book 1065, p. 215, February 9, 1869. The census of 1855 shows a Timothy Linnehan boarding as a farm laborer with Richard T. Fuller on Plain Road. Timothy may have inspired John to come to Wayland.
13. Leary sold this property to James McKay, another blacksmith in 1902. See *Natick Bulletin,* November 21, 1902.
14. Massachusetts Vital Records, *Marriages,* Vol. 110, p. 209.
15. Town of Wayland, *Mortgage Book IV,* 1884—p. 33.
16. Interview with E. Claire McManus May 5, 1979.
17. Ruth R. Wheeler, *Concord, Climate for Freedom,* Concord Antiquarian Society, Concord, Mass., 1967, p. 180.
18. South Middlesex Deeds, *Loker to Wendt,* Book 632, p. 152.
19. *Ibid, Coggin to Groneveldt,* Book 689, p. 503.
20. Town of Wayland, *Mortgages and Militia Roll* Book II, 1859-1875. Boudreau's children's births were not listed in the Wayland vital records.
21. This figure is not comparable with the 22 percent figure for Cochituate cited above. The Cochituate figure includes all family members, whether or not the wives or children were born in Canada. Calculated in this way the percentage of French-Canadians in Marlborough and other towns would be higher than 50 percent.
22. *Natick Bulletin,* December 24, 1880.
23. *Ibid,* April 29, 1881.
24. *Ibid,* February 17, 1882.
25. *Ibid,* March 8 and 15, 1889.
26. *Ibid,* May 2, 1890.
27. *Ibid,* June 22, 1888.
28. *Ibid,* August 3, 1888.
29. *Ibid,* April 11, 1890.
30. *Ibid,* March 15, 1901.

7

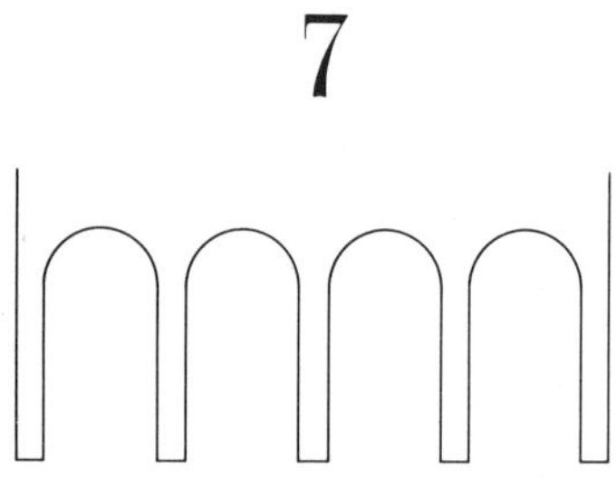

Cochituate Village

WE NOW TAKE up the most important change in the town from 1780 to 1880—the existence in 1880 of the well-defined and recognized village of Cochituate at the southern end of the town. This village had grown up around the shoe industry and in 1880 was thriving and bustling, imbued with justifiable pride in its own growth and stature.

In Part I we have described the addition in 1721 to Sudbury of the land on which Cochituate Village is located.[1] However, in 1721 and again in 1780 when this area became part of East Sudbury, the name Cochituate was not applied. Up to the mid 1840s this area was referred to as "the south part of the town." In the 1840s there were in the south part two clusters of houses and other buildings. Centering on the present corner of Main Street and Commonwealth Road at what for years was known as Bent's Corner but also extending north on Main Street to the intersection with Plain Street (later, during Cochituate's heyday, called Lyons Corner) were village dwellings, shoeshops, and a few stores. By the 1840s this area was known as Bentville, named for the family that was taking the lead in developing the shoe industry. A half mile to the east, at what is now the junction of East Plain Street with Commonwealth Road, was another cluster containing the one-room South schoolhouse which stood at the road intersection. Also, soon to be built (in 1850) was a small church, the Wesleyan Methodist, and a store. The cluster was called Lokerville owing to the number of Lokers who lived in that area, and locally this section continued to be called Lokerville into the twentieth century. This Lokerville is not to be confused with the Lokerville which was a section of Natick appearing by that name as a village in the Massachusetts census of 1895. The only map of Wayland on which the name Lokerville appears is in *Walker's Atlas of Middlesex County*, of which Volume III containing Wayland was published in 1908.

The name Bentville appears on no known map, although this name probably would have appeared had a map of the town been prepared in the early 1840s. An article on transportation in the *Natick Citizen* of September 5, 1884, refers to the Saxonville and Bentville daily mail coach trip beginning in 1844.

The name Cochituate, which superseded Bentville and came vaguely also to encompass Lokerville, was given to the shoe-manufacturing village in 1846 when, having been taken over by the City of Boston for its water supply, Long Pond's name was changed to Lake Cochituate. The story of the lake's name change is interesting. In the seventeenth century the land area at the head of the lake had been called by the Indian name of Cochituate (with variant spellings). However, during the eighteenth century there had been a conscious effort to get away from Indian names, especially in Natick. By the mid-nineteenth century the large body of water on which Wayland, Natick, and Framingham border had for a long time been known as Long Pond, and it was so designated on maps. In March 1846, after a long controversy, it was finally decided that Boston would use Long Pond rather than Spot Pond, north of Boston, as its water supply.

On August 20, 1846, elaborate ground-breaking ceremonies were held for the beginning of the aqueduct and the reservoir gatehouse, which was to be located on land in Wayland. This gatehouse, in somewhat altered form, stands on the east bank of Lake Cochituate near the Lakeview Cemetery. A distinguished group including Mayor Josiah Quincy, Jr., of Boston, and former President of the United States John Quincy Adams, and members of the Boston City Council traveled from Boston to Saxonville by train and marched behind a brass band to the lake. At the banquet luncheon which took place on the edge of the lake after the ground-breaking, Mayor Quincy proposed to the City Council that Long Pond henceforth be known as Lake Cochituate. This name was adopted then and there.

The reason this name change was made is described and documented in the book *Water for the Cities* by N. M. Blake. In the ten-year controversy over whether to use the water of Long Pond or Spot Pond, the matter of Long Pond's water purity had been ques-

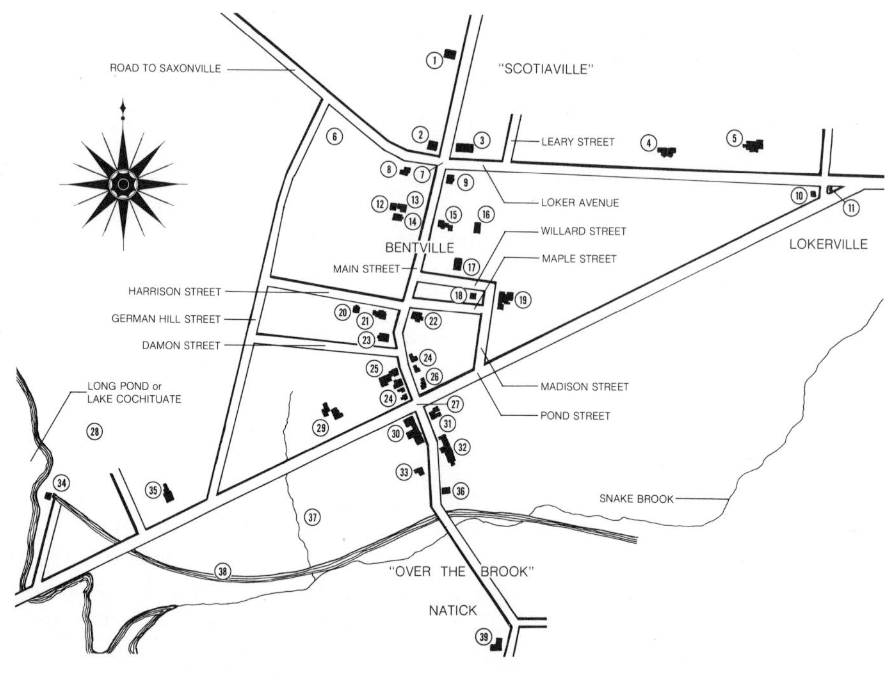

Features of Cochituate Village existing at various times between 1850 and 1900.

Key

1. King Factory
2. Knights of Labor Hall, 1887 (Grange)
3. Horsecar Barn
4. G. L. Loker House
5. J. A. Loker House
6. Ball Field
7. Lyons Corner
8. A. B. Lyon House
9. Fairbanks Block
10. South School House
11. Wesleyan Methodist Church, 1850
12. Beehive, 1891-1913
13. Lyon Factory
14. School, 1873
15. H. C. Dean House
16. H. C. Dean Factory
17. St. Zepherin's Church
18. Beehive until 1891
19. Williams Factory
20. Engine House
21. C. W. Moore Boarding House
22. Mrs. Bond's Store
23. Methodist Episcopal Church
24. Stores
25. William Loker Boarding House
26. J. M. Bent House
27. Bent's Corner
28. Lakeview Cemetery
29. Bryant Factory
30. Bent Factory
31. Bent Boarding House
32. Omnibus Stage Depot
33. First Bryant House
34. Gatehouse
35. G. A. Damon House (later N. Griffin)
36. Blacksmith Shop (P. A. Leary)
37. City Pastures
38. Aqueduct
39. Felch Bros. Factory

tioned. Apparently it was decided that giving the pond an Indian name would connote to Bostonians remoteness in the wilderness and pure, unpolluted water. According to Blake, who did extensive research in the newspapers of the time, "The Mayor's proposal that Long Pond should henceforth be known as Lake Cochituate was enthusiastically adopted. The guests then settled down to a round of eloquent toasts. When ex-President Adams' turn came he proposed 'The waters of Lake Cochituate.—May they prove to the citizens of after ages as inspiring as ever the waters of Halicon to the citizens of ancient Greece.' "[2]

The name-changing banquet took place in late August. On October 1, 1846, a post office called Cochituate was established in the southern part of Wayland and was located on the east side of the southern part of Main Street near the Bent shoeshop, possibly in James M. Bent's store.[3] Correspondence with the Historical Unit of the U.S. Postal Service reveals that petitions to have post offices in village sections and not in the centers of towns were not preserved in the archives of the Post Office Department in Washington.[4] Thus, we cannot find out who asked the Post Office Department to set up this office and who suggested the name. It seems to this writer very likely that James Madison Bent, then a man of thirty-four who had recently formed a partnership with his older brother William to pursue the shoe business already started by the latter, probably had a lot to do with the name change from Bentville to Cochituate. J. M. Bent's obituary in 1888 stated that he was employed by the Boston water board as agent to purchase the land needed for the aqueduct, the gatehouse, and the shore of the lake where farms would be flooded by raising the water level for the reservoir.[5] It can be assumed that he performed these functions in Wayland but not in all towns affected by the aqueduct and the reservoir. He is said to have taken a great interest in the water project, and it is very likely that he attended the ground-breaking ceremony and was at least an onlooker at the banquet at which the name change of the pond was decided upon. It was probably he who favored the name Cochituate for the post office and promoted the change from Bentville.

There was no municipal action to change the name of the village, but it is interesting to note that James Madison Bent served on Wayland's three-man board of selectmen in 1846 and 1847. In looking into the process by which Wayland land was sold to the Boston water board, this writer found a deed signed November 28, 1846, transferring land from Stephen Stanton to Nathan Hale, James F. Baldwin, and Thomas B. Curtis (the Boston water commissioners) termed "a parcel of land with a house and barn and other buildings thereon situated in . . . Wayland in the village of Bentville or Cochituate."[6] This deed shows that as of the fall of 1846 Cochituate was being substituted as a name for Bentville. The earliest use of the place name Cochituate for the southern village found in official Wayland town documents is in a book in which the town clerk recorded chattel mortgages and legal sales of property other than land. A deed of sale records that on June 28, 1848, John McLaughlin bought from Freeman Thomas a barn standing on land owned by Charles Loker "in South Wayland." South Wayland was given as the location of the barn, but the document is headed "Cochituate" in the same way that other documents in this volume are headed "Wayland."[7]

As far as the functioning of the town government went in the mid-1840s, there was one out of three selectmen from the south part of the town, but until April 1845 no effort was made to place notices of town meetings in that part of the town. For the annual town meeting of March 3, 1845, the warrant was posted at the meetinghouses of the First and Second Parishes (meaning at the Unitarian Church and at the Congregational Church), both at Wayland Center. However, on April 15, 1845, the town voted that warrants for town meetings be posted, "one copy at the meeting house of the first and second parishes and one copy at James M. Bent's store in the south part of the town." James M. Bent's store stood on the southwest corner of Main Street and Pond (Lake) Street, now Commonwealth Road, next to the Bent factory. From that time on one copy of the warrant for town meetings was always ordered to be posted in the Cochituate section of Wayland. The warrant for November 13, 1848, was posted "at the Post Office in the south part of the town." Finally, usage by the town clerk and selectmen changed; the warrants for 1849 town meetings were ordered posted "at the Cochituate Post Office."

Size of Cochituate Village

In attempting to depict the size of Cochituate statistically, we shall not confine our analysis to the central village but shall use the broader area, which in 1893 became Wayland's Precinct 2, the area which corresponded to the land added to Sudbury in 1721. Examination of the 1850 census population enumeration indicates that 338 persons were living in that southern area as against 776 in the Wayland or northern area. A census count of 1865 shows that by that year the total population of Wayland had changed little and that proportionally the north and south parts of the town remained about the same—778 in Wayland, 359 in Cochituate. The Civil War had disrupted life in the whole town; the shoe industry in Cochituate had developed, but the great increase in population was yet to come.

In the five years from 1865 to 1870, however, Cochituate began to grow rapidly, increasing (as counted in the 1870 census, which now presented Cochituate and Wayland separately for the first time) from 359 to 480 persons, a 33.7 percent increase. However, as noted above, Cochituate was really to explode in population from 1870 to 1875, growing from 480 to an estimated 1,000.[8] This is a 108 percent increase. Sometime in the early 1870s, perhaps by 1873, Cochituate had come to exceed in population the much larger area of Wayland. The political implications of this growth will be discussed later. As noted before, the growth of Cochituate slowed down in the second half of the 1870s, bringing Cochituate's population in 1880 to 1,161 while Wayland's stood at 801. The rapid growth in the 1870s led to a housing shortage and much building of single-family and multiple-dwelling units, and necessitated the building of the three-story Cochituate School on Main Street.

Articles appearing during December 1874 in the *Framingham Gazette* give us a sense of Cochituate's dramatic growth at that time. In a long article in the December 14 issue, "Quill" wrote that "Cochituate with her energetic manufacturers is bound to maintain an advanced position in the march of improvement with her neighboring manufacturing villages." He then went on to comment on expansion activities in the Bent, Dean, and Lyon shoe companies. Next, he commented on Joseph Moore's hiring of a gang of carpenters to build an addition to his building to provide a larger store area and a better post office. (This store and post office was located on the west side of Main Street a third of the way from Bent's Corner to the Methodist Church. See the 1875 map in *Beers Atlas of Middlesex County.)* He then went on to say that Orrin W. Harris (who had built the Cochituate School) was digging foundations, getting together materials for six new dwelling houses on land purchased from C. W. Richardson,[9] and leasing land on the east side of Main Street from William Moore to erect a building to be used as a tinshop and stove and hardware store. In the *Natick Citizen* of March 1, 1878, the Cochituate correspondent commented as follows: "During the last five years [from 1873] the growth of this village has been wonderful.

The Lt. William Bent House, built in the early 1770s, was a boarding house from 1875 to 1914.

Mr. O. W. Harris, a master builder, has erected an average of one house a month." It cannot be determined whether Harris had actually built sixty houses in Cochituate by this time, but it is clear that he had done a lot of building.

The following unsigned article appeared in the *Framingham Gazette* of December 23, 1874:

During the past week there has been scores of fresh arrivals in our village of workmen seeking employment in our shoe factories. More or less of them have obtained work and will be followed by their families as soon as they can find tenements to live in.

Our new schoolhouse built last year has not accommodations for the increasing number of scholars and an attempt was made at the November town meeting to pass a vote to fit up the new hall [in the Cochituate School, called Schoolhouse Hall] *for a school room resulting in a vote authorizing the town treasurer to borrow money and instructing the school committee to repair and refit the old schoolhouse east of the village for the accommodation of a portion of the scholars.*

In the *Framingham Gazette* two weeks later, on January 6, 1875, Joseph A. Roby wrote a glowing account saying that Wayland (owing to Cochituate's growth) had added $50,000 to taxable property in 1874. To him this was a tremendous increase, and he commented: "This may be for her [Wayland] as much per cent of increase as some of the larger cities and towns of the State can show." Joseph A. Roby had served as town clerk from 1870 to 1874. In the March 12, 1875, issue of the *Waltham Free Press* he pointed out that of thirty-four births in the town in 1874 twenty-eight were in Cochituate and only six in Wayland, six to fathers who were farmers, twenty-four to shoemakers. On the housing shortage "Quill" had written to the *Framingham Gazette* of September 23, 1874: "The building fever seems to be somewhat abating at present notwithstanding every house is filled from basement to attic and the demand for tenements is constantly increasing. Advertising is unnecessary. Four stakes set at right angles upon a lot of land will bring the owner scores of applications for tenements."

Orientation to Natick

As of 1880 Cochituate Village was a thriving place which had grown up around the shoe factories. The Methodist Church, which could be said to stand at the center of the village, is only about one thousand feet north of the Natick boundary. Village life in Cochituate encompassed more than the Cochituate section of Wayland; it included the group of people who lived on the half mile or so of Main Street across the border in Natick and on Pine Street in Natick, in the area known as North Natick or, to Central and South Natick residents, as "the extreme north." This nearby part of North Natick was referred to by people in Cochituate proper as "over the brook," Snake Brook being the boundary between Wayland and Natick. There was much reference to "over the brook" in the Cochituate news in the Natick newspapers of the 1870s, 1880s, and 1890s. The Felches, Hammonds, Bacons, and Coolidges of this area had strong ties to the families of Cochituate. Many of the families attended the Cochituate Methodist Church, and there was considerable moving back and forth over the town border as houses on one side or the other became available. Henry Coggin served as a selectman of Wayland in 1845. Later he was living in North Natick and was no longer politically involved in Wayland, although still included socially. The inclusion of North Natick as an inset on the lithograph entitled "Cochituate, Mass. and North Natick, 1887," drawn and published by George Norris of Brockton was no anomaly. Although under a different political jurisdiction, this area was part of the social and business community.

Cochituate people tended to go to central Natick for shopping and business purposes and took the train from there to Boston and other destinations. Newspaper stories show that they also went to Natick for entertainment and for lodge and social club affiliations, which were a very important element of the social and cultural life of the day. Wayland Center people, on the other hand, went to Waltham for those same advantages.

Urban Aspect of Cochituate

Cochituate Village was more crowded and by 1880 had a much more urban organization than Wayland Center. The valuation list of 1883 shows small house lots of a quarter, a half, or one full acre to have been common in Cochituate, but there were few of these in Wayland Center. The census shows that as of 1880 in all parts of Wayland it was common for more people to dwell in a particular building than is the case today. The north part of Wayland had numerous double houses for two families. Cochituate had these; and also in Cochituate most of the single dwellings, even those of the Bents and Bryants, the shoe factory owners, were fitted up with at least one rental "tenement." There were also boardinghouses which housed single workers in the shoe factories, and sometimes couples. In 1875 the hundred-year-old Bent homestead on the southeast corner of Main and Lake streets had been enlarged and made into what at the time of the 1880 census was called Lovejoy's Boarding House. In June 1880 there were sixteen boarders. Lovejoy's Boarding House was run for ten years, from 1875 to 1885, by Anna Maria Lovejoy, James Madison Bent's daughter and eldest child. In 1885 Mrs. Lovejoy retired from the boardinghouse, and the business was continued by William H. Hardy, who in 1887 enlarged and spruced up the building and called it the Cochituate House.[10] In September 1889 Hardy died, and the Cochituate House was taken over by Joseph Dupuis. The Bent family continued to own the property and to rent it to a succession of proprietors. In the late 1890s the name was changed to the Hawthorne House and again, in 1907, to the Cochituate Tavern. It kept the last name until 1915 when part of the back was removed and the building was renovated and used again by the Bent family and their relatives. This house is still standing at 43 Main Street and to October 1980 was occupied by a member of the Bent family.

Another boarding house was the American House, run by William Loker and later by F. B. Tyler, in a building on the west side of Main

Street halfway between Lake and Damon streets. It burned in 1892 in a spectacular fire which nearly wiped out the center of Cochituate Village. Emily Moore, divorced wife of Charles W. Moore, ran a boardinghouse farther up Main Street north of the Methodist Church. Julia M. Riley was a boardinghouse keeper, as was Levi Curtis's wife. Levi Curtis, a shoe worker from Maine, had the house now standing at 135 Commonwealth Road built in early 1878. The house was close to the Bent factory; at the time of the 1880 census there were six boarders there.

There were also a few multifamily buildings called tenement houses such as the Bent-owned Bee Hive, Wilson House, and Bleak House. These were not large buildings and had little resemblance to slumlike city tenement houses. According to the *Natick Bulletin* of September 19, 1874, Wilson House was the small Natick schoolhouse in which United States Vice-President Henry Wilson of Natick gave his first political speech. In 1874 James M. Bent had acquired it and moved it to his property in Cochituate. It was called a tenement house in the newspapers and parlance of the day, but it probably contained no more than two or three rental units. In nineteenth-century Wayland all rental units were called tenements. Most tenements in Cochituate were on upper floors or in the back wings of private houses and were similar to what we call apartments today. These quarters were heated by coal-fired stoves, and occasionally trouble was reported from coal gas fumes. It is not known what water and, later, plumbing facilities there were in the tenements.

The crowding of persons into houses in Cochituate around 1875 was illustrated and probably exaggerated by "Quill" in the *Framingham Gazette* of August 25, 1875, when he wrote:

To get an idea of the number of occupants of a majority of the houses of this village, the following notice placed on the front door of one of them will illustrate:

Those seeking Mr. Jones these directions will follow
Go round to the back door and hollow.

Those wishing to see Mr. Brown
Knock at the door and he will come down.

For Mr. Smith ascend the first flight
And gently rap on the door on the right.

Stores on the west side of Main Street in Cochituate Village which are now part of the Johnson Pharmacy.

Messrs. White and Green are on the third floor
To find them you will proceed as before.
But at the first landing take the next door
And when you have ascended the topmost stair
Open the door at the left and see if they aren't there.

Stores and Commercial Buildings

In the 1880s most of the commercial buildings in Cochituate Village were concentrated on both sides of Main Street between Bent's Corner and Harrison and Maple streets. Some stores were in existence only briefly or changed hands often, and it would be impossible to catalogue them all. The *Natick Bulletin* of December 20, 1878, published an article on the stores in Cochituate and urged citizens to trade at home. At this time John W. Bigelow had a grocery store in Loker's block on the east side of Main Street, while J. W. Moore ran a grocery and crockery store combined with the post office in his building on the west side of Main Street. Perhaps the best known grocery store, where dry goods were also sold, was Edward P. Butler's store in Bryant's block on the west side of Main Street near the corner of Pond Street. In 1873 Butler, who came to the town from Natick, bought out the Bryant brothers' grocery store. Butler's house, built in 1873, is still standing on the east side of Main Street north of Lyons Corner at number 163.

In late 1878 C. C. Atwood (and later Edward Atwood) had a meat and provision market in the Butterfield building. There were other stores, but only three of these will be mentioned here—Charles F. Bigelow's drugstore in the Bryant block, acquired by purchase in 1878 from James E. Cochran, where a soda fountain was the marvel of the village; N. R. Gerald's news and confectionery store, at that time in the Loker building on the east side of Main Street; and Mrs. Margaret A. Bond's dry-goods, dress goods, and millinery store in her own so-called block or building on the east side of Main Street just south of where Maple Street is now located.

In the later 1880s and in the 1890s French citizens were proprietors of small fish, meat, and grocery stores. There were also, under rapidly changing management or ownership, one or more barbershops and billiard rooms. Most of the commercial enterprises were in "blocks" (buildings) built by the older Cochituate landowners and commercial entrepreneurs who hung on to their land and buildings and leased them for use only. A good deal of the commercial activity on Main Street was on land controlled by Willard Moore[11] and his son, by Charles Damon and his son Charles R. Damon, and by various members of the Loker family. In 1878 James M. Bent had one commercial building on the east side of Main Street in which there was a stove and tinware shop and a tailor. At this period the Bents were not important owners of commercial property. Their original farmlands were sold off or given to married daughters at an earlier time.

Village Atmosphere and Facilities

Cochituate Village shows up in 1880 bird's-eye photographs as a country village landscape. The area was spruce and neat, but it did not have the truly rural aspect which at that time was characteristic of most of the rest of Wayland except for a short stretch of Main Street north and south of the Boston Post Road (now Cochituate Road) in Wayland Center. In the flowery language of the day, a reporter wrote proudly in the *Natick Bulletin* of July 23, 1886, that the roads in Cochituate

The reservoir and 1878 water works gatehouse, with the George Rice House, built about 1810, in the center background.

are beginning to lose their look of ruralness, the hedgerows of raspberry, blackberry and hazel bushes that formerly marked their outline. . . . are in the process of being supplanted by the graceful lattice of refined tastes or the solid masonry of a richer and more prosperous people. The unsightly door and barnyards of a former generation are disappearing before the advance of industry and permanent success, the green lawns, the ribbon beds, and the perfume of exotic flowers fill the landscape with their beauty and enrich the senses with their fragrance and their variety. No one wishes for the return of the old ways, the old hedges and the former conditions, and the new comer sighs for an opportunity to share in the benefits of the changes and better temporal conditions.

Much of what is left in 1980 of old Cochituate is painted white. Exterior white paint was not in style in the 1880s and 1890s; instead there were the browns, buffs, and olive greens of Victorian taste. When the Methodist Episcopal Church was painted in 1882 there was quite a controversy about its color. A newspaper account tells us that at first cardinal red with black trim was tried but seemed too bright. Next trials were made with bronze green and olive green. The building was finally painted in a color described as "old gold."[12] (The Unitarian Church at Wayland Center shows up in photographs to have been painted a color other than white at this time.)

In addition to a neat, suburban landscape, in 1880 Cochituate Village had two urban facilities which were not to come to Wayland Center until the twentieth century, a public water supply and a fire department. The Cochituate water supply was occasioned more by the need for fire protection of the wooden shoe factories than because of a need for more adequate domestic water in the closely settled area, although the latter also was a factor. By the mid-1870s the need for fire protection of the shoe factories, particularly his large one, seemed to obsess James Madison Bent as well it might after a devastating fire in Natick in 1874. Bent took the lead in getting the town to vote for and build the Wayland waterworks. As with all expensive projects, this improvement had to be sold to the whole town. In the summer of 1877 we find an effort being made to connect with Natick's public water supply whose mains then came within a half mile of Cochituate Village.[13] That failed to work, and in the fall of that year at a town meeting held on October 5 the town voted to enlarge the dam on Rice's Pond on Snake Brook to secure a supply of water for the village of Cochituate for fire protection and domestic purposes.

At this meeting a committee headed by James M. Bent with James S. Draper and Hodijah B. Braman of Wayland Center and Thomas Bryant and Albert B. Lyon of Cochituate, all prominent citizens, was chosen to arrange for the water supply. An excellent printed thirty-page document entitled *Report of the Construction Committee of the Wayland Water Works, March 1, 1879,* published by the town in 1880, details the history of the building of the water system. The town was authorized to borrow $23,000, and after a state act created the waterworks in April 1878, a committee of five men, all from Cochituate, was chosen to oversee the construction of the system. James M. Bent headed this committee, which included his son James Alvin Bent, Charles H. Boodey, Charles Fairbank, and Alfred H. Bryant. With the planning supervision of engineer Hiram W. Blaisdell of Concord, a crew of men under George Alonzo Rice (owner of the house now standing at 78 Rice Road near the reservoir, also the man who sold the reservoir property to the town) built the dam and installed a pump procured from the City of Boston. The workers were ready to lay pipe for the initial grid starting at the intersection of Lake and Plain streets by September 26, 1878.

Before the waterworks dam was built, the pond, already dammed

The Cochituate fire station on Harrison Street was built in 1882 and torn down in 1953.

up, covered six acres. When the new dam was finished, the reservoir covered about twelve acres. About four and one-half miles of cast-iron pipe were laid to the twenty-nine original hydrants. The gatehouse, still in existence but not in good repair, is a fourteen-foot-square building constructed of diamond-shaped pieces of red, gray, and black granite. It has not been possible to ascertain who designed this handsome, unique building.

At later junctures the water mains were extended farther north on Main Street and, in 1881, as far as the Simpson mansion on the southwest corner of Dudley Pond. This addition, which was financed by Michael Simpson, brought the public water supply to the households on what is now West Plain Street. The waterworks were well and expeditiously built, but it turned out that the pond dammed up had such a woodsy setting and so much organic matter on its bottom that at certain times of the year the water was unpalatable and, a good bit of the time, because of impurities, poor for washing. The July 15, 1887, *Natick Bulletin* reported that especially in summer the Rice Pond water, considering the presence of algae and iron and other minerals, was not considered fit for drinking or cooking. Families were then falling back on private wells and were drinking milk instead of water. The article went on to advocate use of Lake Cochituate or Dudley Pond for the Wayland water supply. Flushing of the water mains was resorted to at this and other times to try and get rid of the impurities. An amusing note about this is included in the water department report in the 1907 town report, where one finds the following:

Arrangements have been made to flush the mains during the middle of the week so as to have clear water on wash days and not interfere with people taking their Saturday night baths, notice of flushing being given by 5 blasts on the Williams shoe factory whistle one hour previous.

The 1878 waterworks did greatly improve the fire protection as soon as fire equipment (hose, hooks and ladders, and man-drawn carts for them) were purchased and two volunteer fire companies —the James M. Bent Hose Company and the Charles H. Boodey Hook and Ladder Company—were organized.[14] On June 17, 1878, the hook and ladder company went to Felchville to receive its truck. Upon its return to Cochituate, the Cochituate Brass Band participated with the company in a short parade and ceremony. The first fire station was built in June 1878 on the east side of Main Street near Mrs. Bond's store. In May 1882 the fire station was moved to land in front of the town lockup on the south side of Harrison Street where it served for many years as fire headquarters and as a voting place for Precinct 2.

The *Natick Citizen* of June 20, 1879, described a parade held on June 19 to celebrate the fire companies' first anniversary. The article relates that after the parade there were speed trials where the Charles H. Boodey Hook and Ladder Company No. 1 ran one quarter of a mile, spliced ladders, and put a man on a roof in 2 minutes and 10 seconds. The James M. Bent Hose Company No. 1 ran one quarter of a mile, laid 150 feet of hose, and put a stream of water on a roof in 1 minute and 50 seconds. As in all small fire departments of that day, the hose carriage was pulled by the men until 1884 when a set of shafts for horses was acquired.[15]

To support the various activities of the fire department as well as to buy uniforms, firemen's balls were held annually, often at Thanksgiving and Christmastime. Accounts in the Natick newspapers describe these as quite the social events during the 1880s and early 1890s. They were elaborate affairs, sometimes featuring masquerades with costumes rented in Boston. An account in the *Natick Bulletin* of February 10, 1893, describes the masquerade ball of the Bent Hose Company with its preliminary concert, then a grand march followed by dancing into early morning and an elaborate oyster supper. Many of the people at the ball were listed and their costumes described. This writer, who attended Vassar College, wonders what the costume was like which inspired Nellie Gavin to go to that ball as "A Vassar College Girl."

Wayland Center had to wait thirty years—until 1908—for a fire company, and then its only equipment was a chemical truck. Although greatly needed and wanted by that end of the town since the late 1890s, Wayland Center's water supply was still in the distant future.

Another urban amenity which came earlier to Cochituate was electricity. Service was provided as an extension of the Natick utility system. First came five streetlights which were installed on June 13, 1888. The June 15 *Natick Bulletin* reported that the lights—at Lyons Corner, at Bent's Corner, at the Methodist Episcopal Church, at the "old church" (Lokerville), and "on the heights" (German Hill Street)—created quite a sensation. People went out to view them and marveled that they burned for two nights without changing "the carbon." Wayland Center enjoyed its first few streetlights in 1895. In December 1888 the office of the Wm. and J.M. Bent Company was wired, and "the electrics were used for the first time."[16] Electricity came also in late 1888 to certain of the commercial establishments such as the drugstore. Soon thereafter electricity began to be distributed to residences of the village via poles erected in the streets. The first electricity in Wayland Center was installed about 1900. The present Wayland Library was built in 1900 without electricity, but the following year the trustees recommended its introduction and this was soon accomplished.[17]

Transportation

With manufacturing making it necessary to haul raw materials, fuel, and finished product as well as to bring in the commuter workers (to be discussed below), transportation was of great importance to Cochituate as a link to the outside world. It was also important to those on the Wayland end of town who had aspirations to develop that part of the town into more than a simple farming community. The Cochituate Crossing railroad spur of the Boston and Albany Railroad had been established in 1874 as a freight stop across the lake on the border of Natick and Framingham, but this did not constitute railroad service to Cochituate. Although the leaders of the village tried to get it, Cochituate never had its own railroad service.

Up to 1885 passenger traffic in and out of Cochituate to and from Natick and Saxonville was handled by a well-organized system of horse-drawn omnibus coaches or stages. Freight and express were carried in large wagons, mainly to the Natick railroad station but, under some circumstances, to the Stony Brook station of the Fitchburg Railroad line in Weston, as well as to the Massachusetts Central Railroad station in Wayland Center when it was running.

An article in the *Natick Citizen* of September 5, 1884, summed up the history of coach transportation in and out of Cochituate Village. The one daily Saxonville and Bentville mail coach of 1844 has already been mentioned. This mail coach service was run by a man known as Uncle Steve Hayes. In 1856 James M. Moore started a coach line from Cochituate to Natick. Business apparently dropped off during the Civil War period. Moore gave up and there was no coach for a time until a man by the name of Sherman started a line in 1869. According to the *Natick Citizen* article, "After Sherman came Howe and Company and James N. Hammond who did a good business having a little opposition from Loker in 1872. Then came the present proprietor, George F. Keep." Keep came to Cochituate from Oakham, Massachusetts, bought the coach line, and arranged to keep the horses in James N. Hammond's stable. At that time the stage depot and stables were part of a long complex of buildings on the east side of Main Street south of the old Bent house and near the Natick border. The town clerk's chattel mortgage record shows that in October 1873 George F. Keep borrowed $2,850 from George D. Estabrook of Natick, using eight horses, three omnibuses, and two omnibus sleighs as collateral.[18] With the shoe industry growing, there was a need to transport workers. Keep was a good organizer and did so well that by December 1874 four omnibuses with four drivers and fourteen horses were being used between Cochituate and Natick. In April 1882 Keep's line was running seven daily trips each way between Cochituate and Natick. Most trips were to accommodate shoe workers, but two or three trips a day were arranged to connect with passenger trains from Natick to Boston and thus enabled a few Cochituate residents to commute to Boston to work. In January 1880 there was a notice in the *Natick Bulletin* that H. E. Moore was the proprietor of a new coach line between Cochituate and Saxonville, where various workers in the Cochituate shoe factories lived.[19]

In 1885 a group of Natick men decided to build a horsecar line and obtained a charter for the Natick and Cochituate Street Railway. When built and opened for the first time on July 31, the line had two closed cars named for Natick men. The two open cars were named "Lake Cochituate" and "William Bent," the latter for the founder of the large shoe company. George Keep became superintendent of this line, which by the spring of 1886 had seven cars and a comparable number of horses. The expansion necessitated enlarging the stables, which had been built on a lot sold to the company by James N. Hammond, now the site of the Cochituate fire station and library branch. The 1887 Cochituate lithograph shows two horsecars moving along the tracks on their way to the terminus at Lyons Corner. This horse railroad as it was referred to was immediately profitable. The *Natick Bulletin* of July 1, 1887, quoted from a lengthy article about this line which had appeared in the *Framingham Tribune.* This article said that T-rails flush with the ground on the outside were used in open areas. Flat rails were used in thickly settled places and on grades and corners. By 1887 there were three large, open cars, each pulled by two horses for summer use, and three closed cars for winter use. These cars held seventy-four passengers. There was also one small car requiring one horse. In all, nineteen horses weighing an average of 1,050 pounds apiece were owned and, of course, a snowplow. The trip from Natick to Cochituate took a half hour, and the fare was 10 cents. When the horsecar line was opened, it was expected to cut about ten minutes off the trip from Natick to Cochituate.

One cannot read the full weekly news of Cochituate and the lesser amount available for Wayland Center in the Natick, Framingham, and Waltham papers without being aware of the great importance of horses to the functioning of their world in both parts of Wayland in the 1880s. Horses were used not only by the street railway to carry passengers and with wagons to haul freight, but also by stores to make deliveries, by farmers as draft animals (oxen having been given up), and for personal transportation by the more prosperous householders, who used either their own animals or those hired from the livery stables. In addition by the late 1880s there was a considerable craze for trotting horses for recreation and sport. This led the *Natick Bulletin* correspondent to state on January 7, 1887, that "the value of horse flesh [in Cochituate] probably exceeds that of any town of the size in the state." This was in connection with horseraces held that and other winters on a track on the ice on Dudley Pond, which the Boston water board tried unsuccessfully to stop. Participating in these races were Charles Butterfield; Myron, Ralph, and William Harrison

Bent; Ed Marston; John Moore; and Henry Kelley and others.

The newspaper columns on Cochituate were full of illnesses, accidents, losses, and acquisitions of horses. Stories of exciting and sometimes damaging runaways appeared nearly every week. The Wayland town report of 1877-78 stated that in 1877 there were 392 horses in Wayland—perhaps the peak figure.

In due course the horse car line from Natick was converted to trolley cars. In May 1892 the Natick and Cochituate Street Railway began electrifying the railroad and on July 2 the first trip, a free ride for fifty-two people led by Selectman Edwin Marston, took place. The *Natick Review* of July 7 jubilantly reported: "We are 'in it'. Sunday morning . . . the first electric car was started from the stables. The signal was struck by the motor man John Mellon . . . Supt. Keep pulled the bell and away it went spinning gaily over the rails." Later in July there was a celebration in Cochituate with fireworks and a parade when a 5-cent fare was agreed to between the selectmen and the company.

NOTES

1. See page 32.
2. Nelson Manfred Blake, *Water for the Cities*, Syracuse, N.Y., Syracuse University Press, 1956, p. 211.
3. Letter dated March 12, 1979, to Helen F. Emery from National Archives and Records Service, Assistant Chief for Reference.
4. Letter dated April 15, 1979 from Research Administration Historian of the United States Postal Service to Helen F. Emery.
5. *Natick Bulletin*, July 27, 1888.
6. South Middlesex Deeds, *Stanton to Hale, Baldwin and Curtis*, Book 496, page 289.
7. Town of Wayland, *Mortgage Book*, Vol. I., 1840-1859, p. 84.
8. The population enumeration of the 1875 Massachusetts census is not available and the summary volume did not separate Cochituate from Wayland. However, in the *Natick Bulletin* of August 25, 1875 there was an item stating: "This village having increased from a few score of inhabitants within a few years to one thousand at the present time offers a good opening . . ."
9. South Middlesex Deeds, *Richardson to Harris*, Book 1332, p. 418.
10. An earlier Cochituate House had been run by Charles B. Butterfield around 1879 in the Slayton building further up Main Street on the east side.
11. Willard Street was named for him. Note also Madison Street for James Madison Bent and Harrison Street for William Harrison Bent.
12. *Natick Citizen*, June 9, 1882.
13. *Waltham Free Press*, August 17, 1877.
14. In the 1860s several town meetings had been concerned with fire protection. In 1864 a fire department was set up. This mainly entailed purchase of buckets and fire hooks. Whether to keep these in Wayland Center or in Cochituate was a problem.
15. *Natick Bulletin*, January 11, 1884.
16. *Natick Bulletin*, December 7, 1888.
17. *Wayland Town Reports*, 1901-1902 and 1902-1903.
18. Town of Wayland, *Mortgage Book 1859-1875*, p. 185.
19. *Natick Bulletin*, January 9, 1880.

8

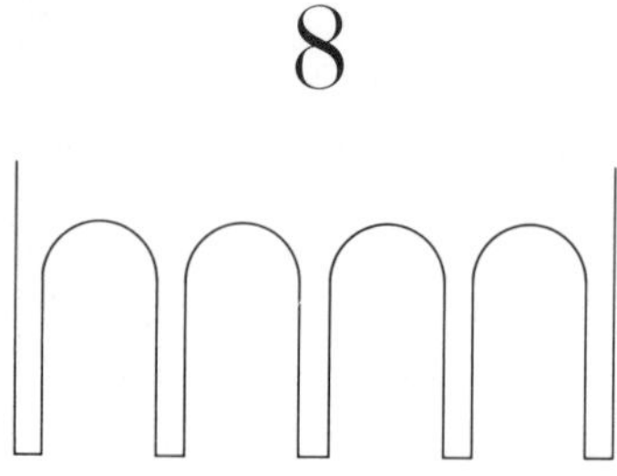

Sectionalism Arises

IN 1880 Wayland was a town growing in wealth, population, and activity, so why was there no energy for, or interest in, celebrating its one hundredth anniversary as a separate town? The answer is that owing to the growth and change we have just described as having taken place in Cochituate Village, the decade of the 1870s had been a time of much pulling and hauling between the north and south parts of the town. Uneven development always brings strains. As population grew in Cochituate and as Wayland Center strove to modernize itself and find a substitute for, or supplement to, farming, there was bound to be friction and jealousy. This was especially the case when it came to paying for facilities which were charged to the whole town but benefited only a part of it. Further, whenever the balance of power between sections changes rather suddenly, as it did when in the 1870s Cochituate was able to outvote Wayland, there tends to be unhappiness and resentment.

One finds in the town clerk's record that the year 1871 saw Cochituate attempting to secure more equal municipal facilities. Also in that year the town began to respond to the need for more school facilities in the south part of the town. After starting to buy land for a cemetery in the south part of town where the present ballfield is located in Cochituate, finally in September the town voted to buy land from Joseph Bullard and John C. Butterfield and to borrow money to lay out Lakeview Cemetery.

Sectionalism Arises

In the annual town meeting of March 1871 Charles R. Damon, a leading figure in Cochituate, and James S. Draper and Edward Mellen were chosen as a committee to try to make Wayland Library books available "so that the citizens of the southern part of the town can avail themselves of the benefits of the Library by receiving and exchanging books at some suitable place in Cochituate Village." This was also the year when, for the first time (November 7) a town meeting was held in Cochituate—in the vestry of the Methodist Episcopal Church. The vote to alternate town meetings between Wayland Center and Cochituate had been taken at the September 16 town meeting.

Cochituate School

Overshadowing the library, cemetery, and other matters in terms of potential expense as well as in practical importance was the town's need for larger and better school facilities in Cochituate. Starting in 1871 with an article in the warrant for the April 13 town meeting about removing the "school house in District No. 1" (Lokerville) to a more central location and suitably repairing it, and with another article to build two new schoolhouses in District 1, finally in March 1873 the town meeting chose Henry C. Dean, Dr. George B. Cochran, and Orrin W. Harris as a committee to purchase land and drew plans for a new schoolhouse and report to the town in April. At the town meeting of April 7 the Cochituate school planning committee reported that they had bought land from Albert B. Lyon on the west side of Main Street south of Lyons Corner and that they proposed to build a two-story building, 52 by 52 feet, with a mansard roof and an unfinished attic. There would be two schoolrooms on the first floor seating fifty-six and sixty-four pupils, respectively, the primary students and the intermediate students. The second-floor space would be available for a grammar school or high school room. The building would be set back on the one-acre lot to allow for play space in front of the building. This report was accepted by the town meeting, and a building committee consisting of Lafayette Dudley, Henry C. Dean, and George B. Cochran was chosen. Apparently there was dissatisfaction with this committee, because at a July 8 town meeting there was a warrant article to add one or more persons to the building committee. No action was taken on this proposal; however, we find a newspaper report of July 12, 1873, that the school was then being built. Ground must have been broken in June, for the correspondent to the

The 1873 Cochituate School with the stack of the Griffin Shoe Factory at the extreme right.

Framingham Gazette of June 25, 1873, wrote: "Our $15,000 schoolhouse is underway . . . It may rival Durant's Seminary.[1] . . . Mr. O. R. Harris is the contractor."

Apparently the building was completed in October. At that point a controversy between the selectmen and the building committee broke out over whether the school was built according to the contract. This led to the dismissal of the building committee and to the formation of a special investigative committee. Henry C. Dean, a selectman of Wayland at the time, seems to have disagreed with Dudley and Cochran and did not participate with the other members of the building committee. Dudley and Cochran worked with Harris, the builder, and T. W. Sulloway, the architect, and finished the school but refused to give the keys to the selectmen. At one of a series of four town meetings in November and December, the town discharged the building committee and chose a committee of five—Chairman James S. Draper, and David Heard, Albert B. Lyon, William Baldwin, and Samuel M. Thomas, all from Wayland except Lyon—to investigate whether the new school had been built according to plans, specifications, and contract.[2]

On December 8 the committee under the chairmanship of Draper reported that to save money the building committee had ignored the specifications and had failed to provide for adequate ventilation of the building. Perhaps members Dudley and Cochran of the building committee held back on presenting the keys to the selectmen because they knew that Henry C. Dean, who disapproved of how they had acted in the matter, would not accept their work and would tell them to rectify the improper ventilation. It is not entirely clear why the controversy arose. The town clerk's record of the town meeting of December 8 does not say what was in the Draper committee report. This report, if written, was not kept with the town records. Thus, one is forced to rely on a newspaper account.

Too long to include in this volume but very interesting and amusing to read is an account in 201 lines of doggerel verse written by "Quill," the unidentified correspondent on Cochituate who wrote for the *Framingham Gazette*. These poems appeared in three December issues of that weekly newspaper, and copies have been made for the files of the Wayland Historical Society. About the report of the special investigative committee Quill wrote:

That they might listen to the special committee then and there
Who had prepared their report with much interest and care.
This report, while it accorded to the building committee good intention
Did not omit their mistakes or shortcomings to mention.
By these mistakes the town loses some hundreds of dollars,
The most noteworthy of which may be stated as follows:
The committee some fifteen thousand dollars have expended
To build the schoolhouse as was originally intended,
With Primary, Intermediate, and Grammar school halls,
And ante room spacious with high towering walls,
Have on the plea of "economy" ignored both plans and specification
And intentionally neglected to provide for ventilation.
God's free air for the children they neglect to provide
By taking stale air through furnaces from the cellar inside.
Why such a culpable negligence on the part of a diplom'd M.D.
Your humble correspondent's vision at present fails to see,
Unless he wishes to engender colds, coughs, fevers and chills,
To increase his practice and sales of quinine and squills.

A complete reading of the Quill series of verses makes one realize that town committees are ever the same.

The 1873 Cochituate School, labeled "Academy" and shown as an important building on the map in *Beers Atlas of Middlesex County*

(1875), gave Cochituate a sense of both pride and identity, as did its successor building in 1911. When it was finished in 1873, there was the prospect in the minds of Cochituate citizens that the second floor would provide a better place for town meetings than the town house in Wayland Center. However, this was to be a place only for alternate town meetings, since the citizens of the north part of the town had no intention of transferring the seat of government to Cochituate.

By 1874, only one year later, the school population had grown so much that it was necessary to consider converting the second-floor Village Hall or School House Hall, as it was more commonly known, to classrooms. As of 1885 there were 198 pupils in the building. The primary school, which had started out with one teacher in one of the two rooms on the ground floor, had that year seventy-five pupils in one room, and the first floor had to be divided into two "schools." The second floor was being used for two intermediate "schools," and the grammar school was occupying the top floor.[3] By 1886 there were also twelve high school students and one high school teacher in this building. By this time the Cochituate facilities had had to be augmented by using the two Lokerville classrooms. In view of the 1873 controversy, it is interesting to note that in 1874 money was voted for ventilation and that in 1890 the cellar of the Cochituate School was dug out and new arrangements made for heating and ventilating the building.

Railroad

The Cochituate School had been a major expense to the town, and a committee composed largely of Wayland Center men had severely criticized its building committee. More bitterly controversial was the sparring that took place in the effort to get direct railroad service to the town and whether it would be to Wayland Center or to Cochituate.

In the "Appendix to The Annals of Wayland" in Alfred S. Hudson's *Annals of Sudbury, Wayland and Maynard*, published in 1891, it is stated that as early as 1843 a railroad was chartered and laid out from Framingham, crossing Wayland to the Stony Brook station in Weston on the Fitchburg line to Boston, and that citizens of Wayland subscribed liberally to its stock.[4] This author has not found contemporary documentation of this project, but nothing came of the venture. In the middle to late 1860s a group of Wayland Center men had become convinced that, compared with its neighbors' railroad service and prosperous industry, Wayland was stagnating or even deteriorating. James S. Draper, the probable author of an article printed in the *Waltham Free Press* of February 7, 1868, had bemoaned the times of earlier-nineteenth-century prosperity for Wayland Center when it was on a through stage line to the west. He then went on to say: "While suffering these depressing conditions and beholding the prosperity of their adjoining sister towns favored with the great miracle of business—The Boston and Worcester and The Fitchburg Railroads and their branches—they cannot but feel a spirit of sadness."

The need to stimulate Wayland Center's economy and the leadership of James S. Draper surely were responsible for the fact that when a group of ten men petitioned the Massachusetts legislature for permission to build a railroad from Mill Village in South Sudbury to Stony Brook in Weston, four were prominent Wayland Center residents. They were: Horace Heard, a large property holder in the center and the town's largest taxpayer in 1872; Edward Pousland, a sea captain who had in the 1860s chosen Wayland as a family residence while still following the sea and had in 1866 built what was then considered one of the most elegant houses in Wayland Center, now the Parish House of the Unitarian Church at 43 Cochituate Road; James Sumner Draper, farmer and surveyor and, because of his large property holdings in the Plains area,[5] also among the top ten taxpayers. There were also Henry D. Parmenter, well-to-do cattle farmer, among the top ten taxpayers; and Charles A. Cutting, a Boston businessman interested in railroad commuting service to Boston who, since marrying a Wayland girl and coming to Wayland as a summer resident on Old Sudbury Road, had been increasing his accumulation of Wayland property.

The locally sponsored Wayland and Sudbury Branch Railroad never materialized, but in 1869 a wider-ranging group in which James S. Draper was included conceived a plan for a railroad from Boston to Northampton through the central part of the state. On May 10, 1869, the Massachusetts legislature chartered the Massachusetts Central Railroad to run ninety-eight miles and authorized capital stock of $6 million. At its first meeting James S. Draper was elected clerk and a director, and Charles A. Cutting was made a director. In the charter the towns were authorized to subscribe to the stock of this railroad up to 5 percent of their assessed valuation. On November 27, 1869, a special town meeting was held to decide what Wayland would do about subscribing to the capital stock of the Massachusetts Central. The voters were strongly in favor of doing so, and a vote passed 103 to

The Wayland Railroad Station, built in 1881.

2 to subscribe for 325 shares of capital stock. Borrowing of up to $32,500 to pay for the stock was authorized. Horace Heard; Edward Pousland; and Thomas J. Damon, a well-to-do farmer from Cochituate, were voted as a committee to negotiate the sale of bonds. Abel Gleason was chosen agent to act in behalf of the town at meetings of the railroad corporation.

The Massachusetts Central Railroad encountered difficulty in raising enough capital and was slow to organize and acquire the right-of-way. Wayland had not yet paid its money and in May of 1873 stalled again about raising the money. Meanwhile, on July 8, 1873, a proposal was made at a town meeting that the town subscribe to the capital stock of the Hopkinton Railroad Company along with the Massachusetts Central in amounts which together would not exceed 5 percent of the town's valuation. This was in response to the desire of Cochituate's shoe factory owners that a railroad come to their village. The *Natick Bulletin* of June 4, 1873, had reported that there was talk of building a railroad from Cochituate to Hopkinton. The *Framingham Gazette* of June 11, 1873, reporting on the attempt to get a railroad to Cochituate, said that the directors of the Hopkinton Railroad had come to Cochituate to look at a proposed route. The article failed to pass on July 8, but ten days later it did pass by a vote of 201 to 18 and the town was authorized to borrow for this purpose, "provided that

The Hopkinton Railroad be located and built through the village of Cochituate . . . within one fourth of a mile from the square on which stands the shoe factory of Wm. & J. M. Bent."

Without anything happening to build either railroad, a real contention within the town developed about the railroad stock subscriptions. In January 1874 there were two town meetings at which the question of rescinding the stock subscriptions was raised. On January 15 the vote to rescind lost 44 to 54, but on January 22 the vote carried. By this time the money pledged to the Massachusetts Central was a sectional issue. At a February 28, 1874, town meeting a vote to instruct the town treasurer to borrow to buy note issues of the Massachusetts Central failed. There had been 91 votes against, all from Cochituate except for two Shermans from North Wayland. The 27 votes in favor of paying the Massachusetts Central were those of Wayland residents, except for Thomas J. Damon of Cochituate.

In the middle years of the 1870s troubles beset the Massachusetts Central and, to quote the book, *The Central Mass.*, published in 1975 by the Boston and Maine Railroad Historical Society, Inc., this railroad "fell into a comatose state for several years." Finally, in 1878 a new board of directors and slate of officers were elected and a more vigorous president, George S. Boutwell, former governor of Massachusetts, was chosen president. James S. Draper was treasurer. This group was better organized and had more capital, and a time limit was set for building the railroad by putting all stock, both town owned and individually owned, in the hands of a trustee for two years.

Construction finally got under way when in October 1880 the first rails were laid from Sudbury both east and west. The track from Sudbury must have reached Wayland by the end of November, because the *Natick Bulletin* of December 3, 1880, noted that "The Massachusetts Central Railroad ran their first train to Wayland on Tuesday [November 30]." Of this event, the *Waltham Free Press* of December 3 wrote:

The first locomotive ever seen in Wayland made its appearance on Tuesday morning on The Massachusetts Central Railroad. The laying of the track, says a Boston paper, is progressing at the rate of one-fourth of a mile per day and the rails will probably be laid to Waltham in about ten days. It is expected that there will be regular railroad communication with Boston early in the coming spring. The large and flourishing village of Cochituate will doubtless send all of its freight and passengers to Boston via The

Massachusetts Central, when completed, thereby making Wayland Centre quite a business point on the road. This quiet old town has been without railroad facilities for the last two hundred years adds the witty reporter.

In his *History of Sudbury, Massachusetts*, published in 1889, Alfred S. Hudson said that on April 20, 1881, a train of cars traveled from Boston to Hudson over the rails. However, the railroad through Wayland was not ready to operate that spring. At last, on October 1 of that year, a grand opening of the twenty-eight miles of road from Boston to Hudson was held with the passage from the Boston and Lowell Railroad station in Boston to Hudson of a train of six passenger cars with one baggage and one smoking car. There were about six hundred passengers aboard, including representatives of the legislature, state officials, and businessmen. Groups cheered the train at decorated railroad stations along the route. A cannon salute was fired by Hodijah B. Braman, a summer resident of Wayland, when the train passed through Belmont.[6] The Tower Hill flag stop shelter was elaborately decorated because of its proximity to James S. Draper's home.[7] The Wayland railroad station, begun in late August and completed in late September,[8] was the scene also of a celebration. When the train arrived in Hudson, there were the usual ceremonies with a brass band and a banquet at the town hall.

As soon as the Massachusetts Central Railroad was in operation with its initial four round trips a day from Wayland to Boston, steps were taken to make the service of this line available to Cochituate. Accordingly, William Loker started a coach line from Cochituate to Wayland. The *Natick Citizen* of October 28, 1881, tells us that "the new coach for the Wayland line arrived Tuesday and is greatly admired. It makes four trips daily in connection with the Massachusetts Central Railroad and the fare from this village [Cochituate] to Boston will be 50 cents." The November 4 issue of the same paper announced a special Saturday excursion from Cochituate to Boston with round trip fare of $1.00 to introduce Cochituate residents to the railroad. In April 1882 a theater excursion to Boston for 50 cents round trip was well patronized.

Meanwhile, in addition to using the passenger service, farmers in Wayland Center were able to ship considerable quantities of milk and receive cattle feed via the railroad. An item in the *Natick Bulletin* in 1883 tells us that instead of buying commercial fertilizer Wayland farmers were importing quantities of manure from Boston via the railroad.[9]

Sectionalism Arises

The Wayland Center interests who had fought to get the railroad were hoping—and it did eventually come to pass—that direct access to Wayland by train from Boston would bring summer residents, visitors, and commuters who would build up the town. Just before the line opened, a long article about the scenic and historic attractions of Wayland had appeared in the *Boston Advertiser* of October 5, 1881, surely inspired if not actually written by James S. Draper. This article was copied in the *Natick Bulletin* of October 7, and ends with the following statement:

A visit to this now quiet place is worth all the effort any one may make to reach it, and its record book of late years shows a growing appreciation of its attractions. Truly a new era of life has opened to those beautiful regions through the advent of the new railroad, not only to scatter blessings to the people here, but to invite thousands yearly to come out from the dusty, noisy city and share them.

Some Wayland citizens had hoped that the railroad would help the north end of the town to develop along industrial lines as Cochituate had. The April 15, 1881, issue of the *Natick Bulletin* carried a brief item reporting that Hodijah B. Braman, who was in the furniture and upholstery business in Boston, was going to start a furniture factory in Wayland. Concerning this prospect, the Cochituate reporter welcomed the arrival of industry in Wayland, since to Cochituate dwellers industry seemed the way to economic betterment and progress. The *Framingham Gazette* of April 15 had a similar notice about Braman's furniture factory. Then its May 13 issue reported that the venture seemed to have fallen through. The article went on to say:

If Mr. Braman should carry into effect this project, it will mark a new era in the manufacturing interests and in the prosperity of the town. Wayland Centre, as is well known, is utterly devoid of manufacturing business and is in every respect an agricultural village with little or no enterprise. Now, as the Massachusetts Central Railroad is sure to be a success, no more valuable field is offered for manufacturers. . . . If Mr. Braman carries this project into effect it will be an initiatory step and it would not be folly to predict for Wayland Centre as rapid and healthy a growth as Cochituate village has enjoyed. The freight facilities . . . are unsurpassed—all around the Centre Village in close proximity to the station are plenty of building sites which are very favorable.

In the spring of 1883 the Massachusetts Central experienced a financial crisis and on May 16 suspended all operations while the property was turned over to trustees of the mortgage bonds.[10] Thus, the railroad ran only nineteen and a half months before closing down for a time. The shutdown lasted twenty-nine months, and on September 28, 1885, the railroad resumed operations through Wayland, having been reorganized as the Central Massachusetts Railroad and an arrangement made to have it operated by the Boston and Lowell Railroad.[11] This time there were seven round trips from Wayland to Boston from Monday through Saturday and one on Sunday. Thousands did not come out from the dusty, noisy city to savor Wayland's rural delights, but by the mid-1880s Wayland Center families were able much more easily to enjoy the cultural resources of Boston. Among the papers given to the Historical Society by descendants of Isaac C. Damon, the well-to-do farmer on Old Sudbury Road, are a number of theater programs which were saved after attending plays in Boston.

It has not been possible to discover how much Cochituate shoe factory freight or express went to or from Boston through the Wayland railroad station. The earlier prediction that most of it would be transferred from Natick did not materialize. After the arrival of the railroad in Wayland, Cochituate shoe-manufacturing interests continued to press for a railroad through or to their village. We have already mentioned that in late 1874 a turnout track for loading freight had been built by the Boston and Albany Railroad on the Saxonville Branch Railroad at Cochituate crossing. Although this did not compare with having a railroad actually in Cochituate, the shoe manufacturers had wanted and had agitated for the turnout.

Much more to be desired, however, was a railroad through the village and really close to the shoe factories. In December 1881 the chief engineer of the Massachusetts Central and a subcontractor went over the route of the survey made when the extension of the Hopkinton Railroad was being proposed. The Massachusetts Central engineer had been persuaded to see if it would be practicable to build a branch from Wayland Center through Cochituate Village and on to the Lakeview Camp Ground in Framingham.[12] It is not known whether financial obstacles or difficult engineering problems were responsible for the fact that nothing was done in this direction during the early 1880s.

In February 1889 the question of a branch railroad from Wayland to Cochituate was discussed in the newspapers.[13] In the July 19, 1889,

Natick Bulletin there appeared a long article describing a meeting at Knights of Labor Hall in Cochituate to try to persuade the Central Massachusetts Railroad to build a branch to Cochituate. At this meeting Myron Bent of the Wm. and J. M. Bent Company made a plea for this railroad and said that if it were built he would take the company teams off the roads and use the railroad exclusively. Nothing came of this effort; perhaps a branch line would have come in the early 1890s if the Bent firm had not got into serious difficulties.

The story of the success (punctuated by temporary failure from 1883 to 1885) of the effort to get a railroad through Wayland, and of the failure ever to get railroad service to Cochituate Village, has been told. It is not known exactly how much lasting bitterness there was about the struggle to finance the railroad and the final location of it through Wayland Center. One can be fairly sure, however, that in 1879 when a man greatly interested in town history and its significance, James Sumner Draper, might have taken the lead in planning a centennial celebration for the town in 1880, Draper was still resentful that the Cochituate shoe manufacturers had made it difficult to get the Massachusetts Central stock paid for by the town.

By the 1890s the existence of frequent commuter trains led to considerable building of village residences at Wayland Center and near the Tower Hill station. The railroad encouraged summer residents such as Edwin Buckingham, Edmund Sears, and Warren G. Roby to make Wayland their home for much longer seasons. The railroad never brought industry to Wayland Center, but the dream that it would do so flourished for some time. In one of the fairly rare columns on Wayland, as opposed to the regular columns on Cochituate, the *Natick Bulletin* of March 30, 1888, said: "It is hoped that the new low price of land and the excellent railroad facilities will induce some manufacturers to locate in our midst."

In 1887 a turntable south of the track and west of the Wayland railroad station was being completed to enable engines to turn around so that there could be eleven trains each way to Boston. A water tank was also being built near the turntable north of the track to provide Mill Pond water for the engines.[14] When Wayland became a terminus for some of the trains, railroad employees became residents of Wayland Center, and some participated in town affairs. Thomas F. Mahoney, who was a selectman of Wayland in 1908, 1909, 1910, and 1912, was an engineer on the railroad.

Wayland was the terminus or a stop on local, daytime commuter trains, but the single track was used also for freight and at night for a link in a through northeastern railroad system. For a short time in the 1890s the Central Massachusetts track was used for trains from Pennsylvania and Washington to the south and to Boston and Bar Harbor, Maine, to the north. This came about when a bridge was finished in 1890 over the Hudson River at Poughkeepsie, New York, making it possible to avoid New York City. As late as the mid-twentieth century, people in town remembered the long-distance trains rumbling through Wayland in the night. These trains did not stop in Wayland, but some stopped in South Sudbury and Waltham.

Town Hall

Returning to the subject of sectional tensions of the 1870s, we find in the town report for the year 1876-77, the first printed and distributed by the town, that the selectmen's report commented that a general town caucus for the nomination of officers had been supported by men of both political parties and that each section of the town had "clearly established as a fact the general interest and desire of the people for the healing of all sectional differences." The selectmen of that year—Luther H. Sherman, Thomas Jefferson Damon, and Abel Gleason—men known for their ability to get along with others, were hoping that the two parts of the town could live happily together.

In 1877 there was a move to obtain a water supply for Cochituate. How this worked out has been described above. We have not yet mentioned that at the town meeting of October 5, 1877, which considered the proposal to secure a supply of water for Cochituate Village, the next article in the warrant was "to see if the town will erect a new building in the central part of the town with accommodations for town meetings, town offices, and the public library at expense not more than $10,000." The juxtaposition of the two articles providing major facilities for the town was no coincidence. In return for getting a water supply for themselves, the citizens of Cochituate, who could now outvote those of Wayland, were willing to trade off and allow the town to build a new town hall at Wayland Center. It will be noted that the town hall article was carefully worded to propose a new building *in the central part of the town*. The cost of this building did not equal that of the Cochituate water supply and fire department, but the prospective expenditure on the stock of the Massachusetts Central Railroad counterbalanced that.

The 1841 town house (now Collins Market) had never been a

completely satisfactory building to house town offices, a town meeting hall, and the library. By 1858 an attempt to run a high school in the new school building on Cochituate Road[15] had faltered for a time. At a town meeting April 15, 1858—it was voted to sell or tear down the 1841 town house and move the library and town offices to the high school building. However, at a town meeting the next day the vote on the high school building was rescinded by a somewhat narrow margin of 123 to 99 votes. The idea of using the high school building for a town hall and library was brought up again in April 1861 but again failed to pass.

Nothing more happened about the town hall during the Civil War period. Cochituate then had not surpassed Wayland Center in population, although by that time the tight center of Cochituate had become much more of an urban place than the central village of Wayland. In any event, in the warrant for a town meeting on November 2, 1869, there was an article "to see if the town will build a town hall in Cochituate." There was no regular newspaper coverage of Cochituate in that year, and there is no clue to where the town hall might have been built or who proposed that it be in Cochituate. In any case, the article was passed over. At a town meeting on October 2, 1871, the town chose Abel Gleason, Charles H. Campbell, and John C. Butterfield as a committee to examine the town house and report the next March on a plan to enlarge it. On March 4, 1872, a report of a plan for the enlargement of the 1841 building must have been made, because the committee was instructed to ascertain the cost. The town clerk's record contains nothing further on this matter. In the warrant for the April 7 meeting of 1873, however, there was an article to sell the old town house and build a new one. This article was passed over. Later that year the idea of using the hall in the new Cochituate School was brought up, passed over at a town meeting on November 4, then voted down on November 29. The town continued to use as its official town hall (but not as the only meeting place—see Chapter 9) the 1841 town house building. In March 1875 the town voted to make Horace Heard agent to patch the roof of that building.

The 1877 article to build a new town hall at a central location passed, and a committee of five—headed by Hodijah B. Braman of Wayland Center with two other Wayland members, Richard T. Lombard, and Horace Heard, and two Cochituate members, Alfred H. Bryant and Thomas J. Damon—was chosen to purchase land if necessary, dispose of the old building, and see to the construction of a building which with land expense would not exceed $10,000 expendi-

The 1800 Grout-Heard House before it was moved in 1878.

ture by the town. A competition was held for architects to design the building. This was won by George F. Fuller of Malden, who designed the high and imposing building which stood in Wayland Center until 1958. In 1879 the town published a seventy-nine-page pamphlet, entitled *Proceedings at the Dedication of the Town Hall, Wayland, December 24, 1878 with Brief Historical Sketches of Public Buildings and Libraries.* In addition to printing the lengthy speeches made at the ceremony and the historical sketches written by James S. Draper, the pamphlet tells about the building committee, choice of architect, builder, and so forth. When the building was well under way but not yet finished and dedicated, an 850-word article about this building, with careful descriptions of both exterior and interior, was published in the *Framingham Gazette* of October 11, 1878. For once a town building project was well documented.

The December 7, 1877, issue of the *Framingham Gazette* reported that the committee of five had decided on the site of the 1841 town house and would enlarge the lot to the north and to the west. No newspaper comment or report states how it came about that the mid-eighteenth-century Grout-Heard house, built in enlarged form in about 1800 across the street from the 1841 town house, came to be moved to a location on the west side of Old Sudbury Road so that the town hall could be built on its slightly higher land where there would be more room for what was hoped would be an imposing structure. The *Framingham Gazette* article simply reports that the "site finally decided upon . . . was about an acre of land located within one-fourth mile of the exact center of the town and within a few rods of the roadbed of The Massachusetts Central Railroad, it being known as the 'Grout Estate.' " Expenditure accounts for the town hall do not show that town money was spent to move the house. It may have been that with the prospect of the railroad station and track nearby, the widow Sarah Heard was glad to move her house to a quieter location. It seems certain that Hodijah Braman, chairman of the town hall committee, saw to it that Mrs. Heard was able to buy a parcel of land near his property for a favorable price.[16]

There are many now in town who remember the 1878 town hall in its later years when it was painted white and housed the Wayland fire department at the north rear. In October 1878 when the building was near completion a press release must have gone out, because both the long *Framingham Gazette* article of October 11, 1878, and the *Natick Bulletin* of the same date describe it as "an odd-shaped structure, beautiful in design and in style bordering on that adopted by the Swiss people." The *Framingham Gazette* described the building as painted in the style of the day, "a grayish shade with chocolate-colored trimmings and brackets under the projecting roof." "Town Hall" in gilt letters was placed over the main entrance and "Library" over the porticoed entrance on the south side of the building. In 1962 the Heard House was returned to this site. Newcomers to the town have wondered why there are two sets of wide granite steps leading to this building. The northerly steps led to the town hall, the southerly steps to the library.

In the town hall part of the building the main hall was up a double flight of stairs, measured 48 by 58 feet, and had a seating capacity of five hundred. It had a rostrum and a balcony called an orchestra gallery. This room was heated by airtight wood stoves and lighted by gas fixtures on the walls. The two library rooms—a reception room with bookcases and desk, and the reading room—were on the first floor, as were about six rooms for the selectmen, town clerk, town treasurer, assessors, a place for lawbooks, and a vault.

Everyone seemed impressed with this building and with the amount and quality of building for the money spent. When its imposing mass was taking shape, a Wayland columnist wrote for the August 30 issue of the *Framingham Gazette*: "The handsomest structure in

The 1878 Town Hall and Library.

these parts is the near completed Town Hall edifice which has a very commanding appearance as it towers 90 feet in height overlooking the village."

The dedication exercises for this building took place the day before Christmas 1878 in what the *Natick Bulletin* described as "blustery weather."[17] After music by the Cochituate Brass Band, James S. Draper, President of the Day, made an introductory speech in which he said that both the waterworks and the town hall were "important, substantial, permanent public works." Following vocal music by a choir, Hodijah B. Braman delivered the keys to Selectman Charles H. Boodey. Then, following band music, there was a dedicatory prayer, more band music, and finally the main address by Elbridge Smith, then principal of the Dorchester High School but a Wayland native. His address was very long; one wonders today how people sat through it. His main theme was praise of the town meeting form of government, and there was quite a bit on education and American history. In his address Smith made the only reference to the town's centennial which this writer has been able to find when he said: "On the eve of your first centennial, ninety-nine years since your separate existence began, you throw open for public convenience these ample apartments."[18]

There are several reasons why James Sumner Draper was chosen as President of the Day. The new building housed the library with which he had been heavily involved. He was an articulate speaker and practiced writer and seems to have enjoyed ceremonies. By working hard to bring the railroad through Wayland Center he had shown that the welfare and sustained prosperity of Wayland were of importance to him. He wanted the building that was to house the seat of town government as well as the public library to be located in Wayland Center, and his wish had been realized. It is quite clear that he did not want Cochituate to supersede Wayland Center as the principal place in the town. He may well have worded the warrant article that said that the new town hall must be centrally located. As the conditions he put on a later gift to the library showed, he wanted to ensure that such institutions as the Wayland Public Library would never move to Cochituate.[19]

It is not known how many Cochituate citizens attended the dedication of the town hall. The *Natick Bulletin* correspondent reported on December 27, 1878, that the building was "most attractive" and commented on portraits of distinguished men on the walls of the library and the plenitude of rooms for town officials, with one room even for a janitor. Other impressive features were the wide stairways and the well-lighted hall with its gas fixtures.

Nine years later, in December 1887, the Cochituate correspondent of the *Natick Bulletin*, in a petulant mood because it seemed as if Cochituate might not be able to get much-needed streetlights, wrote the following:

Any project looking to such an improvement here would meet with opposition from the Centre and farming districts which, receiving some support from the village, would prevent the placing of lights at this part of the town although there are votes enough here to accomplish some improvements. Whenever they have been made it has been accomplished by giving the Centre an equivalent; thus for the water works the Centre got the town house. The water works provides a source of revenue to the town; the town house does not therefore the Centre has gained by obtaining a large, costly and ornamental building at the expense of the outlying districts. What will be demanded if Cochituate wishes for street lights it is not known, but the coming spring will be likely to develop the wants of the Centre. . . . If Cochituate demands street lights and if there is any chance to swap well as the horse trader's parlance goes, Cochituate will not remain long in darkness after the annual town meeting.

NOTES

1. Wellesley College, then being built.
2. *Wayland Record*, Town Meeting November 29, 1873, Article 4.
3. *Natick Citizen*, February 20, 1885.
4. Alfred Sereno Hudson, *The Annals of Sudbury, Wayland and Maynard*, "Appendix to Annals of Wayland," p. 132.
5. The Plains area, home of the Drapers, was to be known as "Tower Hill" after the railroad came through.
6. *Waltham Free Press*, October 7, 1881.
7. The Tower Hill railroad station was not built until 1885. Because of its proximity to the Draper houses, this station was, according to *The Central Mass.*, more expensively built with clapboard exterior rather than the board and batten on the Wayland station. It also had more gingerbread ornamentation.
8. *Framingham Gazette*, August 26, 1881.
9. *Natick Bulletin*, February 23, 1883.
10. Historical Society of the Boston and Maine Railroad, *The Central Mass.*, p. 12.
11. *Ibid*, p. 13.
12. *Framingham Gazette*, December 30, 1881.
13. *Natick Bulletin*, February 8, 1889.
14. *Ibid*, December 30, 1887.
15. Building owned by the Pequod Lodge of Odd Fellows from 1896 until 1979 when sold to the Trinitarian Congregational Church.
16. South Middlesex Deeds, Book 1469, p. 578, *Mary A. Ward to Sarah E. Heard.*
17. *Natick Bulletin*, December 27, 1878.
18. Town of Wayland, *Proceedings at the Dedication of the Town Hall*, 1879, p. 13.
19. See Article 6 of Town Meeting of March 26, 1894 when the town accepted a $500 gift from James S. Draper for the purchase of new books with the proviso that this fund would not continue if the library should be removed from its present location in the central village.

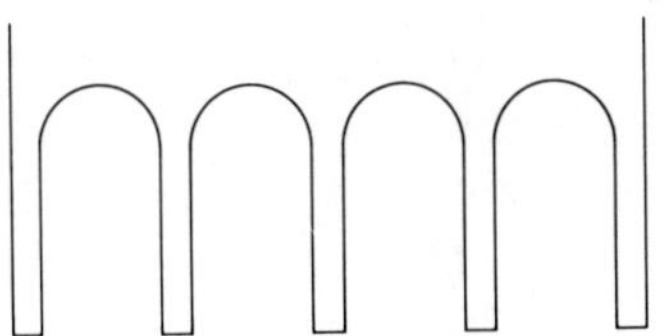

Town Government in 1880

Town Officers

HAVING DESCRIBED the 1878 town hall, the home of the town government, let us next examine the governmental arrangements of the town in 1880 when Wayland had been a separate municipality for one hundred years. Whereas in 1780 the annual spring town meeting had elected five selectmen, in 1880 there were three selectmen, this having been the number elected each year since 1833.

Considerable attention was given in Part I to the makeup of East Sudbury's first board of selectmen, who were the prominent and able leaders of the new town. These men had been nominated on the town meeting floor. By 1880 the important officers of the town were elected by ballot[1] at the beginning of a 10:00 A.M. Monday town meeting in Schoolhouse Hall on the second floor of the Cochituate School on March 1. The men elected as selectmen were Charles H. Boodey and William Hammond from Cochituate and Theodore S. Sherman of Wayland Center. Of the three, only Charles H. Boodey was a man of outstanding ability and leadership, but he had lived in Wayland (the Cochituate part) just under five years. As the nineteenth century progressed, in Wayland as in other Massachusetts towns, the position of selectman had become somewhat less prestigious, but, more significant in terms of change, men sought the job or were nominated because of their ability to be elected, sometimes to represent a section, a faction, a group, or a powerful man, rather than for their own general leadership capacity. No longer was it customary or necessary to choose selectmen from the leading landed property owners, from "old families," or from men who had demonstrated that they could be outstanding leaders by climbing up the ladder of officialdom. Ability to be elected—that is, political weight—and willingness to take office were now the controlling factors.

Charles Hayes Boodey was a bachelor of forty-two in 1880. He had come to Cochituate in 1875, and two years later, in 1877, had been elected selectman. He was to serve Wayland as selectman for eleven consecutive years, 1877-88—a remarkable span of office in the history of the town up to that time. The only man who had served Wayland longer as a selectman was Deacon William Johnson (1775-1828), who was elected selectman sixteen times between 1802 and 1826, the first eight years being consecutive, from 1802 to 1809. William Johnson was a third-generation Sudbury-East Sudbury resident, and his mother was a Rice. He had been a justice of the peace and a deacon of the church. He filled the office of selectman as a part of his position of leadership in the town. Others who had served as selectmen numerous times were Jotham Bullard, with nine terms between 1813 and 1840; and with eight terms each, Richard Heard, Jr., between 1825 and 1847, William C. Grout between 1831 and 1866, and James D. Walker between 1850 and 1873. Of these, Jotham Bullard had been born in Holliston and in 1802 was a newcomer to East Sudbury, where he became a successful farmer. Another newcomer was James D. Walker, born in Milton, who was married in Wayland in 1837 and settled down to farm on upper Glezen Lane. These two men did not have ancestral roots in the town. On the other hand, Richard Heard, Jr., and William C. Grout were descendants of earlier town leaders.

Dr. Boodey was born in New Durham, New Hampshire, in 1838. He studied medicine and graduated from Bowdoin College in Maine. His father was superintendent of the almshouse in Watertown, Massachusetts, in the 1860s and 1870s, and after graduating from Bowdoin, Charles read law and was admitted to the Middlesex County bar. Having done this (good preparation for government service in his town), he decided he preferred medicine, so in the early 1870s he studied with a doctor in New Hampshire, then practiced medicine briefly in Vermont before coming at the age of thirty-seven to the rapidly growing community of Cochituate.[2]

His first office was on the east side of Main Street. An 1877 newspaper account says that he was living in an apartment in Gerald's building, which was then also on the east side of Main Street. In 1880 he had an apartment in Gilbert Bent's house. He never married but in 1888 he finally acquired the Otis Lyon house where he had been living for a time.[3] This house, built in 1849, is still standing at 136 Commonwealth Road and is owned by a descendant of Dr. Boodey's niece.

The only doctor in town was bound to be a well-known person, and Boodey was immediately liked and respected. In 1878 the hook and ladder company of the Cochituate fire department was named for him. He had fine rapport with the people, and in six of the years he served as selectman he was also elected moderator of the annual town meeting. After retiring from the board of selectmen he served for twelve years on the school committee and in 1890 and 1891 as representative to the General Court. It is likely that this man's quick rise to importance in Wayland governmental affairs was backed by James Madison Bent. Boodey died in 1902. He had been an important figure in Wayland for twenty-seven years. The *Natick Bulletin* of October 3, 1902, reported that businesses and the schools in Cochituate and Wayland were closed on the day of his funeral.

William Hammond, Jr., often called "Billy" Hammond, who was the other Cochituate selectman, was born in Sudbury in 1825 and came to Cochituate as a young child in 1828 or earlier. He was a member of the branch of the Hammond family of Newton, which had settled on the edge of Natick and Sudbury around 1760. Hammond's parents may have come to live on what is now West Plain Street near Main in the late 1820s because William Hammond, Sr.'s, wife, Cynthia (Coolidge) Hammond, was a sister of Polly Coolidge who had married William Bent, the father of the two Bent brothers who started the shoe-manufacturing company. At the time of the census of 1880 Billy Hammond was a widower and was called a farmer. However, he had also been one of the early shoemakers in Cochituate. In Volume I of Wayland's personal mortgage records we find him in December 1850, then twenty-five years old, borrowing (as "William Hammond Jr., cordwainer") $25 from John L. Loker, giving as security "a certain shoemaker's shop now occupied by me and situated about two or three rods east of the dwelling house where my father resides."[4] He was still engaged in shoe manufacturing on a small scale in 1886 and was connected with shoe manufacturer Noble Griffin in 1887. He had served as selectman in 1869 and 1870 and from 1877 through 1880. He was well connected in Cochituate; he knew the shoe industry and its problems; and he was a first cousin of James Madison Bent, the leading shoe manufacturer of the town. When he died on March 3,

1904, his obituary in the *Natick Bulletin* of April 8 remarked that in earlier years he had been a familiar figure near Lyons Corner sitting under a very large elm tree in front of his shoeshop.

Theodore Samuel Sherman, the Wayland Center selectman of 1880, was also born in Sudbury and in 1880 was concerned with shoes as the owner of a retail shoestore where Pelham Island Road crosses the Boston Post Road at the center of Wayland Village. He came to Wayland as a young man. It is not known where he received his training as a shoemaker, but the censuses of 1855 and 1860 show him as a shoemaker living in the center of Wayland next to or near Ira Draper, for whom he probably worked. He apparently left Wayland for a time but returned in the 1870s. He was related to the Shermans, who were large landholders in North Wayland, but did not himself own substantial farmland. In 1883 he was taxed on six and three-quarters acres of land, enough on which to pasture his two cows and one horse.

Sherman was elected for the first time as selectman in 1880 after Sylvester Reeves had died in office; he continued with Boodey and William Harrison Bent as selectman from 1881 through 1887. In 1888 he was elected once more to serve with James Alvin Bent and Henry W. Butler. In later years, nearly till his death in 1921, he served in lesser town offices. He was not a prominent or powerful man, but he apparently liked town service and must have been backed for selectman by such important men in Wayland Center as Horace Heard, Hodijah Braman, and James Sumner Draper. He also must have been able to work with the town clerk and treasurer, both Wayland Center men, to hold up the north part of the town's end of things. Theodore S. Sherman can be characterized as the first of a series of selectmen from the north end of the town who were village tradesmen or worker-artisans. They inevitably must have acted as agents for the old-line, more well to do property holders, mostly farmers, dirt or gentleman, who predominated in this part of the town.

It has been pointed out that two of the three selectmen elected in 1880 were from Cochituate Village. Before Bentville or Cochituate became a recognized village in the mid-1840s, there had been a few occasions when a selectman of the town came from the southern end. Isaac Damon, who served as selectman in 1838 had been the only one since Artemas Bond ten years earlier; but, with the southern village growing, its prominent residents came to be recognized and to seek political office. In 1844 and 1845 Henry Coggin of Bentville served as selectman, James M. Bent in 1846 and 1847, and Charles R. Damon in

1848 and 1849. There was no selectman from the south end of the town in 1850, but thereafter, with the exception of 1864 when all were from the northern end of the town, one of the three selectmen was from Cochituate. Coggin, Bent, and Damon were from old families in the area. By the late 1860s and early 1870s such men as Thomas Bryant, Alfred H. Bryant, Albert B. Lyon, and Henry Colburn Dean, of new families to the town and connected with the shoe industry, were serving.

In 1871 when Albert B. Lyon and Alfred H. Bryant were elected to serve with a northend Waylander, Luther H. Sherman, Cochituate began to have two selectmen on the three-man board. And, except for the years of 1877 and 1900 when all three selectmen were from Cochituate, this practice continued until 1902 when a system of having one selectman from Cochituate with two from Wayland again began to prevail. In the 1880s and 1890s it seemed to be a matter of great importance to the self-assertive and self-conscious element in Cochituate that at least two selectmen were from their part of town. Following the town election in March 1892, the Cochituate column in the *Natick Review* reported that Llewellyn Flanders and Edwin W. Marston, both residents of Cochituate, and Thomas W. Frost, resident of Wayland, had been elected selectmen for 1892-93. After giving these and other election results, the newspaper appended the following poem:

The battle's o'er, 'tis won at last
'Tis Thomas, Ed and Lew
Wayland has but only one,
While we have got the two.

We always scoop up all the cake
For Wayland's almost lost.
She had to bustle, scrape and rake
To get her "only Frost."[5]

In discussing the upcoming town election in February 1896, the Cochituate reporter of the *Natick Bulletin* stated that Cochituate had two thirds of the population and should have two selectmen.[6]

From the mid-1870s on, especially in the period when the Bent family was of preeminent importance in Cochituate, the balance of power between Cochituate and Wayland was a matter of apprehension in Wayland and of aggressive pride in Cochituate. Joseph A. Roby made this plain in the *Framingham Gazette* of October 28, 1874, when he reported on the nomination at the Republican caucus of William Harrison Bent for representative of Wayland and its district to the General Court. W. H. Bent had lost this nomination to Horace Heard three years earlier. Roby wrote:

The Cochituate band came down and discoursed sweet music to the astonishment of the natives. The evening was just the most heavenly magnificent ever before known . . . and the Bents went back to their wigwams grinning with ecstacy of unalterable pride, the band playing Hail Columby and Glory Halleluyah till out of sight and out of hearing and quiet and the usual graveyard silence settled down for the next six months on Wayland Centre, broken only by the sighs and sobs of the disappointed aspirants for legislative honors. But the old bachelors of Wayland Centre can now meditate on the political power of a shoe shop that can turn out one hundred voters.

Two years later, writing for the *Waltham Free Press*, Joseph A. Roby made the following remarks about Cochituate's capacity to outvote Wayland when he wrote about the introduction at the town meeting of the idea that a water supply be built for Cochituate. In April 1876 Roby said, "Nothing definite has as yet transpired, but the subject is before the town and as the 'Broganites' have a large majority of voters, the rest of the town must come under the yoke."[7]

Membership on Wayland's board of selectman changed frequently, with a three-year incumbency, not necessarily in consecutive years, being average. During the one hundred years from 1780 to 1880, 110 different men filled 310 slots in the five- or three-man annually elected boards of selectmen. In this time 29 men had held the office of selectman for just one year and 24 men for two years. Eight men of the Heard family had served, as had 7 Reeveses, 7 Shermans, 6 Gleasons, and 5 Johnsons and Rices.

As town clerk in 1880 Wayland had Henry Wight (1820-86), who had served in this capacity from 1851 through 1870. Then, after a short term for Joseph A. Roby, Wight held the office again in 1874, continuing for another ten years, which gave him the record incumbency of twenty-nine years. Henry Wight was the son of the Reverend John Burt Wight who came to Wayland from Rhode Island as minister of the town church in 1815 and eventually led the parish into Unitarianism. Henry's mother was a native of Wayland. Wight never served as a selectman, but in addition to being town clerk for twenty-nine years, he served as town treasurer for nineteen years concurrently with being town clerk. The town clerk's job was a key one in the nineteenth century and earlier, and the holder of the office was important in running the town. Not only did he record the town business, including elections, but he was responsible for running the town meeting, and he coordinated the work of the selectmen and other officers and committees. Furthermore, because he served for a long span of years, he brought continuity to the governmental process. Henry Wight was only the fifth town clerk Wayland had had in one hundred years, his predecessors having been Joseph Curtis, Nathaniel Reeves, Jacob Reeves, and William C. Grout.

None of these men was from the south end of the town. Henry Wight was followed as town clerk by Richard T. Lombard in 1884 and he by Daniel Brackett in 1900. It should be noted that, although adequately represented on the board of selectmen, Cochituate did not provide a town clerk until Warren L. Bishop took office in 1914. One senses the honor it was felt that Cochituate had attained when one reads Bishop's first report as town clerk. A Cochituate citizen, Frank E. Yeager, had become town treasurer in 1903.

The moderator of the annual town meeting was another important position in the town government. James M. Bent had the position in 1857, but with this exception, until 1870, the moderators, all of them men who had served or were to serve as selectmen, were from Wayland Center. In 1870 Lafayette Dudley of Cochituate was elected moderator of the annual town meeting, and he, Charles Boodey, and Lafayette Dudley's son Henry G. Dudley, all from Cochituate, were annual meeting moderators more often than were William C. Grout, Edward A. Pierce, and Hodijah Braman, residents of Wayland Center who also served in this capacity in the decades of the 1870s, 1880s, and 1890s.

Town Meetings

In 1780 and for thirty-five years to come all East Sudbury town meetings took place in the meetinghouse in Wayland Center on the corner of what now is Cochituate and Pelham Island roads. When the new meetinghouse was built in 1814 and dedicated in January 1815, it was decided that future town meetings would be held in a municipal hall rather than in the church. Therefore the town contracted with Jonathan F. Heard and Luther Gleason to move, alter, and rebuild the

1726 meetinghouse on a piece of land on the Boston Post Road east of the new meetinghouse. Town meetings were held in a hall on the second floor of the building, which also contained a store and a dwelling. This building, known for years as "the old green store," was bought in 1888 by Willard Bullard and remodeled into a handsome house known as Kirkside, now standing at 225 Boston Post Road. The large upstairs room in which town meetings took place for twenty-five years is still intact in that house.

In 1841 town meetings were moved to the columned Greek Revival building on Cochituate Road. This building was constructed for the town in 1841 by Deacon James Draper with a meeting room upstairs and schoolrooms downstairs. It is not possible to determine from the town clerk's record when in 1841 or 1842 the first town meeting took place here. All town meetings were held in this building until 1871. Then, at a special town meeting on September 16, an article proposed to alternate the location of town meetings between Wayland Center and Cochituate. This article passed, and it was voted that the next meeting be held in Cochituate. Accordingly, the town meeting of November 7, 1871, was held in the vestry of the Methodist Episcopal Church. All were not satisfied with this arrangement, and at this meeting, under an article about enlarging the town hall, a committee was chosen to look into that possibility. The 1841 town hall was becoming crowded, but at issue also was whether it was fair that the voters of Cochituate Village always be obliged to travel the three miles to town meetings in Wayland.

The annual town meeting of 1872 was held in the town hall at Wayland Center on March 4; the next meeting, called for November 5, was held in Cochituate at the church vestry. Then, at a town meeting on November 30 it was voted to rescind the vote to alternate town meetings. Thus, the first meeting in 1873, the annual meeting of March 3, was again located at the Wayland Center town hall. However, at this time an article was passed which called again for alternating town meetings if the vestry of the Methodist Episcopal Church could be hired for five dollars. Thus, in this busy and contentious year with ten town meetings, five meetings were held in the town hall and five at the church vestry in Cochituate.

With the new Cochituate School building finished in October 1873, it was not surprising that at the town meeting of November 4 (held at the church in Cochituate) there was an article to see if the town would use the upstairs hall in the new schoolhouse for town meetings. The article was passed over. At a meeting three weeks later the same article was introduced and was voted down. At a December 15 town meeting, however, it was voted to use the large room on the second floor of the new school for town meetings until it was needed for school purposes. This upstairs room had been built to house a grammar school, more or less equivalent to the level of a modern junior high school education.

The first town meeting held in the Cochituate School took place on January 22, 1874, in what the warrant called Village Hall. The warrant for the next meeting held here, that of February 28, 1874, called it Schoolhouse Hall, a name used for this hall during the mid-1870s when it served not only for town meetings but for entertainments and meetings of civic organizations in Cochituate. The 1875 and 1876 town meetings alternated at the two places. By 1877 in the minds of some Schoolhouse Hall had become a second town hall. The warrant for the town meeting of April 17, 1877, was ordered placed "at each of the post offices and town houses."

We have already mentioned the vote of October 5, 1877, to erect a new town hall "in the central part of the town," and we have described the resulting building. However, even when this building with its meeting room with a capacity of five hundred or more was finished in the fall of 1878, town meetings continued to alternate between Wayland Center and Cochituate until the annual meeting of 1882, held on March 6. At this time Article 7, "to see if the town will instruct the selectmen to call all town meetings in the center of Wayland until otherwise ordered," was voted in the affirmative.

Two Voting Precincts

From 1882 through 1892 all town meetings were held at the new town hall on the east side of Cochituate Road across from the railroad station. In June 1893 a town meeting took place at which the question was brought up as to whether to accept an 1890 Massachusetts law enabling towns to divide themselves into voting precincts.[8] This article was accepted, and the selectmen were charged with carrying out such a division. This matter may have been brought up at this particular time because it would accommodate Cochituate, and in the warrant for this same town meeting there was an article about remodeling the high school building at Wayland Center. This could have been a trade-off between the two ends of the town, but no newspaper or comment in any other source about trade-off has been found. It did, however, inaugurate a drive for a better school in Wayland Center, which inevitably aroused much sectional feeling. The Wayland Center school building will be discussed later.

At a town meeting held on July 8, 1893, the selectmen brought in a proposal to make two voting precincts, and their plan was accepted. The selectmen drew the line between the precincts exactly where the south boundary of Sudbury had run before the addition of the land of the twelve Natick farmers to the town in 1721. The much larger but less densely populated land north of the line was designated as the First Precinct; that south of the line, the Second Precinct. At the time this division was made, there were 141 voters in the First Precinct and 259 in the Second Precinct. One wonders why this uneven division was made unless to segregate Cochituate from those who considered that they lived in Wayland. Perhaps this was the only acceptable division line. There seems to have been no discussion of this aspect of the precinct division in the newspapers.

This precinct division of July 1893 applied only to state, county, and federal elections. The first separate elections took place on November 7, 1893, with Precinct 1 voting in the town hall and Precinct 2 at the enginehouse in Cochituate Village. It is not surprising that at this election 82.9 percent of the Precinct 1 voters cast ballots while 89.2 percent of the Cochituate voters came to the polls. Distances from the polling place in the Wayland end of the town were much greater. Cochituate was densely populated, and no one lived too far from the firehouse on Harrison Street. In the years to come Cochituate voters were inspired to and found it convenient to turn out in greater strength relative to their registration than did the voters in Precinct 1. Voting in spring town elections was not divided between the precincts until 1908. When this happened, the election had to be held separately from the town meeting, and voting was scheduled for two days ahead.

Very soon after the town was divided into voting precincts and the Cochituate voters no longer had to travel to Wayland Center to cast their votes for governors and presidents, the Cochituate reporters of the *Natick Bulletin* started advocating a return to alternating the town meeting between Wayland and Cochituate. The *Natick Bulletin* of October 13, 1893, said that now that there were two voting precincts there should be a similar provision to facilitate town meeting participation by Cochituate citizens. To this end, the newspaper strongly advocated holding town meetings alternately in Wayland Center and in Cochituate.

Nothing happened immediately, but in 1894 the town was divided on the question of a major expenditure for a new school in Wayland Center. Most voters in Cochituate were opposed to spending a substantial sum on a school at Wayland Center. In order to oppose the school they had to go in large numbers to the town meetings at which the school expenditure was proposed. At a meeting held on June 6 an article was passed providing that all special town meetings be held in Cochituate Village. Thus it was that the town meeting of July 18, 1894, was held in Knights of Labor Hall. Moreover, this meeting was held at 7:00 P.M. to make it possible for the factory workers in Cochituate to attend. In 1895 three town meetings were held in Knights of Labor Hall at Lyons Corner in Cochituate, the time of meeting two o'clock. In 1896 a special town meeting in April was held at Knights of Labor Hall; another on September 4 was held in the enginehouse in Cochituate. Three 1897 town meetings were held in Cochituate in Knights of Labor Hall, two at Engine House Hall. In April of both 1899 and 1900 a town meeting was held in Knights of Labor Hall. Thereafter all town meetings were held in the town hall in Wayland Center. As soon as the trolley car was available to take Cochituate voters to town meetings in Wayland Center, the pressure to have town meetings in Cochituate ceased to exist, and none was held there after April 16, 1900. To accommodate the Cochituate voters all town meetings except the annual March one, which was an all-day affair, were called for 7:45 P.M.

During the last three decades of the nineteenth century in numbers of selectmen and the alternating location of town meetings Cochituate managed to assert its importance in the governmental process. The precinct division of 1893 with the line following the pre-1721 south boundary of Sudbury gave more votes to a much smaller area of the town. Until the shoe industry died out and settlement patterns changed in the twentieth century this imbalance remained and perpetuated the dualism of the town. For those thirty years and well into the twentieth century Wayland Center had a struggle to maintain its status.

As we shall see in Chapter 17, Lydia Maria Child made fun of the supposedly imposing structure built as the 1878 town hall. She perhaps did not realize that by symbols, by the weight of much earlier traditions, and by great effort to stay in control, the northern or rather the central village managed to continue to dominate the government unless some very important issue for Cochituate people forced the south part of the town to organize and throw its weight in the town meeting. The financial balance between the two ends of the town was also important, as we shall see in the next two chapters.

NOTES

1. The practice of electing the top officers by ballot was begun at the town meeting of March 6, 1871.
2. Biographical Review, Vol XXVII *Sketches of Leading Citizens of Middlesex County, Massachusetts*, Boston, 1898, p. 650.
3. *Natick Bulletin*, July 13, 1888.
4. Town of Wayland, *Mortgage Book I, 1840-1859*, page 113.
5. *Natick Review*, March 31, 1892.
6. *Natick Bulletin*, February 21, 1896.
7. *Waltham Free Press*, April 21, 1876.
8. *Massachusetts Laws of 1890*, Section 72 of Chapter 423.

10

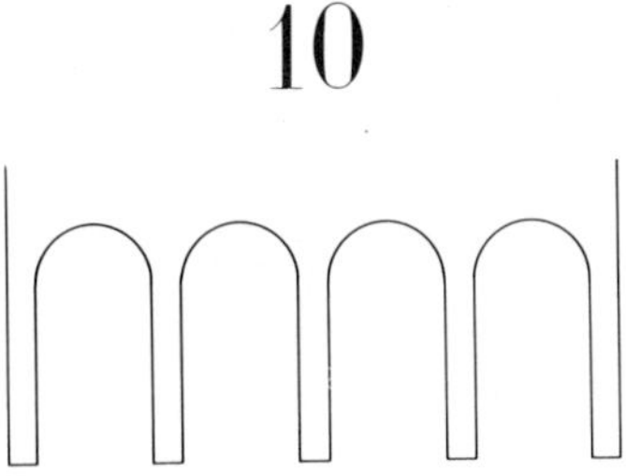

Town Expenses and Income

WITH A POPULATION slightly over two and half times that of one hundred years before, and the existence of a generally higher standard of living, not to mention a changed price level, the level of the town's expenditures was far greater in 1880 than it had been in 1780, and these expenditures covered more services. It is difficult to make a direct comparison between the town's 1780 disbursements and those of 1880. In 1780 there were heavy Revolutionary War expenses, and costs were quoted both in silver-based pounds, shillings, and pence and in the inflated currency of 1780. Other than for the war effort, the chief 1780 expenditures were for schools, for highways, and bridges, as well as for the minister's salary.

The fifth in the series of *Official Reports of the Town of Wayland* covers the year February 1, 1880, to February 1, 1881, and is designated as the report for Wayland's 101st municipal year. It is difficult to reconcile exactly the treasurer's figures in this document with the auditor's report, but this need not concern us. The report indicates expenditures by the town for town purposes of $16,310 for the fiscal year ending February 1, 1881. This was an expenditure per capita of $8.31, low indeed compared with the level of present-day municipal expenditures even after correcting for changes in the price level. The accompanying table gives 1880 town appropriations for broad categories and actual expenditures for those purposes as derived from the auditor's report.

	Appropriation	Expenditure
Schools	$ 4,000	$ 4,437
Highways and Bridges[1]	1,500	1,687
Support of Poor	500	952
Salaries of Town Officers	700	576
Library	300	564
Fire Department	200	507
Town Halls[2]	150	472
Lock-Up	—	40
Water Works	300[3]	952[4]
Cemeteries	100	145
Tax Abatements	232	341
Incidentals	500	519
Interest on Town Debt[5]	4,500	6,143
Collection of Taxes	415	225
Total	$13,397	$17,560

1. Includes separate appropriation for repairs to Bridle Point Bridge.
2. Includes expenses of Schoolhouse Hall in Cochituate School.
3. Maintenance only.
4. Includes $500 to sinking fund.
5. Does not include water department debt.

Expenditures closely followed assessments to a large extent, but in a few cases (as with the library where dog licenses were used for partial support and where in 1880 there was a transfer from contingent funds) expenditures differed substantially from appropriations.

Debt

For the year 1880-81 interest on the town debt amounted to 34.5 percent of the town's expenditures. A sizable town debt had been incurred in the 1870s in order to build the Cochituate School, the town hall, and the waterworks, as well as for other purposes, such as the establishment of the Lakeview Cemetery and to subscribe to the stock of the railroad.

Schools

Of the direct expenditures for services and facilities, schools topped the list, amounting in appropriation to $4,000 and to $4,437 in actual expenditure. This provided ten schoolrooms, each with one teacher. These classrooms accommodated in all between 310 and 339 pupils, depending on whether it was the spring, fall, or winter eleven-week term. At this time the fall term began early in September and ran until the third week of November when there was a vacation of one to two weeks, based on Thanksgiving, which up to the early 1880s was a more important holiday than Christmas.[1] The winter terms ran from sometime in December to the end of February. March was largely a vacation month, probably because of the muddiness of the roads. The spring term began in early April. In 1880 schools and businesses were still observing the old New England holiday of Fast Day as proclaimed by the governor annually for the first Thursday of April.

Of the 332 scholars in the fall term, 214 were in five schoolrooms in the south part of the town and 118 in five rooms in the north part of the town. In the south part there were three primary rooms or "schools," as they were called, the two in the Cochituate School building having enrolled 63 and 42 pupils, respectively, a crowded situation which the school committee report of that year emphasized was very difficult, requiring the addition of at least one more schoolroom if not two. By 1885 Miss Lizzie Moore's primary schoolroom at the Cochituate School had grown to 75 students, at which point it was divided in the spring term into two primary "schools."[2]

The two primary schools were taught by women who were paid $9.00 a week. In the Cochituate School building there was also an intermediate "school" with 40 pupils. A woman teacher was paid $9.50 a week. There was also a grammar schoolroom with 54 scholars in the spring but 36 in the fall, taught by a man who was paid $18 a week. In addition to the 181 pupils attending school at the Cochituate building, there was one room of primary children at the Lokerville School with from 25 to 33 pupils, depending on the term.

In the north part of the town, a man was paid $18 a week to teach grammar school in the building on Cochituate Road, built in 1855 for a high school. In the one-room schoolhouse on Bow Road there were 27 to 29 pupils under a woman teacher. The three schools in the more outlying districts had varying numbers of primary pupils—around 30 at the Rutter School on the west side of Pinebrook Road with Carrie Lee as teacher, paid $9.00 a week. There were fewer pupils at the Thomas School on Old Connecticut Path West in the building still standing but now remodeled and enlarged into a dwelling house just

The Noyes-Morse House on the Boston Post Road was built prior to the Revolution.

south of the present high school driveway. Seventeen pupils were the maximum here, and the teacher was paid $8.50 a week. At the brick schoolhouse on the west side of Concord Road near Lincoln Road, there was in 1880 a maximum of 10 scholars; Miss Eunice Noyes Morse, their teacher, was paid $8.00 a week.

According to the town auditor's analysis, $3,618 went to the ten teachers; $223 for fuel (cord wood except for coal at the Cochituate School); $176 for janitorial services (usually provided by a farmer who lived near the school); $312 for schoolbooks, furniture, repairs, and incidentals; and $110 for superintendence by the school committee.[3] The per pupil expenditure for schools in this year was about $13.45.

Later in the 1880s classes at the high school level were taught both in Wayland and in Cochituate. The building, now standing at 55 Cochituate Road, used for years as the Odd Fellows Hall, had been built in 1855 as a high school. However, in the 1860s, and 1870s, there being little demand for education at this level, the town did not appropriate funds for a high school. Students wanting a secondary school education went out of town to private academies or to the high schools of Weston, Natick, and later Wellesley. The *Natick Citizen* of

September 8, 1882, noted that six girls from Cochituate were attending the Weston High School at a tuition of $5.00 (probably per term). More will be said below about the consolidation of the school population of the north part of the town in a single new building, the Wayland High and Grammar School, more generally known as the Center School, completed in 1897.

The school squadron list of 1781 shows that one hundred years earlier the town schools were entirely district affairs in one-room wooden buildings which were replaced by brick schoolhouses in the years around 1800. At that time a grammar school prepared the very few scholars who wanted that level of education, all boys, for college. Grammar schoolmasters held sessions in different parts of the town at varying times of the year. There were no special building facilities for this upper level of education. By 1880 the majority of pupils in Wayland attended primary and grammar school. High school did not become universal until the twentieth century.

In 1880 several of the teachers were natives of Wayland—Miss Morse, Miss Lee, Miss Rice—they were probably glad to be employed in their own town. Eunice Morse's home was on the Boston Post Road near the town center in the pre-Revolutionary Noyes-Morse house at number 202, but according to Amanda Baldwin's diary, she found it necessary to board near the North schoolhouse when school was in session.[4] In the 1880s and 1890s columns in the Natick newspapers frequently commented on, and deplored the rapid turnover of, teachers at the Cochituate School. In those years Wayland did not pay its teachers well relative to other towns. Teachers often stayed only a year and in some cases left sooner to take jobs elsewhere at higher pay. The newspaper expressed disappointment when a favorite and successful Cochituate teacher was lured away by higher pay to Revere.

Highways and Bridges

The 1880 appropriation of $1,500 for highways and bridges included $1,350 for routine road and bridge work and a special appropriation of $150 for repairs on the Bridle Point Bridge. This segregation of funds for work on a special bridge had been customary during the town's first century, and also in earlier Sudbury history. Wooden bridges over the Sudbury River required frequent repair, depending on flood and winter ice conditions. At least once a decade one of the bridges seemed to need major rebuilding. In 1880 there were two four-arched stone bridges over the river, the Town Bridge (Old

Bridge), in 1880 beginning to be called Baldwin's Bridge, built of stone in 1848; and Stone's Bridge at the New Bridge location, built in 1857 or 1858. These bridges had been more costly to build but required less frequent repairs than the series of wooden bridges going back to the seventeenth century which they replaced.

The town did not have a superintendent of highways until 1889 when Theodore S. Sherman, then no longer a selectman, was appointed for four successive years. In 1880 work on the highways was paid at the rate of 15 cents an hour for a ten-hour day for a man and an additional 15 cents for his horse if used. A load of gravel for the roads cost from 5 to 10 cents, depending on the size of the load. By 1880 the through east-west roads we now know as Routes 30 and 20 had been in existence for roughly half a century. By that same year residential side streets were being developed in Cochituate, but in the north end of the town the road network was not greatly different from that of 1780. At various times in the nineteenth century the town was sued for damages on inadequately maintained highways. Such a suit occurred in 1879 when John A. Wood, Jr., sued the town for damage on the highway on the Saxonville Road (West Plain Street). The town won this case but in 1880 paid out $156.80 in expenses for defending itself. In February 1880 the selectmen recommended a special appropriation to complete grading this road to Lyons Corner. In 1880 Horatio G. Hammond was paid $18 for 360 loads of gravel at 5 cents apiece, so perhaps the recommendation was carried out, although not under a special appropriation.

The Poor

For 1880-81 the town appropriated $500 for the support of the poor. However, the overseers of the poor—John C. Butterfield and Charles Fairbanks of Cochituate and Luther H. Sherman of North Wayland—reported expenditures of more than $900. This was not due to greatly increased poor needs but mostly to timing of payments and accounting difficulties. At this time the overseers were superintending the operation of a town almshouse or poor farm in a very old house dating to the early eighteenth century, just north of the sharp curve on Rice Road, now the entrance of the Mainstone Farm condominium development. This year the town paid David H. Pierce $275 to be the warden and, with his wife, to be in charge of the almshouse where all persons needing the full support of the town were housed. As of February 1, 1881, there were seven inmates, two more than the previous year. All of the running expenses (food, fuel, etc.) for this establishment were met out of receipts from the sale of produce of the farm, but during this year the overseers of the poor had to spend: (1) nearly $100 to house each of two insane and violent inmates at the Worcester Lunatic Hospital; (2) $20 for the burial of an indigent member of the French community in Cochituate; (3) $53 for professional services to Dr. Boodey; and (4) $53 to purchase a cow for the farm. Accounts for this year indicate that the overseers were pursuing a policy voted in October 1879 not to provide partial support or "outdoor relief" to the needy. The report of the overseers of the poor in the town report of 1879-80 had this to say about "partial support":

The custom has obtained in past years of persons in straightened circumstances applying to one of the Overseers and of receiving an order for groceries and provisions. While this plan has afforded great temporary convenience, yet the evils resulting are numerous and serious. It renders support too easily and privately obtained and affords a temptation to secure it rather than apply lessons of economy and self-denial, resulting in a loss of self-respect and independence of character to the recipients, while it places burdens upon tax payers besides tending to fix the settlement of these recipients upon the town.

The town was no longer warning out newcomers as it did late into the eighteenth century to avoid having to assume responsibility if they became indigent, but was trying hard not to assume responsibility by seeming to give settlement rights by aiding the newly arrived poor.

For some time there had been dissatisfaction with the very old and dilapidated poor farm buildings and their somewhat remote location. In 1870 the town meeting of April 4 set up a committee of eight to look into selling the poor farm. Again in 1881 a special committee of seven was appointed to recommend what to do about the poor farm. This committee must have recommended abandonment of the old Cutting farm on Rice Road, because in the warrant for the town meeting of March 17, 1884, there was an article providing for the purchase of a lot on the main road from Cochituate Village to Wayland and to erect a house and stable at an expense not exceeding $1,500. This article failed to pass, and $1,500 was appropriated in April 1884 to build a new barn at the old poor farm.

In 1886 the town failed to act on an article at the town meeting of August 11 to build a new house on the poor farm. In October of that year state authorities visited the Wayland poor farm to look into the conditions under which Addie Moore (who in 1880-81 had been at the Worcester Lunatic Hospital) was confined at the Wayland farm in a small, separate building. The state authorities found very bad conditions for all inmates at the poor farm. It was reported in the *Boston Herald* that the inspectors had found the Wayland establishment to be one of the worst in the state, surpassed in inadequacy only by two such institutions in the Berkshires area. The *Natick Bulletin* of October 22, 1886, quoted from a long article which appeared in the *Lowell Courier* in reply to the *Boston Herald* article explaining that the town had planned to replace the very old, dilapidated building but that the destruction of the Pelham Island Bridge by floods in the winter of 1885 had necessitated putting funds into a bridge-rebuilding project.

The old building was finally replaced by a new poor house in the summer of 1887. The *Natick Bulletin* of July 22, 1887, reported that the location of the new building was to be a little back of the old one. This building was used only for twenty-one years. In 1908 it was decided that it was uneconomical for the town to run a poor farm for a handful of inmates, and the town's full-time dependents were transferred to an institution in Worcester. The town meeting of March 24, 1909, voted to sell the poor farm property, and it was acquired by the owners of Mainstone Farm.

Tramps

The report of the overseers of the poor for 1880-81 stated that 53 tramps were lodged and furnished with food. This number was far less than the 238 tramps lodged in the year ending January 31, 1880. It is not known how early these vagrant men traveling on foot into towns like Wayland had become so numerous. At the time of the first printed town report for the year 1876-77, 239 tramps had been lodged overnight at the poor farm and 318 at the lockup in Cochituate, making a total of 557, with 515 meals given to them. Two years later the report of the overseers of the poor for 1878-79 stated that there were 391 tramps lodged at the almshouse and 459 at the Cochituate lockup, making a total of 850, with 897 meals served. Apparently in mid-1879 the overseers of the poor decided to crack down on tramps. Their report of February 1, 1880, made the following statement concerning the tramp nuisance:

Facts gained from reliable sources convinced us that the town was suffering from imposters. To remedy this evil it was decided that meals and lodging should be furnished only at the almshouse, the meals to consist of one course, viz. crackers and water. The result was immediate and our report on tramps for the year ending January 31, 1880 is as follows:

Tramps furnished with lodging	*238*
Tramps furnished with meals	*141*
Total cost	*$3.52*
	[2 ½ *cents per meal*]

Tramps still wandered into Wayland, and in 1888 we find the town meeting of March 29 appropriating $800 for a shed, a tramp house, and grading at the poor farm. Twenty years later the tramp house, then filthy, was torn down. No tramps were publicly housed after that. The number had climbed again after 1880, and in 1903-4, 306 tramps were lodged at the almshouse. In 1905-6 this number fell to 76, in 1906-7 to 42, and in 1907-8 to 11.

Until the practice was stopped in 1879, John Calvin Butterfield had seen that the tramps lodged at the Cochituate lockup were fed. In his older years he was known as "Gramp" Butterfield. When he died in 1909 at the age of ninety-two, the *Natick Bulletin* called him "the grand old man of Cochituate." Born in Antrim, New Hampshire, he left home at sixteen to learn the trade of shoemaker in Natick. He came to the part of South Wayland that was to become Cochituate before 1840 to pursue shoemaking on his own and by 1853 had purchased land and built one of the early houses on Pemberton or German Hill. During the Civil War, at the age of forty-six, he enlisted with his son as a private in the 39th Regiment of Infantry.[5] He served as superintendent of the Lakeview Cemetery for twenty-one years and as Cochituate's town-appointed undertaker for twenty-one years. He was an overseer of the poor farm from 1878 through 1887 and in 1889.

The Cochituate lockup where tramps were lodged for a few years in the 1870s was built in 1875 when the town meeting of March first appropriated $600 for such a building to be made of brick. William Lovejoy, Lafayette Dudley, and Albert B. Lyon of Cochituate were the committee to plan and have the building erected. It was placed on the back of a lot on the south side of Harrison Street. The lockup, as explained by "Quill" in the August 4, 1875, *Framingham Gazette*, was for drunks. Joseph A. Roby was strongly opposed to permitting the sale of liquor, which led to the need for a lockup in Cochituate. In the *Waltham Free Press* of May 14, 1875, he wrote:

It appears to be good Cochituate economy to keep in full blast some half dozen whiskey dens and then when the night is made hideous, sober men turned to demons, and the devil to pay generally, tax the sober, hard working yeomanry $600 for a brick building which with Cochituate management will cost $1,000 and still let those scoundrels circulate around among decent people and nobody must open their mouths or peep for fear a certain clique will not be voted for for town office.

The 1880-81 town report shows that N. Hayes was paid $25 a year for rent of the land on which the lockup stood.

Library

By 1880 the Wayland Public Library was thirty years old and contained 7,485 volumes. The library committee and the librarian were busy furnishing with busts and pictures of important men the new and better quarters provided when the new town hall was completed at the end of 1878. The library had plans for small, museum-like exhibits, and in the 1880-81 report the library committee recommended appropriating $50 to purchase cases in which to display specimens of minerals, Indian relics, and coins which had been donated. James S. Draper, now approaching seventy, had by this time served as librarian for fifteen years and was to continue for another five. The chief expenditures for the library were $150 paid to Mr. Draper as librarian and for the pay of an assistant; $50 for expressing books between Wayland and Cochituate, a practice begun in 1874; and $304.97 for books purchased.

The history of the founding of the library in 1849 with a gift from the Reverend Francis Wayland, president of Brown University, which was matched by donations in the town, is well known. A reader interested in the details of the founding of the library will find an admirable, in-depth study in a thesis written in 1975 by Sandra S. Schwalm, available at both the library and the Historical Society.

A tablet on a boulder placed on the lawn of the 1878-1901 library, now the grounds of the Wayland Historical Society's Heard House, states that this was the first public library in Massachusetts. Other towns claim this honor. It is hard to define the beginning of what could be called a true public library. Certainly Wayland's town-supported library was one of the first. We also should be aware that an East Sudbury Social Library had been organized in 1796 and that an East Sudbury Charitable Library, supported by private contributions but for the free use of any citizen of the town, was organized soon after 1815 by the Reverend John Burt Wight. Wight was greatly interested in providing libraries and, as Wayland's representative to the General Court in 1851, introduced the important legislation which specifically permitted towns to raise money for public libraries.

James Sumner Draper, who with his father was among the earliest supporters of the library, apparently feared that a larger population in Cochituate than in Wayland Center would create pressure to move the library there. The stipulation on his 1894 gift to the library has already been mentioned. There was a similar stipulation on a gift in 1903 by his son Wallace Draper. James Sumner Draper died in 1896 and thus perhaps did not know of Warren G. Roby's bequest in 1898 of one-half acre of land on Concord Road next to his house and $25,000 to erect a library building as near fireproof as possible.

James S. Draper, born in East Sudbury in 1811, was a Wayland farmer with a literary, intellectual, and bookish bent, and he took special pride in the Wayland Library. As a young man he taught school briefly and throughout his active years did some land surveying. We have already seen that he was the chief proponent for organizing a railroad to connect Wayland with Boston and points west. He served on the board of directors of the Massachusetts Central Railroad for twelve years.

Over many years he studied the history of the eastern part of Sudbury, especially in terms of its layout of roads, houses, and natural features. His map of the town as of 1776 has been mentioned. Many of his historical notes were incorporated into the Wayland portion of Alfred S. Hudson's *Annals of Sudbury, Wayland and Maynard*, published in 1891. Draper's street-by-street and house-by-house listing called "Location of Homesteads," which appeared as part of the "Appendix to The Annals of Wayland" has been invaluable for students of Wayland's history. It is only to be regretted that he did not clarify and confirm the dates cited for the houses with information from the South Middlesex Registry of Deeds and that he did not study the buildings in the village part of Cochituate. It is fortunate that Hudson, a relative, persuaded him to permit his not completely checked listing to be printed. The listing has been a tremendous help to the Wayland Historical Commission in its efforts to identify and date existing older buildings.

Draper never wrote a town history, but he did write historical articles about the town's churches for the *Waltham Free Press*. He

The William Powell Perkins House (Mainstone Farm) in 1895.

believed in recordkeeping and in the compilation of historical material from primary sources. The town honored him with a gold-headed cane when the *Memorial to the Civil War Soldiers* was published in 1871. He had a certain gift for poetry, published one book of poems, and was sought after to write verse for personal and community celebrations. The house he had built in 1834 on land given him by his father for a wedding gift stands (with additions) at 110 Plain Road. At 104 Plain Road, next door, is the house built in 1891 by Edward Marston in the style of the day to replace a house Draper had built in 1856, which was destroyed by fire in 1891. Portraits, furniture, and china owned by James S. Draper and his descendants form an important part of the collection of furnishings at the Wayland Historical Society's Heard House.

Burden of Taxation

To cover town services, to pay $930 in state taxes and $467 for county taxes, and to pay interest on the town debt of $98,906.80, in May 1880 the assessors had assessed $16,442 on polls and estates with a tax rate of $12.70 per thousand. They had determined that the value of real estate was $935,260 and of personal estate $269,103, making a total valuation of $1,204,363. At this time in Natick and various nearby towns there was considerable interest in the tax burden and who paid what. On August 15, 1879, the Cochituate columns of the two Natick papers, the *Bulletin* and the *Citizen*, published identical lists of "Our Heaviest Taxpayers." The 1879 lists covered Cochituate taxpayers only.[6] The *Natick Citizen* of July 30, 1880, published a list of persons in both parts of Wayland who were required to pay more than $50 of taxes in 1880. The top fifteen taxpayers with their reported tax bills were as follows:

William P. Perkins	$1096.51
Wm. & J. M. Bent Company	611.82
J. M. and H. D. Parmenter	455.87
Harriet S. Wyman	300.67
Thomas Jefferson Damon	232.63
Horace Heard	216.53
Hodijah B. Braman	208.52
Warren G. Roby	197.79
Samuel M. Thomas	192.08
Samuel D. Reeves	179.50
James Madison Bent	157.02
Royal M. Flint	150.67
Jude Damon	147.95
James Alvin Bent	147.57
James Sumner Draper	139.80

Ten of these largest taxpayers were from the northern end of the town, five from Cochituate.

William Powell Perkins, who paid much more than the others (7 percent of the entire town's tax), had bought what we now know as Mainstone Farm from the heirs of John Perkins Cushing of Belmont in 1868. In 1873 he had left a large and elaborate estate in Brookline to move to his property in Wayland after the Boston fire of 1872 reduced his fortune, due to his having had fire insurance interests. In 1874 the house crowning Mainstone Hill at 83 Old Connecticut Path was enlarged and remodeled for him by William Fullick of Cochituate to have a third floor and a mansard roof. Wm. and J. M. Bent was the town's large shoe company (about which there will be more in the next chapter). Jonathan Maynard and Henry Dana Parmenter, bachelor brothers who operated as a partnership in cattle and dairy farming, lived in the Parmenter homestead now standing at 28 Concord Road on the corner of Bow Road. Mrs. Harriet S. Wyman, whose maiden name was Hayward, lived in the Hayward house on the Boston Post Road still standing (number 101). Thomas Jefferson Damon was a prosperous farmer living on family lands east of Cochituate Village. Horace Heard was listed in the census as a farmer, but he had prospered enough to be able to invest in considerable Wayland Center real estate such as "the old green store" building and the Pequod Hotel. He also had loaned considerable funds to the town. His home, now standing at 4 Winthrop Place, was then on its original site on the east side of Cochituate Road between the Unitarian Church and Winthrop Road. In 1873 Hodijah B. Braman had built the large Victorian house at 18 Old Sudbury Road (torn down in 1980) while also owning the older house at 10 Old Sudbury Road, which was occupied by his farmer. He had come to Wayland in 1845 as a summer resident. Hodijah B. Braman married the daughter of Samuel Stone Noyes and lived at first in the Noyes house on Old Sudbury Road and Glezen Lane. Warren G. Roby, descendant of a long line of earlier Robys in Wayland, was in the metals business in Boston and lived in Boston during the winter months. The handsome old family homestead in which he lived in 1880 is depicted opposite page 56 of Hudson's *Annals of Sudbury, Wayland and Maynard.* Fire destroyed this historic house in 1887, and it was replaced nearby in 1888 by the house now standing at 11 Concord Road.

Samuel Maynard Thomas was one of Wayland's most prosperous farmers, living in a house (now number 265) on Old Connecticut Path West. Until 1960 this house stood across the road on land taken over by the town when it built the present Wayland High School. Samuel D. Reeves was a widower living with his sister in a house torn down in the 1920s at 28 Boston Post Road in what is now the commercial section as one enters Wayland from Weston. He had been a farmer and owned three houses in that area. By the time of the 1883 valuation list he no longer was in the top group of taxpayers. James Madison Bent was the head of the Bent family at this time. His house, built by the late 1850s but remodeled and enlarged in 1882 to have a mansard roof, stood on the northeast corner of Main Street and Commonwealth Road where an automobile sales agency is now located. Royal M. Flint was a prosperous farmer who had come to Wayland in 1872 from Westfield and lived in a house built in the 1860s on the upper land of what is now the Sandy Burr Country Club. His farm, called Phoenix Farm, contained 132 acres. The house was destroyed by fire in December 1883 and not replaced.

In 1845 Jude Damon, a member of the Cochituate Damon family, had moved to Wayland to the Baldwin Farm on Old Sudbury Road at the corner of Glezen Lane. Damon had invested in this farm after David Baldwin died. The house stood near the road on the front land of what is now 79 Old Sudbury Road. James Alvin Bent was the second son of James Madison Bent and in 1880 a partner in the family shoe-manufacturing business. In 1875 he had built an elegant Victorian house on the south side of Commonwealth Road east of the old Bent homestead. This house, torn down in 1967, stood on land now used for a shopping center.

By 1880 James Sumner Draper owned not only the house he built in 1834 at 110 Plain Road, then occupied by a hired farmer and soon to be remodeled to be rented as a summer residence, but also a house at 104 Plain Road which he had erected in 1856. By this time James S. Draper had inherited his father's house at 116 Plain Road and thus owned three houses on the east side of Plain Road and the farmlands across the road. Eleven of the fifteen largest taxpayers were in the Wayland end of the town. The percentage of the total tax funds paid by these fifteen men was 74.1. Of the entire list of 59 taxpayers paying over $50, 62 percent in dollar amount was paid by Wayland residents; in terms of individual persons, they numbered 33 out of the 59.

In 1882 the *Natick Citizen* published a list of the town's taxpayers whose tax bills exceeded $100.[7] We can, however, best analyze the tax picture for this period by reference to the printed document published and distributed by the town and entitled *Valuation List for the Town of Wayland of Polls, Property, Taxes etc. as Assessed May 1, 1883*. In this report the list of the top fifteen taxpayers is very much the same as for 1880, although the rank of some is slightly different. William P. Perkins still leads, this time with a tax bill of $1,250.68. New and now sixth on the list was a nonresident taxpayer, Michael H. Simpson of Framingham and Boston, whose still unfinished house on Dudley Pond was assessed for $12,000, at that time much the most expensive house ever to have been built in Wayland. This house was reputed to have cost more than $150,000. Michael Hodge Simpson was a winter resident of Boston but was president of the nearby Roxbury Carpet Company and Saxonville Mills in the Saxonville section of Framingham. He was born in Newburyport in 1809 and was quite elderly when he built his large house in the southwest corner of Wayland on Dudley Pond. Before being associated with manufacturing in Saxonville, he had been a successful merchant in Boston. In 1882 he had married as a second wife Evangeline Marrs, the daughter of a family who had lived during the 1870s on Old Connecticut Path near Dudley

The Jude Damon House on Old Sudbury Road was torn down in 1901.

Pond. She was much younger than he and inherited the house when he died in 1884. Eventually she remarried and settled in Minnesota. In 1900 Evangeline Whipple's house was valued at $41,000. Thirty men worked most of 1882 to build the house, the large stable, and a windmill to pump water. This very large and fancy residence was the wonder of Wayland and nearby towns when it was being built. Evangeline Whipple sold the house in the first decade of the twentieth century to a group who converted it into a resort called Mansion Inn. It has already been mentioned that Michael Simpson paid for having the town's water piped out West Plain Street to his house.

By 1883 Samuel D. Reeves had dropped to a considerably lower tax bracket, and James A. Bent and Jude Damon were just below the fifteen-man list. In their places were Charles A. Cutting and Joseph Bullard. By 1883 Cutting owned three adjoining houses along Old Sudbury Road and had begun to buy up woodland properties. In 1885 he remodeled and greatly enlarged the house at 91 Old Sudbury Road, which from 1852 to her death in 1880 had been the home of Lydia Maria Child, the nationally known author and abolitionist. Joseph Bullard built in 1870 a new house on the prosperous farm of his father, Jotham Bullard, on the north or lower part of what is now the Sandy Burr golf course. Joseph Bullard, born in 1804, had lived at this location since 1827. In 1834 he married Harriet Loker, and their son, Willard Austin Bullard, born in 1837, was to become a bank president in Cambridge. In 1888-89 Willard Bullard remodeled "the old green store" next to the Unitarian Church into the residence Kirkside at 221 Boston Post Road. By 1900 he would become the largest property owner in Wayland Center village.

Of the fifteen largest taxpayers, eleven were located in the north end of the town and three in Cochituate. Michael Simpson can best be left out of the calculation because his estate was not in Cochituate Village, nor was it really in the Wayland end of the town. The eleven in Wayland paid $3,173.08 in taxes, while the Cochituate three paid $979.83. If, in 1883, one takes the fifty-two Wayland residents paying $50 or more in taxes to the town and the thirty individuals or companies in Cochituate paying $50 or more, one finds that 67.1 percent, or about two thirds of the tax money, came from the Wayland end of the town.[8] This writer, while unable to identify which end of the town a few of the resident taxpayers were located in, added the entire 1883 tax list for town residents and added those of the nonresident taxpayers who could be identified as in Wayland or in Cochituate and found that 67 percent of the total of taxes paid was on property in the Wayland end of the town. Thus, we find that as of 1883 Wayland, with one third of the population, was paying two thirds of the total tax bill. This fact was not completely understood in Cochituate, although the thoughtful people and the leaders of the community must have known it. Thirteen years later, in 1896, when the tax balance was much the same or showing an even larger share of the tax burden paid by the Wayland end of the town, the "Cochituate Enterprise" contained the following misleading statement in connection with the new school being built at Wayland Center:

We say Wayland was presented with a school building. Yes, she was, but who pays the burden of this present? The town to be sure. But again, what constitutes the town? Wayland itself constitutes one-third while Cochituate represents two-thirds of the population and two-thirds of the tax payers. It follows that Cochituate pays for two-thirds of that new school while she is suffering from the poor school service she is obliged to put up with.[9]

How did it come about that Wayland citizens paid two thirds of the tax bill? In a general way the answer is that the major incidence of taxation in Wayland, as in other towns in the area, was on real estate. Wayland's farmlands, houses, and farm buildings were valued higher in toto than the smaller quantity of land in Cochituate. Added to this

The Hodijah Bramen House on Old Sudbury Road was torn down in 1980.

was the fact that the Cochituate factories, the source of much of the employment and the magnet for the population increase, were not assessed at high figures. The prosperous owners of the shoe factories in Cochituate paid substantial taxes on their homes, especially if they were new and sizable ones, and some taxes on their business property, but most of the Cochituate population were not property holders and were liable only (the men) for the $2 poll tax. Middle-range taxpayers were more concentrated in the Wayland end of the town.

In descending rank, those with the most valuable land in 1883 were William P. Perkins, the brothers Jonathan M. and Henry D. Parmenter, Thomas Jefferson Damon's estate (he had died in 1880), Hodijah B. Braman, Joseph Bullard, Samuel M. Thomas, Royal M. Flint, Charles A. Cutting, and Horace Heard. Of these only the Damon lands were in Cochituate. When it came to individual houses, however, the situation was the reverse. The twelve houses valued at $2,500 or higher were predominantly in Cochituate. Wayland's four houses in this category were those of William P. Perkins ($6,000), Hodijah B. Braman ($4,300), Edward Pousland ($2,500), and Warren G. Roby ($2,500). In Cochituate there were four Bent houses—those of William H. ($3,900), James A. ($3,600), James

Charles R. Damon's mansard roof house, built ca 1870, still stands on Damon Street.

Madison ($2,800), and the boardinghouse (old homestead) then owned by James A. Bent. There were also the Albert B. Lyon house, the Thomas Bryant house on Commonwealth Road, Charles R. Damon's house on Damon Street, George A. Damon's house on Commonwealth Road, Charles Fairbanks' house on Main Street, Adeline Dean's house on Main Street, and Albert F. King's house on Main Street. With the exception of the old Roby house in Wayland Center, all these houses were built in the late 1860s, the 1870s, or the early 1880s; or, as in the case of the Perkins house and the Bent homestead, they were older houses considerably enlarged and modernized. Cochituate Village had been built up in the late 1860s and 1870s. Large Victorian houses were erected there by the shoe manufacturers and a few others. Writing in the *Framingham Gazette* of June 25, 1873, Joseph A. Roby stated proudly that the old Francis house (built by Zachariah Bryant in 1770) now at 10 Old Sudbury Road in Wayland Center had been moved, and went on to say:

and now on the old house site a house that is a house *is understood to be contracted for by the owner Mr. H. B. Braman. . . . Fronting 40 feet on Main Street* [Old Sudbury Road] *and with L 70 feet back, and a Mansard roof, the first one in this village but not the last.*

This house did not have a mansard roof but was of the elegant Victorian stick style. It was torn down in 1980.

It has not been determined when the practice started, but by 1883 the Wayland assessors were taxing intangible personal property as well as livestock and carriages, which were the major items of tangible personal property then taxed. Four persons in Cochituate were taxed from $13 to $37 for money at interest. On the Wayland end of the town three persons with considerable accumulated capital—William P. Perkins, Warren G. Roby, and Mrs. Harriet Wyman—were taxed from $118 to $809 on personal property. We see here the beginning of a trend to get substantial tax assistance from the well-to-do whose fortunes were made outside Wayland.

The assessors' report in the 1878-79 town report analyzes the tax situation in the town. The town obtained 71 percent of its $19,919 total revenue from taxes on real estate amounting to $14,170 and $4,539, or 23 percent, from the personal estate tax. In addition, 566 men paid poll taxes of $2 each; this brought in $1,132, or 5.7 percent of the total. Of the 566 poll tax payers over half (299) paid only the $2 poll tax. From this same assessors' report we see that at this time there was great concern about, and a desire to, publicize the fact that the larger assessments were in the north part of the town. There is in this report the following statement:

In complying with the request of several tax-payers . . . for the assessors to state in this report . . . the comparative amounts of tax paid by parties in the aggregate residing upon either side of a line running from "Stone's Bridge" near the residence of James Adams; thence southerly of the premises of Ephraim Farwell; thence southerly of the farm owned by William R. Dudley; thence northerly of George A. Rice's farm, we find as follows:

Assessed to Residents	*$19,174.46*
Assessed north of said line	*11,644.15*
Assessed south of said line	*7,530.31*
Difference in assessments	*$ 4,113.84*

The report goes on to show that as of November 5, 1878, there were 431 registered voters, 278 south of the line and 153 north of it. The line described in this report approximated the old south boundary of the original Sudbury grant before the addition of the Natick farmers' land and was essentially the same as the line that was drawn in 1893 to divide the two voting precincts.

Town Expenses and Income

NOTES

1. Joseph A. Roby attributed the trend to celebrate Christmas as a major holiday to the influx to the area of Irish people. It is clear from perusal of the local newspapers of this time that merchants played a considerable part in promoting Christmas.

2. *Natick Bulletin,* February 20, 1885.

3. The first professional school superintendant employed by the town was George Pitman who came when Wayland entered into a joint superintendency with West Boylston and other towns in 1895.

4. *Diary of Amanda Patch Baldwin, Wife of Samuel Baldwin of Wayland,* 1871, original owned by David J. Baldwin of Sudbury. Transcription in files of Wayland Historical Society.

5. Town of Wayland, *The Town of Wayland in the Civil War of 1861-1865,* Wayland, 1871, p. 57.

6. The largest taxpayers in Cochituate in descending order were: Wm. & J.M. Bent shoe company, Thomas Jefferson Damon, James Madison Bent, James A. Loker, James Alvin Bent, John L. Loker, Adeline Dean (widow of Thomas A. Dean), Charles Fairbanks, Ellen C. Lyon (wife of Albert B. Lyon) and Fanny Slayton. Of these one company and four individuals were connected with the shoe industry, three were farmers and two were commercial property owners.

7. *Natick Citizen,* July 21, 1882.

8. If one includes the Simpson estate in Cochituate since it was connected with the Cochituate water supply, the figure is 65.6 percent for Wayland.

9. *Natick Bulletin,* December 11, 1896.

11

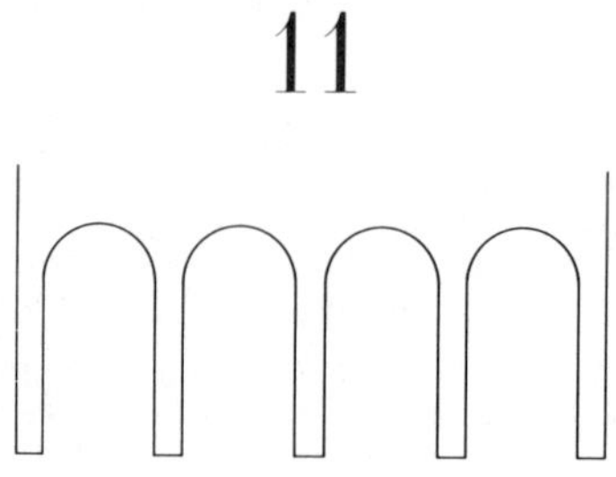

Petitions to Divide the Town

WITH TAXATION weighing more heavily on the Wayland end of the town and the knowledge that the Cochituate end of the town had the larger and growing number of registered voters, so that spending could be controlled there, it is not entirely surprising that frictions built up enough to inspire an attempt to end these imbalances. In the fall of 1881 a petition to the state legislature was drawn up with William P. Perkins, the town's largest taxpayer, as author, asking that Wayland be divided into two towns. The petition, dated October 24, 1881, signed by ninety-five voters of the Wayland end of the town, "respectfully petitioned and represented that the interest and convenience of the inhabitants . . . require that [it] should be divided into two separate towns and that the line of division should run from East to West at points near Stone's Corner at the West to the boundary line between the farms of G. A. Rice and Joseph Rice. That the interests of the two sections are in no way identical, one being manufacturing and the other agricultural, that there is no business or social relations existing between them except for the transaction of Town business."[1]

William P. Perkins's signature came next, with the date, and was followed by the signatures on that page and one other of twenty-nine residents of Wayland Center, including such prominent citizens and large taxpayers as Horace Heard, Jonathan Maynard Parmenter, Jude Damon, Samuel D. Reeves, Royal Flint, James Sumner Draper, Hodijah B. Braman, and Lorenzo K. Lovell. This first list of names is obviously composed of the group who met together with Perkins and decided to prefer the petition. The first signature after that of Perkins is I. C. Damon's. Examination of the original petition in the Massachusetts Legislative Archives suggests that the document is in the handwriting, not of Perkins, but of Isaac Coburn Damon, who may have been the petition's real author and must certainly have been a leading figure in drawing it up. After the signatures of the first thirty, there is an attestation by a constable that on October 25, 1881, he delivered the petition to Henry Wight, town clerk, and to Theodore S. Sherman, selectman. There then appear sixty-five additional signatures, some of them also of prominent citizens like Abel Glezen, Josiah W. Parmenter, and Joseph Bullard, but also men of less importance. This part of the petition contains signatures of persons clustered geographically. Clearly, these names were added when the petition was circulated around the north end of the town.

Nothing was written about this petition in Hudson's *Annals of Wayland* or in the writings of later historians of the town. It is obvious that Hudson and Draper thought that this episode was best forgotten. Newspapers of nearby towns containing Wayland and Cochituate news did, however, discuss the petition, which was taken quite seriously in the town for nearly three months. The *Framingham Gazette* of November 4, 1881, stated under "Cochituate Locals": "Considerable excitement prevails here at present in regard to a petition. . . . The petition has been signed by nearly all the wealthiest men in Wayland Centre." The article then went on to paraphrase the reasons for the division given in the actual petition. The weekly papers came out on Friday. On the same date, under "Wayland," the *Natick Bulletin* reported as follows: "The proposed division of the town of Wayland, which is one of the oldest in the state [sic], and the formation of a new town which shall include Cochituate village, is creating considerable interest among the people here."

Two weeks went by and on November 18 there was further comment. The *Natick Bulletin*'s Cochituate news stated that: "The people here generally think that the citizens of the Centre are somewhat piggish in regard to territory. . . . They seem to be willing to give Cochituate a smaller corner . . . and take the larger portion themselves. A more equal division would be looked upon with more favor." On November 18 the *Natick Citizen* said: "If Wayland wants to divide, why can't an arrangement be made for Natick to marry Cochituate, taking the fair maiden for better or worse . . .?" In that same paper under "Wayland News" the petition was described and it said: "It seems that both sections are agreeable to the change." This article then went on to analyze the town debt as it would have a bearing on a division into two separate towns.

It is not known whether in December there were serious discussions between the leaders of Cochituate and Wayland Center as to the desirability and feasibility of carrying out the division proposal. *The Journal of the House of Representatives* shows that on January 16, 1882, Edward Carter, Wayland's representative to the General Court, who lived in North Wayland and had not signed the petition, presented the petition to the House and that it was immediately referred to the committee on towns.[2] *The House Journal* shows that the next day Representative Dorchester of Natick presented a remonstrance by James Madison Bent and 238 other legal voters of Wayland against the division of Wayland. This document "respectfully and earnestly remonstrated against the granting of . . . the petition of William P. Perkins and twenty-nine others [no mention was made of the other sixty-five signers] for a division of the town of Wayland. We believe that any division of said town would be unwise, injudicious and uncalled for." All but about fifteen of the signers of the remonstrance were Cochituate voters. This group constituted a very large proportion of their electorate and shows considerable organization well before January 17. A few men from Wayland signed the remonstrance. Among them were Henry Wight, the town clerk; his father, the now elderly Reverend John Burt Wight; and Henry's son, George H. Wight, Joseph A. Roby, the former town clerk; and Theodore S. Sherman, Wayland Center's one selectman. There were a few others.

On January 19 a special town meeting, announced before the Perkins petition actually went to the House and before the Bent remonstrance was presented, took place, with its major article "to act on a proposed division of the town." James Madison Bent's remonstrance must have been so impressive that the Wayland Center proponents of the division realized that they were defeated. Most of them seem not to have gone to the meeting. The record shows that when the vote was taken only one person voted for the division—Samuel D. Reeves. One hundred and forty-five citizens voted against the petition, and the town clerk recorded their names alphabetically. Fewer than twenty of these were men from Wayland; the bulk were from Cochituate. Henry Wight, Joseph A. Roby, and Theodore S. Sherman were there to vote against the division, as were three other members of the North Wayland Sherman family.

A group in North Wayland including four Shermans and Representative Edward Carter were strongly against the division. On January 24 George E. Sherman presented a separate remonstrance against the division of the town signed by ten others. A report in the *Natick Citizen* of January 27, 1882, suggests that George and the other Shermans and their neighbors were not only opposed to cutting off Cochituate; they had a different idea in mind. According to this newspaper, "We understand a portion of the people desire a different division than that proposed which includes an addition of a part to the town of Lincoln." This suggestion could not have been serious. As befitted Edward Carter in his position as Representative to the General Court, he had taken the Perkins's petition seriously and had tried to work out a compromise. The Historical Society has a plan written by Carter in late 1881 attempting to draw a more equitable dividing line north of the Cochituate addition line proposed by Perkins.

Apparently in the last week of January, William Perkins asked to have his petition withdrawn from the legislature. Notice of this was recorded in *The House Journal* February 7 when the committee on towns was given leave to withdraw the petition. On February 9 the *Natick Bulletin* said in its Cochituate column: "It is generally believed in this village that the proposed division of the town is a dead issue and will not be resurrected at present, surely not in this session of the legislature."

Very little was ever said again about this division proposal after the withdrawal. However, the outrage engendered in Cochituate could not die down immediately. The March 17 *Natick Bulletin's* Cochituate column, in discussing the prospect of paying for an extension of the Cochituate waterworks and the need to bring the matter before an April town meeting, said:

We understand that a determined opposition will be made to this measure by some of the soreheads who did not succeed in dividing the town. We hope for the best interests of the town that they will not succeed. . . . We can adopt no policy of consideration toward them for the wrath of no one of the notorious thirty could be appeased unless he could be chairman of the board of selectmen every year.

This was enough of a dig so that in the *Natick Bulletin* of the following week (March 24), under "Wayland News" someone wrote:

In your last week's paper your Cochituate correspondent was pleased to style the petitioners for the division of the town "the thirty-five soreheads," not a very complimentary term when in fact the petition was signed by 95 legal voters who represent more than half the valuation of the town instead of three-quarters of the mortgages. . . . The petitioners . . . will not be deterred . . . by the threats that no one who signed the petition can be elected to town office.

Thus ended a rather bitter episode. In the March 6 town meeting in 1882 it was voted to instruct the selectmen to call all town meetings in the center of Wayland until otherwise ordered. It is likely that Cochituate interests were trying to appease the Wayland Center group by allowing the town hall at Wayland Center appear to be the only center of the town government.

The 1881 petition was not the first time the idea of division had come up. At the annual meeting on March 4, 1872, Article 11 had proposed setting off Cochituate and its annexation to Natick. On this article it was voted that the selectmen were authorized to petition the General Court to set off the south part of the town to Natick. No petition to the legislature was forthcoming. The selectmen that year were James D. Walker of Glezen Lane in Wayland and Alfred H. Bryant and George W. Risley of Cochituate. There is no hint in the town clerk's record of who initiated the idea and put it in the warrant or how serious the proponents were. The Framingham and Natick newspapers did not then carry Wayland or Cochituate news, and no comment on the 1872 proposal has been found.

Later, in December 1887 when Natick needed additional population to qualify for a city charter form of government, there was talk in Natick of annexing Cochituate. This was probably mostly the idea of one or more of the Natick newspapers. There was some interest in this proposal on the part of the correspondent of the *Natick Bulletin.* After the Cochituate correspondent discussed the advantages of joining Natick (electric streetlights, better water supply and fire department) and pointed out that there would be higher taxes in Natick, the Wayland column in the *Bulletin* of December 30, 1887, was written, perhaps facetiously, as if the departure of Cochituate was inevitable. It said:

We learn with deep solicitude that Natick wants to gobble up our thrifty little Cochituate and become a city. We understand that a strong feeling exists in Cochituate in favor of the union. People of the centre [Wayland] *will be obliged to submit to the will of the majority. The advent of the central railroad will doubtless add to our numbers and the centre will soon be able to paddle their own canoe. Let us hope for the best.*

In the end, annexation to Natick did not prove to be something the Cochituate people wanted. In the Cochituate news of January 6, 1888, it was reported that the idea of annexation did not interest many in Cochituate and that "very few will vote for annexation." The January 6 column said: "Cochituate will one of these days be a town by itself instead of merging with one of its larger neighbors." Although he did not want Cochituate separated from Wayland in 1882, James Madison Bent is said to have been hopeful that Cochituate could eventually develop as a town by itself. Perhaps he envisioned that someday it might absorb Wayland or the northern part of Natick. There was no further talk of annexation by Natick after the January columns of the *Natick Bulletin* reported little interest in the idea on the part of Cochituate people. During times of strain between the two parts of the town over large expenditures for school buildings, antagonisms flared again. Some of this will be brought out in connection with the building of the Center School in Wayland, which took place in the 1890s. Before advancing to that decade we shall turn our attention to the shoe-manufacturing industry, which was the basis of the development of Cochituate into a powerful and more advanced part of the town.

NOTES

1. Original of petition is in Committee on Towns file, Massachusetts Legislative Archives, State House, Boston.
2. *Journal of the House of Representatives of the Commonwealth of Massachusetts, Special Session, 1881.* Boston, 1882, p. 41.

12

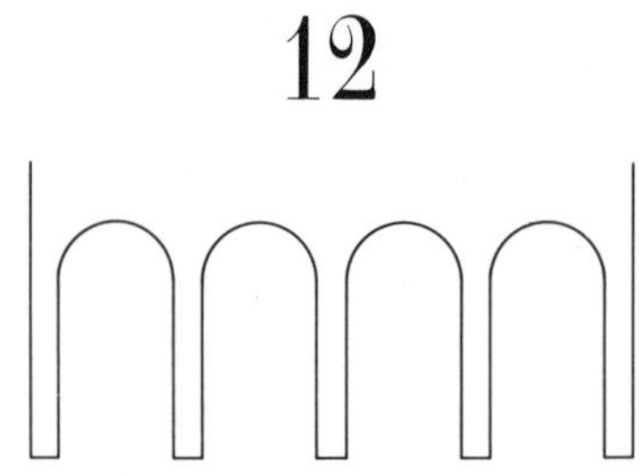

Cochituate Shoe Manufacture in 1880

Availability of Information and Statistics

WE DO NOT HAVE as specific a picture of the shoe industry which existed in Cochituate from about 1830 to 1913 as would be obtainable if company records had been preserved and were available. Several record books of the large Bent company survived until the mid-twentieth century but are now no longer is existence. One volume which remained in the Bent family has been mislaid and could not be consulted for this study. There are, however, photographs of the exterior and interior of the Bent factory at different stages of its development. As statistics of output and employment for the various factories, there are federal and state census figures, but these do not cover some of the short-lived firms. Furthermore, whereas the censuses up through 1880 seem to have contained reasonably correct and complete figures on the shoe industry in Cochituate, shoe manufacturing was not reliably reported for 1885, probably deliberately so.[1] Detail within the state by towns is not extant for 1890, 1895, and 1900, and Wayland employment and production was intentionally left out of the state census of 1905 to avoid disclosure of output by the large company. Trade association figures as published in the *Shoe and Leather Reporter*, a weekly, and in its annual statistical and directory volumes did not give output by companies until around 1900, and then only as shoe-manufacturing capacity expressed in a range. Thus, for the thirty years after 1880 one must use a few scarce statistics to round out the story of the industry as it existed in this town. It is fortunate, however, that for the decades of the 1870s and 1880s, the time of the greatest growth and development of the industry, the Natick newspapers, particularly the *Natick Bulletin*, published several feature articles describing Cochituate's shoe industry.

Shoe Manufacturing in 1880

Let us look first at the shoe manufacturers in 1880. In the original 1880 United States census returns on manufactures, recorded on July 28, 1880, showing products of industry during the twelve months beginning June 1, 1879, and ending May 31, 1880, we find enumerated for the village of Cochituate seven boot- and shoe-manufacturing concerns, varying from two employing a maximum of 10 workers each, to one employing 329 workers.[2] Ranked in descending order of value of product, they are as follows:

	Capital	Greatest no. employed			Value of Product
		Total	Males	Females	
Wm. & J. M. Bent Co.	$ 65,000	329	266	63	$ 736,742
A. B. Lyon Co.	35,000	100	96	4	254,935
A. F. Dean & Co.	7,000	35	35	—	78,000
C. W. & H. C. Dean Co.	5,500	45	44	1	60,000
A. H. Bryant Co.	5,000	45	43	2	32,500
Larrabee & Wesson Co.	2,000	10	10	—	24,040
Henry B. Fischer Jr.	500	10	10	—	7,500
Total	$120,000	574	504	70	$1,193,717

It will be noted that the value of the total product was more than $1 million, which at the going wholesale price of $1.00 for brogans and $2.00 for plowshoes, the two chief products, represented the manufacture of about 955,000 pairs of footwear. The seven firms employed 574 workers at their peak production for the year, most of them men. It will be seen that the Bent company turned out 62 percent of the product, which means that it made more shoes than all the others combined. The Bent company employed 57 percent of the workers and 90 percent of the women. It was the giant on the scene at that time. It is interesting to consider the above firms in terms of information published in a long article on the Cochituate shoe industry which appeared in the *Natick Bulletin* of November 22, 1878. Before we do that, it is worthwhile to compare Cochituate's 1880 figures with those

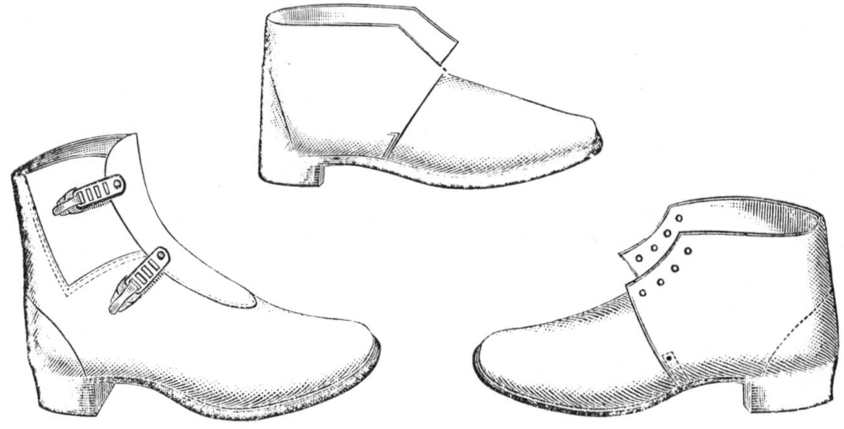

1888 illustrations of Bent brogans and plowshoes. Center, early brogan of the 1840s; left, 1888 plow shoe; and right, 1888 brogan.

of other towns and with that of the state as a whole.

Comparisons can best be simplified by basing them on numbers of workers employed as shown in the United States census of 1880. Within Middlesex County, Wayland's average number of workers—557 in 7 establishments—compared with 3,278 workers (nearly six times as many) in 23 boot and shoe establishments in Marlborough; 1,537 workers (about three times as many) in 33 establishments in Natick; 1,174 workers in 7 establishments in Hopkinton; 1,020 in 5 establishments in Hudson; and 1,122 in 30 establishments in Stoneham. Going outside the county to the large shoe centers in Essex County, we find that at this time there were 7,661 shoe workers in 155 establishments in Haverhill and 10,708 workers in 174 establishments in Lynn. Brockton in Plymouth County had 3,981 workers in 73 establishments, and Worcester had 2,404 in 59. That same year there were 2,286 shoe workers employed in Weymouth and 2,429 in Marblehead.

Massachusetts was preeminent in shoe manufacturing at this time. Total state employment in boot and shoe factories was 51,702. Cochituate's shoe employment constituted roughly 1 percent of the state total. It has often been said that Cochituate was an important shoe-manufacturing center. This was not true in 1880 or at any other time. However, shoe manufacturing was very important locally as the basis of the development of Cochituate Village and was a significant element of Wayland's economy.

Cochituate Shoe Manufacture

The Big Plant

Cochituate's large firm, the Wm. and J. M. Bent Company, which dominated the town's shoe industry, did have industry-wide recognition as a producer of brogans, a type of roughly tanned men's workshoe worn by slave and later free labor on the plantations of the South and in the North by farmers, other outdoor workers, and growing boys. Brogan manufacture had been strong in Natick since the 1830s, and it is not surprising that Cochituate's output was similar. As mentioned earlier in connection with the French-Canadian workers, brogan making began early (around 1810) in North Brookfield in Worcester County. An article which appeared in the November 8, 1888, issue of the *Shoe and Leather Reporter* gave the history of brogans and included line drawings of three types of early brogans made in the 1830s as well as the brogans and plowshoes of 1888. The very earliest brogans were hand-sewn shoes made soon after 1800. By 1811 pegged brogans (soles held on by wooden pegs) had been developed. This gave impetus to the manufacture in Massachusetts and New Hampshire of a cheap enough product to send in large quantities to the South and the West where they were sold in dry-goods and grocery stores. Among the brogans illustrated in the article is a black, laceless, tongueless brogan of the 1830s known as the Bent brogan "made" by Allen, Harris and Potter. The brogan and a plowshoe of 1888 are shown here. When the article referred to Potter, White and Bayley as being one of the two largest brogan manufacturers in the country, it was referring to brogans made in Cochituate by the Wm. and J. M. Bent Company and in one other factory in New Hampshire.

In 1880 James Madison Bent, then sixty-eight years old, was still the senior partner and active director of the business. William Bent, the older of the two original partners, died in 1863. After his brother's death J. M. Bent had taken his two eldest sons, William Harrison Bent (often called "Harry"), born in 1840, and James Alvin Bent, born in 1843, into the firm as partners.[3] Two younger sons, Myron W. and Ralph, also worked for the company, as did William Harrison Bent's son Elmer. By 1880 William H. Bent seems to have been a general executive under his father while, according to an article on the Bent concern in the *Natick Bulletin* of January 30, 1880, James A. Bent was then in charge of dressing and packing the finished product. The November 1878 article stated that the company made about sixty cases of footwear per day. A case contained fifty to sixty pairs. These were mainly brogans and alaskas. The January 1880 article describes the output of the factory as about seventy cases of brogans and plowshoes per day.

In the spring of 1878 an addition had been made to the factory which stood on the southwest corner of Main Street and Commonwealth Road. There was no further expansion until the middle 1880s, so that the 1878 newspaper description would apply also to 1880. According to the 1878 description, the main part of the building was 100 by 40 feet with four stories above the basement. To this were attached two ells, one 40 by 50 feet, the other 40 by 30 feet, both three stories above the basement. By this time the plant had filled the land on which it was built, and photographs show that it had attained a rectilinear shape. These photographs make it difficult to realize that three additions in the 1870s had covered over and all but obliterated a structure that shows in the early photograph on page 204 as a white-painted three-story building of columned Greek revival influence. This factory building was connected to the north by a two-story building to a house-type building on the corner of the roads. This corner building had been James M. Bent's store in the 1850s. The continuous row of second-floor windows in the middle section of the factory as shown in the circa 1860 photograph can still be seen on the facade of the plant with all of its additions in later photographs and in the 1887 lithograph of Cochituate Village. Remodeled and added to numerous times, the wooden building, painted factory red, loomed large on its corner but was never quite as large and impressive as the lithograph made it seem.

The white, columned building was not the earliest plant at that location. It had been placed to the south of an earlier shop, which had been developed on that site using William Bent's grandfather Micah Bent's blacksmith shop. This shoeshop contained a treadmill with a horse going round and round, providing the first source of power other than handpower. William Bent had first made shoes in his own house. Then, before moving his operations across the road, probably in the 1840s, he had had a one-room shop described as being 20 by 20 feet behind his house. According to his great-niece, Margaret Bent Morrell, this building was torn down in 1914.

William Bent had learned shoemaking in Natick as an apprentice to his cousin, Asa Felch, who in 1827 is said to have started the Natick shoe industry.[4] While his brother was learning to be a shoemaker and later setting himself up in business, James Madison Bent had been apprenticed to a cabinetmaker in Framingham. When he went into business with William, he applied his cabinetmaking training and made what was reported to be the first high shoemaker's bench, and also the head block to which lasts were strapped. There is a tradition in the Bent family that, when the older brother took in the younger brother, William insisted that James M. be an apprentice to learn the trade for five years. According to the tradition, it was at this time that James M. built and ran the store on the corner. Different accounts give the dates 1843 and 1846 as the beginning of the William and James M. Bent full partnership.

The exact date is not known, but newspaper accounts written in the 1870s and 1880s tell us that at a rather early date, perhaps in 1842 or in the mid-1840s, the firm began to manufacture exclusively for a company in Boston, then known as Allen, Harris and Potter, later as Potter, White and Bayley. Earlier listings in Boston directories and the 1888 article in the *Shoe and Leather Reporter* call Potter, White and Bayley manufacturers rather than sales agents or dealers. We conclude, therefore, that over the years, certainly in the 1870s and 1880s, decisions as to what the Bent concern would manufacture were made by the Boston firm.

Both the 1878 article on the Cochituate shoe industry and the 1880 article on the Bent factory stressed the excellent appointments of the Bent factory and the presence of much laborsaving machinery, some of it invented by James Madison Bent. In 1880 the plant was run by a 50-horsepower engine with steam furnished by two large boilers which consumed about 1,800 pounds of coal a day. The *Natick Bulletin* of January 2, 1880, tells us that Wm. and J. M. Bent had just replaced the factory whistle with a large gong which could be heard for miles. This gong was sounded at 5:30 A.M. to awaken the Bent workers, and in fact the whole working populace of the village so that they would be ready to arrive at work at 7:00 A.M. six days a week when the factory was running. Not only did the Bent plant dominate shoe production in Cochituate, its signals set the pattern of the village days.

In 1880 the Bent firm was employing about 330 workers. A significant number of them did not live in Cochituate but came daily, mostly from Natick but some from Saxonville, to work in the big plant. The resident population enumeration of the 1880 census for Wayland shows a total of 310 shoe workers living in the town, 295 males and 15 females. Of Bent's 1880 work force half, or perhaps a larger proportion, came daily to the plant from adjoining towns. The *Framingham*

The Bent Shoe Factory about 1860.

Gazette had noted in August 1875 that, notwithstanding the constant building of new houses, there were then some 200 persons working in Cochituate who lived out of town.

Except for those who lived in nearby North Natick who could walk to the plant, the Natick workers came in 1880 on George Keep's line of omnibus coaches or in private teams. In addition to managing a well-run, up-to-date factory taking advantage of new, laborsaving devices, perhaps the reason why the large Bent concern could flourish in a village not on a railroad was the successful public and private transportation arrangements that were worked out. The shoe factories could not have expanded as they did in the 1870s if transportation of workers, raw materials, and the finished product had not been made effective. In September 1874 "Quill" had written in the *Framingham Gazette:*

Our omnibus line is doing a thriving business as in addition to their six regular trips daily they are able to bring into requisition two extra coaches morn and eve to convey the mechanics and laborers living out of town employed by our citizens. Besides these omnibuses there are some half score of private teams that carry from two to twenty workmen each back and forth between Cochituate and Natick and Cochituate and Saxonville daily.[5]

The Bent Shoe Factory about 1880.

In February 1875 the same newspaper reported the addition of a fifth passenger coach for morning and evening trips and the imminent installation of a sixth.[6] We have already described the replacement of the coach line to Natick by the horse railroad which ran from the Natick railroad station to the terminal at Lyons Corner in Cochituate and which opened on July 30, 1885. At the time the horse railroad was being built the *Natick Bulletin* reported that efforts were being made to enable the horses to draw freight cars from the Natick railroad station to the Bent plant.[7] This never proved feasible, although William Harrison Bent was a director of the Natick and Cochituate Street Railroad.

The products of the Bent Company were all sent to Potter, White and Bayley, located in 1880 at 128 and 130 Summer Street in the shoe district of Boston. Earlier they had moved by train from the Natick and at times from the Stony Brook station in Weston. In December 1874 "Quill" had stated in the *Framingham Gazette* that the company had just put on the road "an elaborately finished Concord-built four horse express wagon to convey their freight between their factory and Stony Brook station on the Fitchburg Railroad."[8] But by the summer of 1879 it had been decided that it would be more economical to send the cases of shoes over the road all the way to Boston in large wagons. The *Natick Citizen* of July 11, 1879, carried an article about "a monster freight wagon" recently built for the Bent firm by J. D. Macewen of Natick. This wagon required six horses and had a storage capacity for seventy-five cases of shoes, all of which could be covered. It sometimes required eight horses to pull it through mud and snow.[9] James Madison Bent had a flair for showmanship. He probably enjoyed owning and using "the largest covered team running regularly to Boston."[10] By 1886 the firm had acquired a second very large wagon and at times of rushing business sent two large teams to Boston per day. It was found desirable to change horses on the way to the city, so a stable of replacement horses was kept in West Newton.

Other Factories

Second in size to the Bent factory in 1880 but not nearly as large was what was called the A. B. Lyon Company, named for Albert B. Lyon, then in his forties, who had taken over the business from his father, Otis T. Lyon. Albert Lyon then owned and lived in the house now standing at 14 West Plain Street. The factory, built in 1873, was beside the house toward the school on the west side of Main Street. Otis Lyon had come to Cochituate from Woodstock, Connecticut, with his young family in the mid-1840s.[11] It is not known what brought the Lyons to Cochituate with the Bowleses, Mrs. Lyon's relatives. The census of 1850 lists him as a shoemaker; he probably worked for the Bents, as a deed signed on July 6, 1849, shows William Bent selling him a one-half acre lot of land on the north side of Pond Street (Commonwealth Road).[12] The 1856 map shows O. T. Lyon with a house at this location. Dr. Boodey bought this house in 1888. It is now standing at 136 Commonwealth Road and is owned by Boodey relatives.

The November 22, 1878, *Natick Bulletin* article says that Otis T. Lyon went into business for himself in 1860; probably he had his son as a partner. The first shop was very small, in the backyard of the house on Pond Street. As of 1878 the Main Street shop, already added to once, was 25 by 110 feet with an ell 17 by 25 feet. The factory rose three stories above a basement and had a French or mansard roof. It had a 15-horsepower engine and what the reporter noted to be a very good steam piping system. The products were brogans and plowshoes, and the plant had a capacity of 150 cases per week. In 1878 the company, then called O. T. Lyon and Company, was employing eighty hands. Otis Lyon was sixty-eight years old in 1880 and no longer active in the business. In 1880 Albert B. Lyon was adding machinery to the plant, but two years later he sold the shop and machinery to David Parker and Company of Boston, for whom the Lyons had been making shoes for some time. Albert Lyon had decided to go west, and in June 1882 he assumed a position with the Chicago, Milwaukee and St. Paul Railroad. However, Lyon did not stay long in the Middle West; he returned to work for Wm. and J. M. Bent in Cochituate.[13]

In 1883 the Lyon factory building was leased to Charles H. Felch, who did not make a success of manufacturing shoes there. By 1888 it was being used as a paper-box-manufacturing plant and shows as Herbert Clark's box factory on *Walker's 1889 Middlesex County Atlas* map of Cochituate Village. Twenty girls were employed here around that time. Later uses of this factory building and an addition to it will be described below.

Much smaller in size in 1880 were the two Dean establishments. The Albert F. Dean plant typified the small Cochituate shoe factory, being described in 1878 as a shop of three stories 25 by 30 feet in dimensions. Land was expensive to buy or lease in Cochituate Village, so that the factories here were usually constructed vertically rather than horizontally. On this plan it also was easier to shaft the machinery. As of November 1878 it was reported that an addition of 30 by 20 feet was being planned and that an 8-horsepower engine was soon to be installed. Twenty-five hands were employed in late 1878 with an output of fifty cases per week. This firm failed in April 1882. There had been a previous failure in February 1878, but after offering creditors 15 cents on the dollar, the firm got going again and in April 1879 the addition was being built and steam put in.[14] In April 1882 the company experienced a severe failure, with liabilities of $18,175 and assets of $7,000. Albert Faxon Dean was one of the older sons of Henry W. Dean, who had first come to Cochituate as a shoe worker in the early 1840s[15] and died there in 1898. Henry W. had nine sons, several of whom engaged in shoe manufacturing in Cochituate.

In 1880 two of Albert F. Dean's brothers, Charles W. and Henry Colburn Dean, were in business together on a small scale, employing forty-five workers. This partnership was formed in August 1878. As of November 1878 the shop, located on the east side of Main Street, had three stories and measured 25 by 60 feet, employed sixty hands, and made about sixty cases of footwear a week, mostly brogans and plowshoes. It has not been possible to determine whether the "Colburn Dean" shop referred to in the newspapers several times in the 1890s with various partnerships, such as that of T. L. Sawin, Alfred

Loker, and Edward Moulton locating there in July 1891, was the same plant described in 1878. The *Natick Bulletin* of September 28, 1900, reported that at 3:00 A.M. on September 21 a fire had burned "the old Colburn Dean shop" to the ground. At that time one of the younger Dean brothers, Roscoe, was using the building for shoe manufacturing. We shall hear more of Charles W. Dean at a later point in this story.

The Alfred H. Bryant Company, which employed forty-five workers in 1880, had dwindled from its 1878 level of seventy-five hands and a capacity of sixty cases per week in 1878. Alfred H. Bryant had been taken into his father's (Thomas Bryant) firm as a partner in 1874, and by 1880 the elder Bryant had retired. Thomas Bryant had come to Cochituate in the 1840s, had engaged briefly in meat and other sales, and finally had settled down as a cordwainer. His first house, built for him in 1845, remained in its original location at 24 Main Street until September 1979 when it was moved to Natick to make way for an automobile parking lot. Bryant went to live in Grafton for a few years but returned to Cochituate in the early 1860s. A deed signed in April 1863 shows Thomas Bryant of Grafton, yeoman, buying from William Bent one acre of land and buildings (including a house) on the north side of Pond Street west of another Bent house which later was owned by William and Anna (Bent) Lovejoy.[16] The Bryant house, now standing at 128 Commonwealth Road is one built in 1879 by A. H. Bryant. In 1863 Bryant had built a one-story shoeshop 12 by 17 feet in its backyard. This one-story building was successively lengthened by adding 15 feet, 15 feet, and then 20 feet. At that point this long, low building was known as "Bryant's bowling alley." In this complex, during the Civil War, Bryant finished partly made shoes he purchased from the small shoemakers.

In 1870 a new, three-story plant of 50 by 27 feet was built, also in the backyard. In 1874 this building was enlarged to double its size, and a 12-horsepower steam engine was installed. The Bryant firm did not sell its brogans, plowshoes, and boys' boots through commission houses in Boston. Instead, the Bryants did their own selling, making extensive trips to the West and the South. In the fall of 1878 the shop was again enlarged; then in early 1879 the firm was reported to be in trouble and production was discontinued. In the summer of 1882 the Bent concern was preparing to use part of the idle space in the Bryant factory and Bryant was planning to start up production on his own when, on August 18, fire totally destroyed this building. The firm was dissolved after the fire, and Alfred H. Bryant went to work for the Bent firm as supervisor of the sole leather room.[17] Thomas Bryant had a close friendship with James Madison Bent. In 1885 he built a country house near the Dudley Pond country house of J. M. Bent. He died in 1895.

Larrabee and Wesson Company, which employed ten men in 1880—a partnership between William H. Larrabee and his son-in-law Charles J. Wesson—was a new firm in August 1878. It leased the two-story 40 by 25 foot factory with a mansard roof which Albert F. King had built in the early 1870s near his house "on the Wayland road" north of Lyons Corner. In 1878 the King factory employed twenty workers and had a capacity of twelve cases per week. Larrabee and Wesson were trying manufacturing on their own while King was leading a miner's life at Leadville, Colorado. In December 1883 this factory burned. In early 1884 it was reported that Larrabee and Wesson had hired the A. F. Dean shop, but this did not go through and in February of that year the partners moved to Chelsea where they established a retail shoe business.

The small shoeshop of Henry B. Fischer, Jr., located in the Happy Hollow section of Old Connecticut Path, burned in April 1881. After this fire Fischer went to work for the Bents.

Around 1880 the older firms of Lyon and Bryant were destined to come to their end. Other, lesser single ventures or partnerships came and went, but they were small and very short-lived compared with the Bent firm. A decade before, in 1870, there had been ten firms enumerated in the United States census. Wm. and J. M. Bent, with the only steampower in the town, then employed 205 out of the 319 shoe workers, or 65 percent of the total. Two of the Dean brothers, Thomas A. and Henry C., were then in business together, employing 20 men, 3 women, and 5 children. Thomas Bryant was operating with 24 employees. The others on the list were a different set of small entrepreneurs employing from 3 to 15 workers, all with handpower on two, three, or four machines. There were Alpheus D. Loker making shoes, Sewall Loker making brogans, William Hammond making boys' shoes, and Lafayette Dudley making brogans—all in Cochituate. Making brogans in Wayland was Charles W. Draper,[18] who had taken over from his father, Ira B. Draper, at a small shop on the Boston Post Road opposite the Unitarian Church in the center of Wayland. Wayland also had the tiny firms of Ward and Spofford employing 8 men and C. W. Hodges employing 2 men and a child.

The Puritan Village Evolves

NOTES

1. The volume on Manufactures, Fisheries and Commerce of the Massachusetts Census of 1865 reported that Wayland had three establishments employing 51 persons and producing boots and shoes of a value of $59,000.

2. *Tenth Census of the United States, 1880, Massachusetts, Manufactures,* Vol. 2. Supervisor District No. 60, Enumeration District No. 381, July 28, 1880. Original in Massachusetts Archives.

3. *Natick Bulletin,* November 22, 1878.

4. *Three Hundred Years of Shoe and Leather Making,* pamphlet published 1930 for the Massachusetts Tercentenary Celebration by Gill Publications.

5. *Framingham Gazette,* September 23, 1874.

6. *Ibid,* February 24, 1875.

7. *Natick Bulletin,* May 30, 1885.

8. *Framingham Gazette,* December 2, 1874.

9. *Natick Bulletin,* January 15, 1886.

10. *Natick Citizen,* April 13, 1883.

11. Otis T. Lyon appears first on a Wayland militia list in 1847.

12. South Middlesex Deeds, *Bent to Lyon,* Book 578, p. 572.

13. *Resident and Business Directory of Weston and Wayland for 1887,* Needham, Mass., 1887.

14. *Natick Citizen,* April 11, 1879.

15. Henry W. Dean appears on the Wayland militia roll of 1842. See *Mortgage Book I,* 1840-1859, p. 231.

16. South Middlesex Deeds, *Bent to Bryant,* Book 903, p. 457.

17. *Natick Bulletin,* November 4, 1885.

18. This name is given incorrectly in the manufacturers list in the census. This was either Curtis Warren Draper or Charles R. Draper, both sons of Ira B. Draper. Curtis W. Draper was listed on the 1870 population enumeration as a shoe manufacturer.

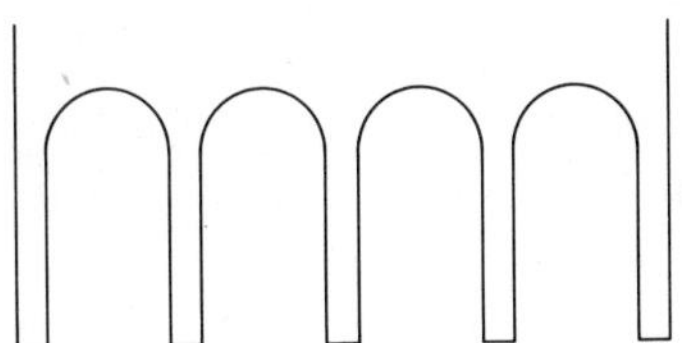

13

Historical Development of Shoemaking in Wayland

BEFORE RELATING the story of the expansion of the Bent company in the later 1880s and the Bent failure and subsequent replacement in the big factory by Charles W. Dean, it is desirable to take a look at the chronological development of Wayland's shoe industry from its beginning to 1880.

William Bent (1808-63), who had been trained as a shoemaker in Natick, built his first, one-room shoeshop in the 1830s behind the family homestead now standing at 43 Main Street in Cochituate. This house had been erected in 1775 by his grandfather, another William Bent, who was a fifth-generation descendant of John Bent, an original Sudbury proprietor. William, the shoemaker's father, had died in 1821, leaving his mother, Polly Coolidge Bent, a widow with three sons ranging from William, age thirteen, to a baby brother. By 1830 William was the man of the family. The first census of manufactures of Massachusetts, taken in 1837, showed a shoe output for Wayland of 29,896 pairs of boots and shoes with a value of $22,419. Employment in shoemaking was stated to be 31 males and 15 females. It is not known whether these figures included shoemaking operations other than by William Bent, but it is likely that there were then a few other small shoemakers making shoes for sale in an outside market, including at least one shoeshop in the northern or Wayland Center part of the town.

In the 1830s and 1840s small shoemaking establishments existed in many eastern Massachusetts towns. Tanneries were quite prevalent as sources of raw material; large sources of power were not needed. Small entrepreneurs developed manufacturing operations in ells of their houses, in barns, or in very small shops near their homes. Often some or all of their few workers, usually young men who did not want to follow farming, boarded with them. The end product could be carted to Boston, so there were no particular locational advantages. At this stage work was done by hand with the large entrepreneurs like the Bents letting out bottoming and other phases of the work by the case (of fifty to sixty pairs) to be worked on in small shops adjoining their homes. These small shops were often known as "ten-footers."

The United States census of 1840 was the first to indicate the number of persons in each household engaged in agriculture, in manufacturing and trade, in commerce, and in "the learned professions." Most of Wayland's working population—221 men—were engaged in agriculture, but there were 62 persons then engaged in manufacture and trade. Some of these were blacksmiths, harnessmakers, and tailors, but on the list one sees numerous early shoemakers. Wayland Center resident Ira B. Draper was already engaged in manufacture, as was Henry R. Newton who, having married a Weston girl in 1837, had moved to Wayland from Southborough where he was related to shoemaking pioneers of that town. First located on Old Sudbury Road, in 1849 he acquired the old, pre-Revolutionary Noyes house on the Boston Post Road opposite the end of Pinebrook Road.[1] Here he engaged in shoe manufacturing on a small scale until about 1870 when he retired to be a "farmer."

Several of the early Cochituate shoemakers are among those listed as engaged in manufacture in 1840, namely, John C. Butterfield, Ezra Howe, Samuel G. Farmer, and Joseph B. Hawes. It is significant that William Bent, who never married and had no family, had six persons engaged in manufacture or trade in his household, as did also James M. Bent who then had two small children but who shows in the 1840 census as having five males age twenty to thirty, one ten to fifteen, and one fifteen to twenty in his household. William Bent's shoemanufacturing operation was growing beyond that of all other such operations in the town, and William and his brother were housing some of their workers.

The United States census of 1850 had a much more elaborate population enumeration, and the "Products of Industry" were recorded for the first time, for the year ending June 1, 1850. For Wayland the only firm of any kind was the Wm. and J. M. Bent Company, shoemakers. Capital invested was given as $6,000, motive power as hand, average number employed as 65 males and 40 females. Annual product was 80,000 pairs of shoes, valued at $57,600. By then, workers must have been coming in from Natick and possibly from Saxonville. The 1850 population enumeration for Wayland listed 34 shoemakers in Cochituate. The Bent firm was the only one of any size in the town in 1850, but there were other very small manufacturers. We find in the chattel mortgage record that on January 31, 1849, William M. Richards, cordwainer, borrowed from Henry R. Newton, shoe manufacturer, on the security of all of his household goods and furniture in a house being leased from Leonard Wood of Wayland.[2]

For Wayland, at least, the census enumerated only the largest manufacturer. It is interesting to note that in 1850 there were twenty-five shoe manufacturers shown in this census for Natick. These firms employed from 4 to 250 workers each, with a total employment of 1,559, and turned out 1,115,000 pairs of boots and shoes, all with handpower.

In the first of a series of censuses taken by the Commonwealth of Massachusetts between the United States decennial censuses—that of 1855—the "Statistics of Industry" stated that during that year 98,500 pairs of shoes valued at $82,600 were produced in Wayland with the employment of 87 males and 42 females. It is not known how many manufacturers were included in these totals.

Under "Products of Industry" the United States census of 1860 listed for Wayland four shoe manufacturers, with the Bent company very much the largest. Wm. and J. M. Bent were reported as making that year 96,700 pairs of shoes valued at $87,000. Next in size was Henry R. Newton, who is reported to have made 25,000 pairs with 10 male and 5 female employees. The population enumeration for 1860 shows various shoemakers in Newton's Boston Post Road area of eastern Wayland. There was Isaac Warren living across the street and Adonirum Puffer living nearby. William Green, Adolphus Ingraham, Charles McDermott, and Terry Brennen were listed as shoemakers living in Newton's household. Also in Wayland Center, Ira B. Draper was a shoe manufacturer who made 1,700 pairs of shoes; and at the edge of Cochituate (the School Street area), Enoch Dudley, who did not operate all year, had made 2,400 pairs.

The *Natick Bulletin* article of 1878 says that Otis T. Lyon started his own shoe-manufacturing firm in 1860. This firm was not listed under "Products of Industry" for 1860. The population census for that year shows Otis T. Lyon, age forty-seven, shoemaker, as head of a household with his son, Albert B. Lyon, age twenty-three, shoemaker. In this household were also Edwin P. Johnson, age twenty-five, a shoemaker born in New Hampshire, and John Grishaler, age twenty-one, shoemaker, born in Württemberg, Germany. Other German-born shoemakers listed as in Wayland in 1860 were Gerhart, Joseph, and Rolff Genter; Simon Schwartz; Ferdinand, Jacob, and Casper Corman; and Sebastian and Leo Jaeger.

The 1860 census summary giving products of industry stated that Wm. and J. M. Bent Company used both hand- and steampower with 4 horsepower. James Madison Bent's obituary written in 1888 stated that steam was first put into the Bent factory in 1862. The census statement belies this, although it is probable that a bigger and more useful steam engine was purchased in 1862. The older partner, William Bent, died in 1863. The inventory of his estate lists "shoe manufacturing shop and 1/3 acre of land with steem [sic] engine and machinery valued at $2600."[3] This accounting implies that William owned the plant and the steam engine. On the other hand, he owned certain machines jointly with his brother. Under personal estate are listed: "½ solather [sole leather] raser, ½ solather cutter, ½ splitting machine, ½ roller, and ½ pegging machine." No sewing machines were mentioned in this inventory; these were usually the first machines owned by a shoe company. According to the chattel mortgage record book, on July 11, 1864, James M. Bent borrowed $1,000 from the Waltham Bank, using as security one engine valued at $1,000, one heater and pipe valued at $100, one boiler valued at $300, and also one pegging machine valued at $300.[4] We also find in 1868 Willard B. Ward borrowing $150 from a man in Sudbury using as collateral "one foot-powered pegging machine . . . used in the shoe shop now occupied by me in Wayland."[5]

An article in the April 28, 1891, *Shoe and Leather Reporter* said that sewing machines were first introduced into shoe factories in 1852. Pegging machines were invented in 1858, and these came to replace hand pegging, which had continued in the outside bottoming shops. Sole sewing machines were introduced in 1862. During the 1860s the industry became mechanized, and the machinery and power sources were increasingly concentrated in the Bent and a few other, smaller factories.

Despite the disruption to southern markets and to local manpower caused by the Civil War, shoe manufacturing grew in Wayland between 1860 and 1865. In the "Statistics of Industry of Massachusetts" in the state census of 1865 Wayland is listed as having a shoe output of

191,844 pairs with a value of $82,760. Male employment was 182, female 39. It is not clear whether these were the figures for the Bent concern only. A statement in the Massachusetts census of 1875, Volume II, *Manufactures and Occupations,* is to the effect that the Wayland figures for 1865 had been for one establishment. The population enumeration for 1865 lists as shoe manufacturers besides the Bents: Henry R. Newton, James N. Hammond, James W. Dudley, Lafayette Dudley, Enoch Dudley, Otis T. Lyon and his son Albert B., Sewall Loker, and Thomas Bryant. Ira B. Draper is listed in this enumeration as a shoemaker and not as a manufacturer.

Appended as Appendix D is a list of the early shoemakers in Cochituate and Wayland, the men designated as such in the census of 1850 in vital records and in the early mortgage records. Some of these men had ten-footer shops to which they took shoe parts to be put together for the Bent company, this being done before all work was concentrated in the factories. The change to all-factory production came gradually, and some work was probably being done outside the main shop well into the 1860s.

There is no reason to believe that the development in Cochituate from a domestic, through a putting-out, to a full-factory system was any different from the evolution described in Hazard's classic book on the early shoe industry in Massachusetts, *The Organization of the Boot and Shoe Industry in Massachusetts Before 1875*, published in 1921. Miss Hazard did not study the Bent company or mention Cochituate, but she did have quite a bit to say about brogans and Natick's development as a shoe-manufacturing center.

In Alfred S. Hudson's *Annals of Sudbury, Wayland and Maynard,* published in 1891, there is an Appendix entitled "The Shoe Business and its Growth in Cochituate." Clearly someone knowledgeable about the development of the shoe business in general and developments in Cochituate in particular was asked to write this section. It would be interesting to know who wrote this three-page piece. It may have been one of James Madison Bent's sons. The part starting with, "Work began to be done in larger shops . . . and the high bench and head block upon which the last was strapped took the place of the low bench when the shoe was pegged on the knees," is very graphic and shows an intimate knowledge of how this work was done when the central shop let out the bottoming work. This writer has not found anywhere in the literature on the early shoe industry anything as clear with as many technical terms explained. This article is well worth reading by anyone interested in the history of the Massachusetts shoe industry.

The article states that "For years William and James Madison Bent let out work from a shop nearly opposite the former residence of William Bent which was on the main street of the village; and there are those who still remember the old man as he leisurely walked from the house to the shop when the work was brought in." The early "Greek Revival" factory, with the four columns, had a tall chimney at the back. The first steam engine may have been placed in this building. Tradition in the Bent family holds that before the acquisition of the steam engine, that is, in the 1850s, animals on a treadmill on the ground floor of the lower, central part of the building connecting to the store provided power for the first machines. The January 30, 1880, *Natick Bulletin* article on the Bent company alludes to "the nag hitched to a cider mill sweep in the cellar of the old 20 by 30 shop." Those first machines would have been sewing machines to put the uppers together so that they could be bottomed by the outside shoemakers.

By the year 1880 the entire shoemaking operation was concentrated in factories which had departments for cutting both sole and upper leather; fitting and stitching departments; as well as lasting, bottoming, and finishing departments. Steampower had come into universal use; Blanche Hazard stated that by 1860 steampower was being introduced into the larger factories.[6] As of 1860 the Bent factory was not large by the standards of such shoe towns as Natick and Lynn. It seems definite that the Bents, led by James Madison who was something of a mechanical genius, were quick to see the merits of, and to acquire advanced equipment for, their factory. James Madison Bent's obituary in the *Natick Bulletin* stated that he was the first in the area to introduce steam into a shoe factory.[7] This statement is not correct. The 1860 census shows that the E. B. Phillips Shoe Company of Natick ran its machinery with a 6-horsepower engine. Also, in Hopkinton the large Claflin, Coburn and Company boot factory was run by steampower.[8]

The shoe industry was quite subject to the ups and downs of the prevalent business cycles of the late nineteenth century. We find that by the early 1880s business had temporarily ceased to boom in Cochituate. In March 1882 the *Natick Bulletin* quoted at length from an article on Cochituate that had appeared in the *Boston Globe*. According to this article:[9]

Some seven years ago [1875] *that village was noted for a boom in the brogan line. . . . Within the past three years this village has shown a noticeable decrease in its industry and upward of forty tenements in the once-filled houses stand idle. . . . Of those . . . doing business, several have suspended. Wm. and J. M. Bent are doing the greater portion of the manufacturing. The outlook toward an increase in the "brogan" line is not very encouraging and many shoemakers have left for other towns. The introduction of steam, labor-saving machinery and the rapid decline of business has tended to throw men out of employment.*

The Massachusetts census of 1875 showed that 69 percent of the Wayland (Cochituate) shoe workers worked as piece hands. The male day hands were paid $2.49 a day, the female day hands $1.02. Pieceworkers earned something more than this—the men $2.71 a day on the average and the women $1.28.[10]

There are no statistics on injuries in the factories, but one cannot read the Cochituate news in the Natick papers without being horrified by the prevalence of accidents in the factories, especially involving workers' hands. Dr. Boodey was kept very busy sewing up these injuries or doing amputations. This statewide situation eventually led to factory safety laws and to the installation of safety devices on the machinery. The *Natick Citizen* of February 20, 1885, carried the story that "William Coggin had the forefinger of his right hand so badly jammed in the rolling machine in the shoe shop Tuesday morning that amputation was necessary. He has already lost a finger on the left hand and has been injured by this machine no less than seven times."

In times of good business strikes were apt to occur. In July 1879 the *Natick Bulletin* reported that the bottomers in nearly all of the factories struck for and received a wage increase of 10 percent. In the same month Bent's blackers also struck and were granted a 5 to 7 percent increase in pay.[11] The *Natick Bulletin* reported that in late September a labor meeting was held in Schoolhouse Hall to hear "speakers in the cause of labor."[12] Small attendance was reported. With depression came wage reductions, and we read in the newspaper that following wage cuts Cochituate shoe lasters had joined the lasters' union recently formed in Natick.[13] There was a certain amount of labor trouble at this time, but in general unions were not yet strong in Cochituate.

Because of fluctuations of orders and the changes in manufacturing runs, work even in the best of times was not absolutely continuous in the factories. From time to time, with almost no notice, the shoe workers were laid off in complete or partial plant shutdowns, and of course the hands were not paid when they were not working. The

Cochituate columns in the Natick newspapers make these shutdowns sound natural and sometimes commented that these times off, often called "loafs," were welcome, enabling the workers to catch up on home chores and engage in recreational activities such as going fishing locally or making trips to the city. Scheduled vacations as such did not exist, with or without pay. There were, however, a certain few holidays—Thanksgiving, Christmas, Fast Day, and July Fourth.

In the late 1870s the plants began shutting down by 3:30 P.M. on Saturdays (as opposed to 5:45 P.M. or 6:00 P.M. on other days) in the summer so that the workers could attend the very popular local baseball games. Baseball was introduced into Cochituate in 1867 when the Live Oak Baseball Club was formed and played against the Natick Eagles.[14] During the next forty years baseball contests on every level took place between Cochituate and other town clubs, between Cochituate and Wayland (Wayland Meadow Hens versus Cochituate Shop Ends),[15] between local plants (the lasters at Bent's and the lasters at Bryant's), and plants in other towns (with the Waltham Watch factory team). There were games between a crack Cochituate team and the Harvard College team.[16] And there were contests between occupants of different boardinghouses (Lovejoy's versus American House). There was even a fat man's nine, which included Dr. Boodey at 230 pounds and Selectman William Hammond at 210 pounds.[17]

Until 1883 baseball games were played at the City Pastures, land south of Pond Street belonging to the Boston water board. In the summer of 1883 the field in back of the Lyon factory began to be used, though not exclusively, for baseball. In August 1883 this field is referred to as the "New Baseball Ground." Elmer Bent, William Harrison Bent's son, was a pitching star and did some coaching of the Harvard College team. He had a chance to become a professional player but chose not to leave his job in the family firm. Alfred ("Bub") Moore, another outstanding Cochituate baseball player, did become a professional.

The only half holidays were not for baseball. Dating back probably to the 1850s or 1860s there was a Bent summer half holiday for the women and for a few of the men to go blueberry picking at Nobscot Hill in Framingham. The *Natick Bulletin* of August 13, 1886, describes that year's event as a great outing, including ninety-three persons, with a Mrs. Bacon winning the prize for picking twenty-three quarts of blueberries. Not everyone went on the berrying expedition, but nearly everyone enjoyed the annual holiday in September to attend the Framingham cattle fair at which Cochituate farmers like Isaac Damon and William Harrison Bent exhibited their cattle and in which Cochituate ladies entered exhibits of all kinds of things from jellies and jams to oil paintings. The Bent firm usually arranged for transportation to the fair.

NOTES

1. South Middlesex Deeds, Book 390, pp. 447 and 449 and Book 574, p. 155.
2. Town of Wayland, *Mortgages*, Book I. 1840-1859, p. 96.
3. Middlesex Probate, William Bent will, 1863, No. 27329.
4. Town of Wayland, *Record of Mortgages of Personal Property*, Book II, 1859-1875, p. 80.
5. *Ibid*, p. 136.
6. Blanche Evans Hazard, *The Organization of the Boot and Shoe Industry in Massachusetts before 1875*, Harvard University Press, 1921, p. 124.
7. *Natick Bulletin*, July 27, 1888.
8. United States Census of 1860, original enumeration in Massachusetts Archives.
9. *Natick Bulletin*, March 9, 1882.
10. *Massachusetts Census of 1875*, Vol. II, Manufactures and Occupations, p. 401.
11. *Natick Citizen*, July 18, 1879.
12. *Natick Bulletin*, October 3, 1879.
13. *Ibid*, November 23, 1883.
14. *Ibid*, July 22, 1887.
15. *Ibid*, August 30, 1889.
16. *Ibid*, April 15, 1887.
17. *Natick Citizen*, May 31, 1878.

14

Further Expansion and the Bent Company Failure

Factory Additions

BY LATE 1882 and early 1883 the worst of the business slowdown was over, and we find talk in the *Natick Bulletin* of adding to the Bent plant. In late 1882 the Bents built a separate building to extract oil from upper leather shoe lifts with naphtha.[1] But no addition to the large factory was reported as actually built until a one-story addition (40 by 56 feet) for the sole-leather-cutting department was constructed at the south end of the factory in the fall of 1885.[2] In order to expand in this direction, in June 1885 the company had bought from Margaret M. Dudley, widow of James Winthrop Dudley, and from other Dudley relatives the property on which stood the 1845 house (24 Main Street) which Thomas Bryant had built.[3] In May 1886 work started on a further 40 by 40 foot addition south of the structure built the previous fall.[4] At this time business was reported as rushing, and plant expansion was the order of the day. This may have been what the *Natick Bulletin* was referring to in describing a *Boston Herald* article about a quickly made addition to the Bent plant. The *Bulletin* stated:

Jesse Jones appreciates a good thing and speaks a good word for the Bent factory in The Herald. *He says "In Wayland in this state a short time ago a manufacturer was so pressed with orders that he engaged a great force of carpenters to put up a four story addition 75 feet long in three weeks, filled it immediately with workers and has now increased his product thereby 75 cases a day."*[5]

This writer could not find the story in the *Boston Herald* and does not know whether it was apocryphal. It at least indicates that the Bent plant was growing spectacularly.

The year 1886 brought further growth to the Bent plant. By July a one-story addition had been completed for the company offices.[6] This created a second floor above a one-story section. The new offices were reported in the *Natick Bulletin* of September 3, 1886, as being "a perfect paradise" with "a host of clerks busily employed constantly. The private office of the firm is in another room and is a model of convenience also." This room may have been the one reported as having stained-glass windows. On May 13, 1887, the *Natick Bulletin* reported that Harry N. Rockwell had been appointed foreman for the ensuing year with John R. Newton and Harry Bond as assistants. Delos W. Mitchell was clerk, E. M. Partridge treasurer, and H. B. Fischer steward.

In October 1886 it was reported that land behind the factory had been bought from Isaac Damon to build a three-story addition on the southwest corner with a basement for the boiler room.[7] This was ready for use in late November. Again, in May 1887 the *Natick Bulletin* reported that "the manufacturing capacity of the big shop is tested to its utmost capacity . . . and it is considered probable that a great addition will be made." Instead of building a large addition, however, there was a report in July 29, 1887, that "the big factory is now producing over 5,000 pairs of shoes in a day using several vacant shops." The rumored large addition was probably not made that year, but in October improvements in the engine and boiler room were mentioned, and it was reported that the roof had been raised to give more light.[8] Next month the November 18 *Natick Bulletin* reported that work had been begun on a small addition. This news item then went on to say: "In the spring an addition that dwarfs all previous attempts to provide quarters will be put up."[9] Business slacked off some in 1888. There is no evidence that any building was started that year. Thus, the additions described above probably produced the plant as it looks in the Cochituate lithograph which was finished very late in 1887.

Bent Family Elegance

From the tone of reports in the *Natick Bulletin*, 1887 may have been the most prosperous as well as the busiest year in the history of the Bent company. For the ten or twelve years leading up to this time the Natick newspapers had been reporting the activities of the Bents as those of a rich and rather glamorous family. They were not, of course, wealthy on the scale of Carnegies and Vanderbilts whose riches and conspicuous consumption and alliances with European titles were then being reported nationwide in the newspapers, but the luxuries the Bents could afford were fairly frequent subjects of press reports.

James Madison Bent's house, built perhaps in the late 1850s or early 1860s diagonally across from the factory on the northeast corner of Main Street and what is now Commonwealth Road, became more and more of a showplace. By 1880 there was a fountain in front of the house. A newspaper item tells us that a pair of rare Pekin ducks had been acquired for the fountain pool.[10] That December small spruce trees were placed in the fountain, and their frozen shapes glistening with ice were described as being "like fairyland." In 1882, following the style of the day, a mansard roof was put on the house. This house was torn down in 1954 to make way for the Cochituate Motors showroom.

Not long after remodeling his "downtown" house James Madison Bent built—in 1883—a summer home on Dudley Pond on a bluff adjoining the Simpson property. In an article in the *Natick Citizen* of September 28, 1883, the house is described as

> *on a high bluff a hundred feet from the lake* [Dudley Pond] *in the midst of an evergreen hemlock grove* [where] *Mr. Bent has erected a summer cottage of the Queen Anne style, surrounded with a broad verandah and arranged with taste and elegance within. . . . The grove surrounding is fitted up with swings, seats, etc. and connected with the cottage by a flight of one hundred steps to the wharf where is moored the steamer "Hannah Dexter."*

The house is shown on the 1887 Cochituate lithograph. It was not very near the Simpson mansion, but the property may have adjoined Simpson land.

The *Hannah Dexter* was a steam-powered launch about which the Cochituate columnists in the Natick newspapers enjoyed writing. The *Natick Citizen* of April 11, 1879, had noted that: "Mr. J. M. Bent's new steamboat arrived last Monday. She is a beauty." On April 25:

J. M. Bent's new steamer was launched last Tuesday in the presence of about three hundred persons. About 1:30 P.M. the fasts which bound her to the shore were loosed and "with a joyous, exulting bound" she leaped into Old Lake Cochituate's arms

"And lo! from the assembled crowd
There arose a shout prolonged and loud."

Mr. Thomas Bryant with his usual forethought had brought along a hod of coal, which, in the bustle and excitement of the occasion others had forgotten. At precisely two o'clock P.M. the engineer, Mr. Nelson Haynes, got up steam, and upon trial, she was found to be a perfect success. She was built for river navigation and Mr. Bent contemplates making several excursions on the Sudbury river as far as Billerica. She is a very pretty craft, and if she is true to his maxim, Madison can "rule the sea, while Martha rules the land."[11]
signed Harry

The Citizen article makes the boat sound sizable. The *Natick Bulletin* of April 11 said that parts had arrived and were being assembled to produce a boat 21 feet long with a 6-foot beam and 34 inches deep. It had a boiler and a 2-horsepower engine. On May 23 Bent and a friend from South Natick who also owned a boat powered by steam went down the Sudbury River to Billerica to the home of Governor Talbot.[12] They launched their boats at Wayland. Apparently the steamer, or steam yacht as it was sometimes called in the newspaper stories, could be put on the big Bent company wagon and taken any distance. There was a report of it being taken to South Boston to be launched in salt water to explore the Boston Harbor area and of it being hauled to Newcastle, New Hampshire, where the James Madison Bents regularly spent summer vacations for a number of years. The *Hannah Dexter* wasn't the *North Star* of Commodore Cornelius Vanderbilt, but the local papers liked to flatter J. M. Bent by writing as if it were.

At the end of the 1883 article about the Dudley Pond summer estate, where in his last years J. M. Bent lived the year round, the author wrote that:

Forty years ago . . . Cochituate Village . . . consisted of less than half a dozen weather-stained houses, no church, no school, no post office, no business,–nothing but squalor and neglect. . . . Today substantial residences, also churches and schools abound, the factory of Bent and Sons is daily turning out its celebrated products, thrift and enterprise are everywhere apparent and the hand whose work is seen in it all is that of James Madison Bent.

The same kind of extravagant admiration is apparent in the following article, which appeared in the *Natick Citizen* of August 18, 1882:

MODEL VACATIONISTS–BENT AND BRYANT ENCAMPMENT

By special invitation from Mr. J. M. Bent Esq., the writer and a few select friends visited, this week, the encampment of the Bent and Bryant families on Reeves Hill, Wayland. These hills are part of the continuous range extending through the towns of Wayland and Weston, terminating in Prospect Hill, Waltham. From this camping place, some two or three hundred feet above the level of the Concord river, which flows within a mile of its base, can be seen Kearsage, Cardigan, Franconia, Monadnock, Moosilauke and Mt. Washington in New Hampshire and Wachuset in Princeton. The Summit House can be distinctly seen with the naked eye while at your feet nestles the village of Wayland, in front of which meanders the majestic Concord river in its onward course to the sea, passing through one of the most fertile sections of all New England.

The farm which this hill forms a part has been in the possession of the Reeves family since the first settlement of the town. Its thrifty fields, well-filled barns and commodious farm house strike the lover of the beautiful sight. The hill is situated about three miles from the village of Cochituate. In reaching it you pass over a shady and somewhat secluded drive, interspersed with hill, dale and romantic scenery. The idea of bringing a mountain resort to your own door was original with the Bent and Bryant families. Being at the head of one of the most extensive shoe factories in the world and knowing the necessity of giving their personal attention to the same, they conceived this idea of being within easy reach of their daily business. Their families and themselves are not deprived of that change of air and recreation so indispensible to the development of the human system and the enjoyment of life.

This encampment consists of some eight families each provided with a water-proof tent, two cook houses, and stable for four horses. They receive daily, milk from their own cows, fruit and vegetables from their own gardens, while, from the parties who frequent the river for the fine perch and pickerel in its waters or hunt the woodcock, duck and teal that inhabit its shores and supply the Parker, Revere, and Tremont of Boston with game and fish, can be procured at any time all the most dainty epicure desires. If fancy dictates, you can do your own hunting and fishing and imagine yourselves in the Adirondack region. For gymnastic exercise you can go to the river and "bend the oarlocks," or if excitement is desirable take a seat in that natty, staunch little steamer "Hannah Dexter" and if Uncle Jim don't pull you along fast enough you are hard to be suited.

As we stood under the stars and stripes that waved over our heads and viewed the sun as it faded from our view behind Wachuset and took leave of our genial hosts, we could but contrast their tastes and situation with those who make pilgrimages to the far off pleasure resorts and endure all sorts of deprivations and extortion that they may appease the wrath of the God of fashion.

signed XYZ

This article describes a practice that went on for several summers in the 1880s—that of the Bents with their friends the Bryants camping for some weeks of the hot weather on Reeves Hill in Wayland on land leased from the Reeves family. After James M. Bent built his Dudley Pond home, his sons William H. and Ralph had small houses built and hauled up Reeves Hill for summer coolness and the enjoyment of this beautiful, rural part of Wayland. In 1885 William H. Bent had a thirty-foot wooden observation tower built by Cochituate carpenter Edwin Marston on the top of Reeves Hill. The Bents appreciated the change of scene from the hot and crowded streets of Cochituate where their houses were very near the big and noisy factory. Other, lesser Cochituate folk camped out by themselves on the shores of Lake Cochituate or Dudley Pond or went to one of the several organized camps on the Natick shore of Lake Cochituate for summer relief. Swimming was not allowed in Lake Cochituate by the Boston water board, but by the original agreement with the towns boating could not be prohibited. J. M. Bent sued to be allowed to run the *Hannah Dexter* on the lake and won. It is not true that no recreation was allowed on or near the Lake. Such camps over the border in Natick as Camp Philip Tray, Camp Pleasant, and Shady Nook housed quite large aggregations of people during the summer months.

James Madison Bent was of the old school. He had started out with nothing but his simple education, native abilities, a willingness to work, and a determination to turn out a good product. Except for his houses and his steam launch, he did not spend generously, and the scale of those items was not lavish. However, inevitably his four sons who were in the company either as partners or as employees acted in some degree like rich men's sons. As was typical of the wealthy of that era in America, they went in for prize livestock. All of the Bents owned and drove fancy horses, but Myron and Ralph were the chief horse fanciers. The *Natick Citizen* of June 28, 1878, announced that Ralph Bent, then twenty-three years old, had been to New York State for another fine-bred colt, "of Hambletonian and champion blood." The brief article went on to say: "The Bents are bound to have good horses." Myron Bent went in for trotting races and on October 24, 1879, he was reported selling his trotting horse, Middlesex, to a man in Detroit. Another item in the *Natick Bulletin* of August 1, 1890, told that James Alvin Bent went to New York "to purchase a new pair of fast horses." James A. Bent also went in for fancy fowl; in 1883 he bought a flock of purebred brahma fowls.[13]

In the mid-1870s William Harrison Bent, who had been married at twenty-one in 1861, was living on the west side of Main Street. In 1880 he had built a new Victorian house just east of Madison (Winter) Street on the north side of Commonwealth Road. The granite steps going up to this house are still to be seen; the house was torn down in 1968 to make room for a modern nursing home building. When his house was in the process of construction, it was reported to be "the finest and most substantial in town."[14] By 1887, however, W. H. Bent had decided to go in for a gentleman's farm in the country and built the house now standing at 67 Loker Street, which the newspapers said he variously called Barney Hill Farm, Cradle Nook Farm, and Lakeview Farm. Here Mrs. Teresa (Loker) Bent entertained her friends and relatives from the village, and her husband built up a herd of blooded Holstein cattle, termed in the May 4, 1888, *Natick Bulletin* "the finest herd of Holstein cattle in New England."

The grandchildren also enjoyed the family prosperity. In 1881 Elmer Bent, William Harrison's son, the athlete of the family, had, after becoming very proficient on a bicycle (bicycling was then all the rage), won races at Cape Cod and the Massachusetts amateur championship.[15] In March 1882 the *Natick Bulletin* related that Elmer Bent had had a half-racer Yale bicycle custom made to order in England.[16]

Death of James Madison Bent

In the early summer of 1888 James Madison Bent, then age seventy-six, fell ill and died on July 24. The *Natick Bulletin* of July 27 carried two articles about him. One, in the Cochituate column, was a

James Madison Bent (1812-1888).

factual account of his life; the other was a flowery and exaggerated obituary article calling him "one of the leading men in this section of Massachusetts, not only in business but in public affairs." The article went on with reasonable accuracy to say that he was responsible for the prosperous and growing village of Cochituate which, before he came along, had been "a widely extended, unoccupied plain, parching under the suns of summer; a black, desolate waste in winter, remote from great lines of travel and far from the marts of trade." Later in the article he was termed "one of the leading shoe manufacturers of the nation"; also, "He gloried in the village because it was Cochituate and as such alone he wanted it to progress." The article ended with the statement: "It may be fairly said that he had been one of the great benefactors of this commonwealth. He brought a new town into existence and made its influence felt as a part of the business world."

A man of outstanding ability had died. James Sumner Draper wrote of him in an article in the "Appendix to The Annals of Wayland" in Hudson's *Annals of Sudbury, Wayland and Maynard* (1891) as follows:

As a result of his success the locality has risen from a mere hamlet of a few dwellings to a thriving and populous village. As a citizen he has won high esteem for his enterprise and public spirit. A vein of humor ran through his mental structure that gave a peculiar charm to his presence socially; many a cloud has been dispelled by his facetious but courteous remarks.

We are reminded by Draper's words of the impish behavior "Quill" described as J. M. Bent's at the town meetings in 1873 regarding the Cochituate School. Alluding to what a good town meeting moderator Sylvester Reeves had been, "Quill" wrote:

We were sorry that our friend Reeves who was there,
Was not elected to the honors of the chair;
Who brought to the office when he was in it
The dignity of a president of the United States senate,
Maintaining good order with parliamentary rule
Like a stern pedagogue of a common district school,
Taking care the old boy on mischief "Bent"
Was duly admonished, and to his seat sent,
The latter seating himself with a refractory sigh,
His gold-bows half concealing the fun in his eye,
Concluding no more the moderator he'd annoy,
But behave himself quietly like a good boy.

The obituary which appeared in the August 2, 1888, *Shoe and Leather Reporter* stressed the excellent quality of James Madison Bent's shoes and the reliability of his business dealings.

By coincidence there had appeared in the July 5, 1888, *Shoe and Leather Reporter* an article set in the form of an interview with a shoe manufacturer who had moved from one of the large shoe-manufacturing centers to a "back country district." The article ends with a question about the workmen's leisure hours. The manufacturer answers by saying:

The shops are gainers by their spending, the church by their contributions; everything is vitalized. As for amusements, after the blow-out whistle sounds and supper is over, an opportunity will be afforded you and me to see some pretty good baseball playing in a field hard by. This game I encourage, believing it to be in the interest of all concerned. Hence the factory is shut down on Saturdays in the summer at 12 o'clock. This evening you will doubtless hear our band rehearsing. They are quite proficient for backwoods players. If you take a stroll, and keep your ears open, no doubt you will hear some piano music from the lassies who in the day time whirl shoe uppers through sewing machines. The factory has been the making of the village, as the citizens have been benefited by my pecuniary means. It is a grand scheme.

Baseball has been said to have been a particular specialty of Cochituate. One can almost hear J. M. Bent talking in the above vein, but there is no evidence that he had anything to do with this so-called interview. We must conclude that baseball was important as recreation in various rural manufacturing villages. As for the band, we have said little about it, but the Cochituate Brass Band figured heavily in news accounts of the village. It probably was started about 1860 under the leadership of E. P. Hartshorn, who was succeeded by Llewellyn Flanders in 1878. It had been an organization separate from the Wm. and J. M. Bent Company, but it was definitely given sponsorship by James M. Bent. We find in the town mortgage records that in 1878 the band had a building on the east side of Madison Street on land leased from James M. Bent.[17] A band created spirit and morale, and it fitted into James M. Bent's flair for publicity. Whenever the Bents entertained, the band was a prominent feature, as in November 1874 when there was a banquet with three hundred guests to congratulate William Harrison Bent on being elected to the state legislature.[18] For the Fourth of July celebration in 1879 the Cochituate Brass Band played on a raft in the middle of the Sudbury River.[19] Instead of being unique in having a band and company baseball teams, Cochituate was in a way the typical example of the rural shoe community.

The Business Continued by the Bent Sons

After James Madison Bent's death, the sons, with William Harrison and James Alvin as the partners, carried on the business. James M. Bent left relatively little property. Before his last illness he had apparently conveyed his interest in the firm to the four sons involved in it. He had also divested himself of all real estate except the Dudley Pond house, which he left to Thomas Dexter Bent, a son who had not been connected with the shoe firm.[20]

In a downturn of trade in the spring of 1889 wages of stitchers and treers in the Bent plant were reduced. This led to the formation of a stitchers' union.[21] Back in November 1883 a wage reduction for the lasters (the most skilled of the shoe workers) had encouraged the Cochituate lasters to join the recently formed Natick lasters' union.[22] In January 1884 a branch of the Lasters' Protective Union was formed in Cochituate with what the *Natick Bulletin* described as a large

The Knights of Labor Hall, built in 1888, when used by the Grange in 1915.

membership.[23] In August of that year the Cochituate lasters' union sent Frank Lupien as a delegate to the Peoples' Convention.[24] In April 1885 the lasters' union was reported hiring a room in the Lokerville School for meetings.[25]

A Knights of Labor chapter had been chartered in Natick in 1882, but it had been of little importance in Cochituate until the Knights settled the lasters' strike at Bent's in 1883. By 1886 the Knights of Labor had been affluent enough to purchase the lot on the northwest quadrant of Lyons Corner with a plan to erect a building for their headquarters and meetings. The *Natick Bulletin* of October 29, 1886, said: "This venture is expected to be successful as Cochituate has no public hall." It took time to collect money, but by January 1888 the frame of the building was up,[26] and by March the structure, though not completed, was closed in enough to make possible a three-day fair to celebrate the opening of the building.[27] Fairs were frequently held in this era to raise money for large local projects. Instead of being held in the daytime, with mainly women involved as workers and customers as they are today, the Knights of Labor and Catholic and other churches held fairs in the evenings so that workers could attend. They offered music and entertainment, often a supper, and there were tables with raffles, handwork, candies, ice cream, and other refreshments on which people would spend money. One evening was often devoted to dancing. By August 1888 two stores in the Knights of Labor building were being finished; then they were rented to a meat market and a general store. The stores and a banquet hall were on the first floor; the main hall, measuring 49 by 54 feet, was on the second floor; it was used for the Knights of Labor and Lasters' Union meetings and for entertainments.[28]

The 1889 downturn did not last long, and the Bent company (still called Wm. and J. M. Bent) continued to expand. In February 1889 the Bents had bought the Lyon factory, planning to use this smaller facility for brogan manufacture while using the large shop exclusively for "the manufacture of button, balmoral and congress shoes."[29] Since 1884 when there had been a so-called brogan depression, which had hit particularly hard in Natick, the Bent firm had been trying to switch at least some of its production to what were called "white lined and lighter shoes." The owners were trying to get away from a product used only in rough outdoor work to one used by urban populations.

In the July 19, 1889, issue of the *Natick Bulletin* there was a long article about a meeting held in the Knights of Labor Hall in Cochituate to try to persuade the Boston and Maine and Central Massachusetts railroads to build a branch linking Cochituate to Wayland and thus to Boston. At this meeting Myron Bent is reported to have said that at this time one thousand hands were employed in the shoe industry in Cochituate. There was also a *Boston Herald* article on the subject. At the meeting Bent is supposed to have said that if the branch were built, his firm would take its teams off the road and use the railroad exclusively. It is not known whether the figure of one thousand shoe workers was an accurate or an exaggerated one. If correct, this represented the peak so far and possibly the all-time high for shoe employment in Cochituate. Unfortunately, there are no census of 1890 figures with which to compare Myron Bent's number. It may be that in his figure of one thousand workers he was including the Felch Brothers Shoe Company then flourishing in North Natick at no distance at all from the Wayland line.[30] This plant would logically have used a railroad branch built to serve the Bent factory. Nothing came of this plea; perhaps it would have resulted in some kind of railroad connection if the events of May 1891 had not occurred.

In the years from their father's death in 1888 to 1891 the Bent sons conducted their lives as usual. James Alvin Bent was reported as going to New York to purchase fast horses, and William Harrison continued to invest in champion Holstein cattle. The Potter, White and Bayley connection continued. With James M. Bent gone, there was probably more direction of the Bent factory by the Boston firm. In the fall after J. M. Bent's death we find the *Natick Bulletin* of September 7, 1888, describing a Labor Day annual banquet tendered by Wm. and J. M. Bent to "the Boston firm for whom they manufacture" at the Hynes place in Wayland (the Thomas Hynes farm, now 74 Moore Road). Things were done in style and

Everything was in readiness when the Boston people, including J. C. Potter and sons, Fred Bayley and others came in carriages from Newton and the banquet which was served by Downs, the caterer, was a sumptuous affair. During the repast music was furnished by a quartette. . . . Many enjoyed a ride in the little steamer while others quietly enjoyed the beauties of nature. The party broke up early and repaired to the residence of M. W. Bent [William H. Bent's former elegant house on Commonwealth Road] *where other friends were met and a social time enjoyed.*

The Bent Failure

Late 1890 and early 1891 was not a good time for shoes and other businesses, but, except for slackened employment and layoffs thought of as brief "loafs," there was no hint of real trouble in Cochituate. Both the *Natick Bulletin* and the *Natick Review* reported that Bent's was installing new machinery in February and in March.[31] In early May the plant shut down, but this seemed to workers and the Cochituate populace like a temporary layoff because of slow sales. The *Natick Review* of May 16 was saying: "It is reported that Bent's shop will start up Monday." The May 15 *Bulletin* had said that James A. Bent had gone to New York to purchase horses. This may not have been true. There is no way of telling when the Bent brothers realized that trouble was looming for their parent firm, Potter, White and Bayley, and for themselves. The *Natick Review* of May 22 carried an item: "If the reports are true, business is assuming a bad outlook and the predictions are that work in the shop may not be resumed before the first of next month or probably later." The *Natick Bulletin* of May 23 said: "Bent's shop is still shut down and there is no certainty as to when it will start up. There is a feeling, however, that business will soon start up and there will be a brighter outlook for the future. While the shop is shut down, most of the workmen are busy repairing and improving their places." The Bent brothers certainly knew by that time that Potter, White and Bayley was in trouble.

The first public report of the failure of Potter, White and Bayley was apparently made in one of the Boston evening newspapers on Monday, May 25. The news came as a surprise to the shoe-manufacturing and business community in Boston and to the people in Cochituate and Natick who worked at Bent's. The *Boston Daily Globe* of Tuesday, May 26, carried an article saying that: "Potter, White and Bayley, boot and shoe manufacturers of 130 Summer Street this city with factories in Cochituate, Mass. and Farmington, N.H., have made an assignment for the benefit of their creditors to George S. Bullens, President of The Revere National Bank . . . [and others]." There was no further mention of Cochituate, but the article referred to the deaths of the elder partners, John Cheney Potter[32] in 1883 and of Franklin White in 1885. An article in the *Boston Herald* of Wednesday, May 27, stated that when a *Herald* reporter asked at the assignees meeting: "Will any other firm be involved in the downfall of Potter, White and Bayley?" and received the answer: "So far as I now know there is but one. The Bents of Cochituate, a large shoe firm who used to do their manufacturing, will have to go to the wall." "Do you know the amount Potter, White and Bayley owe them?" "I do not." This last exchange revealed a complete lack of knowledge of the financial relationship at that time of the Bent firm to Potter, White and Bayley.

The Thursday, May 28, issue of the *Shoe and Leather Reporter* had an article on the Potter, White and Bayley failure which stated that "The Bents have also assigned." The article went on to say that John C. Potter, the senior partner, having paid off the executors of his two partners who died in the 1880s, had been believed to be worth half a million dollars the previous year. The article explained that Potter had had $198,000 tied up in the large Hill Shoe Company of Memphis, Tennessee, which had placed him in debt when the Hill firm failed ten days before.

At this point the *Shoe and Leather Reporter* writer could not believe that a firm of such good reputation as Potter, White and Bayley could be in permanent trouble and went on to say:

If there are no further losses by insolvency and the assignees work at the stock and dispose of the assets judiciously as men of their stamp will be quite sure to do, there is no reason to suppose the creditors will lose much; perhaps they may get their pay in full. This is apparently not a failure caused by the exhaustion of capital. It grows out of the ambition to do a larger business than was entirely prudent, or a spirit of too great trustful-

ness in the ability of the debtors of the concern to pay their bills promptly—a trustfulness strengthened by many years of experience.[33]

The failure of this old, well-known, highly regarded firm of Potter, White and Bayley came as a very great shock to the Boston shoe community.

Some of the Cochituate and Natick people connected with the Bent firm had probably seen the Boston articles, and all of them had no doubt heard about the company failure, with surprise and horror, early in the week. It can be supposed that they did not know much about Potter, White and Bayley and that most of them thought of that firm as a mere sales agent for the well-known Bent firm for which they worked. Thus, they must have read with great interest and anxiety the reports which came out that Friday, May 29, in the *Natick Bulletin* and the *Natick Review*.

The *Natick Bulletin* of May 29, 1891, carried a front-page article about the Potter, White and Bayley failure. The article started by saying that the failure of the Davis Shoe Company of Lynn and the Hill Shoe Company of Memphis, Tennessee, caused the Potter, White and Bayley failure. The writer then went into the history of the Potter, White and Bayley firm and said that the deaths in 1883 and 1885 of two partners had "taken money out of the company." As for the Cochituate reaction:

The report on Monday evening of the failure . . . was a severe shock to the community. Notwithstanding the shop had been closed about three weeks, it was expected by all that work would be resumed at once. The failure was wholly unexpected and has been the cause of many sad faces and much sensational talk this week. Cochituate has had the reputation of having one of the steadiest running shops in New England and the outlook for the next sale is very bright.

Then after a paragraph about the origin of the Bent firm, how important it was to Cochituate and how respected, the article went on to say:

Mr. John C. Potter was held in high esteem by all who knew him, being a constant visitor of the manufactory here to within two years when his son, Mr. Frank Potter, continued to call at the shop weekly. It is universally regretted by all that Cochituate which has had such a prosperous career in the past few years should receive such a set back as, comparatively speaking, the manufactory of Wm. & J. M. Bent is the only business that the town relies upon, but it is hoped for a speedy and satisfactory settlement when it is expected work may be resumed.

Then under "Wm. & J. M. Bent" in the same paper:

The Boston papers report that the firm of Wm. & J. M. Bent will be obliged to settle in insolvency. Their liabilities are estimated at $150,000, two-thirds of which [$100,000] *is owed Potter, White and Bayley. The assets are machinery, factory and real estate. The assignees of Potter, White and Bayley have taken possession of the stock and materials in the Cochituate factory. . . . Up to the time of their failure, Potter, White and Bayley were the financial support so to speak of the Bents as is indeed indicated by the fact that they are their debtors to the large amount of $100,000.*

It can be presumed that few but the Bent brothers, and perhaps not all of them, knew that the Bent firm which had seemed so prosperous owed $100,000 to Potter, White and Bayley. One cannot help wondering whether James Madison Bent would have allowed such a debt to be built up. It was well that the elder Bent did not live to see this failure happen.

The *Natick Review* of May 29, 1891, based an article about the failure on material in the *Boston Globe*. This article stated that the Bent factory in Cochituate employed five hundred workers and that the entire product was handled by Potter, White and Bayley. "They owned all the stock and the Bents produced the finished goods at prices agreed on between them."

Nothing appeared in the Natick newspapers or has been found in any source to explain why the Bent firm was so heavily indebted to Potter, White and Bayley. A large part of the debt must have been incurred to expand and improve the big plant and to buy the Lyon plant. There are extant no account books to explain the position the Bents were in.

Before describing what happened in Cochituate from June 1891 on, it may be revealing to cite what subsequent issues of the *Shoe and Leather Reporter* had to say about the Bents' relationship to the Potter, White and Bayley failure. In the June 11 issue, the stated assets of Potter, White and Bayley were listed with shrinkage figures for each asset and the present estimated value. Listed on Potter, White and Bayley's books as an asset was an item "Accounts receivable from Wm. & J. M. Bent $94,170.49. Shrinkage $85,870.49. Present value $8,300." The creditors and accountants had at that time decided that the Bent firm could realistically pay only 8.8 percent of its debt to Potter, White and Bayley. The Bent firm had other debts of about $50,000, so that the entire value of plant, machinery, and real estate could not be applied to the Potter, White and Bayley debt.

It is not known how much the Bent partnership was able to pay to the Potter, White and Bayley creditors. We have only an article which appeared in an August 1891 issue of the *Shoe and Leather Reporter* with conclusions of the creditor investigatory committee in the Potter, White and Bayley failure. On the subject of the debt of the Bent company to Potter, White and Bayley, this report stated that on May 1, 1886, Potter, White and Bayley owed the Bents $3,681. However, on May 1, 1887, the Bents owed Potter, White and Bayley $6,800; on May 1, 1888, $8,760; on May 1, 1889, $49,700; and on May 1, 1890, $81,000. This rapidly increasing debt is not explained. It suggests that after James M. Bent ceased to control the business and when John C. Potter began, as the report showed, to operate wildly, the Bent brothers, never suspecting that the parent firm would ask payment of the debt, had allowed the company to sink into a deep mire of debt they had no resources to repay.

The Potter, White and Bayley investigatory report reached several conclusions that that concern's assets were nowhere near as great as its liabilities. These conclusions were:

1. *By doing a very large business upon a false credit and without anything like an adequate capital and latterly with no capital whatever.*
2. *By great and increasing store expenses.*
3. *By doing a generally losing business in the Bent and Nute factories.*
4. *By the large withdrawals of the senior member of the firm* [John C. Potter], *including the amount given by him to his son.*[34]
5. *By the application just before the failure of more than $125,000 in stock toward the payment of the outstanding account of Mr. Arnold.*[35]

The relevant conclusion for our story is number three, but they all explain how the Bent company was brought to failure.

Without Bent company accounts and in the absence of any public statements by the Bent brothers, we cannot know whether the Bent concern actually was unprofitable for its owners as it was said to be for Potter, White and Bayley. Wm. and J. M. Bent had expanded its plant facilities tremendously in the later 1880s, around 1890 had installed an electric light system, and in early 1891 had been installing new machinery. They had endeavored to get away from brogans into dressier and more stylish shoes. How profitable their later products were is not known. Their own profitability would have depended in large measure on the agreements they negotiated with Potter, White and Bayley as to what they were paid for each production run.

We know from deeds and from mortgage records in Wayland that the Bent company had its factory and the company real estate, also the partners' own residences, heavily mortgaged. Borrowing on plant and other physical assets was a common way of building up the capital of early New England manufacturers. This worked well if the company did not have serious reverses. The practice of mortgaging everything went back years in the history of the company. William and James Madison Bent had borrowed on their machines, on the new steam engine, and on the real estate back in the early 1860s. When it all crashed in mid-1891, there was a tremendous web of debt for the Bent brothers, William H., James A., Myron W., and Ralph, but particularly for the two partners.

One of the steps taken that summer by the desperate Bents was to borrow $15,000 from George W. Fairbanks, their brother-in-law, on the security of all the machinery, equipment, and tools in the factory.[36] On the same date William Harrison Bent borrowed $1,742.50 from George W. Fairbanks on the security of twenty head of cattle, and on horses, buggies, harnesses, and wagons at Barney Hill Farm.[37] Deeds show that in later 1891 and in the ensuing year or two mortgage interest could not be paid on various parcels of Bent-owned real estate. Some mortgages were foreclosed, and certain parcels went to the town for nonpayment of taxes. One might think that the indebtedness was mainly incurred by the Bent sons who had not known and did not expect adversity. This was not completely the case. Back at the time of the 1881-82 petition to separate Cochituate from Wayland, comment, already quoted earlier, had been made in the *Natick Bulletin* that the Wayland people wanting the separation paid a large share of the taxes in contrast to the holders of heavily mortgaged property in Cochituate.[38] Among those who knew of his financial position, James M. Bent seems to have had a reputation for being a borrower.

Cochituate was in such a state of shock that virtually no news was sent to the Natick newspapers during the last week of May. As soon as the failure came, the newspapers reported that the grocery stores had ceased to grant credit to customers and were doing business only for cash. In June there were increasing reports of individual workers and families leaving town. In the June 12, 1891, *Natick Bulletin* appeared an item that some of the most valuable draft horses of the Wm. and J. M.

Rear view of the Bee Hive and the first Cochituate School in 1911.

Bent Company had been sold to the American Express Company. Some of the Bent workers remained, of course, and had employment in the early summer working on the goods which had been in process and which the creditors of Potter, White and Bayley wanted finished and sold.

By July two or three new shoe partnerships were formed, these by supervisory employees taking advantage of hungry labor. In the *Natick Review* of August 1, 1891, the following appeared:

Quite a number of Bent's old hands are now employed in the Wilson factory at Natick. The statement in Thursday's papers in regard to the condition of the Potter, White and Bayley firm is the subject of discussion here at present. No one here ever suspected such a state of affairs. All idea of Mr. Potter doing business here again is abandoned.

People in Cochituate had by this time learned that the creditors' investigation had shown that John C. Potter, the senior partner, had operated very unsoundly, even dishonestly, and some were bitter about it.

By September so many of the Bent workers had left town, some of them to work in Natick, that the volunteer fire companies were seriously understaffed.[39] Many former Cochituate residents and shoe workers were reported to be working in Millis, Spencer, Brockton, and Marlborough. The *Shoe and Leather Reporter Annuals* of 1891 and 1892, volumes which listed the firms engaged in shoe production in all towns in Massachusetts, listed three Dean firms—E. F. Dean and Company, R. C. Dean, and Charles W. Dean, as well as Noble C. Griffin—all making brogans, so all shoe production in Cochituate did not come to an end when the Bent firm closed down its factory. The Dean and Griffin firms, as well as some which came later, will be described in due course. Let us now continue the story of the Bents.

By the late summer or fall of 1891 the Bent firm had been reorganized into a corporation called Bent Brothers and Company. An advertisement in the *Shoe and Leather Reporter Annual* of 1892 announced this company as "successor to Wm. & J. M. Bent with factory at Cochituate and a Boston office at 95 Bedford Street." Their product was advertised as "men's, boys' and youth's shoes of fine and medium grades in hand, machine and Goodyear welt." By mid-September the new corporation had opened the Lyon shop, known as Shop No. 2, and were making samples. In the November 20, 1891, *Natick Bulletin* Bent Brothers was reported as doing a rushing business. By mid-December business was booming enough to keep the Lyon plant running until 9:00 P.M.

In the December 18 issue of the *Natick Bulletin* we find the report that it had been decided to move the three-story Bee Hive tenement building, owned by the Bents and then empty, to add on to the Lyon plant to make possible an increase of forty shoe workers. In late December the Bee Hive was being readied for its move from near the corner of Willard and Winter streets east of Main Street to the factory west of Main Street.

In January 1892, after a delay owing to deep snow, the building was actually being moved.[40] The January 29, 1892, *Natick Bulletin* stated that "The block [the term used for the Bee Hive] is on its foundation in the rear of Bent Brothers' shop and work is being rapidly pushed. It is expected it will be ready for occupancy in a very short time."

An item in the November 4, 1892, *Natick Bulletin* reported that the shoe business in Cochituate was going well. The big shop was still idle, but Bent Brothers expected to occupy it next spring. In December the mortgage on the large plant having been foreclosed, the big shop was sold at public auction to the Natick Five Cent Savings Bank for $6,000. With the announcement of this, the December 16 *Natick Bulle-*

tin reported that preparations were being made for occupancy of the large plant by Bent Brothers and Company and that Noble C. Griffin had purchased the Lyon plant.

In June 1892 the James Alvin Bents moved out of their house on the south side of Commonwealth Road, and Harold M. Stephens, who had been listed from 1888 through 1891 as a member of the firm of Potter, White and Bayley, took up residence there. He was in Cochituate to help the Bent Brothers manage the marketing of their product, a side of the business they had never been concerned with, and also perhaps to help work off the debt of the Bent partnership to the Potter, White and Bayley creditors. Mortgage records show that at one time there was a firm called Eaton and Stephens which manufactured shoes in Cochituate in the early 1890s. The January 11, 1895, *Natick Bulletin* mentioned that the Eaton and Stephens Manufacturing Company was then in receivership and that Frank A. Bullard, who had worked for Eaton and Stephens, had now entered the employ of Bent and Stephens, "in the office of the big shop." The relationship of these concerns to each other is not clear from the newspaper reports. The January 4, 1895, *Natick Bulletin* had reported that "quite a large force are now at work in the large shop of Bent and Stephens. Let's hope the new year will bring forth renewed prosperity." Apparently Bent and Stephens were not operating the whole factory. In the same issue of the *Natick Bulletin* was the report that "Chessman and Brown have moved machinery into the large factory to manufacture 30 dozens per day and will occupy one of the upper floors."

About 1893 the Bent brothers apparently found that they could not work together running a shoe company. Various members of the family began to engage in their own shoe ventures, often with outside partners. A case in point is reported in the April 14, 1893, *Natick Bulletin* that Mr. Bent (which of the brothers is not clear) was having his barn remodeled to manufacture shoes, and in the April 21 issue was the report that Mr. Scotland and family of Fitchburg had moved into Mr. T. D. Bent's residence on the Plains (the James Madison Bent summer home built in 1883), and that Mr. Scotland was to engage in the manufacture of shoes as a partner of Mr. Bent. In July 1893 work at Bent's was reported as not very flourishing. Depressed business conditions prevailed in the summer of 1893, and both Felch Brothers in North Natick and Bent Brothers closed.

The late summer and fall of 1893 was a time of depression everywhere. A special town meeting was held in December to appropriate money for the poor in Cochituate, "due to unemployment in the factories." It was even reported that entertainments at the Methodist Church were poorly attended because of the bad business situation.[41] The year 1894 was also a poor one for the Bent shoe interests, and the large plant shut down for some months. However, in the December 21, 1894, *Natick Bulletin* it was reported that "work at the large factory has begun. The gong was blown last Monday for the first time for a number of months. Applicants for positions were in large numbers during the day. . . . The starting of the factory is welcome news to all."

In early 1895 Bent and Stephens were operating in the big shop, and there was some selling, on the premises, of men's, boys', and youths' shoes at retail. In August 1895 there was a report that business had been quiet in the big shop all summer.[42] Then September brought news that Bent and Stephens had been dissolved and Harold Stephens had accepted a position as salesman for a large Boston concern.[43] The October 3, 1895, *Natick Review* reported that: "The big shop is silent. Will it ever start up again is often asked." Two weeks later there was an even more lugubrious report:

The big shop will remain idle and the rumors of its starting again are all idle. . . . Business is very quiet here. A large number of people are idle. The prospects of the big shop starting again are as slim as the chances of reopening the Charlestown Navy Yard. Our citizens will be obliged to seek employment elsewhere.

Ralph Bent started a separate factory with Frank A. Bullard. They renovated a building for the purpose and the firm was called Bent and Bullard. In October 1895 the *Natick Bulletin* reported that the barn adjoining the Cochituate House (the old Bent house which had been a boardinghouse since 1875) was being altered and remodeled into a small factory for the manufacture of shoes. "Two different concerns will occupy the building. . . . Messrs. Harry W. [William Harrison] Bent and son Elmer and J. A. Bent will constitute one and N. A. Chessman and T. Brown will form the other."[44]

Meanwhile in November there was a rumor that:

Interested parties were making arrangements for establishing one of the largest shoe manufacturing concerns in the state in the large Bent factory. Cochituate is noted for its skilled workers and, taking into consideration the plant which is one of the best equipped in the state, it would most certainly be advantageous.[45]

The "Big Shoe Plant" when owned by Charles W. Dean in the 1896-1913 period.

Two weeks later it was rumored that a large Marlborough concern would take over the factory.

None of the rumored takeovers came to pass. In January 1896 there was a report that "the large Bent factory was being stripped of its equipment." The February 7, 1896, *Natick Bulletin* carried the news that "the large Bent factory has been advertised to be sold the 24th of the month." By this time all hope that the Bents could operate the factory were gone, but hope continued that an outside concern would buy and operate it.

On February 23, 1896, the Bent factory was sold at a mortgage sale to Melville M. Weston for the sum of $5,000, which covered the mortgage. If in early 1896 the Bents had any hope of getting going again, this was given up by April when the *Natick Bulletin* reported: "On Monday morning [April 13] the fires in the big Wm. & J. M. Bent factory were put out and the watchman and engineer discharged." The dominant position of the Bent factory in Cochituate had ceased to be. The May 15, 1896, *Natick Bulletin* said that:

A large fire gong has been placed on the store of C. S. Williams and Company and a smaller one has been placed in the engine room of the N. C.

Griffin factory. These are both connected with the fire alarm system to take the place of the attachment on the Bent factory.

Then in the June 5, 1896, *Natick Bulletin* appeared the announcement: "C. W. Dean has purchased the factory formerly owned and occupied by Bent Brothers." The *Natick Review* reported that the sale was held on May 29 and that Charles W. Dean outbid "several parties" by paying $7,100.[46] The next week it was announced that Charles H. French had been engaged by Charles W. Dean to act as engineer at the big factory. The report said that "It is expected that Mr. Dean will soon occupy the new plant as his business is cramped for room space."

In the July 30 *Natick Review* it was reported that the factory had been painted and a sign C. W. DEAN & CO SHOE MANUFACTURERS in black-and-red letters placed on the building. Apparently the plant opened for production on September 1. The September 3 *Natick Review* said: "The gong upon the big shop blew loud and long Tuesday morning. It was sweet music to our townspeople who had missed its welcome sound." On September 17 it was announced in the *Natick Review* that C. W. Dean had moved into the big shop and that he expected to make one hundred dozen pairs of shoes per day.

It is sad and ironic that the next weekly issues of the same newspapers—the *Natick Bulletin* of June 12, 1896, and the *Natick Review* of June 11—after the report of the sale of the Bent plant to Dean, carried the story that William Harrison Bent had cut off a thumb while running a crimping machine in the small, so-called factory made from the old barn across the street where he had undertaken to continue in the shoe business with his brother, James Alvin Bent. Eleven days later William Harrison Bent died of blood poisoning caused by his thumb injury. He had been the leading, best liked, and the most capable of the Bent brothers. His obituary was the prominent feature of June 26 issue of the *Natick Bulletin*. The *Natick Review* described his funeral as the largest ever held in the town.

Myron Bent had left Cochituate in February 1896 to superintend a shoe factory in Baltimore.[47] Ralph Bent would soon go to Illinois where he was superintendent of the shoe-manufacturing department of the state penitentiary.[48] James Alvin Bent was the only one of the shoe-manufacturing brothers to stay in Wayland. In 1898 he joined with an already going operation manufacturing wooden boxes (cases) for the shoe output of Cochituate and Natick. Part of his father's large barn was converted for this use. He died in 1910, and his widow continued the box business until 1918. Their daughter, Mrs. Margaret

Bent Morrell, lived for many years until her death in October 1980, in the 1775 Bent homestead which had been used as a boardinghouse from 1875-1913. She was not alive when her father and uncles were engaged in shoe manufacturing in Cochituate, but she remembered the box factory well and was brought up on stories of the Wm. and J. M. Bent Shoe Company.

NOTES

1. *Natick Citizen,* December 8, 1882.
2. *Natick Bulletin,* November 20, 1885.
3. South Middlesex Deeds, *Dudley to Bent,* Book 1711, p. 437.
4. *Natick Bulletin,* April 9, April 16 and May 7, 1886.
5. *Ibid,* August 27, 1886.
6. *Ibid,* July 16 and July 23, 1886.
7. *Ibid,* October 15 and November 26, 1886.
8. *Ibid,* October 21, 1887.
9. *Ibid,* February 3, 1888.
10. *Ibid,* September 3, 1880.
11. J. M. Bent's wife's name was Martha.
12. *Natick Bulletin,* May 23, 1879.
13. *Ibid,* February 9, 1883.
14. *Ibid,* June 11, 1880.
15. *Natick Bulletin,* July 8, 1881 and *Framingham Gazette,* September 2, 1881.
16. *Natick Bulletin,* March 17, 1882.
17. Town of Wayland, *Personal Property Mortgages,* Book III, p. 250.
18. *Framingham Gazette,* November 14, 1874.
19. *Natick Bulletin,* July 11, 1879.
20. Middlesex County Probate, *Will of James Madison Bent,* 1888 No. 24561.
21. *Natick Review,* April 13, April 27, May 4, and May 11, 1889.
22. *Natick Bulletin,* November 23, 1883.
23. *Ibid,* January 25, 1884.
24. *Natick Citizen,* August 29, 1884.
25. *Natick Bulletin,* April 10, 1885.
26. *Ibid,* January 13, 1888.
27. *Ibid,* March 2, 1888.
28. *Natick Review,* May 28, 1887.
29. *Natick Bulletin,* February 19, 1889.
30. The Felch Brothers plant stood about where the Massachusetts Turnpike crosses Route 27 on a bridge.
31. *Natick Review,* February 28, 1891 and *Natick Bulletin,* March 20, 1891.
32. This report was incorrect. Frederick Bayley died in 1883; John C. Potter was still the senior partner of the firm.
33. *Shoe and Leather Reporter,* May 28, 1891, p. 1349.
34. J.C. Potter had given his son a large sum to start a business.
35. Mr. Arnold was the head of a shoe firm in Abington which had earlier manufactured profitably for Potter, White and Bayley.
36. Town of Wayland, *Mortgage Book,* Vol. IV, 1884-1900, p. 441. This gives a detailed description of the machinery and equipment in the plant.
37. *Ibid,* p. 439.
38. See page 196.

39. *Natick Bulletin,* September 4, 1891.
40. *Ibid,* December 18 and 25, 1891, January 15, 22, and 29, 1892.
41. *Ibid,* December 22, 1893.
42. *Natick Review,* August 22, 1895.
43. *Natick Bulletin,* September 26, 1895.
44. *Ibid,* October 11, 1895.
45. *Ibid,* November 8, 1895.
46. *Natick Review,* June 4, 1896.
47. *Natick Bulletin,* February 14, 1896.
48. Allen H. Bent, *The Bent Family in America,* Boston, 1900, p. 221.

15

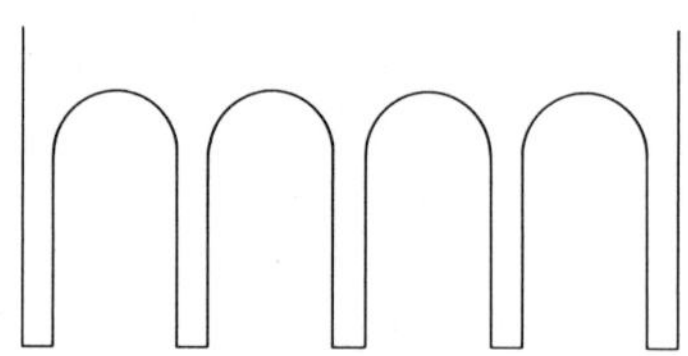

Other Shoe Firms in the 1890s

BEFORE DESCRIBING the years of Charles W. Dean's operation of the large Bent plant, we shall turn our attention to other shoe manufacturers in Cochituate in the 1890s. It has already been mentioned that it has been impossible to find out about all the small and changing partnerships and individual enterprises which existed in Cochituate between 1850 and 1910. Appendix E lists alphabetically the companies encountered by the writer in her research. The list does not pretend to be complete and gives only approximate time periods. These are companies listed in census enumerations up through 1880, in Wayland directories of 1887, 1893, 1897-98, and from 1892 on (with gaps) in the *Shoe and Leather Reporter*. It also includes firms mentioned in the Natick newspapers.

Noble C. Griffin was the most prominent and successful of the smaller shoe manufacturers in Cochituate in the 1890s. In 1868 the Thomas Chipman Griffin family had arrived in Cochituate from Cornwallis, Nova Scotia. T. C. Griffin was a farmer, but several of his six sons went to work in the shoeshops. In the 1870s two of the older Griffin sons tried their hands at operating a small shoe factory. Daniel D. Griffin worked at the Bent factory off and on, but mortgage records show that as of April 1873 he was borrowing $900 on the security of a portable steam engine, three stitching machines, and other equipment in a "shop now owned and occupied by me in Cochituate." In September 1873 a mechanic's lien was placed on Daniel D. Griffin's shoeshop, which was described as a three-story building with a pitched roof. This factory was located on land of Willard Moore east of Main Street.[1] In a *Boston Globe* article about the shoe factories in Cochituate in 1875, there is mention of Dunham and Griffin as a shoe manufacturer. The Dunham brothers, Freeman and Lemuel, were also from Nova Scotia. This concern was short-lived, and no further record of it has been found.

Around 1877 Alonzo Griffin, another of T. C. Griffin's sons, seems to have built a small, three-story shoe factory on what is now West Plain Street, about where Mitchell Street is today. On January 4, 1878, two carpenters placed a mechanic's lien on "Alonzo Griffin's shoe shop for non-payment of their bill for painting a flat roof building three stories high used for the manufacture of shoes."[2] This is probably the three-story Griffin factory which the *Natick Bulletin* of August 2, 1878, reported destroyed in a fire with no loss of life because it was unoccupied except for two workers. Alonzo Griffin moved to North Dakota about 1885 with a group of Cochituate families who settled in or near Ellendale, Dickey County, in that territory. He became a farmer in North Dakota and died there in 1915.

Noble C. Griffin, one of the younger sons, was fourteen when he arrived with his parents in Cochituate. We find him living in his parents' household in 1870 with no occupation given. At a young age he was enterprising; in 1876, when he was twenty-two, he had earned and saved enough money to be able to lend a billiard hall proprietor $574.50.[3] The census of 1880 lists him as a shoe worker living at Emily Moore's boardinghouse on Main Street. By 1882 we find him running his own boardinghouse and opening his own billiard hall over Moore's grocery store. His first venture as a shoe manufacturer came in 1883 when he formed a partnership to make brogans with Colburn Dean. This partnership did not last long; it was dissolved in February 1884. In May 1884 he formed a partnership with William Hammond to manufacture shoes. On February 24, 1888, the *Natick Bulletin* reported that Noble C. Griffin had leased the Dean shoeshop, was fitting it up with a new engine and boiler, and would manufacture boots and shoes. By late March it was reported that he had started production. This business flourished, and in November 1892 it was reported that N. C. Griffin was turning out forty cases of footwear a week. The *Shoe and Leather Reporter Annual* for 1892 describes his product as kip brogans, which were also being made that year by E. F. Dean and Company, R. C. Dean; Charles W. Dean; and Sawin, Croker and Company.

Griffin, who was employing his brother Daniel after the Bent

The Damon-Griffin House, built in 1869, still stands at 92 Commonwealth Road.

failure, was now very successful. Accordingly, in December 1892 he bought the Lyon factory with the attached Bee Hive addition from the Bent brothers when they decided to move back into the large factory.[4] At first Elmer Bent used the Bee Hive for manufacturing shoes, but by late 1894 we find reported in the *Natick Bulletin* that N. C. Griffin "is taking over this space. This will greatly increase the capacity of his present quarters in which he already turns out about 125 dozens a day [1,500 a day]."[5]

The year 1896 was a good one for the N. C. Griffin Company. An addition was built on the plant in March [6] and by fall a new type of rapid sole leather machine was being installed. That same year Ralph Bent had entered Griffin's employ.[7] A record fifty thousand pairs of shoes was reported turned out in July, which indicates that the firm was then employing from 125 to 150 workers.[8]

In the spring of 1897 there was a newspaper report that Noble C. Griffin was putting an addition on his house for an office.[9] Griffin's house is still standing at 92 Commonwealth Road and is now used as a funeral home. This house was built in 1869 by George Alvin Damon, who had been born in Cochituate in 1826. The census of 1850 listed Damon as a blacksmith. In 1868 and 1869, when negotiating to buy the two acres of land near the lake, Damon was living in Boston and working for a firm which transported goods by railroad and ship to New York.[10] He may have built the house on speculation or for investment. We find that the house was being used as a boarding-house by Arabella Tilton in 1876.[11] In October 1882 there were newspaper reports of Damon building a steam laundry at the rear of the house to do contract work for the Boston and Albany Railroad, and he was reported as moving there to live.[12]

George A. Damon died in 1885, and the house was sold in 1888 to Wallace Griffin, one of the Griffin brothers who worked for the Bent company.[13] In July 1890 Noble Griffin bought the house from his brother and, as his business prospered, proceeded to fix up the house as the showplace of a successful shoe manufacturer.

In the spring of 1898 a 50 by 60 foot addition to the Griffin factory was finished, and in 1899 a further addition of 85 by 20 feet was reported.[14] Griffin was then at his peak of success in Cochituate. In September 1899 he bought the Lyon house north of this factory and also the land in back used as the ballfield. By 1899 the Griffin factory, next door to the Cochituate School, had become a great detriment to the school. Actually the noise and the smell had bothered the faculty and students for years. The March 31, 1899, *Natick Bulletin* reported:

> *As to the adjacent factory, it was in the beginning little noticed as a disturbing element. But with its flourishing business, its rapid extension, the multiplication of its machinery, the increase of heavy teaming, the situation though no one's fault becomes very serious.*[15]

In 1900 a cylinder head from one of the Griffin factory engines blew out and landed in the schoolyard. The plant was old and the space crowded, so it was not surprising that in 1902 Griffin took advantage of an opportunity to move his business to a considerably larger and more modern shoe factory in East Pepperell, Massachusetts. This venture was short-lived. In March 1903 the plant burned to the ground. Griffin did not resume manufacturing in Cochituate and in 1904 dismantled his main Cochituate plant but not the ell which had been the Bee Hive. N. C. Griffin continued to live in Cochituate as a well-to-do, retired shoe manufacturer and an important benefactor of the community. In 1900 he ran, was elected, and served as a selectman in a year when all three selectmen of the town were from Cochituate. However, town politics and this kind of service did not interest him, and he refused to run again for office. In June 1900 Griffin offered to provide from his own funds a furnace for the Cochituate fire engine house to keep the chemical fire extinguishers from freezing.

As they had to a greater extent with the Bents, the newspapers wrote up Noble C. Griffin's grand style of living—a steam launch and a boathouse on the lake, one of the earliest automobiles in town, summer band concerts for the public on the lawn, and private whist parties on the broad verandas of the house. As time went on the family spent winters in Boston and Newtonville but continued to use the Pond Street house as a long-season summer home and also to visit their camp on Dudley Pond, then the coming place.

There was one exception. In 1908 N. C. Griffin went to Calais, Maine, to run a new shoe factory there. This was the era when towns everywhere, especially in the northern New England states, were convinced that the route to prosperity was to have a shoe factory in their midst and were actively trying to lure established firms with tax concessions, offers of railroad sidings, and so forth. At the time of the brief venture in northern Maine, the house at 92 Commonwealth Road was rented to a doctor who ran a sanitorium there.

Other Shoe Firms

The 1897-1898 Cochituate directory, incorporated as part of *Shaw's Natick Directory of 1897 and 1898,* listed the following shoe manufacturers:

Elmer Bent
Caswell Brothers
Noah A. Chessman
James Otis Dean
Charles W. and Alfred T. Dean
Elkins and Ewing
Walter Evans
Frank A. Howe
Ricker and Lamarine

The Caswell brothers, Dona and Leander, were sons of a French-Canadian shoe worker, Moses Caswell, who came to Cochituate to work for the Bents in the 1870s. At the time of the disintegration of the Bent firm, they decided to try shoe manufacturing on their own and were in production in a small rented building in early 1895.[16] In November 1895 they were reported building a two-story factory in the rear of the schoolhouse.[17] They were in operation on a small scale up through 1901 but were not listed in the *Shoe and Leather Reporter*

Annual for 1902. By 1905 their shop on Bradford Street was being used for carriage painting.

Noah Augustus Chessman was in charge of the stitching room at Bent's for many years, long enough to be presented with a gold watch by his fellow workers in December 1887.[18] In October 1894, with the Bent operations collapsing, he formed a partnership with a man by the name of Brown to start manufacturing shoes in a barn. In May 1896 the firm of Chessman and Brown was dissolved, and Chessman started to build a small shoeshop on Bradford Street near the Caswell Brothers' shop. The operation was not a great success, and in January 1901 Chessman moved to Ware, Massachusetts. However, he returned a year and a half later to be the foreman of Charles W. Dean's stitching room in the big factory. In 1903 it was reported that Edgar B. Loker had bought Chessman's steam engine and boiler to use for harvesting ice on Dudley Pond.[19]

We see from the above the ephemeral existence of most of the small firms, typical of the history of small business. We also see that quite a few firms were spawned by the collapse of the Bent firm. The small entrepreneurs had had years of experience in shoe work in Cochituate but did not have what it took to grow large and be successful for any length of time.

One more firm of this type will be mentioned—Ricker and Lamarine—which started operating as Ricker, Lamarine and Norris in 1895 in a building 35 by 24 feet in the rear of the Lamarine house on German Hill Street. John Lamarine, a French-Canadian who came to Cochituate in the 1870s when he was about thirty, worked for years at the Bent factory and by the early 1890s was a laster at Bent's shoeshop. Arthur J. Ricker, a Yankee born in Maine, also came to Cochituate in the 1870s. By 1893 he was foreman of the finishing room at Bent's and had a house on Harrison Street. Andrew A. Norris, who had been a cutter at Bent's, dropped out of the firm in its first year of operation. For a few years the shoe firm flourished in a small way, and in 1898 and 1899 additions to the factory were reported. In 1902 the plant was reported shut down,[20] and in April 1904 the shop was being demolished.[21]

A small but increasingly profitable shoe company was the Williams Shoe Company. From the late 1880s Chester B. Williams, from the Taunton area, had been making shoe accessories in Cochituate. The Cochituate Box Toe Company was first reported as beginning operation in the basement of the Lyon shop (then owned by the Bents). By 1891 sole leather counters were being made, George B.

The Williams Shoe Factory was enlarged in 1906 and burned two years later in 1908.

Trumble had joined the partnership, and a branch had been established in Brockton. In 1897 Chester B. Williams, a very enterprising man, purchased Charles W. Dean's old factory on Maple Street and moved it one hundred feet to the east side of Winter Street. The building was to house the box toe company and a shoe-manufacturing firm, the Williams Shoe Company in which Chester Williams participated at first with his brothers Arthur and Ernest who were later to carry on the shoe business.[22] The Williams Shoe Company failed in 1901, but in January 1902 it resumed business[23] on a small scale, being listed in the *Shoe and Leather Reporter Annual* of 1902 as having the capacity of 200 pairs or less a day; in 1905, a capacity of 250 to 500 pairs a day. By 1906 the company, then known as the Arthur A. Williams Shoe Company, was putting on an addition.[24] This factory, with its 1906 addition, shows on the map of Cochituate in *Walker's Atlas of Middlesex County*, and in the nearby illustration. The map makes the Williams plant look almost as large as the Dean plant, but this was not the case. Arthur Williams, now prosperous, owned and occupied the elegant house which William Harrison Bent had had built in 1880 on Commonwealth Road just east of Winter Street. The factory was behind it on the east side of Winter Street between Maple and Willard streets. At 3:00 A.M. on March 13, 1908, a spectacular fire destroyed this factory. Much to the dismay of Cochituate shoe workers, the owner decided not to rebuild or to resume business in Cochituate but to take advantage of an opportunity to move to a much larger plant in Holliston. The Holliston venture was very successful.

Other Shoe Firms

At one time or another five of the Williams brothers of a family of thirteen children of James F. and Hannah J. Williams lived and did business in Cochituate. Chester B. Williams was a leader of men and the most prominent. In 1900 he served as state senator from the district which included Wayland. In 1905, well into adult life, he graduated from Boston University and took bar examinations to become a lawyer. In 1910 he was a county commissioner.

The Griffin and Williams shoe companies enriched their owners and gave a certain amount of employment. Most of the other Cochituate shoe firms of the 1890s and around the turn of the century were small, short-lived, and unsuccessful ventures. The Charles W. Dean firm was in a class by itself and will be taken up in the next chapter.

NOTES

1. Town of Wayland, *Personal Mortgages,* Book II, 1859-1875, p. 182.
2. *Ibid,* p. 177.
3. Town of Wayland, *Personal Mortgages,* Book III, 1875-1883, p. 112.
4. *Natick Bulletin,* December 16, 1892.
5. *Ibid,* December 26, 1894.
6. *Ibid,* March 20, 1896.
7. *Ibid,* October 9, 1896.
8. *Natick Review,* August 6, 1896.
9. *Natick Bulletin,* April 9, 1897.
10. South Middlesex Deeds, Book 1028, p. 581 and Book 1077, p. 270.
11. Town of Wayland, *Personal Mortgages,* Book III, 1875-1883, p. 80.
12. *Natick Bulletin,* October 6, 1882.
13. *Ibid,* July 6, 1888.
14. *Ibid,* April 18, 1898 and November 10, 1899.
15. The original Lyon factory was built in the same year as the school.
16. *Natick Review,* January 24, 1895.
17. *Ibid,* November 14, 1895.
18. *Natick Bulletin,* December 30, 1887.
19. *Ibid,* May 15, 1896.
20. *Ibid,* May 1, 1903.
21. *Ibid,* April 22, 1904.
22. *Ibid,* October 29, 1897.
23. *Ibid,* January 17, 1902.
24. *Ibid,* April 27, 1906.

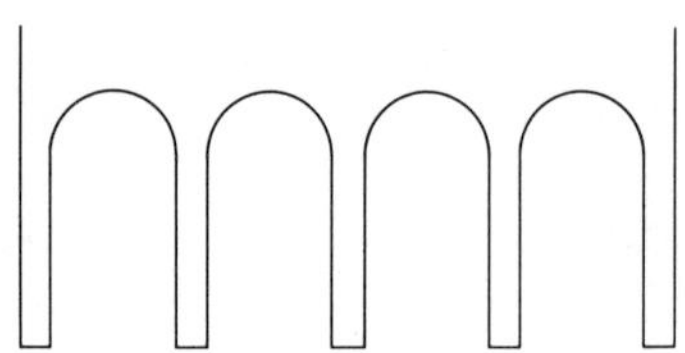

C. W. Dean and the End of Shoe Manufacture

Turn of the Century

WHAT WAS THE OUTPUT and the employment in Cochituate's shoe factories at the turn of the century? And how many workers were then employed? The United States census of 1900 did not publish separate figures for Wayland shoe manufacturing. The manufacturing schedules filled out in the towns and cities were not preserved in the archives in Washington or in Boston. If available, this decennial census would almost surely show the peak production for Cochituate, as this was a year when Charles W. Dean and Company was going strong and when N. C. Griffin was operating his factory at or near its greatest output. The *Shoe and Leather Reporter Annual* for 1900 could not be found in the eastern Massachusetts area to consult. However, the 1902 *Shoe and Leather Reporter Annual* gave the following list of shoe manufacturers in "Cochituate-Wayland":

Chas. W. Dean & Co.	*Daily capacity of 2500 to 5000 pairs*
Felch Brothers [actually in North Natick]	*daily capacity of 1000 to 2500 pairs*
N. C. Griffin	*daily capacity of 1000 to 2500 pairs*

Ricker and Lamarine	*daily capacity 200 pairs or less*
Williams Shoe Company	*daily capacity 200 pairs or less*

The printed volumes of the Massachusetts census of 1905 give a great deal of detail about Wayland, as for all cities and towns in the state. However, in setting forth figures on the manufacture of boots, shoes, and rubbers, those for Wayland were omitted, along with those for fifteen towns, "to avoid disclosing private business." The only published figure bearing on the shoe industry in Cochituate appears in the occupational classification of the resident population, which showed 345 males and 84 females, a total of 429 engaged in manufacture. About 400 of these would have been in shoe manufacturing, but this figure covers only residents of Wayland, some of whom worked in Natick and other places. It gives no hint as to the size of the group who came daily to work in the Cochituate factories from Natick and Saxonville.

The Massachusetts State census of 1895 had given specific figures on the boot and shoe industry in Wayland for the year ending June 1895. This census showed Wayland as having six boot and shoe establishments, with nine partners and capital of $112,666, turning out $638,305 worth of goods, and with an average employment of 263 workers. The year 1895 was a poor one for the Cochituate shoe industry, with the Bent firm disintegrating and the large factory closed most of the time. In this same year 9,391 shoe workers were employed in Lynn and 6,512 in Haverhill, 2,664 in Marlborough, 749 in Natick, and 7,722 in Brockton.[1] It seems probable that around 1900 Charles W. Dean and Company employed from 500 to 800 workers and that N. C. Griffin may have employed 200 to 250. At this peak time Cochituate's shoe industry may have exceeded Natick's dwindling activity by a little, but it was small compared with that of Marlborough and the large shoe centers farther afield.

Charles W. Dean and Company

We turn now to chronicle Charles W. Dean and his rise from running a tiny shoe-manufacturing operation in 1873 to ownership of the "big factory" in 1896 and its operation until the business moved to Natick in 1913. Charles W. Dean was born in 1855 in the Saxonville section of Framingham at a time when his parents, who were to have

1880 view east from Cochituate School roof shows H. C. Dean's house on Main Street at extreme left and his factory directly to the rear.

thirteen children, had temporarily left Cochituate. The family was living in Cochituate at the time of the 1860 census, and Charles attended the two-room South or Lokerville School. According to an article in *Middlesex County and its People*, published in 1927,[2] Charles Dean's introduction to shoemaking came when at a very young age he went to work for his older brother Thomas Dean. The article states that in 1873 Charles went into business for himself making shoes in the basement of a house. According to Margaret Bent Morrell, Charles W. Dean began his shoe manufacturing in the tiny Evans cottage on the hill behind the spring house near Snake Brook, just over the Natick line. This house is still standing.

At the time of the United States census of 1880 Charles W. Dean was in partnership with his eldest brother, Henry Colburn Dean; they were then employing 45 workers. In 1884 the *Natick Bulletin* reported that Hollis Mann, who had earlier worked for the Bents, had formed the partnership of Mann and Dean.[3] Charles Dean had built a house on the north corner of Main and Maple streets in 1878;[4] the plant was behind the house on Maple Street. In March 1886 the *Natick Bulletin* noted that Dean was adding new machinery and increasing his business.[5] In 1890 an ell was added, and in 1891 a basement was excavated. In 1892 an addition was built on the plant allowing production of twenty cases of shoes per day.[6] Late that year it was reported that C. W. Dean's business was flourishing and that he had bought thirty-six feet of land for expansion.[7] The November 30, 1894, *Natick Bulletin* reported that an addition to the Dean factory had been com-

Matching view to the southeast shows C. W. Dean's house (second from left) on the east side of Main Street and the Methodist Episcopal Church at the far right.

pleted, adding 50 hands to the payroll. A year later, when the Bent Brothers Company had collapsed, the *Natick Review* of October 24, 1895, noted that Charles W. Dean's was the only sizable factory then running in Cochituate. Employment there was perhaps between 100 and 150.

We have already chronicled the purchase of the large Bent plant by Charles W. Dean in June 1896 for $7,100. Much of the machinery had been sold, so Dean could not open for business until September. Four months later, the January 22, 1897, *Natick Bulletin* reported: "At the present time business in this town is decidedly good, the best for many years, and the wheel of prosperity seems to revolve in all local enterprise."

Dean made no major changes in the much-added-to wooden plant; there was no room for expansion. In 1903 a new engine and boiler were installed and a large, five-ton smokestack erected.[8]

In inquiring about the shoe industry in Cochituate from family lore and memories of old residents, in 1976 Barbara Robinson received the impression that Charles W. Dean was a difficult employer who underpaid his workers. It is hard to tell from newspaper accounts of Charles W. Dean as a figure in Cochituate what he was like. Major events of the company and certain family items were reported in the *Natick Bulletin* and the *Natick Review*, but there was not the wealth of coverage of Charles W. Dean and his son Alfred, who helped him run the company, that there had been of James Madison Bent and his son, William Harrison Bent. The Deans may have been less colorful people. The shoe industry was by this time an old story in Cochituate, and from the middle 1890s on there were far fewer news stories about what was still the chief business of Cochituate. Certain items appeared about the grand style in which the Deans could afford to live, such as vacationing for a month in Hot Springs, Arkansas, in the winter of 1897, and taking trips around the country in a chauffeur-driven automobile. But these elements of grandeur were not related with the relish which accompanied descriptions of the Bent family luxuries.

James Madison Bent was a showman, and some of the Cochituate reporters of the 1880s were his press agents. William Harrison Bent was genuinely popular, but Charles W. Dean apparently was not a favorite of the working people in Cochituate. In October 1896, just as Charles W. Dean and Company was getting under way to run the large factory and give employment in the village, a fair run by St. Zepherin's Catholic Church awarded a gold-headed cane to "the most popular gentleman" among the shoe company owners, C. W. Dean, N. C. Griffin, and O. A. Felch. Seemingly people attending the fair voted; presumably they paid for the pleasure of doing so. Out of 1,330 votes cast, C. W. Dean was by far the least popular. Noble C. Griffin won the gold-headed cane with more votes than the other two combined.[9]

Instead of being the beloved patriarch of the village and the leader in promoting its interests, which had been the role of James M. Bent, Charles W. Dean seems to have been a sharp dealer who made money and knew how to hang on to it. The selectmen's report in the town report for the year 1898-99 shows evidence of abrasive town relations with Dean in two instances. Apparently the town thought it had an agreement with Dean to blow the fire alarm (attached to the factory) for $150 a year. At the end of the second month Dean presented a bill for $25 a month, double the agreed-upon amount, and demanded payment or the removal of the fire alarm. Soon after that incident, Charles W. Dean demanded that a watering trough and drinking fountain, money to purchase which had been raised by community subscription publicized in the *Natick Review* in 1892, be moved from encroaching one foot on the edge of his factory land on the side of the road at Bent's Corner, or else town rent of $12 a month be paid. The selectmen promptly moved the watering trough a short distance up Pond Street.

The End of Shoe Manufacture

In 1901 an article appeared in the *Natick Bulletin* about the trolley car stop at Bent's Corner. Nostalgically the author wrote:

The name Bent's Corner carries with it a reminiscence of the lustre of Cochituate's palmiest days–when the big shop was managed by the Bents, when every workman earned a good living and did it without making of himself a prison slave, when the land figuratively if not literally flowed with milk and honey. These were the great days and the old folks in our midst love to revert to them in memory. They put a halo about them and exalt them as containing the acme of human happiness gone, alas, to return no more. . . . Bent's Corner is the name that was given to the place at first which has adhered to it for long years and which will continue to adhere to it as long as there are people in Cochituate who remember the better days.[10]

On August 5, 1910, in the midst of tension and fear created by a typhoid fever outbreak in Cochituate, an article appeared on the front page of the *Natick Bulletin* announcing that the Charles W. Dean and Company had arranged to buy land on North Main Street in Natick and to build a five-story cement factory of 300 by 50 feet to which to move the business. This was welcome news for Natick people, as their own shoe industry had dwindled. The article stated that George C. Fairbanks of the Natick Commercial Club had helped secure the land. The following week an article written from Wayland's point of view showed indignation and blamed certain town authorities for driving out the Dean firm. Said this article: "Cochituate has for years enjoyed the distinction of being a shoe town, but one by one firms have left and now the most successful of all its enterprises will soon follow. If there was a desire to drive all manufacturing out of the town it has been accomplished." This article began by claiming that Williams's interests in town politics drove Dean out.[11]

There had been trouble between the Wayland board of health and Dean about pumping the plant's cesspools and dumping sewage. Further, the factory had a water tank for fire protection on one corner of the top floor of the factory. The Wayland water board had cut off water to this reservoir during the day, saying that the company should stop a leak and should fill its tank only at night to avoid disturbing water pressure for the rest of the village.

There clearly had been friction between Dean and the town, but the move to Natick was no sudden decision. In 1895, before the Bent plant was bought, it was rumored in a newspaper that C. W. Dean would buy the Wilson plant in Natick.[12] In 1900 an article in the *Natick Bulletin* of December 14 reported that Cochituate had been considerably stirred up over a report that C. W. Dean and Company was leaving. South Framingham and Natick were mentioned as destinations.

It seems clear that town authorities did not drive the Deans out of Cochituate. The factory building was old, and there was no adequate space nearby in which to expand. Fire protection for an old, wooden building was totally inadequate. The Cochituate water system could not supply enough water or pressure to cope with a major fire. In 1908 there had been an attempt to connect with the Natick water supply, and the Town of Natick had voted to allow the connection. However, the state legislature denied Natick's petition because the Wayland selectmen had opposed this measure at a legislative hearing. Alfred T. Dean was a selectman that year; he would not have been expected to oppose the measure. Albion F. Parmenter and Thomas F. Mahoney, both of Wayland, were the other two selectmen. One or both of them must have opposed the North Natick water connection. The real point of this controversy has not been discovered.

Surely one of the most important considerations in attracting Dean to the Natick location was its available railroad connection. So plans went ahead for building the Natick plant, which is still in existence, housing the Natick Mills at 64 North Main Street.

Full operation of C. W. Dean's new Natick plant began on February 1, 1913. There was no fanfare or complaint about this in the Cochituate news section of the *Natick Bulletin* at the time. The Cochituate shoe workers could take the trolley to continue working for Dean in Natick, as had the Natick workers who had worked at Bent's and then Dean's. Thus, in 1913 all factory production of shoes in Cochituate came to an end, and this happened without too great disruption to the lives of the shoes workers still resident there.

Certain changes in the community followed. The Bent-owned boardinghouse across the street, then called the Cochituate Tavern, which at the end had housed Albanian shoe workers (of the new wave around 1907-12 of cheap labor in the Framingham-Natick-Cochituate area), was closed, fumigated, and returned to the Bent family use. The Albanians had been a somewhat disturbing element for the older ethnic groups. In June 1910 the *Natick Bulletin* wrote of a near riot when two Albanians assaulted two French-Canadian shoe workers on the street in Cochituate.[13] Other Albanians ("Greeks") lived at this time in the Bee Hive building.[14]

When he saw that no other manufacturing concern wanted the old plant, Charles Dean sold the Cochituate factory for its salvage value to avoid taxes. The May 4, 1916, issue of the *Natick Bulletin* reported that "the wreckers have cleaned out the interior of the big shop and have now begun in earnest the tearing down of the building." A week later it was reported that the shipping shed and the office had been purchased by Mr. Nixon of Pleasant Street and moved to the lot adjoining his house. With this, the last and the largest of the Cochituate shoe factories disappeared from the scene. Charles W. Dean and his son Alfred continued to live on Main Street in Cochituate while they ran the business in Natick. Alfred's widow, Hattie, was still in Cochituate in the late 1950s. Even if not working in nearby Natick, some of the shoe workers were slow to leave Cochituate, which had been home for their families for at least two generations. A newspaper item of 1916 stated that quite a group of Cochituate shoe workers were now employed at shoe factories in Marlborough.

NOTES

1. *Massachusetts Census of 1895,* Vol V, Manufactures, pp. 611-612.
2. Lewis Publishing Company, *Middlesex County and its People*, Vol. IV, p. 334.
3. *Natick Bulletin*, February 8, 1884.
4. "Mr. Charles Dean has nearly completed his residence in this village. . . . it will be one of the neatest places in town." *Natick Bulletin*, May 3, 1878.
5. *Ibid*, March 29, 1886.
6. *Natick Review*, May 12, 1892.
7. *Natick Bulletin*, November 4, 1892.
8. *Ibid*, August 14 and September 4, 1903.
9. *Ibid*, October 16, 1896.
10. *Ibid*, February 14, 1901.
11. *Ibid*, August 12, 1910.
12. *Ibid*, November 27, 1895.
13. *Ibid*, June 10, 1910.
14. See photograph title in *Report upon the Town of Wayland, Mass.* by John Nolen, Landscape Architect submitted in 1911 to the Village Improvement Society.

17

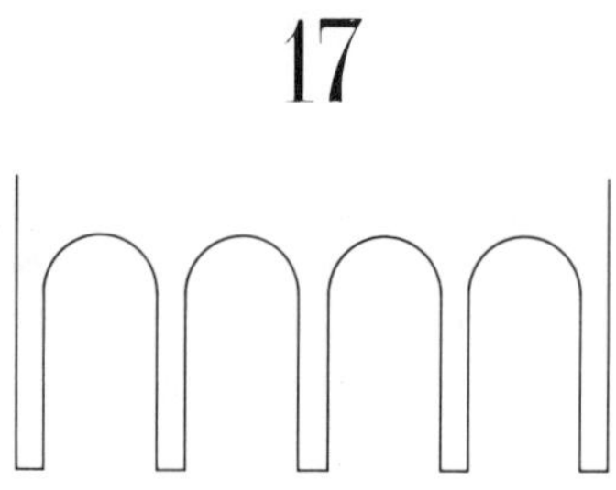

Rural and Agricultural Wayland

Agriculture

IN AN 1890 revised edition of *Nason's Gazetteer of the State of Massachusetts* was published[1] an article that termed Wayland "an agricultural and shoemaking town." We have devoted much space to the shoemaking village. Let us now look at the town's agricultural aspects in the late nineteenth century.

Agricultural statistics were compiled by the censuses showing separate figures for Wayland from 1850 on. Definitions and computations were not consistent, so it is not really meaningful to look at the changes in numbers of farms and in agricultural acreage in the five-or ten-year periods to the end of the century. In the nineteenth century most of the land in the whole town of Wayland was agricultural and woodland. Except for the village residences of shoe manufacturers and workers, a few shopkeepers and artisans in Cochituate Village, and a few village homes in Wayland Center, most of the houses were farmhouses. In 1860 a detailed census enumeration was made of 100 farms containing 5,005 acres of what was called improved land and 2,018 acres of unimproved land. The population enumeration for that year designated 147 men as farmers and 58 men as farm laborers. The United States census of 1880 reported that there were 95 farms with a total employment (farmers as well as farm laborers) of 219. As the second half of the nineteenth century progressed, there were more hired farm laborers on the farms. The presence in this capacity of Irish and Nova Scotia-born men has already been described.

The Commonwealth of Massachusetts censuses of 1875 and 1885 serve us best to give a total picture of agriculture in the town. In 1875 there were reported to be 119 farms on which stood 123 farmhouses. These farms encompassed 6,883 acres. Of this land 2,687 acres were under cultivation with crops; there were 2,247 acres of unimproved land (which included pasture) and 1,949 acres of woodland. There were 150 farmers and 57 farm laborers, making total agricultural employment 207.

In 1885, for a more elaborate census of the state's agriculture, 106 Wayland farms sent in returns showing 3,066 acres under cultivation; 2,339 acres unimproved, mostly pasture; and 2,488 acres of woodland. Recorded were 141 farmers and 110 farm laborers, for a total of 251.

It is not possible to see any trend in the above-cited figures except that the land under cultivation was increasing. This important category of farmland increased to 4,348 acres by 1905, at which time pastureland was down to 1,375 acres with woodland standing at 3,436 acres. More meaningful and illustrative are the absolute figures and trends in crops and livestock shown by the successive censuses.

In the nineteenth century Wayland became progressively more of a dairy-farming town, with milch cows and milk production steadily increasing. The United States census of 1850 showed 384 cows owned on 81 farms; milk production was not reported. The average farm with cows had 4 or 5. Eli Sherman had much the largest herd with 14; others with 9 or more cows were Isaac Damon, Nathan B. Johnson, Daniel Eagan, and Joseph Bullard. All of these farms were in the north part of the town except Isaac Damon's.

In 1860 there were 416 milch cows and 276 other cattle. The Massachusetts census of 1865 was the first to report gallons of milk. A total of 79,332 gallons was reported sold; there were 501 milch cows and 74 heifers reported. By 1870 a group of ten farmers was going seriously into dairy farming with herds of 12 or more cattle. Thomas Jefferson Damon (son of Isaac) of the south end of the town was among these, and in the north end there were Luther Sherman, David Sherman, Christopher Bryden, Nathan B. Johnson, Samuel Maynard Thomas, Charles Cutting, Josiah W. Parmenter, Jude Damon, and Jonathan Maynard Parmenter. Jude Damon, Thomas Jefferson Damon's brother who had moved from Cochituate to the Baldwin lands on Old Sudbury Road in Wayland, had 44 cattle in 1870, while Jonathan Maynard Parmenter was much the largest cattle owner with 84 head.

The J. M. and H. D. Parmenter barns at the corner of Bow and Concord Roads.

The Massachusetts census of 1875 recorded 630 milch cows. Milk production that year was 129,843 gallons, with a value of $20,843, making this item the most important farm product of the town in 1875. Some of this milk was probably shipped to Boston on the trains from Natick and from Stony Brook in Weston. Reports in the *Framingham Gazette* in 1877 tell us that several Wayland farmers delivered milk in Waltham six days a week on a retail basis. Home delivery of milk in Wayland was apparently a new thing that summer. We find a report that "Deacon William Baldwin supplies the Wayland people with milk at their doors which is certainly one of the greatest conveniences we ever enjoyed here."[2] In April 1898 there appeared an advertisement in the *Natick Bulletin* that deliveries of warm milk (right from the cows) were being made in Cochituate mornings and evenings at 5 cents per quart by Dana H. Elkins.[3]

There was a large increase in milk production from 1875 to 1880, when 219,852 gallons were produced. Total number of cattle is given for that year as 831. As soon as the Massachusetts Central Railroad began operating through Wayland, milk was shipped to Boston via rail. The *Natick Bulletin* of November 24, 1882, reported that milk shipments from Wayland were 1,900 cans per week.

By 1885 Wayland's reported milk production had more than doubled that of 1880. The 1883 Wayland valuation list indicates that Jonathan M. Parmenter had the largest herd of cattle with 67 head. Paying taxes on 30 to 37 cattle were Isaac Damon of Cochituate; his uncle, Jude Damon of Wayland; Samuel Maynard Thomas, whose farm occupied the site of the present Wayland High School; and William Perkins on Mainstone Hill. Taxed for between 20 and 29 cattle were Royal Flint and Benjamin Folsom, both relative newcomers to the town, and Dennis McDonald, one of the Irish farmers who had done well. Other Irish farmers who had from 11 to 19 head of cattle apiece were Timothy Malloy, Thomas Hynes, William Eagan, and Michael Rowan, and also the widow Jane Erwin whose husband, Robert, was of Scottish descent from northern Ireland.

The story is well known that Jonathan Maynard Parmenter drove some of his cows to summer pasture in Troy, New Hampshire, for many years. The *Framingham Gazette* of May 19, 1876, noted that:

The annual migration of cattle from this region to South New Hampshire came off this week. Maynard Parmenter [then age forty-four] *was up and on his way with 80 head this morning. S. H. M.* [Samuel Hale Mann] *Heard, late of Cutting's store in Weston, is with him as assistant.*

It is less well known that this was the practice of various dairy farmers in the area. In the town clerk's mortgage and legal record book of 1859 to 1875 there was the following advertisement recorded November 4, 1871:

Found: A part blood jersey cow which fell into my drove while on its way to parture from Wayland, Mass. to Dublin, N.H. Color light red and with short horns, and is about five years old. The owner is requested to prove property, pay charges and take her away immediately.

signed M. French, Wayland, Mass. Oct. 27, 1871 a true copy attest J. A. Roby–Town Clerk & Reg.[4]

Merrill French came to Wayland from New Hampshire and may have promoted the idea of taking Wayland cattle to New Hampshire. The *Natick Bulletin* of November 6, 1891, tells of Isaac Damon's herd of cattle returning to Cochituate after a summer of grazing in New Hampshire. Again in 1902 we find a report of his arrival from New Hampshire with the drove of cattle.[5] Farmers in Sherborn and Dover also drove their cattle to New Hampshire. In the early 1880s and the 1890s there was frequent Natick newspaper comment on the cattle from towns to the south passing up Main Street in Cochituate in May and back down Main Street in October.

With dairy farming the important agricultural activity, it follows

James S. Draper (extreme left) and his crew loading hay.

that the most valuable field crop, one which covered a very large acreage, was hay. The 1855 state census reported that 1,140 tons of English hay had been grown that year on 1,223 acres of Wayland land. In addition, 1,078 tons of wet meadow or swale hay had been cut. Much of this hay was fed to Wayland livestock, but some was delivered to Waltham and places nearer Boston. In 1865, despite the increase in local livestock, acreage and yield of hay were down to 907 tons of English hay on 1,067 acres. In this year only 413 tons of wet meadow hay were harvested. By the 1860s the dam downstream at Billerica and the reservoirs upstream on the Sudbury River had caused sluggish, undrained conditions on the river meadows, and meadow grass was beginning to disappear in many places. In 1875 the total tonnage of hay—1,333 tons of English and 640 tons of meadow—was up considerably. The English hay was valued at $14,918 making it the town's most valuable crop. In 1885 the English hay crop was up, while meadow hay amounted to only 615 tons. By this time meadow hay was not so much sought after. In 1877 a Wayland column in the *Framingham Gazette* had stated: "The farmers do not mourn so much as formerly over the loss of the river meadows but feed English hay, oats, millet, Hungarian and corn stover green or dry to their stock."[6] In 1905, 3,151 acres of Wayland land were devoted to hay, straw, and fodder for the 866 milch cows, 957 total cattle, and 361 horses, of which 104 were on the farms.

For harvesting the large crops of hay, horse-drawn machinery had come to be used in the late 1860s and early 1870s. Writing for the *Framingham Gazette* in July 1875, Joseph A. Roby said this about the use of machinery in harvesting hay:

Well here we are in midsummer. . . . To say nothing of Saratoga and the races, the race here is from field to barn. At the head of this force are Kniffen, Buckeye, Sprague & Co. and it does one good to see an acre of average grass laid flat in one hour, for one dollar, especially if, as in my case, the looker-on has swung the old scythe forty-eight summers. Then at 11 A.M. the American Tedder to scratch and kick, then the spring-tooth rake; and about all the hand work that remains is to pitch it on the wagon.

The article went on to comment on the need to understand and be able to fix the machinery and named some local men who were particularly good at doing this.[7] The farm machinery seems to have been rented out by its Wayland owners to other farmers. The census of 1875 recorded 45 mowing machines, 19 hay cutters, 10 hay tedders, and 50 horse rakes.

In the census of 1875 a dairy by-product, manure, was reckoned as the third most valuable product of the Wayland farms, with 1,388 cords valued at $13,378. Ten years later there were 2,200 cords. In connection with the story of the railroad we have already mentioned that in the 1880s Wayland farmers found it more economical to import manure from Boston on freight cars than to have commercial fertilizer shipped here.

The fourth most important farm product in 1875 was 14,356 bushels of potatoes valued at $11,075. Twenty years before, in 1855, 12,840 bushels had been raised on 214 acres. No acreage figure was given for 1875, but for census years this represents the peak of production in Wayland. The yield per acre was probably higher than in 1855 as a result of more knowledge of fertilizer requirements, so perhaps the 214 acres devoted to potatoes in 1855 was the maximum. By 1880, 8,320 bushels was the potato crop on only 99 acres. As late as 1905 potatoes were being raised on 123 (all but a few) of the Wayland farms. The total that year was 9,878 bushels. The *Framingham Gazette* of September 1876 had commented on the bad scourge of potato bugs of that summer and said: "It is now thought that this is the last year we can raise potatoes."[8]

Next to potatoes in economic importance in 1875 were eggs, with 31,692 dozen produced in Wayland. By 1885 eggs had yielded fifth place to corn, the raising of which declined in acreage from 1855 to 1875. In 1855, 312 acres of Wayland agricultural land had been devoted to Indian corn, that is, corn to be dried and ground to corn meal, with an output of 9,360 bushels. This acreage was second only to that of English hay in that year. By 1875 the crop of Indian corn was down to 3,348 bushels, but there were now grown 2,115 bushels of green and 7 bushels of popcorn. At this time there was considerable interest in corn yields and fertilizing the cornfields. It was reported in the *Natick Bulletin* in November 1882 that whereas W. C. Lyford and the Parmenters, Flints, Damons, Lombards, Heards, and Gleasons got 30 to 40 bushels per acre from their cornfields, Hodijah B. Braman's farm had yielded 80 bushels per acre.[9]

Thomas Jefferson Damon, who died at the age of seventy-one in December 1880, had been Wayland's outstanding farmer. As was his son Isaac after him, he was active in the Middlesex South Agricultural Society. At that society's March meeting in 1880 Damon had said in a speech that he had found corn, hay, and milk to be the most profitable crops. He also found potatoes to be profitable and, with free use of barnyard manure, was able to get upward of 200 bushels of potatoes per acre.[10]

Apples were another large crop in Wayland in the nineteenth century. In 1875 the census recorded 2,132 trees and a crop of 12,400 bushels of fruit. In 1885 three times as many trees were counted, but there was a much smaller crop—5,741 bushels. The year 1885 must have been a poor apple year. Most of the farms had apple trees; however, in land use figures for 1885, only 23½ acres were classified as being cultivated as orchards.

Other uses for the 3,067 acres of cultivated land in 1885 were: 2,321 acres for hay, 628 acres for "principal crops" (potatoes, corn, etc.), 8 acres for market gardens, 10½ acres for nurseries, and 76 acres for other categories. There were four small cider mills which produced 1,705 gallons of cider for sale and 4,452 gallons for home farm use. Of other fruits, strawberries had in 1885 begun to be raised in appreciable quantities, with 17,125 quarts valued at $2,191.

Meat production—of beef, veal, and pork—was not an inconsequential item on the Wayland farms. In 1875, 121,250 pounds were slaughtered; in 1885 the figure was down to 83,407 pounds. This meat production gave rise to small tallow rendering and tripe and fertilizer operations. Isaac S. Whittemore on Old Connecticut Path advertised in the 1875 *Beers' Atlas of Middlesex County* as a "Manufacturer of Tripe and Pure Neats Foot Oil. Tripe, Glue Stock and Coarse and Fine Bone Stock for Sale." More than once the Natick newspapers commented on the smell of the tallow-rendering shop James A. Loker and his son Granville ran on East Plain Street in Cochituate.

By 1890 oxen were no longer used on Wayland farms as they had been in the first half of the nineteenth century and, more importantly, in the seventeenth and eighteenth centuries. These strong animals had been supplanted by horses, partly because the heavy work of clearing stumps from fields and hauling rocks for walls had diminished somewhat, but chiefly because more and better horses were available, and these animals were more adaptable once there were wheeled vehicles, mowing and other machines, and better roads. In 1855 it had been reported that there were 121 oxen more than three years old in Wayland and, in addition, 35 steers under three years. In 1865 there were 87 oxen; in 1875 there were 34; in 1885, only 10. On October 22, 1886, the *Natick Bulletin* noted the sale by Horatio G. Hammond of the last yoke of oxen supposed to be owned in Cochituate. Two oxen in the whole town were reported in 1895.

In 1860, 162 horses were reported in Wayland. In 1885 there were 317 horses, not all of them on the farms. Some horses were being used for sport, some for family transportation, and some for hire at the livery stables. Every once in a while the newspapers reported mistreatment of horses and accidents to persons and to equipment when irresponsible persons hired horses and carriages from the livery stables. On the 1883 valuation list there were 189 carriages, owned by 120 different taxpayers. Warren G. Roby owned 5 carriages; James M. Bent, H. B. Braman, Charles A. Cutting, and Harriet S. Wyman each 4. William H. Bent had 3 carriages, as did William P. Perkins, William H. Campbell, Jeremiah H. Mullen, and W.D.K. Marrs. Except for Mullen and Marrs, who probably rented out their carriages, the above-mentioned citizens enjoyed the prestige and comfort of having several carriages. George F. Keep, who ran a livery stable in Cochituate, had 8 carriages. Other wheeled vehicles like the Bent company's large wagons and the farm wagons were not taxed and not reported.

The census of 1880 classified the 106 farms it identified in Wayland by size. The median farm in size had about 50 acres. Only twelve farms had under 15 acres. There were fifteen farms with over 100 acres, thirteen of them between 100 and 150 acres, one between 150 and 199 acres, and one between 300 and 400 acres. The 1883 valuation list shows William Perkins to be the owner of the largest farm, with

326½ acres. Perkins had two resident farmers and employed various farm laborers, but it is not known how intensively this farm area was worked or how much the owner simply enjoyed protecting his view and being isolated. Next in size was the Thomas Jefferson Damon farm in Cochituate being carried on by his son Isaac Damon. This farm had 208 acres. Charles A. Cutting, the Boston businessman, owned the third largest total of agricultural land, much of it on or near Old Sudbury Road and totaling 197 acres. By this time Cutting had invested heavily in woodland acreage, which raised his total. However, he ran a dairy operation and sold milk. Nathan B. Johnson had 184½ acres; his property included extensive river meadows. Samuel Maynard Thomas had the fifth farm in size with 161 acres. The two brothers Jonathan Maynard and Henry Dana Parmenter, who operated as a partnership, had 157 acres of farmland. They owned a larger-than-usual amount of river meadow. Joseph Bullard had 153 acres.

The most valuable land was that classified as mowing and tillage on which hay and other crops were grown. This type of land was assessed at from $25 to $147 an acre, with $100 an acre fairly standard for good land. William Perkins had 113 acres of mowing and tillage. The Parmenter brothers had 53 acres valued at $119 an acre, indicative of the best farmland in Wayland. Samuel M. Thomas had 45 acres. Alpheus Loker and the Damon farm in Cochituate each had 40 acres of mowing and tillage, as did Royal M. Flint. William H. Campbell on former Heard land on Pelham Island had 36 acres of mowing and tillage; Joseph Bullard, 35 acres.

Thomas Jefferson Damon's son Isaac of Cochituate was well known in the county as a successful and knowledgeable farmer. By the late 1880s Isaac Damon had built up a very fine herd of Holstein cattle which won prizes at the South Framingham cattle shows.[11] Earlier, in 1875, the *Concord Freeman* had reported that Samuel M. Thomas was a prizewinner in plowing contests and for his farm horses at the Middlesex Agricultural Society Fair in Concord, and also that Jude Damon and Robert Erwin won prizes for fat cattle.[12] Another farmer who had outstanding success was Hodijah B. Braman, who employed a farm superintendent because his chief business was that of upholstery and furniture in Boston. His farm, with a house at 18 Old Sudbury Road and a farmer's house at 10 Old Sudbury Road, contained 89 acres in 1883. His 31 acres of mowing and tillage were valued at $147 an acre, the most valuable large piece of land used for farming in the town. He also owned 29 acres of pasture, 9 acres of bow meadow, 6 acres of river meadow, and 14 acres of woodland. For livestock he had 4 horses, 2 oxen, 12 cows, and 2 swine.

Farm Estates

William Powell Perkins died at the age of ninety in Boston in January 1891. The *Natick Bulletin* of January 23 noted: "Mr. Perkins, proprietor of the pin cushion farm of Wayland died. . . . The deceased was the owner of one of the richest farms in the state." In the *Bulletin* of the next week Perkins was termed an "old and respected citizen . . . being proprietor of the 'Cushing estate' . . . one of the richest farms of the state, being valued at about $100,000."[13] This farm was to continue in the ownership of Perkins's nieces and a nephew and to be greatly enlarged in land area in the early twentieth century.

The year Perkins died a new large landowner who went in for gentleman farming came on the scene and immediately made an impact on the town. Francis Shaw, a wealthy Bostonian, nephew of Quincy Adams Shaw who had been the most active of the Bostonian investors associated with the fabulously profitable Calumet and Hecla copper-mining company in Michigan, had a lifelong interest in farming. As a young man he had a large farm in New Braintree in western Worcester County, but in 1890 decided to create a farm estate nearer Boston in Wayland. The area around the Five Paths intersection of Old Connecticut Path with Cochituate Road appealed to him. Very quietly he first bought (apparently using a straw or other device to avoid publicity) the Lewis Bemis house on the corner and the old, eighteenth-century Capt. Joseph Smith house. Then in 1891 he bought Lucy Anna Dudley's farm on Cochituate Road, which had earlier been another Joseph Smith property with a house built in 1817 but owned by Dudleys since 1855.[14] The present house at 194 Cochituate Road was built in 1910 by Francis Shaw as a replacement farmer's house on the foundation of the Smith-Dudley house which burned down that year.

In the summer and fall of 1891 Shaw set to work to have this land cleared. This was the summer of great distress in Cochituate after the Wm. and J. M. Bent Company failure, and Shaw offered work to unemployed shoe workers. We find in the *Natick Bulletin* of September 4, 1891, that "quite a number from here [Cochituate] are employed at the Dudley farm on the Wayland road this week." Shaw's quiet program of buying up property progressed, and we find in early

Aerial view of Francis Shaw's Five Paths House, built in 1892 and torn down in the early 1940s.

January: "The Flint place in Wayland has been purchased by the same parties that purchased the Dudley place. The name or home of the parties is a conundrum to everyone."[15] In the same issue of the *Natick Review* was also the news that the Whittemore brothers, who lived at 214 Old Connecticut Path, had gone into sheep raising and had purchased a farm in Weston. The Whittemore property was taken over by Shaw.

By the fall of 1892 it was known in Wayland that Francis Shaw had assembled a large estate. In September the *Natick Review* reported that "Mr. Shaw of Boston who purchased the old Flint place contemplated building a large barn." In November the *Review* reported that twenty carpenters "were at work on the Shaw mansion which would be ready for plasterers in the spring." Shaw's house was placed on high land with a magnificent view. The twenty-two-room house was designed by the distinguished Boston architectural firm of Little and Browne. Incorporated into the semiclassical house were a staircase, an oval room, fireplace mantels, and dado from the Joseph Barrell mansion built in 1792 in Charlestown and enlarged in 1816 by the famous architect Charles Bulfinch. There were also several exterior features taken from the Barrell mansion, such as an oval porch with two-story columns, the entrance doorway, and Palladian windows.[16] The flagstones in the entrance vestibule came from the Old State House in Boston. And, in keeping with Shaw's socially elite Boston milieu, the dining room paneling came from the old building of the Somerset Club in Boston.[17] This house was torn down in 1942. On its site two successive houses have been built at 57 Shaw Drive.

By 1900 Francis Shaw was taxed for the ownership of 849 acres of land. He was then a resident and voter but also maintained a home in Boston and had property in Maine. Other houses on the property were occupied by the farmer, farm workers, and a large corps of gardeners. Shaw called his estate Five Paths.

Significantly a reporter for Wayland for the *Natick Bulletin* in January 1893 expressed the town's yearning for the tax relief that could be achieved by the presence of the wealthy when he wrote that for the past twenty years Wayland had been at a disadvantage compared with Lincoln and Weston because of "no handful of wealthy men" who had in those two neighboring towns been paying most of the taxes. The article went on to say:

> *At last, however, a Braintree* [sic] *millionaire has made Wayland his residence and, besides adding largely to the real estate valuation by building operations, brings an increase in corporation tax and personal property tax which will meet nearly half of the usual tax level and reduce the rate. . . . The ice being broken in this thorough manner, the town's natural advantages and railroad facilities are expected to start a good-sized real estate boom . . . and to speedily make high taxes, poor schools and sandy highways matters of ancient history.*[18]

In this connection it is interesting to note that the 1874 edition of *Nason's Gazetteer* had called Weston "a picturesque and scenic town" with "hills crowned with mansions of gentlemen doing business in the metropolis." Wayland's reliance on her country squires came to be an important aspect of early-twentieth-century municipal finance.

Wayland Center as a Rural Retreat

Nason's 1890 *Gazetteer* characterized Wayland as "a rural village of much charm and restfulness." Some residents like James Sumner Draper thought of the town as too quiet and backward, worked hard for the coming of the railroad, and as the late 1880s and the 1890s unfolded were acting to promote the town as a haven for city dwellers

1830 house on Old Sudbury Road was the residence of Lydia Maria Child from 1852 to 1880.

in the summers. Others appreciated Wayland as a quiet retreat.

Lydia Maria Child, who died in Wayland in 1880, had been one of the latter category. Characterized as "one of the most prominent women of her time" in recent editions of the *Encyclopaedia Britannica*, Lydia Maria (Francis) Child (1802-80) had come to Wayland in 1852 to take care of her aged and ill father, Convers Francis. He had moved to Wayland in his older age in the 1840s because it had been for some time the home of his son James Francis. Mrs. Child had enjoyed fame as a writer at a young age in Boston. Her marriage to lawyer David Lee Child and their acquaintance with William Lloyd Garrison had led the couple into a controversy-filled and difficult life in the antislavery movement. For Lydia, this included a period of living in New York City to edit the *Anti-Slavery Standard* combined, paradoxically, with David's attempt to grow sugar beets in Northampton, Massachusetts. When the couple stayed on in Wayland after Convers Francis's death, it was to make their home here quietly, almost a retreat from the world.

Lydia Maria wasn't a recluse. She often traveled from Wayland to Boston where, just before and during the Civil War, such important political figures as Massachusetts U.S. Senator Charles Sumner, Governor John A. Andrew, Senator Henry Wilson, and Chief Justice of the Supreme Court Salmon P. Chase are said to have sought her advice. While she was in Wayland she did considerable writing, enjoyed her location on Old Sudbury Road looking out at the river meadows, and cherished friendships with her neighbors. The smaller, older part of the house at 91 Old Sudbury Road was the Child's home until her death. She also devoted herself to helping unfortunate members of the community and preferred this role in Wayland to being an important woman.

Although she had wide acquaintance with sophisticated, wealthy, and intellectual people and was to die quite comfortably off herself, Mrs. Child enjoyed Wayland for its simplicity and rural charm and had no ambition for it to change. Among the sixty-three letters written by her which are owned by the Wayland Historical Society are two in which, when spending winters in Boston after her husband's death, she expressed disapproval of the town's expenditure on the new town hall. In February 1878, writing to Martha Wight, daughter of the Reverend John Burt Wight, she said that this project would "increase the taxes which are already so heavy as to render Wayland an undesirable residence in that particular." The following winter she wrote to Martha Wight on January 5, 1879, from Boston, "I am glad to hear the old gentleman [the Reverend John Burt Wight] was able to sit through all the exercises of dedicating the Wayland Folly. To *what* was the House dedicated? To debt and taxation." Then, later in the letter, "I thank you for your letter. I am sorry you were not able to hop at the Ball [a ball held in the new town hall after its dedication]. I hope the dancers did not run into *debt* for their showy dresses as the town did for building the House which was no more needed than a coach needs a fifth wheel."

In May 1879, when she had just returned from spending the winter in Boston, Mrs. Child who, still concerned with Wayland's debt, quite clearly knew nothing about Cochituate doings and James Madison Bent's plaything, the *Hannah Dexter*, wrote the following to a friend named Emma:

They have started a steam boat in Wayland and they sound a little penny trumpet of a whistle many times a day, like children playing great designs. I shouldn't wonder if they were to raise the price of real estate in consequence of this new enterprise. As my house is not far from the river through which the mightly machine puffs its way, perhaps it may prove a "Silver Mine" to me. If they can get up steam about anything, *it is lucky for Wayland, always provided it does not include debt.*

If one knew nothing about the *Hannah Dexter*, which was launched for the first time in April 1879, one would think that Mrs. Child's letter was telling her friend about a commercial passenger boat. It was in May 1879 that J. M. Bent and his friend from South Natick, who also had a steam launch, went on their trip down the Sudbury to Billerica.

The account of Lydia Marie Child's funeral in Wayland which appeared in the *Framingham Gazette* of October 29, 1880, stressed the contrast between her fame and her quiet life in Wayland. In the eyes of the newspaper reporter:

The funeral was . . . a peculiar one, when we take into consideration the fact that the literary labors of Mrs. Child have been crowned with so much success and also the circumstance of her being so generally known not only in our own, but also in other countries. The last rites occurred in the humble and unpretentious home. . . . To these services the general public was not admitted as one would suppose would be the case when a person so well-known and especially among the rich and the poor of her own community had died.

The article went on to relate that Mrs. Child had written directions for her burial and funeral in June 1879.

In accordance with the terms of these requests, the deceased was laid out in her own clothes with a white cap. . . . The casket was one of the plainest that could be produced, not a silvered handle or screw head could be seen on it. . . . Not a floral offering was laid about the casket.

Both the Unitarian minister of Wayland and Wendell Phillips, the well-known reformer and orator, who was Mrs. Child's longtime associate and her executor, spoke at the service. The casket was then carried on foot for burial next to her husband in the nearby North Cemetery. The *Framingham News* article tells us that "The pall bearers were selected from her old farmer neighbors in Wayland."

Public statements of this era seemed to stress the presence of old farmers in Wayland. There has been no place in this history to tell about an uproar and complicated controversy which took place over a sudden vote to allow liquor licenses in Wayland in 1897 in connection with a clock on the tower of the Cochituate Methodist Church. Because the *Boston Globe* published a story about the controversy with the headline, "Legal Cocktails Will Probably be Mixed in Wayland," Wayland was momentarily given some publicity. Reporters who came to Wayland to interview the town officers involved laid great stress on the farmyards and barns where they interviewed these farmer-officeholders, the hay scales prominent in the center of the town, and so on.

The quiet simplicity which appealed to the Childs brought to Wayland Center, and to some extent also to Cochituate, families who wanted to spend summers in a rural environment. The *Natick Review* of August, 11, 1892, had said that Wayland Center was full of summer boarders and that the inn at the center of the village was full. These people went fishing at Heard's Pond, took carriage rides in the vicinity, and enjoyed simple country pleasures. The *Natick Review* in June 1891 had carried an article taken from a Waltham paper telling of a project afoot to form a stock company to build a resort hotel in Wayland. It featured the Sudbury River with "excellent opportunities . . . for boating, bathing and fishing and the presence on the property of a valuable mineral spring that is known to possess certain medicinal properties."[19] The location of this prospective resort hotel was not identified; it was described as "one of the most beautiful on the river, a high hill commanding an extensive view of the surrounding country, remote, yet conveniently close to the railroad and village and in the midst of a pine grove." It is likely that Francis Shaw bought the hilltop location.

Some summer residents rented houses, as did a Blake family from Dorchester. The *Waltham Free Press* of October 19, 1888, reported that "Mr. Blake and family moved to Dorchester much pleased with Wayland as a summer resort." It is not known whether the Blakes returned for other summers. Others seeking relief from the heat of the city in summer who owned houses in Wayland included the Reverend Brooke Herford, pastor of the Arlington Street Church in Boston, who bought the Deacon James Draper house at 116 Plain Road from James Sumner Draper in 1886. The *Waltham Free Press* of October 26, 1888, reported that Herford stayed in Wayland as late as November 1. Brooke Herford's daughter Beatrice was to marry Sidney Hayward of Wayland and settle down to live in the Hayward house now standing at 101 Boston Post Road. Beatrice Hayward was the originator of the modern dramatic monologue performance. Under the name Beatrice Herford she was well known on the stage and toured Keith's vaudeville circuit. She also went back to England, her native land, for professional engagements and made a successful debut in London in 1895. In 1904 she had built a miniature theater on her property in Wayland for the entertainment of her friends, some of them famous in the theatrical world. This once tiny building is the nucleus of an enlarged theater now owned and actively used by a community dramatic group.

In 1884 Edwin B. Buckingham of Brookline, related by marriage to the Cuttings and Mellens of Wayland, bought Abel Heard's old house on Pelham Island Road (now number 187). Here, after remodeling and putting in heat, the Buckinghams spent longer and longer segments of the year in Wayland. The Buckinghams took what had been a working farm for many generations and turned it into a country residence. They were in the vanguard of a movement. Agriculture was beginning to lose out to country living in the Wayland end of the town. This is what such men as James Sumner Draper had long thought should happen to Wayland and had been his reason for so vigorously promoting the railroad.

NOTES

1. Nason had died in 1887; George J. Varney carried out the revisions for R. B. Russell, the publisher.
2. *Framingham Gazette*, August 3, 1877.
3. *Natick Bulletin*, April 18, 1898.
4. Town of Wayland, *Personal Mortgages 1859-1875*, Book II, p. 161.
5. *Natick Bulletin*, October 24, 1902.
6. *Framingham Gazette*, July 20, 1877.
7. *Ibid*, July 21, 1875.
8. *Ibid*, September 22, 1876.
9. *Natick Bulletin*, November 10, 1882.
10. *Natick Citizen*, March 26, 1880.
11. *Natick Bulletin*, September 23, 1887.
12. *Concord Freeman*, January 30, 1891.
13. *Natick Bulletin*, January 30, 1891.
14. Alfred S. Hudson, *Annals*, Appendix "Location of Homesteads" p. 120.
15. *Natick Review*, January 7, 1892.
16. Society for the Preservation of New England Antiquities, *Old Time New England*, January, 1948, article on the Barrell mansion.
17. See 1940 sales brochure for Shaw estate, copy owned by Wayland Historical Society.
18. *Natick Bulletin*, January 27, 1893.
19. *Natick Review*, May 19, 1892.

18

Modernizing Wayland Center in the 1890s

Center School

THE TOWN could attract a certain number of wealthy or comfortably fixed families for country living in the warmer months of the year, but before there could be a real estate boom bringing middle-class families to Wayland to make the town their year-round home, the schools on the Wayland end of the town needed improvement. The town had had a small high school on Cochituate Road in Wayland Center built in 1855; however, by the late 1880s the building was in such poor repair and so inadequate in its sanitary and ventilation facilities that in early 1892 the state inspector of public buildings had ordered changes made here and also at the one-room Rutter, Center Primary, and North schoolhouses. Moreover, the primary school education was offered in four antiquated, ungraded one-room schools, all but one of which dated back to the earlier half of the century. By the 1880s consolidated schools were the order of the day in progressive communities; accordingly, in 1893 at a town meeting held on June 24, Article 6, "to see if the town will build a new school house at Wayland Centre or remodel the High School building," was put to a vote. This article had been preceded in the warrant by Article 2, "to see if the town will accept Section 72 of Chapter 423 of the Acts of 1890 to divide the town into voting precincts." The school article had probably been carefully placed to come after the voting precinct question as a trade-off of what Cochituate wanted against an expenditure for the Wayland end of the town.

When the poor state of the Wayland High School was about to be brought up in 1892, the *Natick Review* wrote under its Cochituate notes: "We hear that Wayland wants a $10,000 schoolhouse. What next?"[1]

Action provided for by Article 6 introduced on June 24, 1893, would require the committee, constituted in 1892 to repair the high school building, to procure plans for a four-room school building to be heated by steam and to cost not more than $9,000. This committee included Richard T. Lombard, town clerk, attorney and florist who lived at 61 Old Sudbury Road; Hodijah B. Braman; Lorenzo K. Lovell, grocery and dry-goods store proprietor who had bought the 1841 town house to use as a store and who lived next to his store at 11 Cochituate Road; Edward Carter of North Wayland; and Samuel Maynard Thomas. At the same town meeting an article passed which provided for the consolidation of the Thomas, Rutter, North, and Center Primary schools in the new building at Wayland Center.

The next spring, at the annual town meeting of March 26, 1894, the town voted to set aside $4,000 to build a schoolhouse at Wayland Center. It also appropriated $300 to repair the old high and grammar school and to drive an artesian well for that school's use. This was Article 5 in the town meeting warrant. If the articles were taken up in their numerical order, the town at a later point in the meeting voted down an appropriation of $9,000 to build a new schoolhouse at the center. This was slow progress toward constructing a much-needed school at Wayland Center.

The school matter had become urgent, and it now became the subject of a series of special town meetings. A town meeting was held on May 10 when four articles with school proposals for Wayland Center were introduced, but no action was taken on any of them. With their own schools very crowded, most of the Cochituate voters were against spending money for a new school in Wayland. After this meeting the *Natick Review* reported that there was a considerable body of opinion that it would be cheaper and more desirable to add to the old high school building.

To defeat articles for expenditures on a school in Wayland Center the Cochituate voters had to go to Wayland Center to attend the town meetings. This was burdensome, so Article 13 on May 10 proposed that the town hold all special town meetings in Cochituate Village. No action was taken on this article. The selectmen, two of whom were from Cochituate—Edward P. Butler and David P. W. Loker—then called another special town meeting for June 7. This meeting was scheduled for 7:00 P.M., an hour more convenient for the working population of Cochituate. This time groups from Cochituate hired horse-drawn barges to transport voters to the town hall in Wayland, and this time they managed, by a vote of 71 to 59, to pass an article mandating that all special town meetings be held in Cochituate. Again at this meeting all articles providing for a Wayland Center School were defeated.

Apparently the frustration in Wayland Center was very great after the June 7 town meeting. On June 22 the *Natick Bulletin* wrote indignantly that "the present incumbent of two of our most important town offices" had acted very improperly and unfairly when he said after a grass fire in Cochituate that it would be a blessing if every building in the south end of the town burned to the ground. Said the *Bulletin:*

Evidently from the above it is easily concluded that they have not all fully recovered at the North end from the bitter disappointment in regard to the school question which was acted upon at the recent town meeting.

The article ended with:

It is a source of regret that this sectional feeling should continue to exist among the two communities. It is hoped that the question that has developed so much ill feeling will be adjusted satisfactory to all.

On the evening of July 18, 1894, a town meeting was held at the Knights of Labor Hall in Cochituate at 7:00 P.M. Nothing further was voted regarding school facilities at this special meeting or at any town meeting in 1895. An attempt at a November 1895 town meeting to have all town meetings held at Wayland Center again, obviously a move to try to weaken Cochituate's influence, failed to pass.

It has not been determined whether one or more citizens of Wayland Center approached the then new, wealthy, part-time resident Francis Shaw or whether Shaw responded spontaneously when he heard of Wayland Center's inability to have the town vote enough money to build a schoolhouse. In any case, by the time of the annual meeting in March 1896, Francis Shaw had anonymously, as far as the general population went, offered to help with the project. Just before the March town meeting a separately printed school committee report was distributed to the townspeople. This report contained an architect's drawing of the facade and floor plans for the first and

1897 Wayland Center High and Grammar School

second floors of a school building which the committee recommended to the town. These plans had been drawn up by the Boston architectural firm of Dwight and Chandler and had been commissioned and paid for by Francis Shaw. Dr. Boodey had resigned from the school committee in January, and the committee had at the time only two members, both women: Mrs. Lizzie Mitchell of Cochituate and Miss Lucy Anna Dudley of Wayland. The latter part of the committee's report took up the inadequacy of the present school buildings and then went on to say:

Your committee has been enabled through the kindness of a townsman to present for your consideration plans for a house such as we deem necessary and advisable and we ask that one based on these plans shall be built during the coming season.

The report then stated that there would be more room than needed at first, so that the four rooms on the first floor would be finished and furnished, as would the basement playroom. The second floor would be plastered and ready for woodwork and finishing when needed. The cost of the projected building was estimated at from $18,000 to $20,000. The report closed with the statement that if this building was built the two partial high schools being conducted in Cochituate and in Wayland could be consolidated into a complete high school.

Careful planning had gone into the 1896 effort to attain a new school building for Wayland Center. Someone saw to it that the *Natick Bulletin* published on March 20 in its "Cochituate Enterprise" section an article endorsing the need for a new Center School in Wayland.

At the March 26 town meeting the finance committee explained that with $4,000 set aside in 1894 for a school, the $2,000 the town could expect to realize from the sale of the old high school and the four one-room schoolhouses, and an offer of $3,000 by Mr. Shaw, the town would need to raise by borrowing only $11,000. A letter, dated March 20, 1896, from Shaw to an unnamed member of the finance committee was copied onto the town clerk's record at the end of the record of that town meeting. The letter said, in part:

If the plans, as submitted to the people in the report of the School Committee, are in their essential features carried out this year, I will contribute $3,000 towards defraying the cost of building. In other words, if the town will this year appropriate $11,000 in addition to the $4,000 which has already been set aside for this purpose and turn over to the building fund the proceeds from the sale of its school property, estimated at $2,000, I will pledge myself that the school building as sketched in the report of the School Committee shall be completed and furnished and the grounds about it graded without additional expense to the town. This pledge to hold good in case of my death. You will oblige me by reading this letter to the other members of your committee.

The town record goes on to say:

The foregoing letter was read to the meeting and it was voted to tender to Francis Shaw the thanks of the town for his generous gift and pledge as contained in his letter to the town. And the vote was passed unanimously by a standing vote.

Shaw's was a generous offer, too good to turn down. The vote taken on March 26 was 123 to 5 to build the school at a total cost to the town of $17,000. It must have been generally known by then that Francis Shaw had made the gift, because the moderator appointed him to the building committee for the school, in addition to Henry D. Parmenter, a well-to-do Wayland farmer, and Llewellyn Flanders, a man who had come to Cochituate in the late 1870s as a shoe worker and had served as a selectman in 1891 and 1892. At that meeting it also was voted to pay high school tuition for high school students out of town for the school years 1895-96 and to establish a high school as soon as the new building was erected.

In early 1894 an Odd Fellows Lodge had been organized in Wayland Center and included Cochituate membership. This group needed a building and was quick to offer to buy the old high school building to move to a lot it had acquired just south of the school property on Cochituate Road. The Lodge had picked out this lot, undoubtedly with the hope that it would be able to move the old building to it if it became available. When the school building committee began the work of placing the new school on town land, it became apparent that it would be better to locate the structure farther to the south than the town's school lot would allow. Accordingly it was decided to take the Odd Fellows' lot in exchange for a 75-foot piece of the town lot north of the old high school. This exchange of land was voted in a special town meeting held on April 21, 1896. In mid-May the old high school building which had been sold to the Pequod Lodge of Odd Fellows for $200 was moved north so that the new Center School, then called the Wayland High and Grammar School, could be centered behind the two large oak trees.[2]

Ground was broken in 1896, but the new school building was not finished and ready for occupancy until mid-1897. By early 1897 when reports were readied for the 1896-97 town report, $3,519 of the town's $17,000 was unexpended. To finish the building and to grade and landscape the lot, Francis Shaw was said in a newspaper report of November 1897 to have spent, not the $3,000 he originally offered, but $8,000, making the total cost of the new school $25,000.[3]

The new school may have been used for classes in the spring of 1897, but it was not completely landscaped and furnished until that fall. A long article in the *Natick Bulletin* described a rather elaborate dedication ceremony held on October 30.[4] The school was open for inspection from one to five o'clock on a Saturday afternoon. According to the reporter, James Draper, Francis Shaw, and other prominent citizens showed people around. After a tour of the building, guests assembled for refreshments at four long tables in the Odd Fellows Hall. "It was a royal feast to sit down to, and there were hundreds gathered around it from different parts of the state . . . to do honor to mine host the town." The crowd then repaired to the assembly hall on the second floor of the new school where there were elaborate ceremonies. Willard Bullard, who now lived a good part of the year at

Kirkside next to the Unitarian Church, and was by then a large property owner in the center village, was the President of the Day. Elbridge Smith, who had been the main speaker at the dedication of the town hall in 1878, spoke, as did the Honorable Charles F. Gerry of Sudbury. Music was provided by a well-known Boston cellist, and there was a vocal quintet.

The *Bulletin* reporter described the first floor of the building as having four classrooms off the hallway, which was on the east side of the building. Palladian windows of which Shaw was fond were a feature of the staircases and an important element of the facade. In the middle of the hallway, near the east wall, a plaster cast of Hermes was placed, the gift of Lawrence Bond. Enlarged photographs of famous buildings and scenes, gifts of Dwight B. Heard, were on the walls of the four first-floor classrooms, each of which housed two or more grades. The basement contained a playroom for use at recess on stormy days. The building committee had not planned to finish any of the rooms on the second floor; however, before the dedication a private citizen, probably not Shaw, had given $1,000 so that the assembly hall, where the exercises were held, could be finished and furnished. It contained a piano which the newspaper article identified as the gift of Mrs. Wallace Draper. The two classrooms on that floor were unfinished and not then in use, but the next year Francis Shaw gave additional funds so that one of these classrooms and a small science laboratory could be fitted up for use by the high school students.

The dedication seemed an impressive occasion to the Cochituate reporter. He described the building as "commodious," although in terms of classrooms it was hardly so when it was built to replace five other school buildings. Reporters from Cochituate who attended events in the north part of the town seemed frequently to be impressed with the quiet of Wayland Center. The Cochituate resident who covered the dedication exercises wrote:

Wayland has been called a "town where the smoke of the factory never rises" and this . . . becomes at once apparent to every newcomer. Dwelling always in a clear atmosphere, and well away from the harsh discord of machinery, the Waylanders cannot at all realize what music it is to a workingman's ear, in a town where many of the factories are idle more than half the year, to hear the noisy rattle and hum of machinery after long intervals of suspended animation.

The trauma of unemployment after the Bent company failure of 1891 had left its scar. Cochituate reporters enjoyed contrasting the quiet of Wayland with their own more lively area. A piece in the *Natick Review* in 1892, when there was agitation to have town meetings and elections held in Cochituate, shows this reaction. The *Review* correspondent apparently went to a town meeting in Wayland Center on a Saturday afternoon in June and later wrote:

The . . . correspondent arrived at 3:30 P.M., but the meeting had been dismissed ten minutes before and the hall was empty. In vain he tried to find a citizen who attended. . . . The solemn stillness of Wayland Centre was not even broken by a crowing rooster. The streets deserted and desolate caused such a homesick feeling in the bosom of the weary reporter that he made quick tracks over the dusty road to the live and enterprising village, the home of the PEOPLE, to Cochituate.[5]

At the time the Center School was being built the Cochituate School had become very crowded. Jealousy and resentment were present in Cochituate, and these reactions were played on to try to present the case that Cochituate really needed a school much more acutely than Wayland had The *Natick Bulletin* of December 11, 1896, contained a bitter article with false statements about which of the townspeople were paying for the tax-supplied $17,000 for the Wayland Center School:

Cochituate is at present experiencing the inconvenience of overcrowded and incommodious school rooms. Her mother Wayland has just been presented with an enormous, new and modern school house accommodating some one hundred scholars. Wayland, at her present rate of growth of population is supplied with sufficient school rooms for at least fifty years.

The article continued with the familiar two-thirds argument:

Wayland . . . constitutes one third while Cochituate represents two-thirds of the population and two-thirds of the tax payers. It follows that Cochituate pays for two-thirds of that new school while she is suffering from the poor school service she is obliged to put up with. . . . Probably a big mistake was made in erecting such a school house in Wayland. . . . Wayland has the school house and Cochituate has the scholars. It would hardly pay to transport scholars to Wayland. . . . Cochituate must have a new school building sooner or later.

Cochituate did get a new schoolhouse, a brick building started in 1910 and completed in 1911. One of Wayland Center's leading citizens, Edmund H. Sears, helped with anonymous donations to make that building better and more adequate than it would otherwise have been.

In 1897 there was an article in the warrant for the annual March town meeting to have the town buy the Knights of Labor Hall in Cochituate, ostensibly for a school building. Nothing came of this proposal, but the *Natick Bulletin* bristled and began comparing the rather flimsy construction of that building with "the grand and luxurious Wayland School."[6]

In the late 1890s Wayland was rural but struggling to become a residential suburb. In 1899 Dwight B. Heard, who had inherited Horace Heard's landholdings south and east of the Unitarian Church and had moved his grandfather's house to its present location at 18 Winthrop Terrace, planned and advertised a subdivision with eighteen lots of from one half to three quarters of an acre. The sixteen-page brochure with photographs, text, and map gave a prominent place to a photograph of the new high and grammar school across the road from the development. Proudly the brochure said of the school: "The new High and Grammar School building, equipped with the most modern sanitary devices and with its efficient corps of teachers, will convince one of the standing of Wayland from an educational standpoint."[7]

Trolley Car to Wayland

Cochituate people thought of Wayland Center as a scenic, country area of bucolic charms with places to camp on hills and to fish on the river. A year after the trolley line from Natick to Cochituate began operating, a July 1893 issue of the *Natick Bulletin* contained in its Cochituate news an item reporting that there was talk of extending the trolley line to Wayland Center and saying: "Where would there be a pleasanter ride on the Electrics than from here to Wayland during the summer months?" A reporter for Wayland stated in the *Natick Bulletin* in August of that year that "Eighteen new houses have been built in Wayland, north of Cochituate, in the last five years and four have burned. When we get the electric road from Cochituate, we shall expect a boom and shall have street lights in the village."[8]

The September 13, 1893, *Natick Bulletin* reported that there was talk of extending the line from Cochituate to Wayland Center in 1894 with Wayland citizens subscribing to the stock. The Natick and Cochituate

Looking south on Cochituate Road, with the 1835 Trinitarian Congregational Church, Odd Fellows Hall, and Center School facing the trolley tracks on the left.

Street Railway was a prosperous company at this time, and it was not necessary to obtain capital subscriptions in Wayland. The company was in the midst of building extensions to Wellesley and Newton and did not apply to the Wayland selectmen for a franchise until February 1897. On March 23, 1897, the selectmen gave the street railway company permission to build a track from Lyons Corner in Cochituate to the railroad track in Wayland Center. The franchise also allowed the company to build a track on the Boston Post Road to the Weston line and a track from Lyons Corner along West Plain Street and Old Connecticut Path to the Framingham town line on its way to Saxonville. The franchise required that the line from Cochituate to Wayland be completed that summer—on or before September 1, 1897.[9]

There may have been trouble with Francis Shaw about putting the trolley line along Cochituate Road, which cut through his property. The franchise specified that the track be run on the westerly side of Main Street to the Five Paths intersection and cross there to the easterly side of Cochituate Road (then called Main Street) to the Boston Post Road where the track would run up the middle of the street to the railroad track. In May the *Natick Bulletin* reported a rumor that the line could not be built, "owing to a certain piece of woodland which stands in the way." The franchise for building the trolley extension to Saxonville allowed eighteen months. However, that line was built and opened for operation first. The track to Saxonville was started in early June. On July 23 the Saxonville line was opened, and many Cochituate residents took the opening day ride to the muster field.[10]

The street railway company did nothing about building the line to Wayland within the time limit, so the franchise expired. Meanwhile a high school had been instituted at the new Center School in Wayland, and it became necessary to transport Cochituate pupils to Wayland by horse-drawn barges. This situation added to the pressure to build a trolley line to Wayland. In November 1898 the Cochituate news in the *Natick Bulletin* contained a series of articles about the need for a trolley connection. To quote one:

The present mode of conveying the pupils has already become a costly experiment . . . and . . . will in near future become a grievous burden. The lack of proper communication between the two sections is a serious and increasing damage to both. . . . Here are two communities in the same township. Their centers are three miles apart. Their interests are supposed to be mutual. Yet aside from the legal bonds which hold them together, they might as well be at the opposite ends of the state. . . . But for the high school, the annual town meeting, the tax gatherer and the occasional union caucuses, it would hardly be difficult for either to forget that the other existed. Virtually Cochituate is ten times more a part of Natick than of Wayland. The course of business, of trade and of travel is almost entirely in that direction. . . . There are just as convenient and desirable situations for homes upon the Wayland road. But those of moderate means . . . are unable to live there. . . . With a good electric railroad all this would be speedily changed. The whole town would be quickened into new life. The town meetings would be better attended. . . . Not the least of the benefits gained would be the great moral one of a more united and friendly feeling between the two sections, a condition sorely needed at present.[11]

On March 15, 1899, the Natick and Cochituate Street Railway again applied for a franchise to run an extension from Lyons Corner to the railroad track in Wayland. This time the franchise required that the line be completed on or before July 1. The same location as to the sides of the road was proposed at first, but the arrangement was later changed so that the line could run on the easterly side of Main Street from Lyons Corner to Fiske's Corner (School Street). Then, as it crossed the Shaw properties, it would still run on the westerly side of the road.

Certain engineering difficulties were encountered around the Five Paths intersection, and the time limit was extended to August 1. The line was finally finished during the last week of July. On Saturday, July 29, there was a grand opening ceremony, given much publicity in the Natick newspapers. On the front page of the *Natick Bulletin* an article appeared running to one and a half columns entitled "By Electrics to Wayland."

At four P.M. a group of trolleys left Natick bringing about fifty Natick representatives—town officials, the press, and businessmen. They "were soon speeding away to celebrate the union of our coy and bashful maiden sister Wayland to Natick and other towns lying hitherward on our borders." The trip took twenty-five minutes, including a stop at Cochituate where bystanders cheered and a group of people got on. "The greeting we received from the people on reaching Wayland was a perfect ovation . . . the largest number being assembled in front of the Pequod House[12] where the cheering was enthusiastic and long."

A banquet took place, followed by speeches by George F. Keep, superintendent of the street railway; Richard T. Lombard, the town clerk; the Reverend Wright of the Methodist Episcopal Church in Cochituate; and the Reverend Heizer of the Unitarian Church in Wayland. Mr. Heizer said that he had originally objected to having the trolley come to Wayland Center, since he wanted above all to preserve the rural quiet of the town as a retreat for tired businessmen. He had, however, bowed to the inevitable and supported the cause. The president of the street railway, a representative of the Natick National Bank, and the owner-editor of the *Natick Review* all spoke stressing the expected buildup of trade and boom in real estate values.

Before the ceremonies ended tribute was paid to three special, elderly Cochituate guests. They were John C. Butterfield, Kimball Lovejoy, and Sewall Loker. We have commented on Butterfield's long residence in Cochituate and his prestige and popularity there. Born at Hebron, New Hampshire, Kimball Lovejoy came to Cochituate from Boston in the late 1860s. In 1860 his son William had married Anna Bent, James Madison Bent's eldest child. The 1877 voting list calls him a carpenter; in the 1884 list he was a boxmaker. The census of 1880 listed him as "working in a shoe shop." He could have done carpentry work for the Bent company. He was eighty-four years old in 1899.

Sewall Loker (1811-1907) was eighty-eight years old at this 1899 occasion. Grandson of Revolutionary War Capt. Isaac Loker, one of

East Sudbury's first selectmen, he was said to have learned the shoe trade in Natick, much as did William Bent, and then to have driven a mail coach for a while. He took up shoe manufacturing in the late 1840s when Cochituate began to develop in that direction, and from then until the late 1870s he was listed in records as a shoemaker or shoe manufacturer. During these years he also owned farmland and did some farming; he had been born into a farming family and had inherited land. By the census of 1880 he had reverted to being a farmer. He was very vigorous in his older years, and newspapers frequently commented on the distances he walked when he was in his nineties. When he turned ninety in 1901, he was described in a newspaper article as "a prosperous farmer."[13] In him was represented the continuity of the generations from the original settlement of Sudbury, but he had also participated actively in the early stages of the development of the shoe business which changed the southern end of the town.

The "Cochituate Enterprise" reporter for the *Natick Bulletin* of August 4, 1899, waxed very flowery over the significance of the completion of the trolley line to Wayland:

It is a bountiful gift of heaven which has permitted the inhabitants of the good town of Wayland to see the most notable consummations ever wrought in her history. The most fatal stumbling block in the way of her social interest and of her civil and material welfare has after these long years of waiting been forever removed. The two charming hamlets . . . hitherto so locally separated and, worst of all, so alien to each other in feeling have been united with enduring bands of steel.

The article went on to say that Cochituate would have a railroad connection alternative to the Boston and Albany in Natick and, thereby, much better access to the northerly part of the state. It would also be easier to go to the town meetings, and the high school would be more accessible.

To Wayland . . . not the least of the advantages will be the gradual breaking down of the exclusiveness which has been openly boasted in influential quarters there. It is not unreasonable to predict that a new era of life and prosperity will dawn in the near future.

It is not known to this writer how many Cochituate residents or business representatives used the railroad line through Wayland.

After initial difficulties about school pupils' fares on the trolley, transportation to the high school was offered to Cochituate pupils. If they attended the high school, the young people from both ends of the town would become acquainted. Because the passenger service to Wayland on the trolley was not profitable, there were after 1900 to be two unsuccessful attempts to carry freight and express items between Cochituate and Wayland Center.

In eastern Massachusetts the era of trolley lines between rural towns and villages lasted only into the 1920s. At a Historical Society program in 1955 a former conductor on this line, Alvin Neale, said that the trolley from Cochituate to Wayland was discontinued in 1921 after a severe ice storm knocked down the wires. When reminiscing in the late 1950s about his younger years in Wayland, Henry Patterson was sure that the trolley from Wayland to Natick was running as late as 1923. Some of the track was taken up at the time town water was put in during the late 1920s. The selectmen's report in the 1930 town report tells us that "at the suggestion of the Board the Middlesex and Boston Street Railway Company removed practically all the rail and ties remaining in the highways."

The trolley between the two villages of Wayland may be said to have existed in the first quarter of the twentieth century. We shall look at the major twentieth-century changes in the town in the Epilogue. A future historian may want to do exhaustive research on this very interesting era of our town's history. There is space here only to paint the picture with a broad brush.

NOTES

1. *Natick Review*, May 19, 1892.
2. *Natick Bulletin*, May 15 and May 22, 1896.
3. *Ibid*, November 13, 1897.
4. *Ibid*, November 6, 1897.
5. *Natick Review*, June 16, 1892.
6. *Natick Bulletin*, March 19, 1897.
7. Booklet entitled *Wayland*, printed by Heintzemann Press, Boston. No date (probably 1899).
8. *Natick Bulletin*, August 11, 1893.
9. Town of Wayland, *License and Franchise Book*, pp. 39-45.
10. *Natick Bulletin*, July 30, 1897.
11. *Ibid*, November 18, 1898.
12. Site of the present Public Safety Building at 38 Cochituate Road.
13. *Natick Bulletin*, April 19, 1901.

Epilogue

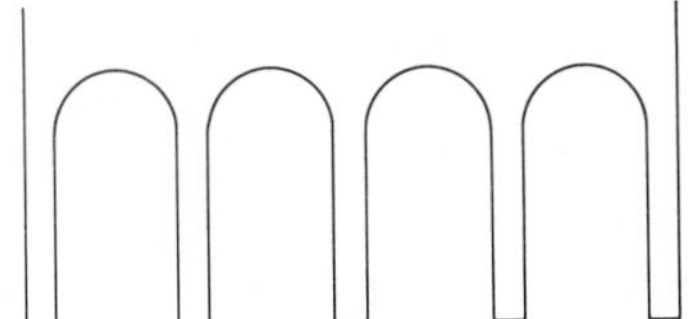

Twentieth Century Overview

TREMENDOUS CHANGES took place in Wayland in the twentieth century, especially after World War II when the population increased enormously, so that by 1970 there were six times as many residents as there had been in 1900. As time went on Wayland was no longer an agricultural town, although some dairy farming and market gardening continued. After 1912 the town's southern section, Cochituate, was no longer a manufacturing center, but in the mid-1950s one large industrial research facility, the Raytheon Laboratory, became an added feature of Wayland Center. A gazetteer would probably characterize Wayland in 1980 as a well-to-do residential suburb mainly of single-family dwellings on the outer fringe of the Boston metropolitan area.

This section will summarize the events and influences of the first eight decades of the century as they brought the late-nineteenth-century town described in Part II to be the town Wayland now is, a place no longer of two rather distinct and somewhat incompatible sections—the northern part, a rural farming community with a sparse and spread-out population on 78 percent of the land, the southern part, built up around shoe manufacturing.

Wayland End of the Town—Early Decades

Part II ended with the arrival of the trolley car in Wayland Center when the Natick to Cochituate line was extended in 1899. This facility, which was supposed to have brought the two ends of the town together, did not change the pattern much. The trolley line was not greatly patronized and ceased to run to Wayland in the early 1920s. It had brought high school students from Cochituate and enabled Wayland residents to do business in Natick and Framingham rather than remain oriented completely to Waltham and other places on the railroad to Boston.

At first the railroad with its peak twelve daily round trips to Boston dominated the development of Wayland Center. The railroad and the automobile made the town more generally accessible and led to the building of houses whose owners could use the Wayland and Tower Hill stations to go to Boston—and in some cases, if they made Wayland their year-round home instead of being summer residents, as many were at first—they could send their children to school in Weston or to private schools nearer the city.

Country Estates

During the first three decades other country estates emerged in addition to the Shaw estate and Mainstone Farm, the latter where relatives of William Powell Perkins had enlarged the land area, increased the number of residences on the hill, and expanded the prize dairy herd. We can mention only a few of the estates established between 1900 and 1930.

In 1900 Henry Whitely Patterson, a man in his thirties not then active in business but with wealth from a Pennsylvania fortune, bought the brick Abel Glezen house which had been built in 1803 (now 74 Glezen Lane) with fifty-five acres of farmland. The house was considerably enlarged with wings and ells; the largest wing, on the west end, was a two-story library, the front of which was as long as the original house. That wing was torn down in the 1930s; another was detached and made into a separate house later. On the land stretching to the north a dairy farm was started which in the 1940s was to become the Watertown Dairy, named for the hometown of Hyman Shick who then acquired it. Henry Patterson died in 1907, but his widow and children continued to live in the house, Mrs. Patterson remaining until her death in 1950.

Within a few years of the arrival of the Pattersons the adjoining Capt. Isaac Glezen house (now 50 Glezen Lane) was bought by Charles A. Hardy. Mrs. Hardy and Mrs. Patterson were sisters. The house was enlarged and converted into an elegant residence which was used at first as a summer home. In 1918 this estate, with its chauffeur's house and eighty-nine acres of land, was sold to a semiretired New York investment banker, Albert H. Beck, who soon bought the dairy farm from Mrs. Patterson.

Not far from these two old houses which were converted to estate properties, Harry E. Morrell, a Boston publisher, tore down an old house at the corner of Glezen Lane and Old Sudbury Road and built a stylish three-story Federal-type house looking toward the Sudbury River over forty acres of farmland and river meadows. This house no longer exists.

There is not space in this section to mention all of the professional and businessmen, mostly working in Boston and Cambridge, who chose to have country places in Wayland during the first decades of the century. As did the Pattersons and the Hardys, many of them acquired and improved late-eighteenth- and early-nineteenth-century farmhouses and their surrounding lands. Two families who were particularly public-spirited contributors to the town were the Stones and the Searses. By 1921 J. Sidney and Dorothy Stone, who in 1915 acquired the Benjamin Adams house built about 1775 (now 34 Lincoln Road), owned 90-odd acres of land in the vicinity and their property included the old brick North schoolhouse.

Edmund H. Sears, grandson of the much-beloved mid-nineteenth-century Unitarian minister of both Wayland and Weston, Edmund Hamilton Sears, married as his first wife Leslie Buckingham. They lived in the Buckingham house near Heard's Pond, a house built about 1715 by Samuel Stone, owned by Bents in Revolutionary times, and for a long time after that by members of the Heard family. Sears was in the felt business, but during the early decades of the century he found time to serve as a selectman and was also very active on the committee to build the 1910 Cochituate School. He also helped to acquire land for public purposes for the town. By 1921 Sears owned 336 acres of land and several houses and was the fourth largest taxpayer in the town. His second wife, Sophia Bennett Sears, who died in 1980, deeded her grandfather Judge Mellen's law office and the land it stood on to the town for a nominal sum in 1971.

Wayland never became a town predominantly of big estates, but the estates and the well-to-do people who owned them were a definite feature of the town in the early part of the century. Most spectacular as a gentleman's country estate was Greenways, now owned by the heirs of Frank Paine and occupied by his widow Virginia Paine. In late 1909

1715 Samuel Stone House on Pelham Island Road at the end of the Heard occupancy.

Francis Shaw sold 219 acres west of the Five Paths intersection sweeping down to the Sudbury River to his friend Edwin Farnham Greene, a wealthy Boston businessman who was treasurer and chief executive officer of Pacific Mills. Greene had a home on Beacon Hill and was a leading figure in the cultural and social life of Boston, serving as a trustee of such institutions as the Museum of Fine Arts, the New England Conservatory of Music, and Wellesley College. Samuel Mead of Weston, who had designed other country houses in the area and had been the architect of the Wayland Public Library, was engaged to design the large, formal Georgian brick house flanked by matching wings overlooking a bend in the Sudbury River.

The Greenes did things in grand style and on June 20, 1910, had an elaborate cornerstone-laying ceremony. The block of marble brought by the Greenes from Asia Minor contains an intriguing array of Wayland mementos such as a 1910 railroad timetable, Indian arrowheads found on the place, and various poems including one entitled "To a Wayland Youth of about the year 2110 A.D."

The house was ready for occupancy in the spring of 1911, and for sixteen years the family used it as its country residence from late May until November. The Historical Society owns the leather-bound

The Samuel Stone House after its embellishment by the Buckinghams and Sears.

guestbook kept for this house through 1926. In this book Ferris Greenslet, author and publisher, once an associate editor of the *Atlantic Monthly* and eventually editor in chief at the Houghton Mifflin Publishing Company, wrote a dedicatory poem which begins: "There is a small village called Wayland. . . ." Entries in this guestbook came to an end in 1926 when the Greenes sold what is still called Greenways to the Frank Paines of Weston. Stephen Greene who founded the Stephen Greene Press of Brattleboro, Vermont, was one of the three Greene sons who spent youthful summers in Wayland.

At the time when Francis Shaw became known as a wealthy property owner of Wayland, a Natick newspaper commented on what a boon it was to have wealthy residents able to pay a significant proportion of Wayland's tax bill. A newspaper account of 1911 decried the fact that the death in 1907 of Henry Patterson and the final settlement of his estate diminished the extent to which Wayland's roster of rich residents would contribute to support the town. The 1914 valuation list, printed two years before the introduction of a Massachusetts State income tax and the concomitant change in the state law which forbade towns to tax intangible personal property, shows that in 1914 Wayland was getting 48 percent of its tax revenue from the intangible assets (stocks, bonds, etc.) of its wealthy residents. This kind of revenue came not only from the estate owners and Boston business and professional men who lived all or part of the year in the Wayland section of the town but also from Charles W. Dean, who had moved his business from Cochituate to Natick but was still a Cochituate resident. From 1916 to the present the town has been able to tax as personal property only tangible items like furniture. In 1914 the largest sums paid to the town on intangible property were $1,700 by Jane N. Patterson and trustees; $1,776 by Francis Shaw and trustees; $1,302 by the Greenes; and $1,588 by Jonathan Maynard Parmenter, Wayland's wealthy farmer about whom more will be said later. These four individuals were then paying 21 percent of Wayland's total tax bill by the levy on their intangible wealth alone.

Cochituate—Early Decades of the Century

After the closing of the last factory in early 1913 some shoe workers took the trolley to continue to work for Dean in Natick. Others used the interurban trolley system and trains to travel to and from factories in places like Marlborough and Boston. Still other shoe worker families moved out of town to more distant manufacturing centers. Some stayed on in Cochituate and found other local work. There were very few of the original French shoe worker families left in Wayland in 1980, but as late as the mid-1940s there were more than forty families who carried down the names of the French-Canadian shoe workers who came to Cochituate in the 1870s and 1880s.

According to George G. Bogren, a lifelong resident, devoted public officeholder, and keen observer of the town, Cochituate by 1920 had become a residential village of commuters who reached their jobs in Boston and elsewhere mostly by taking the trolley to the Natick railroad station. By 1916 Bent's Corner was changed by the tearing down of the Bent-Dean factory. The Lyons Corner area changed also. In 1913 the old wooden Cochituate School was torn down. In 1904 Noble Griffin had demolished the Lyon shoe factory which he owned and ran and in 1913 the Bee Hive, which had been attached to the Lyon factory and then later used as tenements for Albanian shoe workers at Dean's, was torn down.

Meanwhile, with the shoe industry gone, the Knights of Labor were no longer active in Cochituate and rented their building on the northwest corner of West Plain Street and Main Street to the Patrons of Husbandry, a Grange organization which called the building Grange

Hall. The Grange movement did not last long in Cochituate, and as soon as World War I was over the returning veterans were able to rent the premises from the Knights of Labor for an American Legion Hall. This building, a landmark on the corner since 1889, burned in a spectacular fire in 1925. Quickly, private individuals, members of the Legion, and the town churches helped collect funds so that a yellow brick hall could be built for the Legion on the site of the Knights of Labor Hall. This building existed until 1972.

The Damon farm continued in operation in the early decades of the century, and later the Anzivino family acquired land in that general area and began market-gardening operations. Further, as was also the case in nearby towns, floriculture became a locally based business for several Cochituate entrepreneurs who built greenhouses and supplied such things as pansies to the Boston market. One notable horticulturist of that era was George Fullick, son of William Fullick, one of the important builders when Cochituate was in its boom years of 1870-90. George Fullick, who had florist's greenhouses on Damon Street, made quite a name for himself as a landscape gardener outside Wayland. Between 1910 and 1915 he performed extensive landscape work for Percy Rockefeller in Greenwich, Connecticut; did the original planting for the outdoor theater on the campus of Vassar College at Poughkeepsie, New York; and planted trees at the Christian Science Church in Boston.

There was little open space within the confines of Cochituate Village for residential development, although there were a few attempts to build on land which had been acquired at the turn of the century by the Griffin family. One example of a residential development in Cochituate Village was an area called Cochituate Park on a tract of land on the south side of East Plain Street between the Fairbanks block (Dath's liquor store) and Hill Street. It is not known how many houses were built in this development, the plan for which was submitted to the Registry of Deeds in June 1915. Edward Dammers of Cochituate, related to the Butterfields, who had seen, been inspired by, and participated in, real estate developments in many locations including Florida, was involved in this venture.

Summer Cottage Developments on Dudley Pond and Elsewhere

Much more important for the southern segment of Wayland in terms of residential expansion was the rash of camps and summer cottage developments, mostly around Dudley Pond but also on the shore of Lake Cochituate and along the Sudbury River near Stone's Bridge. Between 1900 and 1915 the newspapers commented on individuals building summer cottages and camps on Dudley Pond, and there was a report that in June 1915 there were then thirty-six cottages located around the pond. The earliest cottages had been built by local people for their own use or had been constructed in groups of two or three to rent to Boston residents for the summer. In 1905 Clarence Dudley was reported as building two rental cottages. Boating was then allowed on Dudley Pond but not swimming as the pond was then a part of the Boston water supply.

A considerable group of sizable developments financed and managed by outside speculators started in 1913 and reached a peak by 1918. By June 1916 when this movement was well under way the *Natick Bulletin* referred to a "small army of summer residents." A few food stores were built to accommodate these visitors, but these families were in Wayland only during the summer months and did not send children to the schools or expect much town service.

The chief developers were D. Arthur Brown and John F. Stackpole, outsiders who had offices on Tremont Street in Boston and a land office on Old Connecticut Path opposite the Mansion Inn. They made sales of lots and cottages mostly to Boston-area people and also advertised in the newspapers of neighboring towns. The acquisition of land for them around Dudley Pond was managed to a considerable extent by Henry C. Mulligan of Natick.

The earliest such development was known as Wayland Manor with 301 lots on the eastern shore of Dudley Pond. Some single lots in this development were as small as one twentieth of an acre. By 1927 there were 34 cottages, 6 houses, 10 garages, and 40 unsold lots in this development. The average parcel which had been sold contained two 2,000-square-foot lots (roughly one tenth of an acre), although individual ownership ranged from one to eight lots.

Much the largest development organized by Brown, Stackpole and Mulligan was Woodland Park, registered in 1914. This area of 85 acres was to the north of Dudley Pond, encompassing a network of roads and paths (some just on paper) based on present Maiden Lane. The development had 969 lots, some as small as 1,200 square feet or one thirty-sixth of an acre.

Woodland Park was followed by Shore Acres, Lakewood, Castle Gate North, and Castle Gate South. The Castle Gate projects were developed by the Cochituate Real Estate Trust, as Brown and Stackpole's development company for these was called, on the southwest and south shores of Dudley Pond.

A few other developers built on Dudley Pond at such locations as Beechwood Point (now Dudley Road). Also along the river near Stone's Bridge the most notorious of Wayland's waterside developments, Riverview Terrace, was created in 1924 by an outside group, the Bay State Realty Corporation. In subdividing this area into 301 lots there was little consideration of the fact that much of the land would be under water when the river was in flood.

The people who bought small parcels of land or finished cottages in the woods or fields around Dudley Pond, Lake Cochituate, or near the river from 1913 to 1928 were mainly interested in primitive cottages or camps where they could live in the summer months. At first, access to the cottage areas was advertised to be by the trolley from Natick on its way to Wayland or by the branch of the Natick and Cochituate Street Railway, which went from Cochituate up West Plain Street. As automobiles became more plentiful, cottage owners somehow drove over tortuous dirt roads or paths to reach their cottages where some of them built garages.

Then came the depression in 1929. Many cottage owners lost their jobs and their city homes, and a considerable number moved out to try to live in their summer abodes. Most of the cottages had been designed for warm weather living and were not heated; nor were the roads suited to be driven on in icy, snowy, or muddy conditions. Many of these people were destitute and needed welfare aid from the town. Moreover, speculators bought up cottages and took advantage of the town's welfare by encouraging impoverished families to rent these dwellings. The burden of welfare for these not truly Wayland people became so great that the welfare agency had to make a rule that town funds could not be used to pay rent of more than $15 a month for one of these cottages.

Construction of a good many of the summer cottages had been flimsy, and some people who tried to live in their cottages during the winter attempted to keep warm by using packing cases to help insulate the thin walls. This practice gave rise to the name "Cardboard Village" for the Riverview Terrace area.

It is no wonder that by 1930 those who were trying to make Wayland a well-managed and livable town felt that a zoning ordinance must be adopted to halt the growth of such thickly settled developments, poorly planned for the land on which they were placed. In 1926 Wayland had instituted a planning board made up of a capable group of men, the leader of whom was Howard S. Russell, who had moved to Wayland Center from Arlington in 1920. This group saw the need for zoning and for a higher type of residential development.

Public Water Supply and Other Municipal Improvements

Before continuing with the achievement of Wayland's first zoning ordinance in 1934, we shall return to Wayland Center and tell the story of the attainment of a public water system in the northern part of the town. Since 1902 when a serious study was made, it was realized that a public water system was needed in Wayland Center both for fire protection and to encourage residential building. However, various committees had not found it financially or physically feasible to enlarge the Cochituate water system, to try to pump water from driven wells, or to tie into the Metropolitan District Commission water system. All that changed when in 1921 Jonathan Maynard Parmenter died leaving four legacies to the town: a fund for the library, a fund for the care of the cemeteries, $225,000 to build a water supply for Central and North Wayland, and $220,000 to build a hospital in or near Wayland.

Construction of the Wayland water system was started in 1926 and completed in 1928. It was based on wells near Baldwin's Pond with a pumping station to force water to a standpipe on Reeves Hill. In the 1920s it was not thought by the town fathers or by Parmenter's executor, the Harvard Trust Company, that a hospital in Wayland was a suitable facility, so the hospital legacy was reinvested and its use deferred until 1953 when the Parmenter Health Center was built and endowed. In addition, certain hospitals in neighboring towns were given funds.

Jonathan Maynard Parmenter (1831-1921), descendant of an original proprietor of Sudbury, was the greatest private benefactor of the town. The hardworking cattle farmer and thrifty Yankee had been guided in making shrewd stock market investments by his friend and neighbor Willard A. Bullard, a Cambridge banker. Parmenter's wealth and legacies amazed the town when they became known.

In this era there were others who used their private resources to benefit the town. Around 1910 there was a movement spearheaded by a private Park and Playground Association to set aside land for play

Jonathan Maynard Parmenter (1831-1921).

areas for children. Edmund Sears took the lead in acquiring land for a large playground in Wayland Center. No sooner did the wealthy Edwin Farnham Greene become a property owner in Wayland than Sears persuaded him to help buy in 1910 thirty-three acres of land behind the Odd Fellows for use as a park and playground area. Edmund Sears also was a leader in acquiring land in the center of Wayland Village to beautify the area and make room for expansion of public facilities in the future. In 1912 Noble Griffin had given land on Main Street from the Cochituate School to Lyons Corner for skating and this was managed by the Playground Association. In 1919 the four-acre Griffin ballfield was bought by the town. Then in 1920 Arthur Williams, who had been very successful in business after leaving Wayland in 1908, along with his brothers, bought store properties on the east side of Main Street and created a young children's playground, naming it for their mother, Hannah Williams. This property was privately owned and managed by local trustees until bought by the town in 1966.

The Depression Years

Although it was not an industrial or commercial town, Wayland, like most American cities and towns, experienced unemployment as soon as the depression started to deepen in 1930. There were no breadlines as in the cities, but the town found its welfare resources severely strained. It must be realized that when the Great Depression started towns had not had access to state funds except for support of war veterans or their relatives, and for certain road purposes. Further, the federal government was not even dreamed of as a source of aid to a Massachusetts town where people were out of work and unable to pay their rent or mortgages or to buy food.

Wayland expected to go it alone in taking care of its poor, as it had for nearly three hundred years. In 1931 it was decided to help the unemployed and to benefit the town at the same time by digging and laying miles of water pipes to tie the new Wayland water supply into Cochituate. In order to give the maximum employment to needy citizens it was decided that all the digging to bury the pipes would be done by hand. In 1932 citizen labor was used to reconstruct Cochituate Road and Main Street, using at various times 135 unemployed Wayland citizens.

By 1934, with the Roosevelt administration agencies coming into operation, federal aid helped with unemployment and tight money problems in Wayland, as in most other communities. In that year a federal grant was obtained to help build a new high school, nucleus of the large building which is now the Wayland Town Building. Special permission was granted by the state legislature to use some of the park and playground land bought for the town by Greene and Sears in 1910 as its site.

In 1935 town records were being classified with the assistance of funds made available by the Emergency Relief Appropriations Act. Later, in 1937, the Federal Writers' Project transcribed and tried to bring order to some of the scattered and ill-kept historical records of the town. As the depression worsened, efforts to combat it were increasingly mentioned in the selectmen's reports. The hurricane of 1938 was devastating to the trees in Wayland, and both as a fire safety measure and to provide employment massive programs were undertaken to clean up the woods along roadsides and on private property. In 1939 it was arranged that local people would be employed by the Works Progress Administration (WPA) in building the Hultman Aqueduct as it crossed Wayland. Thus, the depression decade was endured with more and more federal help, while the town reports began to sound as if unemployment and large relief loads had become a permanent feature. This author has not studied all of the depression measures carefully, but her impression is that, except for the controversy which began in 1930 about whether to build a new high school in Cochituate where more of the students who attended it lived and ended in 1935 with a new building in Wayland Center, the whole town pulled together very well in the depression era. This also was the case in the difficult years of World War II when men and a few women from all parts of the town volunteered for service or were drafted, while gasoline and other restrictions severely curtailed certain local activities.

The World War II period saw a slightly stepped-up population growth. With gasoline rationing and only limited bus and train transportation, some residents moved nearer to the city, but other hardy souls, many of them of a particularly creative and public-spirited breed, moved to the town between 1940 and 1945. Their energy and talents did much for the town in the postwar era of enormous growth.

Planning for a Better Town

Early in the century well-to-do citizens used their own resources when they saw the need and opportunity for town improvements. Some of the private efforts were made by organized groups such as the Wayland Village Improvement Society. A Village Improvement Society, part of a national movement, had existed in the 1880s and had then addressed itself to planting roadside trees. In 1909 a revived society tried to meet the need which came along with the use of the automobile and rural free delivery of mail to induce the town to adopt a uniform and consistent set of street names in the northern part of the town to take the place of vague names like "Road to Sudbury" and "Road to Concord." The following year this organization, no doubt with money from such residents as E. H. Sears, E. F. Greene, and Francis Shaw, engaged a Cambridge landscape architect to suggest changes to beautify the two village centers and the approaches to Wayland. Suggestions were made to landscape the railroad station parking lot and to remove trash, signs, and unused buildings from the triangular village green.

Public planning was to come when in 1926 the town organized a planning board, the early years and activities of which were so graphically described in a *Town Crier* article of March 1980, written by Howard S. Russell just before his death. Russell described, as do the official planning board reports, the earlier efforts in the late 1920s to make turns into country lanes more suitable for automobile traffic and then the plunge into the big job of arranging land use zoning for Wayland. Before a zoning ordinance could be drawn up and presented to the town it was necessary to make a modern map of the town showing streets by their current names, the bodies of water, and the wetlands. A firm of Waltham civil engineers was hired to compile a town map, which was completed in 1932.

The idea of arranging zoning for Wayland was first proposed to the town by the planning board in 1931. In 1932 the town appointed a zoning committee consisting of Howard Russell as chairman, Charles T. Fullick and Clarence S. Williams from Cochituate, and Chester H. Hobbs and Theodore W. Harrington from Wayland Center. In the town report of 1933 the committee's plan was set forth, advocating the zoning of the entire town as a single-residence district except for two areas: a business district in Wayland Center and, behind it to the northwest, as it extended to Russell's crossing of the railroad track, a small triangle of land to be used for light manufacture. Added at the last minute, owing to controversy and to quell strong opposition to zoning by a property owner, was a strip 900 feet long and 300 feet deep on the north side of the State Road East from Bigelow's Corner at the Weston line. In Cochituate the four corners of the intersection of Plain and Main streets were zoned for business, as was the land on both sides of Commonwealth Road for a distance west of School Street, strips at Bent's Corner from Damon Street, and the Hannah Williams playground south to the Natick line.

The first zoning ordinance required that all new residences be on lots containing 10,000 square feet with a frontage of 80 feet. This ordinance passed at a special town meeting held on September 5, 1934. In 1939 minimum lot sizes were raised in certain parts of the town. Wayland had been one of the last towns within twenty miles of Boston to adopt zoning. It had come too late to save much of the area around Dudley Pond, but it was a landmark event for Wayland. Howard Russell's great contribution to the town was to guide the planning board in these crucial days and to head the zoning committee.

During World War II the planning board, still chaired by Howard Russell, continued to plan well for the future of Wayland. That board's report in the 1945 town report is worth reading in toto, but only a small portion of it can be quoted here. Written in early 1946 under the heading "Unprecedented Developments Ahead," this report starts with the statement:

With the end of the war and the release of materials for construction, the Planning Board believes that the Town . . . is facing an era of unprecedented development. Our people have been accustomed to think of Wayland as a country town with the pleasing features of small numbers, neighborliness, natural beauty and plenty of space. Yet as a result of the westward march of population in the Boston area these very features that we enjoy have caused many people to cast longing eyes at Wayland. Hence, continuing growth of the town is inevitable. What the townspeople can do is to try to guide this growth so as to retain the village atmosphere and the charm of the ponds, river, woods, farms and natural features, while fitting into the environment the new neighbors who hope to join us.

The report goes on to describe the assessors' maps (town atlas) and subdivision controls which were worked out by the board in the war years. After the discussion of other matters of concern, the report ends with the statement:

Changes are bound to come . . . and with the end of the war some are immediately before us. Yet if the people of the town wish it strongly enough (and we believe they do) both its natural beauties and those desirable features that have been added through three centuries of the town's life can be preserved along with the growth and improvement that will take place and everyone who lives or works here will gain in the process.

This was an inspiring statement of the philosophy of this able board's membership of Howard S. Russell, Allan R. Finlay, Chester H. Hobbs, Frank S. Tarr, Frederick S. Whiteside, and Carl T. Emery. One can say in 1980 that this policy was amazingly well carried out in view of the great increase in the population.

Howard S. Russell served as a correct, dignified, efficient, and gracious moderator of town meetings from 1939 through 1959. In later years he wrote for the local weekly newspaper historical articles about New England and others on general philosophy; by the time of his nineties he had become the sage of Wayland. His greatest contribution to the town had been heading the planning board from its founding in 1926 to 1950, when he decided to resign and not finish an elected term. He was Wayland's early mid-century hero; his death occurred in 1980.

Second on the list of the 1945 planning board was Allan R. Finlay, a Boston investment counselor, who in 1941 had moved his family and an old house, which had been built in 1713 in Kingston, to 75 Old Sudbury Road. In 1945 Finlay was on the planning board and had already been serving on the school committee for two years. Allan Finlay's contribution to the improvement and growth of the Wayland school system will be described later.

While serving on the planning board during the World War II years, Finlay and others became concerned with what kind of development would occur on Wayland's extensive open lands, and in particular with what would happen to the large Shaw estate, which came on the market in 1942. Francis Shaw had died in 1935, and by 1942 his heirs had decided to sell the 720-acre Five Paths estate. This was a strategic piece of land lying as it did astride the main road between Wayland Center and Cochituate Village. Sales of such properties were slow in wartime, but the land was attractive, in a good town near Boston, and an appealing piece for any developer willing to cope with hilly and ravine-creased land. About 1943 one subdivision plan for dividing this area into 10,000-square-foot lots encompassing a whole community with stores, a motion-picture house, and other facilities came to the attention of the planning board and was given publicity in a national architectural magazine.

Post-World War II Residential Developments

Finlay saw that as the Shaw property went so very definitely would go Wayland's postwar residential character. He found others with similar worries, and they decided to form the Wayland Real Estate Company. The principals, all from Wayland, included Finlay and Nathaniel Hamlen, who with family members owned Mainstone Farm on the other side of the hill on which the Shaw house had stood. Another principal was Gerald Henderson, a resident of Wayland from early childhood. The Hendersons owned key property in the Tower Hill section of Wayland, having bought the Deacon James Draper property and other lands on Plain Road. The fourth principal was Roger Ela, a lawyer whose wife was a member of the Dickson and Bennett families which had had considerable landholdings in Wayland for some time.

Except for one piece which had already been sold, the entire Shaw estate was acquired by this group in 1948 under an agreement with the trustees that the peripheral land would not be sold off first but the area developed with a network of roads from the inside out. The Shaw land as developed in several successive sections by the Wayland Real Estate Company was known as Woodridge and included the area called Happy Hollow, west of Cochituate Road (Woodridge No. 6). All house plans were submitted to a Woodridge approval committee, but there were no architectural restrictions and there was no predesign. The Town of Wayland made no attempt to tell the Wayland Real Estate Company how to develop the curving roads which on the undulating land gave the area a varied and nondevelopment character. In upper Woodridge lots tended to comprise at least two acres and there were a few much larger ones; in Happy Hollow the average lot was under an acre.

In the late 1950s Allan Finlay, with Woodridge now well along, began participating in the new, large residential development not then given a definite name but now known as the Claypit Hill section, and stretching northeast from Claypit Hill Road to Glezen Lane and the Weston border. In the early 1950s Gerald Henderson had begun to sell house lots on Plain and Claypit Hill roads. By 1953 most of this land was zoned for 60,000 square feet with 210 feet of frontage. At first Henderson sold these 60,000-foot lots or larger pieces subject to thirty-year subdivision restrictions to individual buyers who planned and built their own houses. By 1956 a new subdivision road, Adams Lane, had been added off Claypit Hill Road; and beyond Adams Lane there eventually branched a long subdivision road called Sears Road, which went through what had been woodlots to upper Draper Road. Development of the Henderson land, which had been acquired over a generation, began with sales to private individuals who could build according to their own plans. Gerald Henderson died suddenly in early 1957. Eventually Allan Finlay and Roger Ela became interested in developing Dickson land in this area, and more and more the houses began to be built by the Swiedler Building Company. As time went on, various companies were formed to acquire land in the Claypit Hill area.

When the Claypit Hill development moved beyond the first houses on Sears Road, and especially when it crossed Draper Road to the east, Allan Finlay was arranging the layout of the roads and lots; and Edward Swiedler, who then lived in Wayland, was buying lots on a wholesale basis and building some houses as custom residences for purchasers and others on speculation. Funds for acquiring the land

and capital for roads and utilities were supplied by a Boston resident and business associate of Allan Finlay. This same group of three went on to develop similar housing in Weston.

Allan Finlay did not devote all his energies to the Woodridge and Claypit Hill residential developments, nor did he or his associates by any means constitute the only developer in Wayland. There were numerous other builders who put in one or two subdivision streets. Two 1951 examples were the Estates Development Company, which received approval for 49 lots on two new roads off Old Connecticut Path West, Old Farm Road, and Rolling Lane, and a subdivision called Memorial Park near Lake Cochituate in the southwest part of the town encompassing Charles Street, Maguire Road, Gage Road, and Grace Road with 52 lots.

From 1951 through 1953 the planning board approved more than 250 subdivision lots each year. During 1954 there was a slowdown to 50 lots, but in 1955 the figure was up to 208 new lots. In the ten years from 1955 through 1964, 824 new lots in subdivisions were granted planning board approval. Permits to build new houses, not necessarily all of them on newly subdivided land but some on lots on long-established roads, are another indication of how rapidly new residential housing was built in Wayland in the postwar years. In the decade from 1950 through 1959, 1,449 building permits were issued for new houses, 466 in Cochituate and 983 in Wayland. The peak year for these permits was 1953 with 181, 97 in Cochituate and 84 in Wayland; 1953 was also the year Daymon Farms and other Cochituate developments were started. In the 1960-69 decade 846 permits were granted for new houses.

Considering the amount of building cited above, it is not surprising that from 1950 to 1955 Wayland's population increased by nearly 3,000 people—from 4,393 in 1950 to 7,359 in 1955. The rate of increase slowed a little in the second half of the decade, but with 10,444 in the town in 1960 the population had more than doubled in the 1950s, having increased by about 6,000 people, or 137.7 percent.

School Expansion

Such an influx of population created enormous pressures on Wayland's public facilities, and most of all on the schools. When the postwar influx started the Wayland schools did not rate high among school systems. Some of the families that moved here did not care about the quality of the schools; others were ignorant of their quality;

while still others encountered deficiencies and became determined to improve the schools. Improvement and expansion went hand in hand. By the late 1950s, under the superintendency of Edward Anderson, a publicist, Wayland's schools had improved enough and had acquired such a good reputation that more families came to live in the town, especially a considerable number of couples who were well educated themselves and had several children of school age. This factor prolonged the town's rapid growth into the 1960s. It also brought to the town a large number of young and beginning families, so that in 1961, 26 percent of the Town of Wayland's population was in the public schools compared with 16 percent in the average Massachusetts town. This was the more striking when one realizes that Wayland did not then have kindergartens.

In 1943 Allan R. Finlay and Charles F. Moore, Jr. (the latter soon to leave Wayland to become a vice-president of the Ford Motor Company), were elected to the three-member school committee. They saw the need to improve the schools and stressed in their report to the town the desirability of paying teachers high enough salaries to be able to compete for and hold good ones. By 1946 conditions in the Wayland schools were very crowded. There were 261 pupils in the eight grades in the Center School; 289 in the Cochituate School; and 188 in the high school building, which was then eleven years old. This led to discussion in 1947 of having double sessions. A school building committee under the headship of Allan Finlay was constituted in 1947. On its recommendations the town voted in 1948 to add the north, gymnasium wing, and library-cafeteria section to the high school and to enlarge the Cochituate School.

As soon as the existing school plant was enlarged, however, residential building and the resulting increase in population with large numbers of preschool children made it apparent that there would have to be new school buildings. Accordingly, the town voted in 1953 to build a new elementary school in a center of increasing population—the Happy Hollow School. This buildiing was ready for use in 1955 and ten years later was enlarged with a ten-room addition.

The Happy Hollow School eased the pressure temporarily, but by the mid-1950s Wayland was growing so fast that its school enrollment, which had been 728 in 1946, had doubled to 1,498 by 1955. The need for school expansion was so acute and the way to plan it fraught with such problems that in 1954 a consultant firm, Englehart, Englehart and Leggett, was retained to advise the town on how to proceed with an orderly and feasible school expansion to go along

The new Wayland High School, built in 1960.

with the home building, which was then in full flood. So crowded was the elementary school in Wayland Center at that time that schoolrooms were rented from the Weston school system and pupils bused there.

The Englehart report recommended that the town plan several more schools. A school site committee had been appointed, and on the recommendation of this committee the town voted to acquire six school sites and to proceed immediately to the construction of two more new elementary schools. The plan to have six postwar elementary schools in addition to the Cochituate and Center schools was based on the idea that moderate-sized elementary schools were best for young children and that by having neighborhood schools many children could walk to school.

In 1956 the Claypit Hill and Loker schools were started. In 1957 Claypit opened with 385 students; Loker, with 275. (Each of these schools was added to by ten rooms in the early 1960s, and the Claypit Hill School had another addition in 1972.)

Meanwhile it was clear that the high school at Wayland Center would never be adequate when the younger children advanced to higher grades. In 1956 a site on Old Connecticut Path West was bought. In December 1958 the town appropriated $2,275,000 to build the campuslike facility of six buildings with its domed field house designed by The Architects Collaborative. This complex of buildings was ready for use in 1960, added to in 1967 with money authorized in 1964, and again altered to contain a media center in 1972.

When in 1960 the high school classes were moved out of the Wayland Center High School, that building became a junior high school with its nearby annex, the Center School, which had been released when the 1960s additions were made to the modern elementary schools. In the mid-1960s projections of a rapidly increasing school population indicated that even more school space would be needed. At first it was proposed that the junior high school be added to, but the land on which that building stood did not provide suitable leaching fields for a larger building. Thus, in 1967 it was decided not to enlarge the Center Junior High School but to place a new junior high school on a site at the north end of Cochituate Village. The town voted $4 million for this facility in the fall of 1969. The building was ready for use in the fall of 1972.

With the completion in 1972 of the new junior high school, Wayland's long and expensive postwar effort to increase its school plant came to an end.

From 1947 when the additions to the Cochituate School and the Wayland High School were being planned until 1967, Allan Finlay worked hard on both policy and detail and did an outstanding job as head of the school building committee. At the town meeting held on March 15, 1967, the town paid him a tribute for his valuable service. He had ceased to serve on the school committee in 1952 but had continued to work closely with the school committee and administration in planning the school expansions. The modern school plant and the way it accommodated the burgeoning school population was Allan Finlay's public contribution to Wayland's growth.

The expansion and upgrading of the Wayland schools was the dominating phenomenon of the middle years of the twentieth century. In 1920 total school enrollment had been 364 pupils in two buildings, and the town's per pupil expenditure had been $73.82. Fifty-five years later, in 1975, four years after the peak enrollment came, there was just under ten times as many pupils enrolled, but the per pupil cost of $1,785.22 was twenty-four times greater than it had been in 1920. The price level had changed, but not to that extent. Schooling in Wayland had become an expensive commodity. Between 1915 and 1925 there had been various warrant articles in the town meetings proposing to discontinue the Wayland High School because it was a marginal institution in inadequate quarters, some of it in an attic. By the 1960s and 1970s Wayland had one of the fine high schools of the country with an elaborate curriculum, almost lavish facilities, and a superior student body. The town had changed in ways that made all these features possible, albeit at a great cost to the town's taxpayers as well as involving failure to keep up other institutions such as the public library.

Alternatives to Residential Expansion

So large was the increase in population in the early 1950s that the town tried various measures to cut down the possible further growth and limit the pressure on the schools. In 1953 a zoning change was adopted raising minimum area and frontage requirements and adding a new zone in the rural, undeveloped areas in which it was required to have 60,000 square feet and 210 feet of frontage.

In a report to a town meeting in November 1953 the planning board said:

The present state of growth of the Town is considered abnormal and caused by an unusual pace of new housing developments rather than by a normal desire of new families to select Wayland over other communities. The pressure for development in Wayland is at least in part caused by the fact that in neighboring towns having comparable areas available for development the zoning requirements are higher. . . . As a result Wayland is favored for speculative building over its neighboring communities.

In the same crisis year—1953—the planning board and others of the administration began proposing that land be rezoned so that an industrial plant could be placed north of the railroad track between State Road West and Old Sudbury Road. The argument presented to the town was that an industrial facility would bring tax revenue into the treasury and broaden the tax base. Actually, the particular piece of land which was before the town for rezoning was one for which an outside developer was bidding and upon which he would have built at least forty houses, which would have added greatly to the town's school burden.

After hearings where it was explained that the Raytheon Manufacturing Company wished to have built a large industrial research laboratory using the open river meadows as its test area, the zoning change came before the town at the annual town meeting on March 3, 1954. A group called Home Owners of Wayland violently opposed the laboratory and warned that the voters would be deciding whether the town "would remain a town of homes and farms or become a questionable center for industry." A careful campaign by the principal members of the finance committee and that committee's argument that the arrival of Raytheon would reduce the tax rate by $3 to $8 won. At midnight the 900 voters present in the gymnasium of the high school voted 733 to 167 for the rezoning change.

Old and new residents hated to see an industrial facility near the village center and in sight across the fields from some of the choice residential locations looking across the river meadows. But the tax revenue from a plant like that proposed was a deciding argument, as was the idea that residences alone could probably not support schools and other facilities. The original plant was finished in 1955; several additions have been made since, and in 1980 it employed two thousand persons. For fiscal 1980-81 Raytheon supplied 3.7 percent of Wayland's tax revenue—a much large contribution than would have been made by forty-odd houses on that land—and did so without increasing school costs.

Raytheon brought to Wayland numbers of families of highly educated and intelligent scientists who added much to the town's population mix. The company also gives employment in non-scientific positions to a considerable number of local residents. However, the big plant added to the town's need to expand its police and fire departments, and it also increased the already difficult traffic congestion on the Boston Post Road.

Fire and Police Departments

In 1948 Wayland's fire department was a primitive organization, a volunteer department with thirty-five callmen who received 83 cents an hour for answering alarms while the five engineers received $20 a year if officers and $10 if privates. The alarm system worked through the local women telephone operators who responded to the town's crank telephones and who tended to know the whereabouts of many townspeople, especially the firemen. (The automatic dial telephone system did not come to Wayland until 1953.)

Wayland Center's fire engines were housed in the back of the 1878 town hall; the Cochituate equipment, in the 1882 fire station on Harrison Street. In 1952 the town built a new, brick Cochituate Town

Building on the northeast corner of Main and Plain streets on horsecar barn land bought in 1944 from the Middlesex and Boston Street Railway. This building contained a fire station, library branch rooms, a police room, and an office for the welfare department. At a November 1953 town meeting it was voted to demolish the old Harrison Street station which had served for years as Cochituate's polling place.

The year 1956 saw the beginning of a full-time professional fire department with funds voted for four permanent, full-time fire fighters, two for Wayland and two for Cochituate. In 1957 a fire chief (Francis Hartin) replaced the board of five fire engineers. In 1960 there were seven full-time firemen and thirty-three callmen. By 1971 the permanent fire department force numbered twenty-eight men, but there were still some part-time call firemen. In 1979 the fire department was almost fully professional with twenty-five full-time men; the town had been wired for fire alarm boxes; and the department owned an ambulance for citizen rescue operations.

As late as 1952 Wayland had only one full-time policeman, Chief Ernest Damon, who with a number of auxiliaries had constituted the police force since 1917 and became chief in 1945. In 1953 an additional full-time officer was appointed, and one more was added in 1954. In 1956 three patrolmen were added to make a department of five policemen and a chief. By 1959 there were seven police patrolmen who, with the chief and some communications officers, made up a department of eleven. In 1980 there were twenty-four officers in the department.

As early as 1953 the finance committee report was saying that a brick building of a type like the Cochituate fire station was needed to house Wayland's town offices, the police department, and the Wayland part of the fire department. At a special town meeting in December 1954 the town appropriated funds for plans and specifications and in 1956 made an appropriation of $270,000 for the Wayland Town Building, which was placed on the northeast corner of the intersection of the Boston Post Road with Cochituate Road on land acquired for this purpose in 1920.

In 1920, with a desire to improve the center of Wayland Village and the knowledge that the 1878 town hall would not be adequate for a growing town, a private group had purchased the then decaying Wayland Inn or Pequod House. This group was spearheaded by Edmund H. Sears, Walter B. Henderson, and J. Sidney Stone and had additional financial aid from Edwin F. Greene, Charles A. Phipps, Wallace S. Draper, and Francis Shaw.

After considering using the old inn as a teachers' lodge or a community house, it was decided in 1928 to tear down the 1771 building and deed the land and a piece behind it owned by Edmund Sears to the town to be used for park purposes until a town hall could be built. Also in the 1920s Francis Shaw and Edmund Sears had bought and torn down unsightly buildings on the land southwest of the intersection.

These generous acts by a group of well-to-do private citizens had been the high water mark of the era when private citizens used their own resources to beautify and provide improved facilities for the town. The depression years made it less possible for private benefactors to provide needed municipal facilities. By the 1940s those in a position to make large gifts to the town were dying, or their ability to provide benefits for the town was greatly reduced by heavy federal and state taxation.

The brick, one-story colonial Wayland Town Building was ready for occupancy in September 1957, and the same year the town voted to demolish the 1878 town hall. When the Town Building was dedicated on February 23, 1958, it was stressed that the structure had been built without borrowing.

Bob Morgan

Achievement of a fine town headquarters and police and fire station with a minimum of expense and difficulty and, more importantly, the translation of all large-scale town projects of this era into reality with a minimum of debt and trouble was in great part due to Robert M. Morgan, who served on the finance committee from 1938 to 1971 and made that committee the powerful center of government in Wayland which it still is today. Morgan had moved to Wayland in 1932 as a fairly young man connected with a Boston bank. He rose to be president of one of New England's largest and most successful banking institutions. His leadership of the finance committee went forward year after year as if he had nothing else to do but work for Wayland. After holding many hours of budget discussions and mastering the pros and cons of every warrant article for each town meeting, Bob Morgan saw that the necessary articles passed in town meeting and that the needed funds were made available.

All those who lived in Wayland and were aware of its governmental affairs during Bob Morgan's period of leadership know that he was the giant of mid-twentieth-century leaders of the town. They are proud to have known him and grateful that he guided the town through its days of explosive expansion so ably and that the town which his vision and tenacity created turned out so well. At the town meeting of March 8, 1972, Robert M. Morgan was honored with a plaque and other gifts from the town. Those present were saying good-bye to "Mr Wayland," who was dropping the reins and leaving his beloved hometown because of ill health.

Changes in the 1970s

The year 1971, when Bob Morgan decided to retire, was a turning point for Wayland in various other, unrelated respects. After ninety years of operation, passenger service on the railroad was discontinued. That year, after a League of Women Voters' study had advocated it in 1969, and a town committee had considered the question, the number of selectmen was increased from three to five. One of that first board of five selectmen was Catherine Seiler, the first woman to hold the office of selectman in Wayland. In the latter part of the nineteenth century women had served on the school committee and as library trustees, but in the early years of the twentieth century very few women attended the town meetings and none held the traditional men's jobs except that of town clerk, which was held by Alice Neale from 1926 to 1951 and by Leila Sears from 1951 to 1970. In 1902 it had been reported that six women had voted at the annual town meeting. In 1980 there were two highly competent women selectmen, well able to hold their own with the men. Other women have been and are the leaders of important committees and commissions, and at this writing a woman is for the first time chairman of the finance committee.

To the surprise of those who had projected further school growth, 1971 was the peak year for school enrollment with 4,014 pupils, more than ten times as many as in 1920 when the town was quite small. In 1962 the planning board had forecast that Wayland's population would reach 18,620 in 1980; the school department's projection of 1968 had been that in the fall of 1980 there would be 5,395 children in the Wayland schools instead of the 2,600 who entered school in September 1980.

Census figures show that the total population of Wayland declined after 1971. The town clerk's figures show 1980 total population down from 1975 but households increased. (See Appendix A.) Now, in 1980, Wayland's total population has reached a plateau, while the school population is declining, owing to smaller families and the presence in the town of older households with children past school age. In recent years two schools have been given up. Sadly for the Cochituate Village population who had loved their school, the Cochituate School was discontinued in 1978, and town officials worked to convert that building into apartments for elderly and low-income persons. By the fall of 1980 the schools could operate more economically if the Loker School were taken out of service. This building was being retained on a standby basis for future school use should another bulge in the school population occur.

When it became obvious that the school population had passed its peak, plans to remodel the old junior high school into an elementary school were scrapped. The town meeting of March 28, 1974, voted to form a municipal building planning committee to decide whether it was feasible to move the town and school department offices to that building to provide more room in the 1957 Town Building for the police and fire departments. The latter building is now known as the Public Safety Building, and the original 1935 high school with its various additions is now the Wayland Town Office Building with offices for the regular employees; meeting rooms for town boards and commissions; a large room for hearings, public events, and meetings of civic organizations; a gymnasium for recreational activities; an area for senior citizen activities; and a large suite of offices for the school committee and school administration. The remodeled building was ready for use in April 1978.

In 1980 the administration of a town of about 13,000 people under modern conditions entailed the employment of about 480 full- or nearly full-time paid employees, most of them working under collective-bargaining agreements. The government was conducted under a system of numerous and complicated controls. The administration of a large school system in charge of a plant worth $21 million and fairly elaborate recreational facilities as well as the older town facilities (roads, bridges, and water supply) constituted a large operation.

During the daytime the Town Office Building is manned by a corps of paid employees. On weekday evenings the lights burn late while unpaid elected and appointed boards meet to carry on their business. There is an office machine room, a computer, and a large fireproof vault. All this is in great contrast to what seemed to the town to be palatial quarters in the 1878 town hall. The world has changed and people's expectations have risen tremendously. Wayland is no longer a small, backward, rural town but has become one of Massachusetts' affluent residential communities.

In October 1959 the League of Women Voters conducted a survey which showed that the population at that time contained only 9 percent who were natives of Wayland but that 75 percent were natives of New England. It showed that 70 percent of Wayland's adults had moved to the town in the previous ten years, that the overwhelming reason why those newcomers moved to Wayland was to enjoy the rural atmosphere, and that 86 percent of the households had at least one person who went out of town for his employment. Now, twenty years later, the statistics of a similar survey might be different but not greatly so. There is considerable turnover in the existing housing, and there are many newcomers.

By the 1970s Wayland's population was not only much larger but was also more diverse than that of the two-village town of one hundred years before and completely different from the homogeneous Protestant Yankee town born in 1780. There was a handful of black and Oriental families, but the bulk of the population was white and born in the United States. By the 1970s the town contained a significant number of persons of Italian descent who, like the Irish and Germans of the nineteenth century, had moved out from Boston.

To accommodate larger membership the two Roman Catholic parishes built new and larger churches—St. Zepherin's in 1960 and St. Ann's in 1963. As of this writing, a Jewish temple has been holding services in the First Parish (Unitarian) Church for nearly two years and is now planning to buy and remodel a building where it can have its own temple and school. Added to the older Protestant roster were a Lutheran Church and a Protestant Episcopal Church, both completed in 1964.

Owing to shorter work hours and modern conveniences, there is much more leisure for breadwinners and housewives, although, as is true all over the nation, many housewives have found outside employment and there are numbers of two-income families. Meanwhile, so numerous are the local clubs and organizations based on educational, cultural, social, sports, and political interests that an energetic segment of the population goes on a hectic round of activities, some church-related, many not. These are too numerous and varied to enumerate, ranging from participation in, or attendance at, the Vokes Players theater productions, in what started out as Beatrice Herford

Hayward's tiny private theater, to civic beautification projects which are an important focus of three women's garden clubs.

Today sports facilities abound, with two golf courses and a town-run bathing beach on Lake Cochituate, rented from the state in 1949 as soon as Lake Cochituate was discontinued as a stand-by source of Boston water. This beach replaced earlier, simpler beaches at Baldwin's Pond and Dudley Pond. A private organization with an interesting history runs a large indoor swimming pool in a building near the high school. There are a private curling club and a swimming and tennis club, both with fairly elaborate facilities. Except for the golf course and the earlier beaches, these facilities were developed after World War II.

Wayland is no longer a summer resort, and it is hard for some to believe that it ever was. There is now enough affluence that quite a few families have second homes at the seashore or mountains for use on weekends and for summer and winter vacations. A large number of families take vacations away from Wayland in the summer season, and except for outdoor recreation much of the organized activity ceases.

Motor vehicles average slightly more than three per household in Wayland, a measure of our citizens' wealth and also an indicator of the present almost complete dependence of the town on the automobile. The automobile was chiefly responsible for the changes Wayland underwent from 1910 on; for better or worse, we have a town dependent on a device which was a toy only eighty years ago.

New Trends in Housing

In 1934 Wayland was zoned for single residences with village business zones and a small light industry area. In the 1970s new trends have dominated the residential planning. One trend has been that of multiple housing. Multiple housing has become a recognized need for low-income elderly persons or couples who no longer can or wish to maintain houses. Bent Park in Cochituate, opened in 1974 with fifty-four units, served a great need but was not adequate for the demand. The Cochituate School will add apartments when remodeled for that purpose in a neighborhood where residents can walk to the churches and stores.

Another kind of multiple housing has been provided in Wayland—a large, modern, luxury condominium development. In the fall of 1972 Devens Hamlen of Mainstone Farm went to the planning board with preliminary plans for an open-space multiresidence development which would necessitate a new type of zoning. Instead of selling off his highly taxed land for single-family homes on standard lots, Hamlen and his uncle Robert Gannett decided to create a condominium development on 362 acres of land, the southern half of the large Mainstone Farm estate. The planning board spent well over a year researching, holding hearings on, and devising this zoning change. Wisely, they considered whether this Mainstone plan could be considered as a single case. They decided that if the zoning laws were to be changed to allow this type of multiple housing, a zoning ordinance should be created to cover all five of the large open areas in the town, owners of which might in the future ask permission to put up multiple housing of this or any other type. For Mainstone it was worked out that the buildings would be low and clustered, that large areas of land in the development would have to be left as open, natural land, and that certain sections of the land would be deeded to the town as conservation land. The Planned Development Bylaw was finally passed by the town meeting in March 1974.

The Mainstone Farm condominium, begun on Rice Road near the Episcopal Church of the Holy Spirit, was in late 1980 a successful and going concern. One hundred and twenty-nine out of a total of 435 units had been finished and sold, and roads, recreational facilities, and additional buildings were rapidly being added. Of the families living there, many were retired couples whose children had left home, and there were very few children of school age in the complex. The development was designed to discourage families with more than one child and to encourage occupancy by people affluent enough to make a net contribution toward the town's tax burden.

The four other open tracts, none as large as this one, whose owners may decide to come before the town for planned multiple-residential development, must obtain individual approval of their specific plans.

There is still open land in Wayland and various individual pieces of land with frontage and area sufficient to allow further building. Twenty-five permits for new, single-family houses were granted in 1979. However, unless zoning restrictions are changed further explosive development of single-family residences will not occur, and building can now take place only on suitable land. Building in the flood plain of the Sudbury River was forbidden by a zoning ordinance in 1958.

Conservation

In the past twenty years retaining Wayland's rural atmosphere and natural physical assets has become more and more of a challenge but has continued as a dream which in some measure is being realized. In the north and central part of the town the Sudbury River meadows give a wonderful feeling of openness. Fortunately, the wetlands on the banks of the river have been made part of a National Wild Life Refuge. On flat, drier land toward the river from Old Sudbury Road the old cow common has been acquired for the town by the conservation commission.

An early effort had been made to preserve one of Wayland's natural assets when in 1928 a town committee was formed to consider acquiring a town forest. This project came to naught. In the 1950s a recreation site committee of the planning board suggested acquiring five swampy, wooded land areas near streams and ponds. The significant conservation effort started in Wayland when in 1961, as called for by a state law, the selectmen appointed a conservation committee which by its second year became the conservation commission. This agency, now one of the town's most dedicated and effectively run bodies, had in its early years remarkably good leadership by Allen H. Morgan, a citizen of long standing and a nationally known conservationist. He was with the commission from its inception until his resignation in 1973.

In its first report the conservation committee indicated that it would concern itself with water resources, woodlands and wildlife, and recreation and open space. Work was begun early to devise a master plan of lands it was hoped the town could acquire to protect the streams and water table and also to provide open land in crowded areas. The first detailed plan was finished in 1966 and publicized in 1967, and a revision was brought out in 1977.

There have been some gifts of conservation land to the town, a significant early one (1962) of twenty-one acres along Pine Brook being made by the Sears family of Weston. By 1980 561.7 acres had been transferred to the conservation commission. A large part of this was purchased directly from owners or, while awaiting town meeting action, through the help of an interim owner—the private, nonprofit Sudbury Valley Trustees, which had been incorporated in 1953 for the preservation of open land in the Sudbury River valley. By 1980,

Early 1900s photo of Wayland Center from the Unitarian Church belfry shows the 1771 Pequod House at lower right, the Town Hall in the background, and stores on the green at the left.

$866,340 had been spent for acquiring conservation parcels in Wayland, but with federal and state reimbursement this represented a net expenditure by the town of $384,172.

When it was drawn up it was hoped that the 1967 master plan, which was considered by its authors to be a modest one adapted to the financial resources of the town, could be completed in ten years. The 1967 plan called for the acquisition of, or placing conservation restrictions on, 1,351 acres of Wayland land. The commission has had greater difficulties than had been anticipated in negotiating with owners.

Recreational and educational trails have been cleared and marked through the woodland area; open farm fields have been leased to farmers; and on part of the cow common more than 150 individuals or families, a few nonresidents, are using plots in a community garden area.

As evidenced by a favorable vote in an October 1980 town meeting to purchase restriction rights to a piece of agricultural land in a crowded section of the south part of the town, the townspeople have demonstrated that the preservation of open space is something they are willing to pay for if a suitable program is presented to them.

Historic Preservation

In addition to conserving natural features and protecting the water supply, the town embarked in the 1960s on a historic preservation effort in Wayland Center. In 1965 fourteen parcels constituting about twenty-one acres with thirteen buildings were zoned as a town historic district, which meant that exterior changes to the buildings visible from the road could be made only with the approval of the historic district commission. The majority of the buildings are examples of early-nineteenth-century village architecture. In 1970 the town purchased the railroad station within the district to preserve it as a historic structure. In 1975 this district was placed on the National Register of Historic Places, which meant that architecturally and historically valuable buildings such as the First Parish Church were eligible for federal grants for structural repairs and renovation.

Thus, after the building boom of 1949-65 which inevitably changed the landscape, the town took positive steps to preserve both its natural features and a concentration of structures, some of them historic, at the village center which grew up around the fourth and fifth meetinghouses. Measures also were taken by the town to preserve and protect the two picturesque four-arch stone bridges over the Sudbury River which were built in the mid-nineteenth century and no longer carried traffic to Sudbury and Framingham.

Urbanization and Absorption in the Metropolitan Area

In the 1972 town report the selectmen had said: "Whether Wayland can retain the character of a small community with rural overtones becomes an increasingly important subject as outside pressures mount." In the same report the planning board stated that the early 1970s was a "pivotal period in which pressure for more intense development and urbanization will increase. Creeping commercialism, more traffic and concern for moderate income housing are some of the symptoms."

In other reports of the 1970s the selectmen and planning board dwelt on the interdependence between Wayland and the larger metropolitan area. They suggested that one of the town's most important duties was to try, through joint public transportation responsibilities, and sharing of area resources like refuse disposal facilites, to fit Wayland into the larger eastern Massachusetts metropolitan area.

About twenty years ago this writer attended a lecture by the author of a new book on the history of Milton, Massachusetts, which is about the same distance from Boston as is Wayland. That historian said that he considered that by the middle of the twentieth century his town had ceased to exist as an individual entity, although it continued as a separate municipality. This writer shares Howard Russell's thought expressed in a *Town Crier* article of May 10, 1979, that towns that are as far as Wayland is from Boston still have their own distinctive personalities. To a great extent the personality and individuality of a town like Wayland is the result of its earlier history and of the efforts that have gone into steering the town through the past forty or fifty years. Wayland has not grown haphazardly. What shaped the town was the efforts of the planners—at first public-spirited private citizens, later town officials.

Out of our population of between 12,500 and 13,000 there is now scarcely anyone whose ancestors have lived here from generation to generation since the founding of Sudbury. Margaret Bent Morrell was one of the last. Including this writer, there is a considerable group living here now who are descendants of one or more of the original proprietors through ancestors who moved away. Many belong to this group without being aware of their ancestral connection with Wayland's earliest days. In general, however, our population consists of twentieth-century newcomers who chose the town as an abode and, in a comparatively few cases, as a place to work. Many do not stay long, but most have some curiosity about, and take at least a passing interest in, the history of the town.

Much detail, many interesting anecdotes, and mention of hundreds of citizens and officials who have made important contributions to the town have had to be left out of this section. The author has tried not to slight the most important persons and events. She hopes that she has given some idea of how Wayland became the place it is today. There has not been space in this section to discuss how the cleavage and imbalance between the south and north parts of the town faded in the twentieth century to almost a dim memory, but that did happen.

As Wayland arrived at the ninth decade of the twentieth century and its two hundredth anniversary as a separate town, it contained over ten thousand more people than it did when the twentieth century began. No town can grow this way and still be characterized as small and rustic. Providing schools, fire and police protection, garbage and refuse facilities, recreation facilities, and all the amenities expected of a well-to-do community is big business, and in 1978-79 town expenditures of its own funds amounted to $14.6 million. Of this amount about 70 percent was for salaries, a far cry from the days when the town hired only a minister and a small number of poorly paid schoolteachers.

The open town meeting still prevails as the ultimate source of decisions about what the town will spend and how the possible revenue shall be allocated. For those interested enough to participate in the town meeting and to serve on town committees and boards, there is still the framework of American town democracy in the development of which *Puritan Village's* author, Sumner C. Powell, considered his Sudbury (now in part our Wayland) to have been an especially successful pioneer.

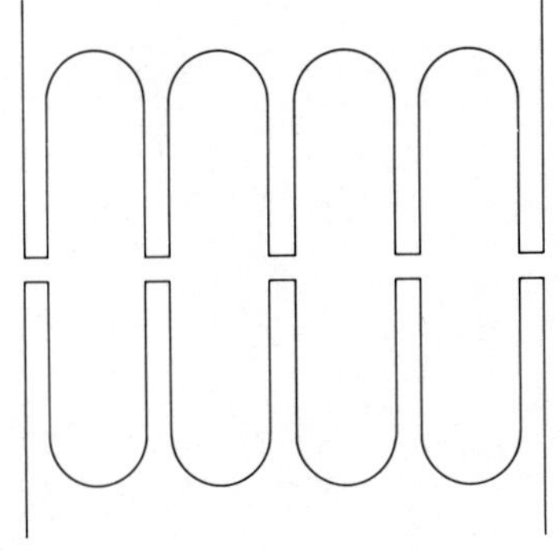

Appendices

APPENDIX A

Population of East Sudbury and Wayland / 1780-1980

Year	Population[1]	Numerical Change	Percentage Change in Decade	5 Years	Population in North[2]	South	No. of Houses[3]
1780	775						
1790	801	+26	+3.3%		721	80	112
1800	835	+34	+4.2%				
1810	824	−11	−1.3%				
1820	962	+138	+16.7%				
1830	944	−18	−1.9%				141
1840	998	+54	+5.7%		773	225	
1850	1,115	+117	+11.7%		777	338	205
1855	1,178	+63		+5.7%			
1860	1,188	+10	+6.5%	+0.8%			215
1865	1,137	−51		−4.3%	778	359	209
1870	1,240	+103	+4.4%	+9.1%	760	480	215[4]
1875	1,766	+526		+42.4%	766	1,000	291
1880	1,962	+196	+58.2%	+11.1%	801	1,161	331
1885	1,946	−16		−0.8%			368
1890	2,060	+114	+5.0%	+5.9%			388
1895	2,026	−34		−1.6%	752	1,274	413
1900	2,303	+277	+11.8%	+13.7%			440
1905	2,220	−83		−3.6%	827	1,393	459
1910	2,206	−14	−4.2%	−0.6%			479
1915	2,033	−173		−7.8%	872	1,161	544
1920	1,935	−98	−12.3%	−4.8%			795
1925	2,255	+320		+16.6%			959
1930	2,937	+682	+51.8%	+30.2%			1,162
1935	3,346	+409		+13.9%			1,125
1940	3,505	+159	+19.3%	+4.7%			1,253
1945	3,901	+396		+11.3%	1,558	2,343	1,318
1950	4,393	+492	+25.3%	+12.6%			1,489
1955	7,359	+2,966		+67.5%			2,171
1960	10,444	+3,085	+137.7%	+41.9%	5,245	5,199	2,825
1965	12,192	+1,748		+16.7%	6,314	5,878	3,325
1970	13,992	+1,800	+34.0%	+14.8%	7,641	6,351	3,591
1975	13,282	−710		−5.1%	7,251	6,031	3,627
1980[5]	12,633	−649	−9.7%	−4.9%	7,010	5,623	4,081

1. Figures from 1790 on are from U.S. censuses for decades and Massachusetts censuses for 1855, 1865 and so on. Figure for 1780 is an estimate.

2. *North* and *South* parts of the town are the areas designated in 1893 as Precinct 1 [North] and Precinct 2 [South], sometimes referred to in this history as Wayland Center and Cochituate. Before 1895 figures are counts from census enumerations with margin for error as the exact location of every family was not known to compiler. U.S. Censuses of 1870 and 1880 enumerated Wayland and Cochituate separately. Massachusetts Census of 1875 enumeration not available. Figure for South part of town taken from a newspaper article.

3. Earlier counts of houses are from census records; later ones from Assessors Reports in Wayland Town Reports.

4. The Assessors Report for 1872 has the figure 253 for number of houses as does *Nason's Gazetteer* published in 1874.

5. Wayland Town Clerk's figures.

APPENDIX B

Houses Built by 1780 Still Standing in Wayland / 1981

	Year Built	Householder in 1780
Noyes-Parris House 204 Old Connecticut Path	1669	Deacon Samuel Parris
John Goodenow House 3 Water Row	1680-1700	Jonathan Carter
John Noyes House 71 Old Sudbury Road	1704-1715	Capt. John Noyes
Hopestill Bent Tavern 252 Old Connecticut Path	1710	Lt. John Whitney
Stone-Heard-Sears House 187 Pelham Island Road	ca 1715	Zachariah Heard
Reeves Tavern 126 Old Connecticut Path	ca 1715	Jacob Reeves
Samuel Griffin House 184 Glezen Lane	ca 1720	Samuel Griffin
Brintnall-Loker House 36 Loker Street	ca 1740	Capt. Isaac Loker
Josiah Bridge Parsonage 47 Old Sudbury Road	1761	Rev. Josiah Bridge
Benjamin Adams House 34 Lincoln Road	1750-1775	Benjamin Adams
Zachariah Bryant House 10 Old Sudbury Road	ca 1770	Zachariah Bryant
Timothy Sherman House 24 Sherman Bridge Road	1763-1771	Timothy Sherman
Isaac Damon House 357 Commonwealth Road	1765-1790	Isaac Damon
Luther Moore Tavern 318 Concord Road	ca 1770	Luther Moore
Noyes-Morse House 202 Boston Post Road	ca 1772	Widow Anna Noyes
Jonathan Parmenter House 28 Concord Road	ca 1775	Maj. Jonathan Parmenter
William Bent House 43 Main Street	ca 1775	Lt. William Bent
Jonathan Sherman House 62 Oxbow Road	ca 1780	Jonathan Sherman
Nathaniel Rice House 29 River Road	ca 1780	Nathaniel Rice
Ephraim Sherman House 206 Oxbow Road	ca 1780	Ephraim Sherman

APPENDIX C

Buildings Erected by 1880 Still Standing in Cochituate Village / 1981

Location	*First Owner*	*Year built*
92 Commonwealth Road	George A. Damon	1869
100 ″	Elbridge J. Carter	by 1870
106 ″	James B. Stone	ca 1850
117 ″	John L. Place	by 1875
118 ″	Richard Hammond	1846
119 ″	S.B.H. Whitney	ca 1863
120 ″	Charles Damon	by 1850
123 ″	Lafayette Dudley	by 1850 (?)
124 ″	Stephen Stanton	1863
127 ″	Henry Coggin	by 1860
128 ″	Alfred H. Bryant	1879
131 ″	Theodore L. Sawin	by 1866
132 ″	Phineas Wheelock	1845
135 ″	Levi B. Curtis	1878
136 ″	Otis T. Lyon	1849
152 ″	Charles R. Damon	by 1850
178 ″	George W. Fairbanks	1879
187 ″	Alfred C. Loker	1878
200 ″	George Keep	by 1877
221 ″	Elbridge J. Carter	ca 1874
227 ″	Colin Ward	1873
235 ″	George L. Hixon	1873
9 Cormans Lane	George Risley	by 1872
16 Damon Street	Charles R. Damon	by 1872
17 ″	Orrin W. Harris	1874
9 Dunster Avenue	Alonzo Griffin	by 1875
13 ″	Alonzo Griffin	by 1875
38 East Plain Street	Patrick Leary	1874
44 ″	David Flint	1872
50 ″	Alonzo Griffin	by 1875
72 ″	Granville Loker	1879
84 ″	James A. Loker	by 1860
9 French Avenue	Joseph W. Moore	1879
9 Harrison Street	Edwin W. Marston	1878
14 ″	Arthur J. Ricker	1874
15 ″	Charles D. Ricker	1877
20 ″	Albert W. Goodnow	by 1875
21 Leary Street	Frank Lupien	1879
33-35 Main Street	Hammond & Howe Beer Brewery	by 1856
43 ″	William Bent	by 1775
52-58 ″	Ambrose Bryant Store	by 1870
80 ″	Meth. Episc. Church	1868

Location	*First Owner*	*Year built*
86 Main Street	Charles W. Moore	ca 1868
93 ″	Joseph M. Moore	by 1872
111 ″	Dean (?)	by 1875
163 ″	Edward P. Butler	1873
174 ″	Albert F. King	by 1874
182 ″	Edward P. Loker	ca 1879
186 ″	Joseph A. Wing	ca 1873
7 Maple Street	John R. Moore	by 1880
7 Pemberton Road	Adonirum Puffer	1867
9 ″	Lewis C. May	1866
10 ″	Evinson Stone	by 1875
14 ″	John C. Butterfield	by 1850
15 ″	Charles Damon	by 1860
21 ″	Marshall Garfield	by 1875
26 ″	John G. Schleicher	1851
37 ″	William H. Bolles	1870
44-46 ″	Frederick Wendt	1851
47 ″	John Lamarine	1880
56-60 ″	James Murphy	by 1875
*76 ″	William Garfield	by 1875
12 Shawmut Avenue	William H. Bent	1867
5 Stanton Street	Sarah Crofut	1876
11 ″	Edy Coaldwell	1876
12 ″	James Davis	1879
13 ″	Francis Stanton	1879
14 West Plain Street	Albert B. Lyon	ca 1868
39 ″	Charles Trumbull	by 1875
*45 ″	Myron W. Bent	1873
60 ″	Charles W. Whitney	by 1875
61 ″	Alonzo Griffin	by 1877
65 ″	Marcus Mitchell	1878
67 ″	Charles M. Bowles	1873
91 ″	Throop B. Hawes	by 1856
10 Willard Street	Charles B. Dascomb	by 1875

*House moved from another location.

Sources: Maps, deeds, valuation lists, newspaper notices, census population enumerations, and photographs taken in 1880.

The Puritan Village Evolves

APPENDIX D

Early Shoemakers in Cochituate and Wayland / 1840-1850

John Q. Adams
Joseph N. Alexander
John W. Bemis
William H. Bemis
Gilbert Bent
James M. Bent
William Bent
Edwin P. Bond
Augustus Brigham
Elijah Brigham
Thomas Bryant
William Bullard
Elias B. Burrows
John C. Butterfield
James Cain
Albert P. Carter
Elbridge Carter
Henry Coggin
William Crowley
Daniel Cutting
Mirick F. Damon
Luther S. Dearth
Ira B. Draper
Edwin A. Dudley
Enoch H. Dudley
Lafayette Dudley
Lewis Dudley
James W. Dudley
Joseph M. Dudley
George Fairbanks
Solomon G. Farmer
Patrick Fay
James Gillespie
Edwin Hammond
Richard E. Hammond
William Hammond Jr.
Antipas Hanibal
Joseph B. Hawes
Ebenezer Hersey
Benjamin L. Howe
Edward K. Howe
Ezra Howe
Stephen Jameson
Joseph Jessup
Alpheus D. Loker
Jefferson Loker
John L. Loker
John W. Loker
Sewall Loker
Otis T. Lyon
David Massure
Solomon T. Melman
Josiah R. Mills
Jeremiah Munro
Henry R. Newton
Charles G. Pratt
Benjamin F. Reed
James H. Reeves
Joseph A. Rice
William M. Richard
Charles B. Roberts
Calvin H. Saunders
Joseph K. Sawin
Joseph Swain
Evinson Stone
Benjamin Ward
William Ward Jr.
Thomas J. Ware
Charles Weston
H. Phineas Wheelock
Joseph R. Winch

Source: Wayland vital records, mortgage records, and Census of 1850.

APPENDIX E

Wayland and Cochituate Shoe Manufacturers / 1849-1913

Adams Brothers 1895
Wm. & J.M. Bent Company ca 1842-1891
Bent Brothers Company 1891-1895
Bent and Stephens [Howard] ca 1893-1895
Elmer and James A. Bent 1893
William H., Elmer and James A. Bent 1895
Bent [Ralph] and Bullard [Frank A.] 1895-1896
Bent [Ralph] and Fairbanks [George W.] 1896
A[lfred] H. Bryant Company 1880-1882
Thomas Bryant Company ca 1860-1879
Henry [William H.] Butterfield 1886-1890
Caswell [Dona H., Leander, & George] Brothers 1895-ca 1903
Noah A. Chessman 1896-1901
Chessman [N.A.] and Brown [T.] 1894-1896
Clarke [William W. & Herbert] Shoe Company 1892
Albert F. Dean ca 1875-1882
Charles W. Dean Company ca 1873-1913
T.A. [Thomas A.] and H.C. [Henry Colburn] Dean 1870-1880
Dean [Henry Colburn] and Howe [Frank K.] 1891
Roscoe C. Dean 1882-1890
J. [James] O. [Otis] Dean 1896
Dean [Charles W.?] and Griffin [Noble C.] 1884
Dean and King 1873-1878
Abby H. Draper 1870
C.W. [Curtis Warren] Draper 1870
Ira B. Draper ca 1855-ca 1871
Enoch Dudley 1860
Lafayette Dudley 1865-1870
James W. Dudley 1865
Dunham and Griffin [Daniel D.] ca 1877-ca 1882
Eaton and Stephens [Howard] 1893
Ewing [Orlando] and Elkins [Dana] 1893-1895
Fairbanks [George W.] and King [Albert F.] 1895
C. H. Felch 1883-1884[1]
Henry B. Fischer ca 1875-1881
Alonzo Griffin 1877-1878
Daniel D. Griffin 1872-1873
N. [Noble] C. Griffin 1884-1902
Hammond [James N.] and Howe [Ezra L.] 1856
William Hammond 1850-1886 (intermittent)
Charles W. Hodges 1870
Frank A. Howe 1895
Hunting [W.] and Dean [?] 1896
Charles Keyes 1885-1886
Larrabee [William H.] and Wesson [Charles J.] 1878-1883
A. [Albert] F. King -1878
Alpheus D. Loker 1870
Sewall Loker 1870
Lovejoy [William] and Damon [Charles R.] (finishing firm) 1873-1875
A. [Albert] B. Lyon Company ca 1880-1882
Otis T. Lyon & Son ca 1860-ca 1879
Mann [Hollis] and Dean [Charles W.] 1884
Maud Brothers 1893
Moulton [Edward H.], Sawin [Theodore L.] and Loker [Alfred] 1891
Henry R. Newton 1849-ca 1865
Ricker [Arthur J.] and Lamarine [John] 1895-1903
Ricker [Arthur J.], Lamarine [John] and Norris [Andrew] 1894
Sawin [Theodore L.] and Loker [Alfred] 1892
Scotland [William] and Campbell [William] 1894-1895
Veazey [Damon C.] and Loker [David P.W.] (factoring business) 1878
Willard B. Ward 1868
Ward and Spofford 1870
Ward and Ewing [Orlando C.] 1890-1893
Williams Shoe Company [Chester B., Arthur A. and Ernest] 1897-1908

Note: In all but a few cases dates are not exact as to the beginning and end of a firm. As shown in text, only a handful of firms had life spans of more than four or five years.

[1]*The Shoe and Leather Reporter Annual* lists as in Cochituate in 1891 O.A. Felch, and W.L. Felch in 1905 and 1910. These are believed to have been in North Natick.

APPENDIX F

Bibliography

A. SECONDARY MATERIAL BEARING DIRECTLY ON WAYLAND

Printed books and pamphlets on Wayland before 1920

Cutting, Alfred Wayland, *Old Time Wayland,* Boston, 1926.

____________, *A Hundred Years of the Old Meeting House,* address in First Parish Church, Wayland, January 15, 1915.

Federal Writers Project of W.P.A., *A Brief History of the Towne of Sudbury in Massachusetts 1639-1939,* rev. ed. by Sudbury Historical Society, 1968.

Harvard Trust Company, *The Parmenter Story,* Cambridge, 1960.

Hudson, Alfred Sereno, *The Annals of Sudbury, Wayland and Maynard,* 1891. (Contains 90-page Appendix on Wayland.)

____________, *The History of Sudbury, Massachusetts, 1638-1889,* Sudbury, 1889, also 1968 reprint edition.

Hurd, D. H. *History of Middlesex County with Biographical Sketches,* Philadelphia, 1890, 3 Vols.

League of Women Voters of Wayland, Massachusetts, *Wayland, a Community Handbook,* revised edition, 1968.

Merrill, Truman Allen, *Sermon Commemorative of the Formation of the Evangelical Trinitarian Church, Wayland, Mass.,* delivered May 21, 1878 on its 50th anniversary, Boston, 1878.

Powell, Sumner Chilton, *Puritan Village–The Formation of A New England Town,* Wesleyan University, 1963, also Anchor Books paperback edition, New York, 1965.

Wayland Bicentennial Committee, Barbara Robinson, editor, *Wayland Historical Tours,* Wayland, 1976.

Wayland, Town of, *Proceedings at the Dedication of the Town Hall, Wayland December 24, 1878, with Brief Historical Sketches of Public Buildings and Libraries,* Wayland, 1879.

____________, *Report of the Committee of the Wayland Water Works, March 1, 1879,* Natick, 1880.

____________, *The Town of Wayland in the Civil War 1861-1865,* Wayland, 1871.

Unpublished reports and papers available at the Historical Society and/or at the Library

Baldwin, Amanda Patch, *Diary for 1871*, transcription in files of the Wayland Historical Society.

Emery, Helen F., *Date of Building of Stone's Bridge,* Report to Massachusetts Historical Commission, 1976 with 1979 additions.

____________, *"The Town that Bears his Name"–An Attempt to Document the Change in the Town's Name from East Sudbury to Wayland in 1835,* Report to Historical Society, 1957.

____________, *Wayland's Town Seal–Its Historical Accuracy,* Report to the Wayland Board of Selectmen, 1971.

Hamlen, Elizabeth Perkins, *Wayland; A Sketch* (Mainstone Farm) 1948.

Sawyer, Kenneth W., *A Graveside Memorial Service for Lydia Maria Child, October 18, 1980*, Wayland, 1980.

Schwalm, Sandra, *The Town of Wayland, Massachusetts, A Microcosm of and Unique Contribution to the Development of the Free Public Library Movement in Massachusetts,* Wayland, 1975.

True, Palmer D., *In Memory of the Revolutionary War Soldiers Buried in the North Cemetery, Wayland,* Wayland 1975.

Wight, John Burt, *Reminiscences,* Wayland, 1865.

B. CHIEF PRIMARY SOURCES OF EARLY SUDBURY AND WAYLAND HISTORY TO 1915

Official Town Sources

Sudbury — *Town* [Clerk's] *Records, 1639-1790,* 6 vols., on microfilm, also Mary Heard handwritten transcriptions made 1855-6 for Town of Wayland, 3 vols., 1639-1760 (Vol. 4 missing).

____________ — *Proprietors Records, 1706-1805,* on microfilm.

____________ — *Book of Grants, 1706-1802,* on microfilm.

____________ — *Westerly Precinct Record, A.D. 1722-1732.*

New England Historic Genealogical Society, *Vital Records of Sudbury, Massachusetts to the Year 1850,* Boston, 1903.

Wayland — *Town* [Clerk's] *Records, 1780-1919,* 5 vols. (East Sudbury Records 1780-1835 contained in first 2 vols.)

____________ — *Vital Records,* copies in several vols. of records through 1843, original registers 1843-present.

New England Historic Genealogical Society, *Vital Records of Wayland Massachusetts to the Year 1850,* Boston, 1910.

Wayland — *Register of Voters in the Town of Wayland 1877-1882.*

____________ — *Register of Voters 1884-1914.*

____________ — *General Register of Voters Opened October 30, 1892.*

____________ — *Town Clerk's Chattel Mortgage and Legal Agreements Records,* 4 vols., 1840-1900. (Early vols. contain militia lists and boundary perambulations.)

____________ — *East Precinct Record,* (Original lost. Transcription made in 1937 by W.P.A. owned by Historical Society.)

____________ — *Assessors Records* Handwritten valuation lists for 1801, 1811, 1821, and 1831. Printed valuation lists for 1850, 1860, 1872, 1883, 1900, 1914, 1921, 1927, 1941, 1945, 1951, 1952, 1955, 1958, 1961, and 1970.

____________ — *Treasurer's Reports,* 2 printed reports of receipts and expenditures, printed in 1850s.

____________ — *Auditors Reports,* 9 printed reports of 1860s and 1870s.

____________ — *Official Reports of the Town of Wayland,* printed annually from 1876 to present.

Middlesex County Records

Deeds
Probate Records
Plan Books
Court Records

The Puritan Village Evolves

Commonwealth of Massachusetts Records

Legislative Archives

Petitions, lists and other documents photocopied from originals and bound by subject (e.g. "Ecclesiastical") in large vols., also unindexed original material.

Massachusetts Censuses of 1855, 1865, 1875, 1885, 1895, 1915 in printed vols. (also available at libraries), and population enumerations for 1855 and 1865 on microfilm.

Original copies of population enumerations and products of industry and agriculture from United States censuses of 1850, 1860, 1870, and 1880.

Early maps (see below under maps).

Acts and Resolves of Massachusetts, printed volumes, some annotated with petitions and other relevant historical materials.

National Archives of the United States

Decennial Census Enumerations of Population, 1790-1880 and 1900, on microfilm.

Maps

Plan of Sudbury, 1707, by John Brigham, Massachusetts Archives Maps and Plans No. 228.

Sudbury, [1708 by John Brigham], Massachusetts Archives Maps and Plans No. 230.

Wayland [East Sudbury] by Matthias Mossman, 1795, Massachusetts Archives Maps and Plans No. 1181.

Map of East-Sudbury surveyed March, 1831 by Wm. C. Grout, Massachusetts Archives Maps and Plans No. 2047.

Map of Middlesex County, Massachusetts by Henry F. Walling, wall map published by Smith and Bumstead, Boston, 1856.

Map of the City of Boston and Environs by H. F. Walling, wall map published by Baker and Tilden, New York, 1866.

F.W. Beers County Atlas of Middlesex, Massachusetts, J.B. Beers & Company, New York, 1875. Map of Town of Wayland and Plans of Villages of Wayland and Cochituate.

Walker's Atlas of Middlesex County, George Walker Co., Boston, 1889. Map of Town of Wayland and Plans of Villages of Wayland and Cochituate.

Atlas of Middlesex County, Vol. III, published by George H. Walker & Co., Boston, 1908. Map of Town of Wayland and Plans of Villages of Wayland and Cochituate and Tower Hill.

Wayland in 1775 by James Sumner Draper, Wayland, circa 1875. (A reconstruction map) Reprints are entitled "Plan of the Town of Wayland in the year 1776."

Lithograph and Photographs

Cochituate, Mass and North Natick, 1887, lithograph by George Norris, Brockton, 1887. Reprinted 1975 by John F. Yeager.

Photograph collection of the Wayland Historical Society; framed photographs, albums and unmounted photographs.

Collection of photographs and postcards of Wayland in library of Society for the Preservation of New England Antiquities, Boston, Massachusetts.

Album of photographs of Wayland scenes taken by Alfred Wayland Cutting of Wayland, in Wayland Public Library.

Margaret Bent Morrell photograph collection, Wayland, Mass.

Photograph files of the Wayland Historical Commission.

Appendices

Commercially published Town Directories

Resident and Business Directory of Wayland and Weston for 1887.

1893 Directory of Wayland, Weston and Lincoln.

Shaw's Natick Directory, 1897-98, (includes Cochituate).

Waltham Suburban Directories for 1906-07, 1909, and 1911-12.

Newspapers

Natick Observer (weekly) Apr. 15, 1856-Mar. 28, 1857; May 7, 1857-Aug. 17, 1861.

Natick Times (weekly) Oct. 28, 1865-Feb. 13, 1869.

Natick Bulletin, (weekly) Nov. 27, 1869 to present. Edition called *Cochituate Enterprise* started Sept., 1882.

Natick Citizen (weekly) Dec. 29, 1877-Dec. 25, 1895.

Natick Review (weekly) 1886 to 1910 or later. Edition called *Cochituate Review.*

Framingham Gazette (weekly) June 7, 1871-Dec. 26, 1913.

Waltham Free Press (weekly) Dec. 2, 1863-Dec. 28, 1877.

Waltham Sentinel (daily) Jan. 7, 1870-Dec. 25, 1874.

Waltham Daily Free Press-Tribune, Sept. 4, 1888-June 30, 1923.

Waltham Record, (semiweekly) from 1864.

The Puritan Village Evolves

APPENDIX G

Illustrations and Credits

The illustrations in *The Puritan Village Evolves* came from many sources. The 1976 Bicentennial Collection of photographs reproduced for town display, and the archives of the Wayland Historical Society and the Wayland Library proved to be invaluable sources, and these collections were augmented by material from local residents and the archives of historical institutions within the state. The author is deeply grateful to all who helped provide such a broad range of subject matter for consideration and final selection.

In the following, all illustrations are listed chronologically as they appear in the book. The abbreviated title of each is followed by the photographer or delineator's name where such information was available, the source, and the page number on which the illustration appears.

Jacket photo: Lovell's Store, formerly the 1841 Wayland Town House / Wayland Town Collection.

INDEX

A

B

Index

C

Index

D

Index

E

F

H

M

Index

N

O

Q

R

U

V

W

Y

Z

To the honorab

of Representatives o

Bay, in New-Eng

The Petition o

-tants of the easterly

humbly sheweth.

That whereas

Inconveniencies in ti

Consequence of our p

being united in all

westerly Part of s.d

and heavy Weight u

hereafter endeavour

in as clear and just

thing will possibly a